WORLD
FACTS
& PLACES

WORLD
FACTS
& PLACES

ANTONY MASON
ANNE MAHON
ANDREW CURRIE

TIGER BOOKS INTERNATIONAL
LONDON

© Geddes & Grosset Ltd 1993

This edition published in 1993 by
Tiger Books International PLC, London

ISBN 1-85501-327-4

Printed and bound in Slovenia

A

Aachen (Aix-la-Chapelle) a historic university city and spa town in western GERMANY. (Pop. 250,000)

Aargau a northern canton in the relatively low-lying MITTELLAND of SWITZERLAND; its main town and capital is Aarau. (Pop. 465,000)

Aarhus *see* **Århus**.

Aba an industrial town in southern NIGERIA. (Pop. 210,700)

Abadan a major oil-refining port on an island in the SHATT AL ARAB waterway, southern IRAN. (Pop. 296,000)

Abéché a trading centre for nomad caravans in the semi-desert southeast of CHAD, and the capital of the prefecture of Quaddai. (Pop. 54,000)

Abeokuta an industrial town in western NIGERIA. (Pop. 301,100)

Aberdeen a city and fishing port in northeast SCOTLAND, and the administrative centre of the GRAMPIAN region. (Pop. 214,000)

Aberdeenshire *see* **Grampian**.

Aberystwyth a resort and university town on CARDIGAN BAY, 132 km (82 miles) north of CARDIFF, and main commercial centre for Mid-Wales. (Pop 10,290)

Abidjan a major port and the chief city of CÔTE D'IVOIRE. (Pop. 1,850,000)

Abkhazia an autonomous republic of GEORGIA, lying on the BLACK SEA coast in the north of the state. (8600 sq km/ 3320 sq miles; Pop. 513,000)

Åbo *see* **Turku**.

Abruzzi (Abruzzo) a region of southern central ITALY; its capital is Aquila. (Pop. 1,246,600)

Abu Dhabi the largest sheikhdom of the UNITED ARAB

EMIRATES, of which the city of Abu Dhabi is the capital. (67,350 sq km/26,000 sq miles; pop. emirate 535,700/city 244,000)

Abuja the new capital of NIGERIA, in the centre of the country, still under construction but inaugurated in 1992. (Forecast pop. 2,000,000 by the year 2000)

Abu Simbel the celebrated site of temples of ancient EGYPT, by Lake NASSER.

Acapulco a large port and beach resort on the PACIFIC coast of MEXICO. (Pop. 800,000)

Accra the capital and main port of GHANA. (Pop. 1,045,400)

Aconcagua the highest mountain of the ANDES, in ARGENTINA. (6960 m/22,834 ft)

Acre (1) a state in the extreme west of BRAZIL, bordering on PERU. (152,590 sq km/58,900 sq miles; Pop. 386,200) **(2) ('Akko)** a city and trading port since the days of the Phoenicians, and now in the state of ISRAEL, 13 km (8 miles) north of HAIFA. (Pop. 37,700)

Adan *see* **Aden**.

Adana a city and province in southern TURKEY. (Pop. city 776,000)

Ad Damman *see* **Damman**.

Ad Dawhah *see* **Doha**.

Addis Ababa (Adis Abeba) the capital of ETHIOPIA, in the centre of the country. (Pop. 1,500,000)

Adelaide the state capital of SOUTH AUSTRALIA. (Pop. 969,000)

Aden (Adan) a major port in southern YEMEN, formerly the capital of South Yemen. (Pop. 264,350)

Adirondack Mountains a mountain range in NEW YORK State, USA. The highest peak is Mount Marcy (1629 m/ 5344 ft).

Adis Abeba *see* **Addis Ababa**.

Admiralty Islands a group of about 40 coral and volcanic islands in the southwest PACIFIC; part of PAPUA NEW GUINEA. (2000 sq km/800 sq miles; Pop. 30,200)

Adriatic Sea a branch of the MEDITERRANEAN SEA, between

ITALY, SLOVENIA and CROATIA.

Aegean Sea a branch of the MEDITERRANEAN SEA between GREECE and TURKEY.

Afghanistan is a landlocked country in southern ASIA. The greater part of the country is mountainous with several peaks over 6000 m (19,686 ft) in the central region. The climate is generally arid with great extremes of temperature. There is considerable snowfall in winter which may remain on the mountain summits the year round. The main economic activity is agriculture, and although predominantly pastoral, successful cultivation takes place in the fertile plains and valleys. Natural gas is produced in northern Afghanistan, and over 90% of this is piped across the border to the former USSR. Other mineral resources are scattered and so far underdeveloped. The main exports are Karakuls (Persian lambskins), raw cotton and foodstuffs.

Area : 652,090 sq km (251,772 sq miles)

Population : 15,810,000

Capital : Kabul

Other major cities : Herat, Kandahar, Mazar-i-Sharif

Form of government : People's Republic

Religions : Sunni Islam, Shia Islam

Currency : Afghani

Africa the second largest continent in the world, with the MEDITERRANEAN SEA to the north, the ATLANTIC OCEAN to the west and the INDIAN OCEAN to the east. There are 52 nations within Africa, excluding WESTERN SAHARA. (30,335,000 sq km/11,710,000 sq miles; pop. 614,000,000)

Agadez a Saharan oasis town in the centre of the AïR mountainous region of NIGER. (Pop. 21,000)

Agadir a port and popular tourist resort in MOROCCO. (Pop. 111,000)

Agincourt *see* **Azincourt.**

Agra a city in central INDIA, and site of the Taj Mahal, considered by many to be the world's most beautiful building, and certainly one of its finest examples of Mogul architecture. It was built in 1632–43 by emperor Shan Jehan as a white marble mausoleum for his favourite wife. (Pop. 747,000)

Agrigento (Girgenti) a town on the south coast of SICILY, and one of the great cities of classical antiquity. (Pop. 53,400)

Aguascalientes a state in central MEXICO; its capital has the same name, meaning "hot waters", after the hot mineral springs of this high plateau region. (Pop. state 556,000/city 239,000)

Agulhas, Cape the southernmost point of the African continent, 170 km (105 miles) southeast of CAPE TOWN.

Ahaggar *see* **Hoggar**.

Ahmadabad (Ahmedabad) an industrial city in western INDIA. (Pop. 2,548,000)

Ahmadi an oil town and commercial centre 35 km (21 miles) south of KUWAIT city. (Pop. 25,000)

Ahvaz a port on the Karun River in southern IRAN. (Pop. 471,000)

Ahvenanmaa *see* **Åland**.

Ain Salah *see* **In Salah**.

Aïr (Azbine) a mountainous region of the SAHARA DESERT in north-central NIGER, rising to 1500 m (5000 ft) and covering about 78,000 sq km (30,000 sq miles).

Aix-en-Provence a university city in southern FRANCE. (Pop. 129,000)

Aix-la-Chapelle *see* **Aachen**.

Ajaccio the capital and main port of CORSICA, on the west coast of the island. (Pop. 55,300)

Ajman the smallest emirate of the UNITED ARAB EMIRATES. (65 sq km/25 sq miles; pop. emirate 42,000/ town 27,000)

Ajmer an industrial city about 340 km (210 miles) southwest of DELHI; noted for its mosques, forts, and artificial lake. (Pop. 375,600)

Akita an industrial city near the northwest coast of HONSHU ISLAND, 440 km (275 miles) north of TOKYO. (Pop. 296,400)

'Akko *see* **Acre**.

Akron a city in northeast of the state of OHIO, USA. (Pop. city 226,900/metropolitan area 650,100)

Akure a cocoa-trade centre and capital of Ondo state in southwest NIGERIA. (Pop.114,400)

Akureyri a port and third largest town in ICELAND, situated at the head of the 60-km (37-mile) long Eyjafjördur inlet, on the north coast of the island. (Pop.13,750)

Akyab (Sittwe) a major rice market, port and state capital of ARAKAN, BURMA. (Pop. 143,200)

Alabama a state in southern USA. The state capital is MONTGOMERY. (133,667 sq km/51,606 sq miles; pop. 4,021,000)

Alamein *see* **El Alamein**.

Alamo, The an old Spanish mission near SAN ANTONIO, TEXAS, USA. Davy Crockett and 186 other Texans died defending the fort here against a Mexican army in 1836.

Åland (Ahvenanmaa) a group of over 6000 islands in the central BALTIC at the entrance to the Gulf of BOTHNIA. More than 100 of them are inhabited, by Swedish-speaking people who have a large measure of home rule from Finnish sovereignty, conferred in 1921. (Pop. 22,800)

Alaska the largest and most northerly state of the USA. The state capital is JUNEAU. (1,518,800 sq km/ 586,400 sq miles; pop. 521,000)

Alaska, Gulf of extends between the Alexander Archipelago and the Alaska Peninsula as the most northeasterly part of the PACIFIC OCEAN. It is a region of tectonic instability where there have been several major earthquakes and volcanic eruptions. (5200 sq km/2000 sq miles)

Alaska Highway a road extending 2452 km (1523 miles) from DAWSON CREEK in BRITISH COLUMBIA to FAIRBANKS, ALASKA; built by the US Army in 1942 and originally called the Alcan Highway.

Alba the Gaelic name for SCOTLAND.

Albacete a town and province of southeastern SPAIN. (Pop. town 177,100)

Albania is a small mountainous country in the eastern MEDITERRANEAN. Its immediate neighbours are GREECE and the former Yugoslavian republics of SERBIA and MACEDONIA, and it is bounded to the west by the ADRIATIC SEA. The climate is typically Mediterranean, and although most rain falls in winter, severe thunderstorms frequently occur on the plains in summer. Winters are severe in the highland areas, and heavy snowfalls are common. All land is state-owned, with the main agricultural areas lying along the Adriatic coast and in the Korce Basin. Industry is also nationalized and output is small. The principal industries are agricultural product processing, textiles, oil products and cement. Most trade is with neighbouring Serbia and Macedonia of the former Yugoslavia.

Area : 28,748 sq km (11,100 sq miles)

Population : 3,200,000

Capital : Tirana (Tiranë)

Other major cities : Durrës, Shkodër, Elbasan

Form of government : Socialist Republic

Religion : Constitutionally atheist but mainly Sunni Islam

Currency : Lek

Albany the capital city of NEW YORK State, USA. (Pop. 99,500)

Al Basrah *see* **Basra**.

Albert, Lake a lake in the GREAT RIFT VALLEY in East AFRICA, shared between UGANDA and ZAÏRE. (Also known as Lake Mobuto Sese Seko.) (5180 sq km/ 2000 sq miles)

Alberta a province of western CANADA; EDMONTON is its capital. (661,190 sq km/255,285 sq miles; pop. 2,238,000)

Ålborg a city and port in northern DENMARK. (Pop. 160,000)

Albuquerque a university city on the RIO GRANDE in NEW MEXICO, USA. (Pop. 350,600)

Albury-Wodonga an industrial twin-city straddling the

MURRAY river and state border, Albury being in NEW
SOUTH WALES and Wodonga in VICTORIA, AUSTRALIA. (Pop.
50,000)

Alcalá de Henares a town in central SPAIN, birthplace of
Miguel de Cervantes (1547-1616), author of *Don Quixote*.
(Pop. 142,900)

Alderney one of the CHANNEL ISLANDS.

Aldershot a town in HAMPSHIRE, ENGLAND, and site of a
large military camp. (Pop. 53,665)

Alençon an early lace-making centre, and capital of the
Orne département in northwestern FRANCE, 48 km (30
miles) north of LE MANS. (Pop. 32,500)

Aleppo (Halab) an industrial city of ancient origins in
SYRIA. (Pop. 905,944)

Ålesund a port and market town in western NORWAY, on
an island between BERGEN and TRONDHEIM. (Pop. 34,650)

Aleutian Islands a chain of over 150 volcanic islands,
extending southwestwards from the ALASKA Peninsula
between the North PACIFIC OCEAN and the BERING SEA.
The most westerly island, Attu, as part of the USA, is only
88 km (55 miles) across the BERING STRAIT from the
RUSSIAN FEDERATION.

Alexandria (El Iskandariya) the main port of EGYPT, on
the NILE delta. (Pop. 2,320,000).

Al Fujayrah the second smallest emirate in the UNITED
ARAB EMIRATES and also the name of a small town in the
emirate. (117 sq km/45 sq miles; pop. emirate 38,000/
town 760)

Al Furat *see* **Euphrates, River.**

Algarve the southern province of PORTUGAL.

Algeria is a huge country in northern AFRICA, which
fringes the MEDITERRANEAN SEA in the north. Over four-
fifths of Algeria is covered by the SAHARA DESERT to the
south. Near the north coastal area the ATLAS MOUNTAINS
run east-west in parallel ranges. The climate in the
coastal areas is warm and temperate with most of the
rain falling in winter. The summers are dry and hot with

temperatures rising to over 32°C. Inland beyond the Atlas Mountains conditions become more arid, and temperatures range from 49°C during the day to 10°C at night. Most of Algeria is unproductive agriculturally, but it does possess one of the largest reserves of natural gas and oil in the world. The main exports are oil-based products, and some fruit and vegetables.

Area : 2,381,741 sq km (919,590 sq miles)

Population : 25,360,000

Capital : Algiers (Alger)

Other major cities : Oran, Constantine, Annaba

Form of government : Republic

Religion : Sunni Islam

Currency : Algerian dinar

Algiers (El Djazair, Alger) the capital of ALGERIA, on the MEDITERRANEAN coast. (Pop. 1,800,000)

Al Hufuf *see* **Hofuf**.

Aliákmon, River the longest river in GREECE. (Length 297 km/184 miles)

Alicante a port and popular beach resort, and also the name of the surrounding province, on the MEDITERRANEAN coast of SPAIN. (Pop. town 251,400)

Alice Springs a desert settlement in the NORTHERN TERRITORY of AUSTRALIA. (Pop. 18,400)

Aligarh a university town in central INDIA. (Pop. 321,000)

Allahabad a holy city in INDIA on the confluence of the rivers GANGES and YAMUNA. (Pop. 650,000)

Allegheny Mountains the most northwesterly range of the APPALACHIANS, stretching 800 km (500 miles) through VIRGINIA, MARYLAND and PENNSYLVANIA in northeastern USA, rising from 600 m (2000 ft) to over 1480 m (4860 ft).

Alma-Ata (Almaty) a trading and industrial city and capital of KAZAKHSTAN. (Pop. 1,046,100)

Al Madinah *see* **Medina.**

Al Manamah the capital and main port of BAHRAIN. (Pop. 115,054)

Al Mawsil *see* **Mosul**.

Almeria a port in southern SPAIN, 275 km (170 miles) east and slightly north of GIBRALTAR. (Pop. 140,800)

Alps, The a mountain range in southern central EUROPE that spans the borders of SWITZERLAND, FRANCE, GERMANY, AUSTRIA, SLOVENIA and ITALY.

Alsace a region in the northeast of FRANCE.

Altai (Altay) an area of high mountain ranges in central Asia on the borders of CHINA and the RUSSIAN FEDERATION where they meet at the western end of MONGOLIA.

Altun Shan a mountain range with peaks in excess of 4000 m (13,000 ft) forming the northwestern outer edge of the TIBETAN PLATEAU in Central ASIA.

Amager a fertile island to the south of COPENHAGEN, in DENMARK.

Amalfi a small, picturesque town on a spectacular part of the west coast of ITALY. (Pop. 6100)

Amarillo an industrial city in northwest TEXAS, USA. (Pop. 162,900)

Amazon, River (Amazonas) with the River NILE, one of the world's two longest rivers. It rises in the ANDES of PERU and flows east through BRAZIL to the ATLANTIC OCEAN. (Length 6516 km/4050 miles)

Amboina *see* **Ambon**.

Ambon (Amboina) an island and the capital of the so-called Spice Islands in the MALUKU group in eastern central INDONESIA. (813 sq km/314 sq miles; pop. 73,000)

America the continent lying between the ATLANTIC and the PACIFIC OCEANS. For convenience it is divided into three zones: North America (USA, CANADA, MEXICO and GREENLAND: 23,500,000 sq km/9,071,000 sq miles; pop. 354,000,000), Central America (the area between the southern MEXICO border and the PANAMA-COLOMBIA border together with the CARIBBEAN: 1,849,000 sq km/714,000 sq miles; pop. 63,000,000), and South America (the area to the south of the PANAMA-COLOMBIA border: 17,611,000 sq km/6,798,000 sq miles; pop. 284,000,000).

American Samoa *see* **Samoa, American**.

Amiens an industrial city and capital of the SOMME department of northern FRANCE. (Pop. 159,600)

Amindivi Islands *see* **Lakshadweep**.

Amman the capital of JORDAN, in the northeast of the country. (Pop. 1,232,600)

Amoy *see* **Xiamen.**

Amritsar an industrial city in northern INDIA and home of the Golden Temple, the most sacred shrine of the Sikhs. (Pop. 595,000)

Amsterdam the capital and commercial centre of the NETHERLANDS, a historic port set on the IJSSELMEER. (Pop. 712,300)

Amudar'ya, River a central Asian river forming much of the border between TAJIKISTAN and AFGHANISTAN before flowing through UZBEKISTAN into the ARAL SEA. Its ancient name was OXUS. (Length 2620 km/1630 miles)

Amundsen Sea an arm of the South PACIFIC in ANTARCTICA.

Amur, River (Heilong Jiang) a river which runs along the border between CHINA and the RUSSIAN FEDERATION, flowing east into the PACIFIC OCEAN. (Length 4416 km/2744 miles)

Anatolia (Anadolu) the Asian part of Turkey, occupying the large rectangular peninsula between the BLACK SEA, eastern end of the MEDITERRANEAN SEA and the AEGEAN SEA, consisting of mountain ranges and plateaux with numerous large salt lakes in the interior; sometimes referred to as ASIA MINOR.

Anchorage the largest city and port in ALASKA, USA, on its southern coast. (Pop. 226,700)

Ancona a sea port in central ITALY, on the ADRIATIC, founded by Greeks from SYRACUSE in about 300BC. (Pop. 106,500)

Andalusia (Andalucía) a region of southwestern SPAIN, with a coast on the MEDITERRANEAN and ATLANTIC. (Pop. 6,441,800)

Andaman and Nicobar Islands two groups of islands

in the Bay of BENGAL, administered by INDIA. (Pop. 188,700)

Andaman Sea a branch of the Bay of BENGAL, lying between the ANDAMAN ISLANDS and BURMA.

Andes a high mountain range that runs down the entire length of the western coast of South AMERICA. The highest peak is Mount ACONCAGUA, in ARGENTINA (6960 m/22,835 ft).

Andhra Pradesh a state in southeast INDIA. The capital is HYDERABAD. (275,088 sq km/106,184 sq miles; pop. 53,549,700)

Andorra is a tiny state, situated high in the eastern PYRÉNÉES, between FRANCE and SPAIN. The state consists of deep valleys and high mountain peaks which reach heights of 3000 m (9843 ft). Although only 20 km (12 miles) wide and 30 km (19 miles) long, the spectacular scenery and climate attract many tourists. About 6 million visitors arrive each winter when the cold weather with heavy snowfalls makes for ideal skiing. In summer when the weather is mild and sunny the mountains are used for walking. Tourism and the duty-free trade are now Andorra's chief sources of income. Natives who are not involved in the tourist industry may raise sheep and cattle on the high pastures.

Area : 453 sq km (175 sq miles)

Population : 51,400

Capital : Andorra-la-Vella

Form of government : Co-principality

Religion : RC

Currency : Franc, Peseta

Andorra-la-Vella the capital of ANDORRA. (Pop. 14,000)

Andros the largest of the islands of the BAHAMAS (4144 sq km/1600 sq miles; pop. 8900)

Angara, River a river in the RUSSIAN FEDERATION flowing from Lake BAIKAL into the YENISEY River. (Length 1825 km/1135 miles)

Angel Falls a narrow band of water falling 979 m (3212

ft) from a high plateau in southeastern VENEZUELA to form the world's highest waterfall.

Angers a commercial and industrial centre in western FRANCE, on the Maine River, a tributary of the LOIRE, 80 km (50 miles) upstream from NANTES. (Pop. 141,000)

Angkor the ruined ancient capital of the Khmer empire in CAMBODIA.

Anglesey an island off the northwestern tip of WALES. (715 sq km/276 sq miles; pop. 69,000)

Angola is situated on the ATLANTIC coast of west-central AFRICA and lies about 10° south of the Equator. It shares borders with CONGO, ZAÏRE, ZAMBIA and NAMIBIA. Its climate is tropical with temperatures constantly between 20°C and 25°C. The rainfall is heaviest in inland areas where there are vast equatorial forests. The country is also rich in minerals, but deposits of manganese, copper and phosphate are as yet unexploited. Diamonds are mined in the northeast, and oil is produced near LUANDA. Oil production is the most important aspect of the economy, making up about 80% of export revenue.

Area: 1,246,700 sq km (481,351 sq miles)

Population : 10,020,000

Capital : Luanda

Other major cities : Huambo, Lobito, Benguela

Form of government : People's Republic

Religions : RC, Animism

Currency : Kwanza

Angoulême a historic fortified city and capital of the Charente départment in western FRANCE. (Pop. 109,400)

Anguilla an island in the LEEWARD ISLANDS group of the CARIBBEAN, now a self-governing British dependency. (91 sq km/35 sq miles; pop. 6500)

Angus *see* **Tayside**.

Anhui (Anhwei) a province of eastern CHINA. Its capital is HEFEI. (130,000 sq km/50,000 sq miles; pop. 48,030,000).

Anjou a former province of western FRANCE, in the valley of the River LOIRE.

Ankara the capital of TURKEY, in the eastern central part of Asian Turkey. (Pop. 2,252,000).

Annaba (Bone) a historic town and seaport on the MEDITERRANEAN coast of ALGERIA. (Pop. 245,000)

An Nafud (Nefud; Great Sandy Desert) a vast area of sandy desert in north-central SAUDI ARABIA that crosses imperceptibly into JORDAN and SYRIA.

Annam the old name used by the French for the central MIEN TRUNG region of VIETNAM.

Annapolis the capital of the state of MARYLAND, USA. (Pop. 31,900)

Annapurna a mountain of the HIMALAYAS, situated in NEPAL. (8091 m/26,545 ft)

Annecy an Alpine resort and capital of the Haute-Savoie départment in southeastern FRANCE. (Pop. 115,700)

Anshan a steel-manufacturing city in LIAONING province, northern CHINA. (Pop. 11,000,000)

Antakya (Antioch) a city of ancient origins in southern TURKEY. (Pop. 109,200)

Antalya a port and resort on the MEDITERRANEAN coast of TURKEY. (Pop. 258,100)

Antananarivo the capital of MADAGASCAR, in the centre of the island. (Pop. 663,000)

Antarctica an ice-covered continent around the SOUTH POLE consisting of a plateau and mountain ranges reaching a height of over 5000 m (16,500 ft). It is uninhabited apart from temporary staff at research stations. (14,000,000 sq km/5,100,000 sq miles)

Antarctic Circle Latitude 66° 32' south. At the southern winter solstice, the sun does not rise, nor does it set at the summer solstice, at this line, or in higher latitudes.

Antarctic Ocean (Southern Ocean) the waters that surround ANTARCTICA made up of the southern waters of the ATLANTIC, INDIAN and PACIFIC OCEANS.

Antarctic Peninsula a largely ice-covered and mountainous scimitar-shaped extension of ANTARCTICA, projecting some 1300 km (800 miles) towards South AMERICA.

It is also known as Graham Land, and remains a disputed territory claimed by ARGENTINA, CHILE and the UNITED KINGDOM.

Antibes a MEDITERRANEAN port and resort in southeastern FRANCE, once an important Roman town. (Pop. 63,250)

Antigua and Barbuda is located on the eastern side of the Leeward Islands, a tiny state comprising three islands—Antigua, Barbuda, and the uninhabited Redonda. Antigua's strategic position was recognized by the British in the 18th century when it was an important naval base, and later by the USA who built the island's airport during World War II to defend the CARIBBEAN and the PANAMA CANAL. The climate is tropical although its average rainfall of 100 mm (4 inches) makes it drier than most of the other islands of the WEST INDIES. On Antigua, many palm-fringed sandy beaches make it an ideal tourist destination, and as a result tourism is the main industry. Barbuda is surrounded by coral reefs, and the island is home to a wide range of wildlife.

Area : 440 sq km (170 sq miles)

Population : 85,000

Capital : St. John's

Form of government : Constitutional Monarchy

Religion : Christianity (mainly Anglicanism)

Currency : East Caribbean dollar

Antilles the major chain of islands in the CARIBBEAN SEA, divided into two groups: the Greater Antilles (which includes CUBA and PUERTO RICO) to the west; and the Lesser Antilles (including eg MARTINIQUE and BARBADOS) to the east.

Antioch *see* **Antakya.**

Antofagasta an important rail centre and copper exporting port in northern CHILE; it is the capital of the region of the same name. (Pop. city 170,000/region 342,000)

Antrim a county and town in NORTHERN IRELAND. (2831 sq km/1093 sq miles; pop. county 642,267/ town 22,242)

Antwerp (Antwerpen, Anvers) the capital of the

province of Antwerp and the main port of BELGIUM. (Pop. 488,000)

Anuradapura an ancient Sinhalese royal capital founded in 500 BC, 160 km (100 miles) northeast of Colombo in present-day SRI LANKA. Its fine ruins lay beneath the jungle for over 800 years until the British uncovered them in the 19th century. An important place of Buddhist pilgrimage. (Pop. 32,600)

Anvers *see* **Antwerp**.

Anyang a city of ancient origins in the HENAN province of eastern CHINA. (Pop. 500,000)

Aomori a port on HONSHU Island, JAPAN. (Pop. 294,000)

Aosta an iron and steel-making town in the French-speaking VALLE D'AOSTA region of ITALY, 80 km (50 miles) north of TURIN. The modern city follows the original Roman street plan, and there are many important ancient remains. (Pop.37,200)

Apatity a mining town 120 km/75 miles north of the ARCTIC CIRCLE in the KOLA PENINSULA of the RUSSIAN FEDERATION; its name recognizes the world's largest deposit of apatite, which is nearby. (Pop. 74,100)

Apeldoorn a town in the NETHERLANDS, in the central Gelderland province; nearby is the summer residence of the Dutch royal family. (Pop. 140,800)

Apennines (Appennino) the mountain range which forms the "backbone" of ITALY. The highest peak is Monte Corno (2912 m/9554 ft).

Apia the capital of WESTERN SAMOA. (Pop. 34,000)

Appalachian Mountains a chain of mountains which stretches 2570 km (1600 miles) down eastern North AMERICA from CANADA to ALABAMA in the USA. The highest peak is Mount MITCHELL (2037 m/6684 ft).

Appennino *see* **Apennines**.

Apulia *see* **Puglia**.

Aqaba the only port in JORDAN, situated at the head of the Gulf of Aqaba. (Pop. 35,000)

Aqaba, Gulf of an arm of the RED SEA that is part of the

GREAT RIFT VALLEY system, and separates the SINAI and ARABIAN PENINSULAS; it is 160 km (98 miles) long and 19–27 km (12–16 miles) wide.

Aquitaine a region and former kingdom of southwestern FRANCE.

Arabian Gulf *see* **Gulf, The.**

Arabian Peninsula (Arabia) a great peninsula in southwest ASIA, between the RED SEA and The GULF; it consists chiefly of a desert plateau, including the vast "Empty Quarter" (RUB AL-KHALI), and with mountains rising over 3000 m (10,000 ft) in the western HEJAZ region. It is, however, rich in oil deposits, especially along The Gulf coast. The total area of the peninsula is greater than that of GREENLAND: 2,600,000 sq km (1,000,000 sq miles).

Arabian Sea a branch of the INDIAN OCEAN between INDIA and the Arabian Peninsula.

Arafura Sea a stretch of the PACIFIC OCEAN between NEW GUINEA and AUSTRALIA.

Aragón a region and former kingdom of northeast SPAIN.

Arakan a coastal state of BURMA, on the Bay of BENGAL, that is cut off from the rest of the country by the Arakan Yoma (hills) which rise over 1700 m (5600 ft). The main town and state capital is AKYAB. (36,778 sq km/14,200 sq miles; Pop. 2,046,000)

Aral Sea a large, salty lake, to the east of the CASPIAN SEA, which lies on the border between UZBEKISTAN and KAZAKHSTAN. (64,750 sq km/25,000 sq miles)

Aran Islands (Oileáin Arann) three small islands Inishmore, Inishmaan and Inisheer off County GALWAY in the Republic of IRELAND. (44 sq km/18 sq miles; Pop. 1380)

Ararat, Mount (Büjük Agri Dagi) the mountain peak in eastern TURKEY where Noah's Ark is said to have come to rest after the Great Flood. (5165 m/16,945 ft)

Arauca, River a major tributary of the ORINOCO River which forms part of the border between COLOMBIA and VENEZUELA. (Length 1000 km/620 miles)

Arbroath a port and resort on the NORTH SEA coast of eastern SCOTLAND, in TAYSIDE region, famed for its "smokies" (smoked haddock) and its abbey, the scene of the barons of Scotland's *Declaration of Independence* to Pope John XXII in 1320. (Pop. 24,093)

Archangel (Arkhangel'sk) a port on the DVINA Delta on the WHITE SEA in the RUSSIAN FEDERATION. (Pop. 403,000)

Arctic Circle latitude 66° 32' north. The sun does not set above this line at the northern summer solstice, nor does it rise above this line at the winter solstice.

Arctic Ocean the ice-laden sea to the north of the ARCTIC CIRCLE. (14,056,000 sq km/5,426,000 sq miles)

Arctic, The the regions that lie to the north of the ARCTIC CIRCLE.

Ardabil a town in IRAN, famous for its knotted carpets. (Pop. 222,000)

Ardennes a hilly and forested region straddling the borders of BELGIUM, LUXEMBOURG and FRANCE.

Arendal a port on the SKAGERRAK coast of southern NORWAY, 65 km (40 miles) northeast of KRISTIANSAND; its main trade is in timber, shipbuilding and ferry traffic to DENMARK. (Pop. 25,100)

Arequipa a city and department of PERU. (Pop. city 448,000)

Arezzo a city and province in TUSCANY, ITALY, 60 km (35 miles) southeast of FLORENCE. (Pop. city 91,700/province 313,600)

Argentina, the world's eighth largest country, stretches from the Tropic of Capricorn to Cape HORN on the southern tip of the South American continent. To the west a massive mountain chain, the ANDES, forms the border with CHILE. The climate ranges from warm temperate over the PAMPAS in the central region, to a more arid climate in the north and west, while in the extreme south conditions although also dry are much cooler. The vast fertile plains of the Pampas once provided Argentina with its main source of wealth, but as manufacturing industries were established in the early 20th century agriculture suffered badly, and food exports were greatly reduced. A series of military regimes has resulted in an unstable economy that fails to provide reasonable living standards for the population.

Area : 2,766,889 sq km (1,068,296 sq miles)

Population : 32,690,000

Capital : Buenos Aires

Other major cities : Cordoba, Rosaria, Mendoza, La Plata

Form of government : Federal Republic

Religion : RC

Currency : Austral

Argos a city in the PELOPONNESE, GREECE, and one of the oldest ancient sites, with Mycenaean remains dating from the 14th century BC. Legend says Jason and the Argonauts set sail from here to seek the Golden Fleece.

Argyllshire *see* **Highland**; **Strathclyde**.

Århus a port and the second largest city in DENMARK. (Pop. 246,700)

Arica a port in the extreme north of CHILE, outlet for Bolivian and Peruvian trade. (Pop. 123,300)

Arizona a state in the southwest of the USA. The capital is PHOENIX. (295,024 sq km/113,902 sq miles; pop. 3,137,000)

Arkansas a state in the south of the USA. The state capital is LITTLE ROCK. (137,539 sq km/53,104 sq miles; pop. 2,359,000)

Arkansas, River a tributary of the River MISSISSIPPI in the USA, flowing from the ROCKY MOUNTAINS through the states of KANSAS, OKLAHOMA and ARKANSAS. (Length 2335 km/1450 miles)

Arkhangel'sk *see* **Archangel**.

Arles an ancient Roman provincial capital situated in southeastern FRANCE on the east bank of the RHÔNE River. It is now a centre for agricultural marketing and tourism, as well as having associations with the last and most productive years of the Dutch painter, Vincent Van Gogh (1853-90). (Pop. 50,800)

Armagh a county and city in NORTHERN IRELAND. (1254 sq km/484 sq miles; pop. county 118,820/city 12,700)

Armenia (1) the former independent kingdom that straddled the borders of modern TURKEY, IRAN, GEORGIA, and AZERBAIJAN. **(2)** the smallest republic of the former USSR and part of the former kingdom of Armenia which was divided between Turkey, Iran and the former USSR. It declared independence from the USSR in 1991. It is a landlocked Transcaucasian republic, and its neighbours are Turkey, Iran, Georgia and Azerbaijan. The country is very mountainous with many peaks over 3000 m (13,418 ft). Agriculture is mixed in the lowland areas. The main crops grown are grain, sugar beet and potatoes, and livestock reared include cattle, pigs and sheep. Mining of copper, zinc and lead is important, and industrial development is increasing. Hydro-electricity is produced from stations on the river Razdan as it falls 1000 m (3281 ft) from Lake Sevan to its confluence with the River Araks.

Area : 29,800 sq km (11,500 sq miles)

Population : 3,267,000

Capital : Yerevan

Other major city : Kumayri (Leninakan)

Form of government : Republic

Religion : Armenian Orthodox

Currency : Rouble

Arnhem a town in the NETHERLANDS, scene of a battle in 1944 between British (and Polish) paratroops and the German army. (Pop. 128,600)

Arnhem Land an Aboriginal reserve in the NORTHERN TERRITORY of AUSTRALIA.

Arno, River the main river of TUSCANY in ITALY, flowing westward through FLORENCE to PISA on the coast. (Length 245 km/152 miles)

Arran a mountainous island on the west side of the Firth of CLYDE and separated from the KINTYRE peninsula by the Kilbrannan Sound; its main industry is tourism. (430 sq km/166 sq miles; Pop. 3844)

Ar Riyad *see* **Riyadh**.

Artois a historical area in the extreme north of FRANCE, acquired from Spain in 1659, occupying a chalk plateau between FLANDERS and PICARDY, and now the region of NORD-PAS DE CALAIS.

Aruba a CARIBBEAN island off the coast of VENEZUELA, formerly one of the NETHERLANDS ANTILLES. The capital is ORANJESTAD. (193 sq km/75 sq miles; pop. 67,000; cur. Aruba guilder)

Arunachal Pradesh a union territory of northern INDIA, bordering TIBET. The capital is Shillong. (Pop. 631,800)

Arusha a regional capital of northern TANZANIA; it is a tourist centre at the foot of Mount Meru (4565 m/14,977 ft) and lies in a coffee-growing area. (Pop. 55,300)

Ascension Island a tiny volcanic island in the South ATLANTIC OCEAN, forming part of the ST HELENA DEPENDENCIES. (Pop. 1625)

Aseb (Assab) a RED SEA port in ERITREA, EHTIOPIA, 60 km (35 miles) north of the border with DJIBOUTI; it has the country's only oil refinery. (Pop. 25,000)

Ashdod a port and industrial centre on coast of ISRAEL about 30 km (19 miles) south of TEL AVIV; it is the site of an ancient Philistine harbour, fort and temple. (Pop. 68,900)

Ashkhabad the capital of TURKMENISTAN. (Pop. 347,000)

Ashqelon a port and resort on the MEDITERRANEAN coast, 50 km (30 miles) south of TEL AVIV, ISRAEL; it was originally a Philistine city-kingdom, captured by the Romans, and later, in the 12th century, by the Crusaders. (Pop. 54,700)

Asia the largest continent, bounded by the ARCTIC, PACIFIC and INDIAN OCEANS, plus the MEDITERRANEAN and RED SEAS (43,608,000 sq km/16,833,000 sq miles; pop. 3,075,000,000). East Asia is taken to mean those countries to the northeast of BANGLADESH (eg CHINA); Central

Asia comprises the five Islamic republics, formerly of the USSR and independent since 1991, that lie east of the Caspian Sea (eg KAZAKHSTAN); South Asia refers to the countries on the Indian subcontinent (eg INDIA); and South-East Asia includes those countries to the south-east of China, including the islands to the west of NEW GUINEA (eg INDONESIA).

Asia Minor the historical name for ANATOLIA.

Asmara (Asmera) the main city of ERITREA in ETHIOPIA. (Pop. 430,000)

Assab *see* **Aseb**.

Assam a state in northeastern INDIA. (99,680 sq km/38,476 sq miles; pop. 19,900,000)

Assisi a small town in UMBRIA, central ITALY, and birth-place of St Francis (1182-1226). (Pop. 24,400)

Assyria an empire of ancient MESOPOTAMIA founded around 3000 BC and reaching the height of its power in the 7th century BC. Its main cities were Assur and NINEVEH on the River TIGRIS, now in modern IRAQ.

Astrakhan a port near the CASPIAN SEA, situated on the delta of the River VOLGA. (Pop. 487,000)

Asturias a region of northern SPAIN. The capital is OVIEDO. (Pop. 1,227,000)

Asunción the capital and the only major city of PARAGUAY. (Pop. 456,000)

Aswan a city in southern EGYPT by the River NILE. The Aswan High Dam, completed 1971, is 13 km (8 miles) to the south. (Pop. 200,000)

Asyut an ancient city in central EGYPT, on the River NILE; it was Lycopolis in classical times. (Pop. 214,000)

Atacama Desert an extremely dry desert lying mainly in northern CHILE.

Atbara an industrial town in northern SUDAN, standing at the confluence of the NILE and the Atbara river (Black Nile) and strategically located on the junction of two major roads ánd railway lines to KHARTOUM (from WADI HALFA and PORT SUDAN). (Pop. 73,100)

Athabasca, River a river in CANADA which flows north from the ROCKY MOUNTAINS to Lake Athabasca. (Length 1231 km/765 miles)

Athens (Athinai) the historic capital, and the principal city, of GREECE. (Pop. city 885,700/metropolitan area 3,027,300)

Athlone (Baile Atha Luain) a market town in WEST-MEATH, at almost the exact centre of IRELAND. (Pop. 9410)

Athos a group of monasteries on Mount Athos (2033 m/ 6670 ft) on a peninsula in northern GREECE.

Atlanta the capital and largest city of the state of GEORGIA in the USA. (Pop. 426,100)

Atlantic Ocean the second largest ocean, lying between North and South AMERICA, EUROPE and AFRICA. (82,217,000 sq km/31,736,000 sq miles)

Atlantic Provinces *see* **Maritime Provinces.**

Atlantis 'the lost continent' which, according to ancient legend, sank beneath the ATLANTIC OCEAN west of the Strait of GIBRALTAR.

Atlas Mountains a series of mountain chains stretching across North AFRICA from MOROCCO to TUNISIA.

Attica (Attiki) the ancient region of the ATHENS city-state, and today an administrative department of modern GREECE, occupying the south-projecting peninsula that extends from the Isthmus of CORINTH to Cape SOÚNION and surrounding Athens. (2496 sq km/964 sq miles; pop. 342,093)

Auckland the largest city and chief port of NEW ZEALAND, on NORTH ISLAND. (Pop. 769,600)

Augsburg a historic city in BAVARIA, GERMANY. (Pop. 245,000)

Augusta (1) a city and river port on the Savannah River in GEORGIA, USA. (Pop. city 46,000/metropolitan area 368,300). **(2)** the state capital of MAINE, USA. (Pop. 22,000)

Augustow (Avgustov) a boating and sailing centre in the Suwalki lake district of northeast POLAND. (Pop. 25,600)

Auschwitz (Oswiecim) a small town in POLAND and site of the biggest of the Nazi concentration camps 1940-45. (Pop. 35,600)

Austerlitz *see* **Slavkov**.

Austin the capital city of the state of TEXAS, USA. (Pop. city 397,000/metropolitan area 645,400)

Australasia a general term for AUSTRALIA, NEW ZEALAND and neighbouring islands.

Australia, the world's smallest continental landmass, is a vast and sparsely populated island state in the southern hemisphere. The most mountainous region is the GREAT DIVIDING RANGE which runs down the entire east coast. Because of its great size, Australia's climates range from tropical monsoon to cool temperate and also large areas of desert. Central and south QUEENSLAND are subtropical while north and central NEW SOUTH WALES are warm temperate. Much of Australia's wealth comes from agriculture, with huge sheep and cattle stations extending over large parts of the interior. These have helped maintain Australia's position as the world's leading producer of wool. Cereal growing is dominated by wheat. Mineral extraction is also very important.

Area : 7,686,848 sq km (2,967,892 sq miles)

Population : 17,100,000

Capital : Canberra

Other major cities : Adelaide, Brisbane, Melbourne, Perth, Sydney

Form of government : Federal Parliamentary State

Religion : Christianity

Currency : Australian dollar

Australian Capital Territory the small region which surrounds CANBERRA, the capital of AUSTRALIA. (2432 sq km/939 sq miles; pop. 240,000)

Austria is a landlocked country in central EUROPE and is surrounded by seven nations. The wall of mountains that runs across the centre of the country dominates the scenery. In the warm summers tourists come to walk in the forests and mountains, and in the cold winters skiers come to the mountains, which now boast over 50 ski resorts. Agriculture in Austria is based on small farms, many of which are run by a single family. Dairy products, and beef and lamb from the hill farms, contribute to exports. More than 37% of Austria is covered in forest, resulting in the paper-making industry near GRAZ. Unemployment is very low, and a good strike record has attracted multinational companies in recent years. Attachment to local customs is still strong, and in rural areas men still wear lederhosen and women the traditional dirndl skirt on feast days and holidays.

Area : 83,853 sq km (32,376 sq miles)

Population : 7,600,000

Capital : Vienna (Wien)

Other major cities : Graz, Linz, Salzburg

Form of government : Federal Republic

Religion : RC

Currency : Schilling

Auvergne a mountainous region of central FRANCE.

Avgustov *see* **Augustow**.

Avignon a historic city on the River RHONE in southern FRANCE, the seat of the Pope, 1309–77. (Pop. 177,500)

Avila a town and province in the mountainous central region of SPAIN, famous as the birthplace of St Teresa (1515-82). (Pop. Town 41,800)

Avon a county in the west of ENGLAND; the county town is BRISTOL. (1338 sq km/517 sq miles; pop. 936,000)

Axios, River a river flowing through the BALKANS to GREECE and the AEGEAN SEA. (Length: 388km/ 241miles)

Axum an important historic town in ETHIOPIA, once a royal capital where the Queen of Sheba is said to have ruled. (Pop. 20,000)

Ayers Rock a huge rock, sacred to the Aborigines, rising sharply out of the plains in the NORTHERN TERRITORY of AUSTRALIA. (348 m/1142 ft)

Aylesbury the county town of BUCKINGHAMSHIRE, in southeast central ENGLAND; it is situated on a plain below the northern escarpment of the CHILTERN HILLS. (Pop. 51,999)

Ayr a former county town and coastal resort on the Firth of CLYDE, 50 km (30 miles) southwest of GLASGOW, SCOTLAND. The poet Robert Burns was born in 1759 in the Ayr suburb of Alloway, where his cottage is now a memorial museum. (Pop. 49,481)

Ayrshire *see* **Strathclyde**.

Ayutthaya a town with the extensive ruins of the city that was the capital of THAILAND from 1350 to 1767. (Pop. 113,300)

Az Zahran *see* **Dhahran**.

Azad Kashmir a disputed area in the former princely state of JAMMU AND KASHMIR, which has been governed by PAKISTAN since the United Nations ceasefire between INDIA and PAKISTAN in 1949; *Azad* means "free". The KARAKORUM Highway, built with Chinese aid, passes through the towering HIMALAYA peaks of the area to connect Pakistan with the XINJIANG region of CHINA.

Azarbaijan a region of northern IRAN. Its population shares the same language as the people of neighbouring AZERBAIJAN. (Pop. 4,613,000)

Azbine *see* **Aïr**.

Azerbaijan, a republic of the former USSR, declared itself independent in 1991. It is situated on the southwest coast of the CASPIAN SEA and shares borders with IRAN, ARMENIA, GEORGIA and the RUSSIAN FEDERATION. The Araks river separates Azerbaijan from the region known as AZARBAIJAN in northern Iran. The country is semi-arid, and 70% of the land is irrigated for the production of cotton, wheat, maize, potatoes, tobacco, tea and citrus fruits. It has rich mineral deposits of oil, natural gas, iron and aluminium. The most important mineral is oil, which is found in the BAKU area from where it is piped to Batumi on the Black Sea. There are steel, synthetic rubber and aluminium works at Sumgait just north of the capital Baku.
Area : 87,000 sq km (33,600 sq miles)

Azincourt

Population : 6,506,000
Capital : Baku
Other major cities : Kirovabad, Sumgait
Form of government : Republic
Religions : Shia Islam, Russian Orthodox
Currency : Rouble

Azincourt (Agincourt) a village in the Pas-de-Calais département of northern FRANCE, 48 km (30 miles) southeast of BOULOGNE, that was the site of the famous victory in 1415 by King Henry V of ENGLAND, over the French, in his conquest of NORMANDY.

Azores three groups of small islands in the North ATLANTIC OCEAN, belonging to PORTUGAL. The capital is PONTA DELGADA. (2335 sq km/901 sq miles; pop. 336,100)

Azov, Sea of (Azovskoye More) a shallow, almost enclosed sea, east of the CRIMEA peninsula, connected to the BLACK SEA by the Strait of KERCH.

B

Baalbek a ruined city dating back to Phoenician and Roman times in the BEQA'A VALLEY in LEBANON.

Babylon one of the great cities of ancient MESOPOTAMIA, situated in modern IRAQ.

Badajoz a brewing, distilling and food-processing town 325 km (200 miles) southwest of MADRID, on the Spanish side of the border with PORTUGAL. It has many fine Roman remains and was the capital of a Moorish Kingdom in the 11th century. (Pop. 114,400)

Baden-Baden a famous spa town in southwest GERMANY dating from Roman times. (Pop. 50,000)

Baden-Württemburg the southern state of GERMANY bordering FRANCE and SWITZERLAND. (Pop. 9,241,000)

Bafatá the main commerical centre for the interior of GUINEA-BISSAU, lying at the highest navigable point on the GÊBA River, about 110 km (70 miles) east and slightly north of BISSAU. (Pop. 116,000)

Baffin Bay a huge bay within the ARCTIC CIRCLE between BAFFIN ISLAND in CANADA and GREENLAND.

Baffin Island a large, mainly ice-bound island in northeast CANADA. (507,451 sq km/195,927 sq miles)

Baghdad the capital of IRAQ, in the centre of the country, on the River TIGRIS. (Pop. 3,300,000)

Baguio a popular hill resort and summer capital of PHILIPPINES, located on northern LUZON, about 210 km (130 miles) north of MANILA. (Pop. 119.010)

Bahamas, The consist of an archipelago of 700 islands located in the ATLANTIC OCEAN off the southeast coast of FLORIDA. The largest island is ANDROS (4144 sq km/1600 sq miles), and the two most populated are Grand Bahama and New Providence where the capital, NASSAU, lies. Winters in the Bahamas are mild and summers warm. Most rain falls in May, June, September and October, and thunderstorms are frequent in summer. The islands have few natural resources, and for many years fishing and small-scale farming were the only ways to make a living. Now, however, tourism, which employs over two-thirds of the workforce, is the most important industry and has been developed on a vast scale. About three million tourists, mainly from North AMERICA, visit the Bahamas each year.

Area : 13,878 sq km (5358 sq miles)

Population : 256,000

Capital : Nassau

Other important city : Freeport

Form of government : Constitutional Monarchy

Religion : Christianity

Currency : Bahamian dollar

Bahawalpur a town and former princely state on the SUTLEJ River, about 345 km (215 miles) southwest of LAHORE. (Pop. 178,000)

Bahía Blanca an inlet and port about 550 km (340 miles) southwest of BUENOS AIRES on ARGENTINA's ATLANTIC coast; trade out of here is mainly produce from the southern PAMPAS. (Pop. 223,800)

Bahia *see* **Salvador**.

Bahrain is a Gulf State comprising 33 low-lying islands situated between the QATAR peninsula and the mainland of SAUDI ARABIA. Bahrain Island is the largest, and a causeway linking it to Saudi Arabia was opened in 1986. The highest point in the state is only 122.4 m (402 ft) above sea level. The climate is pleasantly warm between December and March, but very hot from June to November. Most of Bahrain is sandy and too saline to support crops, but drainage schemes are now used to reduce salinity, and fertile soil is imported from other islands. Oil was discovered in 1931, and revenues from oil now account for about 75% of the country's total revenue. Bahrain is being developed as a major manufacturing state, the first important enterprise being aluminium smelting. Traditional industries include pearl fishing, boat building, weaving and pottery.

Area : 678 sq km (262 sq miles)

Population : 486,000

Capital : Manama

Form of government : Monarchy (Emirate)

Religions : Shia Islam, Sunni Islam

Currency : Bahraini dollar

Baia Mare the capital city of the Maramures region of northwest ROMANIA. (Pop. 117,800)

Baikal, Lake (Ozero Baykal) the world's deepest freshwater lake, and the largest by volume, situated in southeast SIBERIA in the RUSSIAN FEDERATION. (31,500 sq km/ 12,150 sq miles)

Baikonur *see* **Baykonyr**.

Baile Atha Cliath *see* **Dublin**.

Baja California a huge 1300 km (800 mile) long peninsula of MEXICO, which stretches south from CALIFORNIA in the USA into the PACIFIC OCEAN. (Pop. 1,400,000)

Bakhtaran formerly called Kermanshah, a large city in IRAN on the old trading routes between TEHRAN and BAGHDAD. (Pop. 531,000)

Baku (Baky) a port on the CASPIAN SEA and the capital of the republic of AZERBAIJAN. (Pop. 1,661,000)

Bakwanga *see* **Mbuji-Mayi.**

Balaklava *see* **Sevastopol**.

Balaton, Lake a lake in western HUNGARY, famous as a tourist resort. (601 sq km/232 sq miles)

Bâle *see* **Basle**.

Baleares, Islas (Balearic Islands) a group of islands in the western MEDITERRANEAN SEA belonging to SPAIN and famous as tourist resorts. The main islands are MAJORCA (Mallorca), MINORCA (Menorca), IBIZA (Iviza), Formentera and Cabrera. (Pop. 685,000)

Balearic Islands *see* **Baleares, Islas.**

Bali a small island lying off the eastern tip of JAVA, distinguished by being the only island in INDONESIA to have preserved a predominantly Hindu culture intact. The main town and capital is DENPASAR. (5591 sq km/2159 sq miles; pop. 2,470,000)

Balkans the southeastern corner of EUROPE, a broad, mountainous peninsula bordered by the ADRIATIC SEA, the IONIAN SEA, the AEGEAN SEA and the BLACK SEA. ALBANIA, BULGARIA, GREECE, ROMANIA, SLOVENIA, CROATIA, BOSNIA-HERZEGOVINA, the rest of the former YUGOSLAVIA and the European part of TURKEY are all in the Balkans.

Balkan Mountains (Stara Planina) a range of mountains extending east-west for about 320 km (200 miles) in a gentle arc across BULGARIA, from the BLACK SEA to the border with SERBIA. The highest point is Botev Peak, 2375 m (7792 ft).

Balkhash, Lake (Ozero Balkhash) a massive lake in KAZAKHSTAN, near the border with CHINA. (22,000 sq km/ 8500 sq miles)

Ballarat a historic gold-mining town in VICTORIA, AUSTRALIA, the scene of the 1854 rebellion known as the Eureka Stockade. (Pop. 62,600)

Balleymena a town in County ANTRIM, NORTHERN IRELAND, in a fertile farming region, and with linen, wool and engineering industries. (Pop. 55,400)

Baltic Sea a shallow sea in northern EUROPE, completely surrounded by land masses except for the narrow straits that connect it to the NORTH SEA.

Baltimore the largest city in the state of MARYLAND, USA. (Pop. city 763,000/metropolitan area 2,244,700)

Baluchistan a province of southwestern PAKISTAN, bordering IRAN and AFGHANISTAN. (Pop. 4,332,000)

Bamako the capital of MALI. (Pop. 405,000)

Bamberg a town in northern BAVARIA, GERMANY, seat of prince-bishops of the Holy Roman Empire (1007–1802). (Pop. 70,000)

Banbury a market town on River Cherwell, 35 km (22 miles) north of OXFORD, ENGLAND. (pop. 37,460)

Bandar Abbas a port in southern IRAN on the Strait of HORMUZ, at the neck of THE GULF. (Pop. 89,200)

Bandar Seri Begawan the capital of BRUNEI. (Pop. 50,000)

Banda Sea a part of the PACIFIC OCEAN, in eastern INDONESIA.

Bandundu a busy commercial centre in the southwest of ZAÏRE, and capital of the region of the same name. Formerly called Banningville in days of the colonial Belgian Congo. (Pop. city 120,000/region 4,120,000)

Bandung a large inland city in western JAVA, INDONESIA. (Pop. 1,462,700)

Banffshire *see* **Grampian**.

Bangalore a large industrial city in central southern INDIA. (Pop. 2,921,800)

Banghází *see* **Benghazi**.

Bangkok (Krung Thep) the capital of THAILAND, on the River CHAO PHRAYA. (Pop. 5,900,000)

Bangladesh was formerly the Eastern Province of PAKISTAN. It is bounded almost entirely by INDIA and to the south by the Bay of BENGAL. The country is extremely flat and is virtually a huge delta formed by the GANGES, BRAHMAPUTRA and Meghna rivers. The country is subject to devastating floods and cyclones which sweep in from the Bay of Bengal. Most villages are built on mud platforms to keep them above water. The climate is tropical monsoon with heat, extreme humidity and heavy rainfall in the monsoon season. The short winter season is mild and dry. The combination of rainfall, sun and silt from the rivers makes the land productive, and it is often possible to grow three crops a year. Bangladesh produces about 70% of the world's jute, and the production of jute-related products is a principal industry.
Area : 143,998 sq km (55,598 sq miles)
Population : 113,340,000

Bangor

Capital : Dhaka (Dacca)
Other major cities : Chittagong, Khulna
Form of government : Republic
Religion : Sunni Islam
Currency : Taka

Bangor (1) the largest seaside resort in NORTHERN IRELAND and an attractive residential satellite town for BELFAST, only 20 km (12 miles) to the southwest. (Pop. 46,500) **(2)** a university town in GWYNNED, North WALES, situated on the mainland side of the MENAI STRAIT. (Pop. 12,174)

Bangui the capital of the CENTRAL AFRICAN REPUBLIC, in the south of the country. (Pop. 387,000)

Bangweulu, Lake a large lake in northern ZAMBIA. (9800 sq km/3784 sq miles)

Banja Luka a city of ancient origins on the Vrbas River in northwest BOSNIA-HERZEGOVINA. (Pop. 183,000)

Banjarmasin a port on the southern coast of KALIMANTAN, INDONESIA. (Pop. 381,300)

Banjul the capital of the GAMBIA. Formerly called Bathurst. (Pop. 42,000)

Banningville *see* **Bandundu**.

Barania Gora *see* **Beskidy**.

Barbados is the most easterly island of the WEST INDIES and lies well outside the group of islands which makes up the Lesser ANTILLES. Most of the island is low-lying, and only in the north does it rise to over 340 m (1116 ft) at Mount Hillaby. The climate is tropical, but the cooling effect of the northeast trade winds prevents the temperatures rising above 30°C (86°F). There are only two seasons, the dry and the wet, when rainfall is very heavy. At one time the economy depended almost exclusively on the production of sugar, and its by-products molasses, and rum, and although the industry is now declining, sugar is still the principal export. Tourism has now taken over as the main industry, and it employs 40% of the island's labour force. The island is surrounded by pink and white sandy beaches and coral reefs which are visited by almost 400,000 tourists each year.

Area : 430 sq km (166 sq miles)

Population : 260,000

Capital : Bridgetown

Form of government : Constitutional Monarchy

Religions : Anglicanism, Methodism

Currency : Barbados dollar

Barbuda *see* **Antigua and Barbuda**.

Barcelona the second largest city in SPAIN, and the name of the surrounding province. It is a major port on the MEDITERRANEAN SEA. (Pop. city 1,754,900)

Barents Sea a part of the ARCTIC OCEAN to the north of NORWAY.

Bari a major port on the ADRIATIC coast of ITALY. (Pop. 370,000)

Barnsley a town in South YORKSHIRE, 18 km (11 miles) north of SHEFFIELD; it was a leading coal-mining centre for over a century. (Pop. 74,000)

Baroda *see* **Vadodara**.

Barossa Valley a wine-producing region in SOUTH AUSTRALIA, 50 km (30 miles) north of ADELAIDE.

Barquisimeto an industrial city in western VENEZUELA. (Pop. 600,000)

Barra the southernmost inhabited island (including Vatersay, linked by causeway) of the WESTERN ISLES of SCOTLAND. (52 sq km/20 sq miles; Pop. 1264)

Barranquilla the largest port on the CARIBBEAN coast of COLOMBIA. (Pop. 1,067,000)

Barren Desert (Dasht-e Lut) *see* **Iranian Plateau.**

Basel *see* **Basle**.

Bashkiria (Baskir Republic) a republic of the RUSSIAN FEDERATION, in the southern URALS. The capital is UFA. (143,500 sq km/55,400 sq miles; pop. 3,860,000)

Basilan an island with principal town of same name (formerly Isabela) lying off the southern tip of Zamboanga peninsula of MINDANAO, PHILIPPINES. (Pop. city 171,000)

Basilicata the remote region of mountainous and desolate hill country at the bottom of ITALY's "boot". The regional capital is POTENZA. (992 sq km/3850 sq miles; Pop. 618,200)

Basle (Basel, Bâle) a city in northern SWITZERLAND and the name of the surrounding canton. (Pop. city 200,000)

Basque Provinces (País Vasco) an autonomous region of northern SPAIN, comprising the provinces of Alava, Guipúzcoa and Vizcaya; they are inhabited mainly by Basques, who have retained virtual autonomy from the 9th century. The chief town is Bilbao. (7250 sq km/2800 sq miles; pop. 2,141,809)

Basque Region (Basque Country) an area straddling the border of SPAIN and FRANCE on the ATLANTIC coast at the western end of the PYRÉNÉES, whose native people have a unique language—unrelated to any other European tongue. .

Basra (Al Basrah) the second city of IRAQ, and its main port. (Pop. 1,200,000)

Bassein a trading city on the delta of the IRRAWADDY River in BURMA. (Pop. 355,600)

Basse Normandie *see* **Normandy.**

Basseterre the capital of ST KITTS AND NEVIS. (Pop. 16,000)

Basse Terre the capital of the French island of GUADELOUPE, situated on the island called Basse Terre. (Pop. town 14,000/island 141,000)

Bass Strait the stretch of water spanning the 290 km (180 miles) which separate the mainland of AUSTRALIA from TASMANIA.

Bastia the main commerical and industrial city of CORSICA, 105 km (65 miles) northeast of AJACCIO. It is also an important port, exporting wine and fish. (Pop. 51,700)

Basutoland the former name (until 1966) of LESOTHO.

Bata a port and chief town of mainland EQUATORIAL GUINEA. (pop. 30,700)

Bath a beautifully preserved spa town in the county of AVON, southwest ENGLAND. (Pop.85,000)

Bathurst *see* **Banjul**.

Baton Rouge the state capital of LOUISIANA, USA, situated on the MISSISSIPPI River. (Pop. city 238,900/ metropolitan area 538,000)

Battambang a town in the centre of CAMBODIA's main rice-growing region, of the same name, that lies beside the shores of the TONLE SAP lake. (Pop. city 40,000/province 551,860)

Batumi a tourist resort, seaport and naval base on the east coast of the BLACK SEA in GEORGIA. (Pop. 130,000)

Bauchi a tin-mining and tobacco-producing state in northeast NIGERIA; its chief town and state capital has the same name. (Pop. city 60,800/state 2,432,000)

Bavaria (Bayern) the largest state in GERMANY. (70,553 sq km/27,241 sq miles; pop. 10,958,000)

Bayern *see* **Bavaria**.

Bayeux a market town in NORMANDY, FRANCE, and the home of the huge 11th-century Bayeux tapestry depicting the Norman conquest of ENGLAND. (Pop. 15,300)

Baykonyr (Baikonur), a remote district of KAZAKHSTAN, some 240 km (150 miles) northeast of the ARAL SEA, was the main Soviet missile and rocket-testing site and the launching pad for most of the former USSR's space probes and satellites.

Bayonne the capital of the French BASQUE region. (Pop. 129,730)

Bayreuth a town in BAVARIA, GERMANY, famous for the theatre built by the composer Richard Wagner (1813-83), where his operas are still staged every summer. (Pop. 71,800)

Bear Island (Bjørnøya) an uninhabited island in the ARCTIC OCEAN, 386 km (240 miles) north of NORWAY to whom it was eventually granted in 1925 after a long history of territorial dispute. (178 sq km/69 sq miles)

Beaufort Sea a part of the ARCTIC OCEAN to the north of North AMERICA.

Beaujolais a famous wine-producing region of FRANCE situated on the River SAONE between LYONS and Macon.

Beaune a town in the Côte d'Or départment in east-central FRANCE, the centre of the BURGUNDY wine-producing district. (Pop. 21,100)

Beauvais the capital of the Oise départment 65 km (40 miles) northwest of PARIS, FRANCE, famed for its 13th-century cathedral, with massive buttresses. (Pop. 57,600)

Béchar an oasis town in northwest ALGERIA, 467 km (290 miles) southwest of ORAN; it is an administrative centre at the start of two main trans-Saharan routes: one south to MALI via Tanezrouft, the other west to MAURITANIA via Tindouf. (Pop. 65,100)

Bechuanaland the former name of BOTSWANA (until 1966).

Bedfordshire a county in central southern ENGLAND; the county town is Bedford. (1235 sq km/477 sq miles; pop. 75,000)

Beersheba (Be'er Sheva) the capital of the NEGEV (the southern part of ISRAEL), about 72 km (45 miles) southwest of JERUSALEM. (Pop. 114,300)

Beijing (Peking) the capital of CHINA, situated in the northeast of the country. (Pop. 9,231,000)

Beira a deep-water port in the south of MOZAMBIQUE, developed as an outlet for landlocked countries like ZIMBABWE and MALAWI, with which there are rail links and also an oil pipeline to the former. (Pop. 113,800)

Beirut (Beyrouth) the capital and main port of LEBANON. (Pop. 938,000)

Belarus (Belorussia, Byelorussia), a republic of the former USSR, declared itself independent in 1991. It borders POLAND to the west, UKRAINE to the south, LATVIA and LITHUANIA to the north, and the RUSSIAN FEDERATION to the east. The country consists mainly of a low-lying plain, and forests cover approximately one third of it. The climate is continental with long severe winters and short warm summers. The main economic activity is agriculture, the main crops being flax, potatoes and hemp. The main livestock raised are cattle and pigs. The production of peat is the main industry and provides the republic's main source of energy. Other developing industries include oil refining, food processing, woodworking, chemicals, textiles and machinery.

Area : 207,600 sq km (80,150 sq miles)

Population : 9,878,000

Capital : Minsk

Other major cities : Gomel, Vitebsk, Mogilev

Form of government : Republic

Religions : Russian Orthodox, RC

Currency : Rouble

Belau a republic consisting of a group of islands in the western PACIFIC formerly known as Palau. It has an agreement of free association with the USA. Copper is the chief export and the main language is English. The capital is KOROR. (494 sq km/191 sq miles; pop. 14,000; cur. US dollar)

Belém a major port of BRAZIL situated to the north of the mouth of the River AMAZON. (Pop. 934,000)

Belfast the capital and by far the largest city of NORTHERN IRELAND. (Pop. 360,000)

Belfort a town and region lying between the VOSGES and JURA in southeast FRANCE, and on an important route that links France to GERMANY and SWITZERLAND. (Pop. town 76,200/ region 132,000)

Belgian Congo *see* **Zaïre.**

Belgium is a relatively small country in northwest EUROPE with a short coastline on the NORTH SEA. The MEUSE River divides Belgium into two distinct geographical regions. To the north, the land slopes continuously for 150 km (93 miles) until it reaches the North Sea where the coastlands are flat and grassy. To the south of the river is the forested plateau area of the ARDENNES. Between these two regions lies the Meuse valley. Belgium is a densely populated industrial country with few natural resources. Agriculture is based on livestock production but employs only 3% of the workforce. The metalworking industry, originally based on the small mineral deposits in the Ardennes, is the most important industry, and in the northern cities new textile industries are producing carpets and clothing. Nearly all raw materials are now imported through the main port of ANTWERP.

Area : 30,519 sq km (11,783 sq miles)

Population : 9,930,000

Capital : Brussels (Brussel, Bruxelles)

Other major cities : Antwerp, Ghent, Charleroi, Liege

Form of government : Constitutional Monarchy

Religion : RC

Currency : Belgian franc

Belgrade (Beograd) the capital of SERBIA, on the confluence of the Rivers DANUBE and Sava. (Pop. 1,407,100)

Belize is a small Central American country located on the southeast of the YUCATAN Peninsula in the CARIBBEAN SEA. Its coastline on the Gulf of HONDURAS is approached through some 550 km (342 miles) of coral reefs and keys (cayo). The coastal area and north of the country are low-lying and swampy with dense forests inland. In the south the Maya Mountains rise to 1100 m (3609 ft). The subtropical climate is warm and humid, and the trade winds bring cooling sea breezes. Rainfall is heavy, particularly in the south, and hurricanes may occur in summer. The dense forests that cover most of the country provide valuable hardwoods such as mahogany. Most of the population make a living from forestry, fishing or agriculture. The main crops grown for export are sugar cane, citrus fruits (mainly grapefruit), bananas and coconuts. Industry is very underdeveloped, and many people emigrate to find work.

Area : 22,965 sq km (8867 sq miles)

Population : 193,000

Capital : Belmopan

Other major city : Belize City

Form of government : Constitutional Monarchy

Religion : RC

Currency : Belize dollar

Bellinghausen Sea a part of the Pacific Ocean off Antarctica, due south of South America.

Belmopan the capital of Belize. (Pop. 5000)

Belo Horizonte an industrial city, and the third largest city of Brazil, in the southeast of the country. (Pop. 1,777,000)

Belorussia *see* **Belarus.**

Belostock *see* **Bialystok**.

Benares *see* **Varanasi**.

Benbecula a low-lying island in the Western Isles of Scotland, between North and South Uist. (Pop. 1880)

Bendigo a mid 19th-century gold-rush town in Victoria, Australia, 130 km (80 miles) northwest of Melbourne. Originally called Sandhurst, the town was renamed in 1891 after the nickname of a local shepherd. (Pop. 52,700)

Benelux the acronym referring to the customs union that was formed by Belgium, the Netherlands and Luxembourg in 1948 and that became an economic union in 1960. The term is often used generally to describe these Low Countries.

Benevento an ancient city in southern Italy, 50 km (30 miles) northeast of Naples; it has many splendid Roman remains. (Pop. 76,600)

Bengal a former Indian state which was divided at the partition of India in 1947 into two parts: West Bengal in India, and East Pakistan (now Bangladesh).

Bengal, Bay of the massive bay occupying the broad sweep of the Indian Ocean between India and Burma, to the south of Bangladesh.

Benghazi (Banghazi) a major port at the eastern end of the Gulf of Sirte in Libya. (Pop. 485,000)

Benguela an important seaport on the Atlantic coast of southern Angola, over 400 km (250 miles) from Luanda. Together with Lobito, 29 km (18 miles) to the north, it is at the seaward end of a 1415 km (880 mile) long rail network linking the mineral rich interior regions of Zaïre and Zambia with the coast. (Pop. 41,000)

Benidorm one of the most popular MEDITERRANEAN sea-side resorts of SPAIN. (Pop. 25,600)

Benin on the southern coast of West AFRICA is an ice cream cone-shaped country with a very short coastline on the Bight of Benin. The coastal area has white sandy beaches backed by lagoons and low-lying fertile lands. In the northwest the Atakora Mountains are grassy plateaux which are deeply cut into steep forested valleys. The climate in the north is tropical and in the south equatorial. There are nine rainy months each year so crops rarely fail. Farming is predominantly subsistence, with yams, cassava, maize, rice, groundnuts and vegetables forming most of the produce. The country is very poor, and lack of foreign investment prevents diversification of the economy. The main exports are palm oil, palm kernels, and cotton. Tourism is now being developed but as yet facilities for this are few except in some coastal towns.
Area : 112,622 sq km (43,483 sq miles)
Population : 4,760,000
Capital : Porto-Novo
Other major city : Contonou
Form of government : Republic
Religions : Animism, RC, Sunni Islam
Currency : Franc CFA

Benin City the capital of the present-day Bendel state of NIGERIA, 240 km (150 miles) east of LAGOS. It was the capital of the ancient Kingdom of Benin (10th-16th centuries) and famed for its craftsmen who produced exquisite cast bronzes and carved ivories. (Pop. 161,700)

Ben Nevis *see* **Grampian Mountains**.

Benue, River a river which flows through CAMEROON and NIGERIA to the Gulf of GUINEA. (Length 1390 km/865 miles)

Benxi an industrial city in LIAONING province in northern CHINA. (Pop. 1,200,000)

Beograd *see* **Belgrade**.

Beqa'a a long, fertile valley running north to south in

LEBANON, between the Lebanon and Anti-Lebanon Mountains.

Berbera the second largest port of SOMALIA, after the capital MOGADISHU, on the north coast on the Gulf of ADEN. The population of the town was swollen in the 1980s by refugees from the drought-stricken interior (Pop. 40,000–70,000)

Bergamo a historic and industrial city in northern ITALY. (Pop. 121,000)

Bergen (1) an old port in southwest NORWAY, and now that country's second largest city. (Pop. 181,000). **(2)** *See* **Mons**.

Bering Sea a part of the PACIFIC OCEAN between ALASKA and eastern RUSSIAN FEDERATION.

Bering Strait the stretch of sea, 88 km(55 miles) wide, that separates the RUSSIAN FEDERATION from ALASKA in the USA.

Berkshire a county of central southern ENGLAND; the county town is Reading. (1256 sq km/485 sq miles; pop. 708,000)

Berlin the capital of GERMANY, situated in the north of the country on the River Spree. Until 1990 it was divided in two by the infamous Berlin Wall. The re-united city is one of the 16 states (länder) of the new enlarged Federal Republic of Germany. (883 sq km/341 sq miles; pop. 3,400,000)

Bermuda consists of a group of 150 small islands in the western ATLANTIC OCEAN. It lies about 920 km (572 miles) east of Cape HATTERAS on the coast of the USA. The hilly limestone islands are the caps of ancient volcanoes rising from the sea bed. The main island is Great Bermuda, and it is linked to the other islands by bridges and causeways. The climate is pleasantly warm and humid, with rain spread evenly throughout the year. Bermuda's chief agricultural products are fresh vegetables, bananas and citrus fruit. Many foreign banks and financial institutions operate from the island to take advantage of the lenient tax laws. Its proximity to the US and the pleasant climate have led to a flourishing tourist industry.

Area : 53 sq km (21 sq miles)

Population : 59,066

Capital : Hamilton

Form of government : Colony under British administration

Religion : Protestantism

Currency : Bermuda dollar

Berne (Bern) the historic capital of SWITZERLAND, and also the name of the surrounding canton. (Pop. city 150,000)

Bernese Oberland a high mountain area of the central ALPS, south of BERNE, SWITZERLAND, dominated by the massif that includes the Eiger (3970 m/13,025 ft), Jungfran (4158 m/13,642 ft), and Finsteraarhorn (4274 m/14,022 ft).

Berwickshire *see* **Borders**.

Besançon a town of ancient origins in the JURA region of eastern FRANCE. (Pop. 120,800)

Beskidy (Beskids, Beskydy) a series of forested ranges along the border of SLOVAKIA and POLAND that form the northern outer arc of the CARPATHIAN MOUNTAINS, and rising to the highest peak, BABIA GÓRA (1725 m/5659 ft).

Bethlehem a town in the WEST BANK area of ISRAEL, celebrated by Christians as the birthplace of Jesus Christ. (Pop. 30,000)

Béthune an industrial town in northeastern FRANCE. (Pop. 259,700)

Beuten *see* **Bytom**.

Beyrouth *see* **Beirut**.

Béziers the leading centre of the LANGUEDOC wine trade in southern FRANCE, situated on a hill 60 km (37 miles) southwest of MONPELLIER. (Pop. 83,200)

Bhopal an industrial city in central INDIA. It was the scene of a massive industrial accident in 1984 in which some 3000 people were killed by gas leaking from a major chemical plant. (Pop. 671,000)

Bhutan is surrounded by INDIA to the south and CHINA to the north. It rises from foothills overlooking the BRAHMAPUTRA River to the southern slopes of the HIMALAYAS. The Himalayas, which rise to over 7500 m (24,608 ft) in Bhutan, make up most of the country. The climate is hot and wet on the plains, but temperatures drop progressively with altitude, resulting in glaciers and permanent snow cover in the north. The valleys in the centre of the country are wide and fertile, and about 95% of the workforce are farmers. Yaks reared on the high pasture land provide milk, cheese and meat. Rice is grown on the lowest ground. Vast areas of the country still remain forested as there is little demand for new farmland. Bhutan has little contact with the rest of the world, and the number of visitors is limited to 1500 each year.
Area : 47,000 sq km (18,147 sq miles)
Population : 1,400,000
Capital : Thimphu
Form of government : Constitutional Monarchy
Religion : Buddhism
Currency : Ngultrum
Biafra *see* **Iboland**.
Bialystok (Belostock) an industrial city in northeast POLAND producing primarily textiles. (Pop. 240,000)
Bianco, Monte *see* **Blanc, Mont**.
Biarritz a fashionable coastal resort and fishing port 8 km (5 miles) southwest of BAYONNE, on the Bay of BISCAY, FRANCE. (Pop. 26,700)
Bielefeld an industrial city in western GERMANY. (Pop. 310,000)
Bielsko-Biala (Bielitz) an industrial city in southern POLAND. (Pop. 172,000)
Bihar a state in northeast INDIA. The capital is PATNA. (Pop. 69,914,700)
Bikini an atoll in the MARSHALL ISLANDS famous as the site of US nuclear weapons tests between 1946 and 1962. This invited joking comparison with the effect on male

onlookers of women's twopiece swimwear, to which the name bikini was applied.

Bilbao a port and industrial city in the BASQUE region of northern SPAIN. (Pop. 433,000)

Billings a market town and agricultural produce-processing centre on the YELLOWSTONE River in MONTANA, USA, 85 km (53 miles) north of the WYOMING border. (Pop. city 69,800/ metropolitan area 118,700)

Billund a village and commercial airport 26 km (16 miles) east of VEJLE in southeast JUTLAND, DENMARK. It is the home of Legoland, a 10-hectare (25-acre) theme park containing model villages and other constructions built with over 30 million Lego bricks—the toy invented by carpenter Ole Kirk Christiansen in 1954. (Pop. 4000)

Bioko an island in the Gulf of GUINEA, formerly called Fernando Póo, and now governed by EQUATORIAL GUINEA. (2017 sq km/780 sq miles; pop. 57,000)

Birkenhead an industrial town and port on the WIRRAL peninsula, near the mouth of the River MERSEY, ENGLAND. It is 2 km (1.25 miles) southwest of LIVERPOOL, to which it is linked by two road, and one railway, tunnels, as well as numerous ferry crossings. (Pop. 123,907)

Birmingham (1) the main city of the industrial WEST MIDLANDS and the second largest city in the UK (Pop. 976,000). **(2)** the largest city in the state of ALABAMA, USA. (Pop. city 279,800/metropolitan area 895,200)

Biscay, Bay of the broad bay, notorious for its rough weather, formed by the ATLANTIC OCEAN between northern SPAIN and BRITTANY in northwest FRANCE.

Bishkek, formerly Frunze, the capital of KYRGYZSTAN. (Pop. 577,000)

Biskra an oasis town and communications centre, 190 km (118 miles) southwest of CONSTANTINE, ALGERIA. It lies at the beginning of the eastern Algerian trans-Saharan routes to NIGER. It is also a fashionable resort because of its good climate, hot springs and interesting ancient remains. (Pop. 90,500)

Bismarck the state capital of NORTH DAKOTA, USA. (Pop. city 47,600/metropolitan area 86,100)

Bismarck Archipelago a group of mainly volcanic islands off the northeast coast of PAPUA NEW GUINEA; it includes NEW BRITAIN, NEW IRELAND and the ADMIRALTY ISLANDS. The population is mainly Melanesian, but there is a significant Chinese and European element. (Pop, 315,000)

Bismarck Sea a branch of the PACIFIC OCEAN to the north of PAPUA NEW GUINEA.

Bissau (Bissão) a port and the capital of GUINEA-BISSAU. (Pop. 109,000)

Bitola the southernmost city of the former YUGOSLAVIA, lying 110 km (68 miles) south of SKOPJE, in the republic of MACEDONIA. Just south are the ruins of Heraclea (Lyncestis), a Roman town with famed mosaics. (Pop. 137,800)

Bitter Lakes the two lakes—the Great and Little Bitter Lakes—that form part of the SUEZ CANAL, EGYPT.

Biwa the largest lake in JAPAN; it lies just northeast of KYOTO, on HONSHU ISLAND. (675 sq km/260 sq miles)

Bizerte (Bizerta, Binzert) a port and naval base on the north coast of TUNISIA at a canalized outlet of Lake Bizerte. Its natural safe harbour attracted one of the earliest Phoenician settlements in 800–700BC. (Pop. 94,600)

Bjørnøya *see* **Bear Island.**

Blackburn an industrial town of LANCASHIRE, in northwest ENGLAND, that dates back to Saxon times (6th century) and significantly expanded as a cotton-making centre in the 18th and 19th centuries. (Pop. 88,000)

Black Country the industrial area of the British MIDLANDS around BIRMINGHAM.

Black Forest (Schwarzwald) an extensive area of mountainous pine forests in southwest GERMANY.

Black Hills a range of hills rising to 2207 m(7242 ft) on the border between the states of SOUTH DAKOTA and WYOMING in the USA.

Blackpool the largest seaside holiday resort in the UK, in LANCASHIRE. (Pop. 147,000)

Black Sea a sea lying between southeast EUROPE and western ASIA; it is surrounded by land except for the BOSPHORUS channel, leading to the MEDITERRANEAN SEA.

Blagoevgrad the capital of the province of same name, on the Struma river 70 km (44 miles) south of SOFIA, BULGARIA. Formerly Gorna Dzhumaya, it was renamed in 1950 after Dimitar Blagoev (1856-1924), founder of the Bulgarian Marxist movement. (Pop. 68,000)

Blagoveshchensk the capital of the RURRISAN FEDERATION's far eastern region of AMUR, and situated on the river of that name. (Pop. 192,000)

Blanc, Mont (Monte Bianco) the highest mountain in Western EUROPE, on the border between FRANCE and ITALY, just to the south of CHAMONIX. (4808 m/15,774 ft)

Blantyre the largest city in MALAWI. (Pop. 333,800)

Blida (El Boulaida) an administrative and trading centre in the middle of a major citrus fruit-growing area, 48 km (30 miles) southwest of ALGIERS in ALGERIA. (Pop. 195,000)

Bloemfontein the judicial capital of SOUTH AFRICA, and the capital of the ORANGE FREE STATE. (Pop. 256,000)

Blue Mountains (1) a range of mountains rising to 1100 m (3609 ft) in NEW SOUTH WALES in AUSTRALIA, some 65 km (40 miles) from SYDNEY. **(2)** the mountains in eastern JAMAICA rising to 2256 m (7402 ft) at Blue Mountain Peak. The region has given its name to the high quality coffee produced there.

Bluff the southernmost settlement on SOUTH ISLAND, NEW ZEALAND, 40 km (25 miles) southeast of INVERCARGILL. It has the country's only aluminium smelter, which uses cheap hydro-electricity from nearby FIORDLAND to process bauxite imported from AUSTRALIA. (Pop. 2720)

Bo the southern regional capital of SIERRA LEONE, situated at the edge of the Sewa river swamps, about 180 km (115 miles) southeast of FREETOWN. It is a market town for tropical crops, including palm kernels and ginger.

Bobo Dioulasso the second largest town of BURKINA, after the capital, OUAGADOUGOU, from which it lies some 310 km (193 miles) to the southwest. It is a trading and industrial centre with many processing plants for local produce. (Pop. 148,000)

Bochum an industrial city in the RUHR region of western GERMANY. (Pop. 410,000)

Bodensee *see* **Constance, Lake.**

Bodh Gaya a small town in eastern INDIA which is the site of Buddhism's most revered shrine. Gautama, the Lord Buddha, achieved enlightenment here in about 500BC. (Pop. 15,700)

Bodrum a port on the southeastern MEDITERRANEAN coast of TURKEY. Known in the ancient world as Halicarnassus, its Mausoleum (since destroyed) was one of the Seven Wonders of the Ancient World. (Pop. 13,090)

Bodø a port, administrative centre and "midnight sun" tourist resort at the head of the Saltfjorden, on NORWAY's Nordland coast, 80 km (50 miles) north of the ARCTIC CIRCLE. (Pop. 27,600)

Bogor a city in west JAVA, INDONESIA, 80 km (50 miles) south of the national capital, JAKARTA. It was a Dutch colonial hill station and has a famous tropical botanical garden. (Pop. 250,000)

Bogotá the capital of COLOMBIA, set on a plateau of the eastern ANDES in the centre of the country. (Pop. 5,789,000)

Bo Hai (Po Hai) a north-western arm of the YELLOW SEA, off the east coast of CHINA. It was formerly called the Gulf of Chihli. It contains major oil fields. (139,200 sq km/ 54,000 sq miles)

Bohemia formerly an independent kingdom (9th to 13th centuries), now a western region of the CZECH REPUBLIC which includes the capital PRAGUE. In the mistaken belief that Gypsies came from Bohemia, the term Bohemian came to be applied to artists and writers with unconventional lifestyles.

Bohol

Bohol one of the VISAYAN ISLANDS in the central area of the PHILIPPINES. (3862 sq km/1491 sq miles; pop. 759,370)

Boise the state capital of IDAHO, USA (Pop. city 107,200/ metropolitan area 189,300)

Bolivia is a landlocked republic of central South AMERICA through which the great mountain range of the ANDES runs. It is in the Andes that the highest navigable lake in the world, Lake TITICACA, is found. On the undulating depression south of the lake, the Altiplano, is the highest capital city in the world, LA PAZ. To the east and northeast of the mountains is a huge area of lowland containing tropical rainforests (the Llanos) and wooded savanna (the Chaco). The northeast has a heavy rainfall while in the southwest it is negligible. Temperatures vary with altitude from extremely cold on the summits to cool on the Altiplano, where at least half the population lives. Although rich in natural resources, eg oil, tin, Bolivia is not rich because of lack of funds for their extraction. Agriculture produces foodstuffs, sugar cane and cotton for export, and increased production of coca, from which cocaine is derived, has resulted in an illicit economy.

Area : 1,098,581 sq km (424,162 sq miles)

Population : 6,410,000

Capital : La Paz (administrative capital), Sucre (legal capital)

Other major city : Cochabamba

Form of government : Republic

Religion : RC

Currency : Boliviano

Bologna the capital of the EMILIA ROMAGNA region in northeastern ITALY. (Pop. 455,900)

Bolton a textile manufacturing town in the county of LANCASHIRE, ENGLAND. (Pop. 147,000)

Bolzano an industrial Alpine town in ITALY, about 55 km (34 miles) south of the Brenner Pass and the Austrian border, and, as such, a meeting place of Latin and Germanic cultures. (Pop. 104,600)

Bombay a major port, the capital of MAHARASHTRA state in central western INDIA, and now India's most important industrial city. (Pop. 8,234,400)

Bonaire a Caribbean island off the coast of VENEZUELA, formerly administered by the Dutch and still a part of the NETHERLAND ANTILLES (288 sq km/111 sq miles; pop. 9700)

Bondi Beach a famous surfing beach in the suburbs of SYDNEY, AUSTRALIA.

Bone *see* **Annaba**.

Bonin Islands a group of small volcanic islands in the PACIFIC OCEAN belonging to JAPAN. (Pop. 2300)

Bonn the capital of former West Germany, which will remain the administrative centre of GERMANY until the government moves to BERLIN. (Pop. 300,000)

Bophuthatswana one of the homelands declared by the government of SOUTH AFRICA to be an independent republic in 1977. It consists of seven separate territories. (44,109 sq km/17,030 sq miles; pop. 1,935,000)

Bordeaux a major port on the GIRONDE estuary in southwestern FRANCE. The region is famous for its wines. (Pop. 650,125)

Borders an administrative region of southern SCOTLAND, created in 1975 out of the former counties of Berwickshire, Peeblesshire, Roxburghshire, Selkirkshire and part of Midlothian. (4662 sq km/1800 sq miles; pop. 101,000)

Borkum *see* **Friesian Islands**.

Borneo one of the largest islands in the world, now divided between three countries. Most of the island is known as KALIMANTAN, a part of INDONESIA. The northern coast is divided into the two states of SARAWAK and SABAH, which are part of MALAYSIA, and the small independent Sultanate of BRUNEI. (751,900 sq km/290,320 sq miles)

Bornholm a detached island in the south BALTIC SEA, belonging to DENMARK and consisting mostly of rugged granite rocks. The main economic activities are concerned with agriculture and tourism. (587 sq km/227 sq miles; Pop. 47,300)

Borno the largest state of NIGERIA, in the extreme northeast. It is sparsely populated. In the 10th and 11th centuries the vast plain beside Lake CHAD was the centre of the powerful Bornu Empire and joined the Kingdom of Kanem in the 13th century. (116,400 sq km/44,942 sq miles; Pop. 2,998,000)

Borobodur the great Buddhist temple near YOGYAKARTA in southern central JAVA, INDONESIA, dating from *c.* AD750.

Borås the textile centre of SWEDEN, situated 69 km (43 miles) east of GOTHENBURG (Pop. 99,900)

Bosnia-Herzegovina, a republic of former Yugoslavia, was formally recognized as an independent state in 1992. It is a very mountainous country and includes part of the Dinaric Alps, which are densely forested and deeply cut by rivers flowing northwards to join the Sava river. Half the country is forested, and timber is an important product of the northern areas. One quarter of the land is cultivated, and corn, wheat and flax are the principal products of the north. In the south, tobacco, cotton, fruits and grapes are the main products. Bosnia Herzegovina has large deposits of lignite, iron ore and bauxite, but there is little industrialization.

Area : 51,129 sq km (19,736 sq miles)

Population : 4,124,000

Capital : Sarajevo

Other major cities : Ban ja Luka, Tuzla

Form of government : Republic

Religions : Eastern Orthodox, Sunni Islam, RC

Currency : Dinar

Bosphorus the narrow strip of water, some 29 km (18 miles) long and no more than 4 km (2.5 miles) wide, which provides the navigable link between the MEDITERRANEAN SEA and the BLACK SEA by way of the Sea of MARMARA. The Bosphorus separates the European part of TURKEY from its Asian part.

Boston an ATLANTIC port and the state capital of MASSA-CHUSETTS, USA (Pop. city 570,700/metropolitan area 2,820,700)

Bosworth Field the site, 16 km (10 miles) west of LEICES-TER in south-central ENGLAND, where Henry Tudor and his Lancastrian army defeated King Richard III and his Yorkist troops to end the War of the Roses (1460–85).

Botany Bay a bay now in the suburbs of SYDNEY, AUS-TRALIA, discovered by Captain James Cook in 1770.

Bothnia, Gulf of the most northerly arm of the BALTIC SEA, bordered by FINLAND and SWEDEN.

Botswana is a landlocked republic in southern AFRICA which straddles the Tropic of Capricorn. Much of the west and southwest of the country forms part of the KALAHARI Desert. In the north the land is marshy around the OKAVANGO BASIN, home to a wide variety of wildlife. With the exception of the desert area, most of the country has a subtropical climate. In winter, days are warm and nights cold while summer is hot with sporadic rainfall. The people are mainly farmers, and cattle rearing is the main activity. After independence in 1966, the exploitation of minerals started. Diamonds became an important revenue earner and the copper from the nickel/copper complex at Selebi-Pikwe was also exported. Mineral resources in the northeast are now being investigated. About 17% of the land is set aside for wildlife preservation in national parks, game reserves, game sanctuaries and controlled hunting areas.

Area : 581,730 sq km (224,606 sq miles)

Population : 1,260,000

Capital : Gaborone

Other major cities : Mahalapye, Serowe, Francistown

Form of government : Republic

Religions : Animism, Anglicanism

Currency : Pula

Bouaké the second largest city of the CÔTE D'IVOIRE. (Pop. 640,000)

Bougainville the easternmost island belonging to PAPUA NEW GUINEA, and a part of, though politically separate from, the chain of islands forming the SOLOMON ISLANDS.

Boulogne the largest fishing port of FRANCE, situated on the ENGLISH CHANNEL in the north of the country. Ferries provide the busy link to BRITAIN. (Pop. 98,900)

Bourgogne *see* **Burgundy**.

Bournemouth a coastal resort in the county of DORSET in southern ENGLAND. (Pop. 145,000)

Boyne, River a river flowing into the IRISH SEA on the east coast of the Republic of IRELAND. Famous for its prehistoric remains, it was the site of the battle (1690) in which Protestant William of Orange defeated Catholic James II. (Length 115 km/70 miles)

Boyoma Falls a series of seven cataracts over 90 km (56 miles) where the LUALABA River beomes the ZAÏRE River. They were formerly called Stanley Falls after the British explorer Sir Henry Morton Stanley.

Brabant the central province of BELGIUM around the capital, BRUSSELS. (3358 sq km/1297 sq miles; pop. 2,200,000)

Brac *see* **Dalmatia**.

Bradford a city in the county of West YORKSHIRE, ENGLAND, which came to prominence as the centre of the woollen industry in the 19th century. (Pop. 281,000)

Bragança a small inland town of medieval origins in PORTUGAL, and the original home of the family which ruled Portugal from 1640 to 1910. (Pop. 13,900)

Brahmaputra a major river of South ASIA, flowing from the HIMALAYAS in TIBET through ASSAM in northern INDIA to join the River GANGES in BANGLADESH. (Length 840 km/765 miles)

Braila a port in ROMANIA on the River DANUBE, 140 km (87 miles) inland from the BLACK SEA. (Pop. 214,000)

Brandenburg (1) one of the re-unified GERMANY's 16 states (*Länder*) covering a large area of former East Germany around, but not including, BERLIN; the state capital is POTSDAM. (29,059 sq km/11,220 sq miles; pop. 2,700,000) **(2)** a port and industrial town on the Havel river about 60 km (35 miles) west of BERLIN. (Pop. 95,100)

Brasília the capital, since 1960, of BRAZIL. (Pop. 412,000)

Bratislava (Pressburg) the second largest city in the former CZECHOSLOVAKIA, and the capital of the newly independent SLOVAKIA. (Pop. 402,000)

Bratsk an industrial town on the ANGARA river, about 460 km (285 miles) northwest of IRKUTSK. (Pop. 236,000)

Braunschweig *see* **Brunswick**.

Brazil is a huge South American country bounded to the north, south and east by the ATLANTIC. It is the fifth largest country in the world and covers nearly half of South AMERICA. The climate is mainly tropical, but altitude, distance from the sea and prevailing winds cause many variations. In the Amazonia area it is constantly warm and humid, but in the tropical areas winters are dry and summers wet. Droughts may occur in the northeast, where it is hot and arid. About 14% of the population is employed in agriculture and the main products exported are coffee, soya beans and cocoa. Brazil is rich in minerals and is the only source of high grade quartz crystal in commercial quantities. It is also a major producer of chrome ore, and it is now developing what is thought to be the richest iron ore deposits in the world.

Area : 8,511,965 sq km (3,285,470 sq miles)

Population : 115,600,000

Capital : Brasília

Other major cities : Belo Horizonte, Porto Alegre, Recife, Rio de Janeiro, Salvador, São Paulo

Form of government : Federal Republic

Religion : RC

Currency : Cruzeiro

Brazilian Highlands (Planalto Brasil) a large area of mountain ranges and plateaux of east central BRAZIL, lying between the capital, BRASÍLIA and the ATLANTIC coast near SALVADOR; rising to 1500 m (4920 ft).

Brazov an industrial city in central ROMANIA. (Pop. 304,000)

Brazzaville the capital of the CONGO, on the River ZAÏRE. (Pop. 425,000)

Breconshire *see* **Powys**.

Breda a historic and manufacturing city in the NETHER-LANDS. (Pop. city 118,000/Greater Breda 153,000)

Bremen a major port on the River WESER, near to the NORTH SEA coast of GERMANY, and also the name of the surrounding state. (Pop. 550,000)

Bremerhaven a port on the NORTH SEA coast of GERMANY, 55 km (34 miles) to the north of BREMEN. (Pop. 135,000)

Brescia a city in northern ITALY. (Pop. 206,000)

Breslau *see* **Wroclaw**.

Brest (1) a important naval port situated on an inlet on the tip of FINISTERE in northwestern FRANCE. (Pop. 205,000). **(2) (Brzesc)** an inland port in BELARUS situated on the River BUG on the border between Belarus and POLAND. (Pop. 214,000)

Bretagne *see* **Brittany**.

Brezhnev *see* **Naberezhnyye Chelny**.

Bridgeport a manufacturing city on the coast of the state of CONNECTICUT, USA. (Pop. city 142,000/ metropolitan area 441,500)

Bridgetown the capital of BARBADOS. (Pop. 97,000)

Brighton a famous seaside resort on the south coast of ENGLAND in the county of East SUSSEX. (Pop. 149,000)

Brindisi a port on the east coast of ITALY at the southern end of the ADRIATIC SEA. (Pop. 92,000)

Brisbane a port on the east coast of AUSTRALIA, and the state capital of QUEENSLAND. (Pop. 942,400)

Bristol a major city and port in southwest ENGLAND, and the administrative centre of the county of AVON. (Pop. 399,000)

Britain *see* **Great Britain**.

British Columbia the western seaboard province of CANADA. The capital is VICTORIA. (929,730 sq km/358,968 sq miles; pop. 2,744,000)

British Indian Ocean Territory the Chagos Archipelago, a group of five coral atolls in the middle of the INDIAN OCEAN. (52 sq km/20 sq miles)

British Isles the name given to the group of islands in northwestern EUROPE formed by GREAT BRITAIN and IRELAND, and the surrounding islands.

British Virgin Islands *see* **Virgin Islands, British**.

Brittany (Bretagne) the region of FRANCE which occupies the extreme northwestern peninsula, overlooking the ATLANTIC.

Brno (Brünn) an industrial city in the southeast of the CZECH REPUBLIC. (Pop. 381,000)

Broads, The *see* **Norfolk Broads.**

Broken Hill a mining town in NEW SOUTH WALES, AUSTRALIA, 920 km (570 miles) west of SYDNEY and 420 km (260 miles) northeast of ADELAIDE. It is known as "Silver City" and has some of the richest deposits of silver, zinc and lead in the world. (Pop. 26,900)

Broken Hill *see* **Kabwe.**

Bromberg *see* **Bydgoszcz.**

Broome a small port on the remote northwest coast of WESTERN AUSTRALIA, about 1650 km (1030 miles) north and slightly east of PERTH. Its main industry is the production and export of mother-of-pearl. (Pop. 3600)

Bruges (Brugge) a historic town and capital of the province of West FLANDERS, BELGIUM. (Pop. 120,000)

Brunei is a sultanate located on the northwest coast of BORNEO in South-East ASIA. It is bounded on all sides by the SARAWAK territory of MALAYSIA, which splits the sultanate into two separate parts. Broad tidal swamplands cover the coastal plains and inland Brunei is hilly and covered with tropical forest. The climate is tropical marine, hot and moist, with cool nights. Rainfall is heavy (2500 mm/98 inches) at the coast but even heavier (5000 mm/197 inches) inland. The main crops grown are rice, vegetables and fruit, but economically the country depends on its oil industry, which employs 7% of the working population. Oil production began in the 1920s and now oil and natural gas account for almost all exports. Other minor products are rubber, pepper, sawn timber, gravel and animal hides.

Area : 5,765 sq km (2,226 sq miles)

Population : 267,000

Capital : Bandar Seri Begawan

Other major cities : Kuala Belait, Seria

Form of government : Monarchy (Sultanate)

Religion : Sunni Islam

Currency : Brunei dollar

Brünn *see* **Brno**.

Brunswick (Braunschweig) a historic town in northern GERMANY, and the capital of the Dukes of Saxony. (Pop. 255,000)

Brussels (Brussel, Bruxelles) a historic city and the capital of BELGIUM. It plays a central role in EUROPE as the administrative headquarters for the European Community. (Pop. 1,000,000)

Bryansk an industrial city in the west of the RUSSIAN FEDERATION. (Pop. 424,000)

Bubiyan Island a large island belonging to KUWAIT situated in the very north of The GULF and close to the border with IRAQ.

Bucaramanga a city in the north of COLOMBIA, close to the border with VENEZUELA. (Pop. 516,000)

Bucharest (Bucuresti) the capital of ROMANIA, in the southeast of the country. (Pop. 1,861,000)

Buckinghamshire a county in central southern ENGLAND; the county town is AYLESBURY. (1883 sq km/727 sq miles; pop. 609,000)

Budapest the capital of HUNGARY, comprising Buda and Pest, which lie on opposite sides of the River DANUBE. (Pop. 2,064,400)

Budweiss *see* **Ceské Budejovice**.

Buenaventura the largest PACIFIC coast port of COLOMBIA, about 330 km (205 miles) west and slightly south of

BOGOTÁ. It is the principal outlet for the export of coffee. (Pop. 190,000)

Buenos Aires the capital of ARGENTINA. (Pop. city 3,325,000/ metropolitan area 9,948,000)

Buffalo a city and port in NEW YORK state situated at the eastern end of Lake ERIE. (Pop. city 339,000/metropolitan area 1,205,000)

Bug, River a river which flows northwest from the UKRAINE, forming the border with POLAND before turning west into Poland and joining the Narew and VISTULA rivers. (Length: 813 km/480 miles)

Büjük Agri Dagi see **Ararat, Mount**

Bujumbura the capital of BURUNDI, situated at the northern end of Lake TANGANYIKA. (Pop. 180,000)

Bukhara an old trading city in UZBEKISTAN. (Pop. 204,000)

Bulawayo the second city of ZIMBABWE, in the southwest of the country. (Pop. 414,000)

Bulgaria is a southeast European republic located on the east Balkan peninsula and has a coast on the BLACK SEA. It is bounded to the north by ROMANIA, west by SERBIA and MACEDONIA of the former YUGOSLAVIA, and south by GREECE and TURKEY. The centre of Bulgaria is crossed from west to east by the Balkan Mountains. The south of the country has a Mediterranean climate with hot dry summers and mild winters. Further north the temperatures become more extreme, and rainfall is higher in summer. Traditionally Bulgaria is an agricultural country, and a revolution in farming during the 1950s has led to great increases in output. This was due to the collectivization of farms and the use of more machinery, fertilizers and irrigation. Each agricultural region now has its own specialized type of farming. Increased mechanization led to more of the workforce being available to work in mines and industry. Now Bulgaria is the third most urbanized country in eastern Europe.

Area : 110,912 sq km (42,823 sq miles)

Population : 8,970,000

Buraydah

Capital : Sofia (Sofiya)
Other major cities : Burgas, Plovdiv, Ruse, Varna
Form of government : Republic
Religion : Eastern Orthodox
Currency : Lev

Buraydah an oasis town in the centre of SAUDI ARABIA, 450 km (280 miles) northwest of RIYADH, noted for its grain and dates. (Pop. 75,000)

Burgas a major port on the BLACK SEA coast of BULGARIA. (Pop. 183,000)

Burgenland the southeasternmost state of AUSTRIA noted for its rich farmland and wine making. It was formerly part of HUNGARY, and only transferred to Austria in 1921 following a referendum. The capital is Eisenstadt. (3965 sq km/1531 sq miles; pop. 272,568)

Burgos an industrial town in northern SPAIN, and the name of the surrounding province. (Pop. town 156,000)

Burgundy (Bourgogne) a region of central FRANCE, famous for its wine.

Burkina (Burkina Faso) a landlocked state in West AFRICA, on the southern fringe of the SAHARA DESERT; it was known as Upper Volta until 1984. The country is made up of vast monotonous plains and low hills which rise to 700 m (2297 ft) in the southwest. Precipitation is generally low, the heaviest rain falling in the southwest, while the rest of the country is semi-desert. The dusty grey plains in the north and west have infertile soils which have been further impoverished by overgrazing and overcultivation. About 90% of the people live by farming, and food crops include sorghum, beans and maize. Some cotton, livestock and oil seeds are exported. There is a great shortage of work, and many of the younger population go to GHANA and CÔTE D'IVOIRE for employment. The only main industries are textiles and metal products.

Area : 274,200 sq km (105,869 sq miles)
Population : 8,760,000

Capital : Ouagadougou
Form of government : Republic
Religions : Animist, Sunni Islam
Currency : Franc CFA

Burma (Myanmar) the Union of Myanmar (formerly Burma) is the second largest country in South-East Asia. The heartland of the country is the valley of the IRRAWADDY. The north and west of the country are mountainous, and in the east the Shan Plateau runs along the border with THAILAND. The climate is equatorial at the coast, changing to tropical monsoon over most of the interior. The Irrawaddy river flows into the ANDAMAN SEA, forming a huge delta area which is ideal land for rice cultivation. Rice is the country's staple food and accounts for half the country's export earnings. Burma is rich in timber and minerals, but because of poor communications, lack of development and unrest among ethnic groups, the resources have not been fully exploited.

Area : 676,578 sq km (261,227 sq miles)
Population : 39,300,000
Capital : Yangon (formerly Rangoon)
Other major cities : Mandalay, Moulmein, Pegu
Form of government : Republic
Religion : Buddhism
Currency : Kyat

Bursa a city in northwestern TURKEY, and also the name of the surrounding province, of which it is the capital. (Pop. city 614,100)

Burundi is a small densely populated country in central east AFRICA, bounded by RWANDA to the north, TANZANIA to the east and south, and ZAÏRE to the west. It has a mountainous terrain, with much of the country above 1500 m (4921 ft). The climate is equatorial but modified by altitude. The savanna in the east is several degrees hotter than the plateau, and there are two wet seasons. The soils are not rich, but there is enough rain to grow crops in most areas. The main food crops are bananas, sweet potatoes, peas, lentils and beans. Cassava is grown near the shores of Lake TANGANYIKA. The main cash crop is coffee, accounting for 90% of Burundi's export earnings. There is a little commercial fishing on Lake Tanganyika, otherwise industry is very basic.

Area : 27,834 sq km (10,747 sq miles)

Population : 5,540,000

Capital : Bujumbura

Form of government : Republic

Religion : RC

Currency : Burundi franc

Buryat Republic an autonomous republic of the RUSSIAN FEDERATION, situated in the southeast, between Lake BAIKAL and MONGOLIA. (351,300 sq km/135,600 sq miles; pop. 985,000)

Bushmanland (1) a sparsely populated district of northeastern NAMIBIA; a wooded savannah region on the edge of the KALAHARI DESERT that is the home of the hunter-gatherer San (Bushmen) peoples. The only settlement is Tsumkwe. (18,468 sq km/7130 sq miles; pop. 500) **(2)** an equally remote region of semi-desert scrub, in the interior of northeastern CAPE PROVINCE, SOUTH AFRICA, lying to the south of NAMIBIA and the ORANGE river.

Butare the second largest town of RWANDA, after its capital KIGALI, and 20 km (12 miles) from the border with BURUNDI. It is the seat of Rwanda's only university. (Pop. 30,000)

Bute *see* **Strathclyde**.

Butte a mining town in the ROCKY MOUNTAINS in southwest MONTANA, USA, about 110 km (68 miles) from the IDAHO border. It is one of the country's leading producers of copper, lead, zinc, silver and gold. (Pop. 34,500)

Butterworth a port on the north-west coast of Peninsular MALAYSIA, facing PENANG ISLAND, to which it is linked by the world's third longest bridge (13.5 km/8.4 miles). It has an oil refinery and tin smelters. (Pop. 78,000)

Buzau an industrial city in south-central ROMANIA, about

100 km (60 miles) northeast of Bucharest. It produces chemicals, textiles and processed food and drinks. (Pop. 112,800)

Bydgoszcz (Bromberg) a historic and industrial city in central Poland. (Pop. 357,700)

Byelorussia *see* **Belarus**.

Bytom (Beuthen) an industrial city in southwest Poland. (Pop. 238,100)

Byzantium *see* **Istanbul**.

C

Cabinda a coastal province of ANGOLA separated from the rest of the country by a 30-km (19-mile) wide corrider of ZAÏRE; its capital, also called Cabinda, is about 390 km (242 miles) north of LUANDA. The province produces three quarters of Angola's oil output, following the discovery of major offshore reserves in 1966. (7270 sq km (2807 sq miles); Pop. province 81,000/town 13,500)

Cabora Bassa the site on the ZAMBESI River in northern MOZAMBIQUE of the largest dam in southern AFRICA. (1600 sq km/620 sq miles)

Cáceres a market town in a province of same name, about 240 km (150 miles) southwest of MADRID, SPAIN, famous for *embutidos*—red sausages. (Pop. town 71,900/province 414,700)

Cadiz a port of Phoenician origins on the ATLANTIC coast of southern SPAIN; also the name of the surrounding province. (Pop. town 157,800)

Caen a city in NORMANDY, FRANCE. (Pop. 187,600)

Caerdydd *see* **Cardiff**.

Caernarfon (Caernarvon) a port and resort in northwest WALES, in GWYNEDD on the mainland shore of the MENAI STRAIT. It has medieval city walls and a large 13th-century castle, in which the investiture of Charles as the Prince of Wales took place on 1 July 1969. (Pop. 9506)

Caernarfonshire *see* **Gwynedd**.

Cagayan de Oro a trading and transport centre on the north coast of MINDANAO, PHILIPPINES; and capital of the region. (Pop. 163,000)

Cagliari the capital of the Italian island of SARDINIA. (Pop. 232,800)

Caicos Islands *see* **Turks and Caicos Islands**.

Cairngorm Mountains a range forming part of the GRAMPIAN MOUNTAINS in SCOTLAND.

Cairns a port on the northeast coast of QUEENSLAND, AUSTRALIA and a tourist resort catering for visitors to the GREAT BARRIER REEF. (Pop. 48,000)

Cairo (El Qahira) the capital of EGYPT, in the north of the country on the River NILE; it is the largest city in AFRICA. (Pop. 8,540,000)

Caiseal *see* **Cashel**.

Caithness *see* **Highland Region**.

Calabria the region which occupies the southern "toe" of Italy. The main town is REGGIO DI CALABRIA. (Pop. 2,121,700)

Calais an old port in northern FRANCE situated on the narrowest part of the ENGLISH CHANNEL, opposite DOVER in ENGLAND. Nearby is the site of the French terminal of the CHANNEL TUNNEL. (Pop. 101,500)

Calcutta the largest city in INDIA, a major port and industrial centre situated in the northeast of the country, on the HUGLI River. (Pop. 9,194,000)

Caledonia the ancient Roman name for SCOTLAND.

Caledonian Canal a canal in northern SCOTLAND, linking the ATLANTIC with the NORTH SEA by the joining up of natural lochs through the GREAT GLEN.

Calgary the second largest city in the province of ALBERTA, CANADA. (Pop. 593,000)

Cali an industrial city in southern COLOMBIA. (Pop. 1,755,000)

Calicut (Kozhikode) a port on the west coast of southern INDIA. (Pop. 546,100)

California the most populous state of the USA, on the PACIFIC coast. The state capital is SACRAMENTO, but LOS ANGELES is the biggest city. (411,015 sq km/158,693 sq km; pop. 26,365,000)

California, Gulf of the narrow inlet which separates the mainland part of MEXICO from the peninsula of BAJA

CALIFORNIA. It is also known as the Sea of Cortes.

Callao the port serving LIMA, the capital of PERU. (Pop. 440,500)

Calvados a department of northern FRANCE, part of NORMANDY. It is famous for its apple-based liqueur. (Pop. 590,000)

Camargue the broad, flat area of sea marshes in the delta of the River RHONE in the centre of the MEDITERRANEAN coast of FRANCE.

Cambodia is a South-East Asian state bounded by THAILAND, LAOS and VIETNAM, and its southern coast lies on the Gulf of Thailand. The heart of the country is saucer-shaped, and gently rolling alluvial plains are drained by the MEKONG river. The Dangrek Mountains form the frontier with Thailand in the northwest. In general Cambodia has a tropical monsoon climate, and about half the land is tropical forest. During the rainy season the Mekong swells and backs into the TONLE SAP (Great Lake), increasing its size threefold. Almost 162,000 hectares of land are flooded by this seasonal rise of the Mekong and this area is left with rich silt when the river recedes. Crop production depends entirely on the rainfall and floods, but production was badly disrupted during the civil war, and yields still remain low. Industry, also, has not recovered from the ravages of war.

Area : 181,035 sq km (69,898 sq miles)

Population : 8,300,000

Capital : Phnom Penh

Other major cities : Kampong Cham, Battambang

Form of government : People's Republic

Religion : Buddhism

Currency : Riel

Cambrian Mountains a range of mountains which forms the "backbone" of WALES.

Cambridge (1) a famous university city in eastern ENGLAND. (Pop. 95,300) **(2)** a city in MASSACHUSETTS, USA, home of Harvard University and the Massachusetts Institute of Technology. (Pop. 103,000)

Cambridgeshire a county in eastern ENGLAND; the county town is CAMBRIDGE. (3409 sq km/1316 sq miles; pop. 578,700)

Camelot the legendary English town where King Arthur's palace and court were situated. Camelford in north CORNWALL, ENGLAND is claimed according to local legend to be the real site of the Arthurian royal seat.

Cameron Highlands an upland area of MALAYSIA where tea and and vegetables are grown.

Cameroon is a triangular-shaped country of diverse landscapes in west central AFRICA. It stretches from Lake CHAD at its apex to the northern borders of EQUATORIAL GUINEA, GABON and the CONGO in the south. The landscape ranges from low-lying lands, through the semi-desert SAHEL, to dramatic mountain peaks and then to the grassy savanna, rolling uplands, steaming tropical forests and hardwood plantations. Further south are the volcanoes, including Mount CAMEROON, and the palm beaches at Kribi and Limbe. The climate is equatorial with high temperatures and plentiful rain. The majority of the population lives in the south where they grow maize and vegetables. In the drier north, where drought and hunger are well known, life is harder. Bananas, coffee and cocoa are the major exports although oil, gas and aluminium are becoming increasingly important.

Area : 475,442 sq km (183,568 sq miles)

Population : 11,540,000

Capital : Yaoundé

Other major city : Douala

Form of government : Republic

Religions : Animism, RC, Sunni Islam

Currency : Franc CFA

Cameroon, Mount an active volcano in west CAMEROON. (4095 m/13,435 ft)

Campania a region of central southern ITALY, on the west coast around NAPLES. (Pop. 5,623,400)

Camp David the US president's retreat in the APPALA-

CHIAN MOUNTAINS, MARYLAND; it was the scene of the Camp David Agreement of 1978 between EGYPT and ISRAEL that outlined a framework for establishing peace in the MIDDLE EAST.

Campeche a port on the western coast of the YUCATÁN peninsula, MEXICO, where in 1517 the Spaniards first set foot on Mexican soil. Today, it is the capital of the surrounding state of the same name. (Pop. city 99,000/ state 408,000)

Campeche, Bahia de (Campeche, Gulf of) the southwest part of the Gulf of MEXICO, situated west of the YUCATÁN peninsula.

Campina Grande a market town 160 km (100 miles) inland from RECIFE in northeast BRAZIL, and gateway to the large inland semi-arid zone known as the *sertão*. (Pop. 248,000)

Campinas a modern industrial town 75 km (47 miles) north of SÃO PAULO in BRAZIL. (Pop. 665,000)

Campo Grande a market and transportation centre and capital of the Mato Grosso du Sul state of southwest BRAZIL. (Pop. 282,844)

Campos an industrial town 230 km (144 miles) northeast along the coast from RIO DE JANEIRO. It services BRAZIL'S main oil fields in the offshore Campos basin. (pop. 349,000)

Cam Ranh Bay a naval base in VIETNAM developed by the US Navy which subsequently played an important part in the Soviet military presence in South-East ASIA.

Canaan an ancient region between the River JORDAN and the MEDITERREAN, corresponding roughly to modern ISRAEL; the biblical "Promised Land of the Israelites".

Canada is the second largest country in the world, and the largest in North AMERICA. Canada is a land of great climatic and geographical extremes. It lies to the north of the USA and has both PACIFIC and ATLANTIC coasts. The ROCKY MOUNTAINS and COAST MOUNTAINS run down the west side, and the highest point, Mount Logan (5951 m/19,524 ft), is in the YUKON. Climates range

range from polar conditions in the north, to cool temperate in the south with considerable differences from west to east. More than 80% of its farmland is in the prairies that stretch from ALBERTA to MANITOBA. Wheat and grain crops cover three-quarters of the arable land. Canada is rich in forest reserves, which cover more than half the total land area. The most valuable mineral deposits (oil, gas, coal and iron ore) are found in Alberta. Most industry in Canada is associated with processing its natural resources.

Area : 9 ,976,139 sq km (3,851,787 sq miles)

Population : 26,600,000

Capital : Ottawa

Other major cities : Toronto, Montreal, Vancouver, Quebec

Form of government : Federal Parliamentary State

Religions : RC, United Church of Canada, Anglicanism

Currency : Canadian dollar

Canal Zone a former administrative region of the US on the Isthumus of PANAMA around the PANAMA CANAL, and bordered on each side by the Republic of Panama, into which it was incorporated in 1979. (1453 sq km/533 sq miles)

Canarias, Islas *see* **Canary Islands**.

Canary Islands (Canarias) a group of islands belonging to SPAIN, and one of its 17 regions; situated some 95 km (60 miles) off the coast of WESTERN SAHARA. The main islands are Gran Canaria, Tenerife, La Palma, Fuertaventura, Gomera, Lanzarote. (7273 sq km/2808 sq miles; pop. 1,444,600)

Canaveral, Cape a long spit of land on the east coast of the state of FLORIDA, USA. It is the USA's main launch site for space missions and the home of the John F. Kennedy Space Center. For a time it was known as Cape Kennedy.

Canberra the capital of AUSTRALIA, lying about halfway between SYDNEY and MELBOURNE in the southeast of the country. (Pop. 255,900)

Cancún

Cancún a tiny island just off the YUCATAN coast of MEXICO, connected to the mainland by a causeway, and now a popular holiday resort. (Pop. 70,000)

Canna a conserved island off the west coast of SCOTLAND, lying 6 km (4 miles) northwest of Rum; it is one of the Small Isles group of the Inner HEBRIDES. (16 sq km/6 sq miles; Pop.11)

Cannes a famous beach resort on the CÔTE D'AZUR in southern FRANCE. (Pop. 72,800)

Cantabria a province on the ATLANTIC coast of northern SPAIN. (Pop. 510,800)

Cantabrian Mountains *see* **Cordillera Cantabrica**.

Canterbury a small cathedral city in the county of KENT in southern ENGLAND. (Pop. 36,000)

Canterbury Bight a small but broad sweep of the south PACIFIC OCEAN on the east coast of SOUTH ISLAND, NEW ZEALAND.

Canterbury Plains the grasslands on SOUTH ISLAND, NEW ZEALAND, stretching more than 150 km (90 miles) along the east coast, back to the foothills of the SOUTHERN ALPS.

Can Tho a town at the centre of the intensive rice-producing MEKONG delta in south Vietnam, 150 km (94 miles) southwest of HO-CHI-MINH CITY

Canton *see* **Guangzhou**.

Cape Breton Island an island off the eastern coast of CANADA which forms part of the province of NOVA SCOTIA. (10,349 sq km/3970 sq miles; pop. 170,000)

Cape Province the southernmost and largest of the Republic of SOUTH AFRICA'S provinces. It was also the area that was first settled by Europeans in 1652, and became the Cape Colony under the British in 1806, and later the Cape of Good Hope Province of the Union of South Africa in 1910. (645,767 sq km (249,331 sq miles; pop. 5,373,800)

Cape Town a major port on the southwestern tip of SOUTH AFRICA, and the country's legislative capital. (Pop. 1,912,000)

Cape Verde, one of the world's smallest nations, is

situated in the ATLANTIC OCEAN, about 640 km (400 miles) northwest of SENEGAL. It consists of 10 islands and 5 islets. The islands are divided into the Windward group and the Leeward group. Over 50% of the population live on São Tiago on which is PRAIA, the capital. The climate is arid with a cool dry season from December to June and warm dry conditions for the rest of the year. Rainfall is sparse and the islands suffer from periods of severe drought. Agriculture is mostly confined to irrigated inland valleys, and the chief crops are coconuts, sugar cane, potatoes and cassava. Bananas and some coffee are grown for export. Fishing for tuna and lobsters is an important industry, but in general the economy is shaky, and Cape Verde relies heavily on foreign aid.

Area : 4033 sq km (240,534 sq miles)

Population : 369,000

Capital : Praia

Form of government : Republic

Religion : RC

Currency : Cape Verde escudo

Cap-Haitien (Le Cap) a port and second largest city of HAITI, after PORT-AU-PRINCE. Founded by the French in 1670 on the north coast of HISPANIOLA, it was the former colonial capital. (Pop. 75,000)

Cappadocia an area of eastern TURKEY to the southeast of ANKARA, noted for the extraordinary sugar-loaf shapes of its volcanic rock formations, into which cave houses have been carved.

Capri a rocky island at the southern end of the Bay of NAPLES on the west coast of ITALY, famous as a fashionable holiday retreat. (10.4 sq km/4 sq miles; pop. 16,500)

Caprivi Strip a narrow corridor of land, 450 km (280 miles) long, which belongs to NAMIBIA and gives it access to the ZAMBEZI River along the border between BOTSWANA to the south and ANGOLA and ZAMBIA to the north.

Caracas the capital of VENEZUALA, in the northeast of the country. (Pop. 3,500,000)

Carcassone an ancient walled town founded in the 5th century BC, situated 73 km (45 miles) northwest of PERPIGNAN in southwest France. Its medieval fortifications were restored in the 19th century. (Pop. 46,000)

Cardamom Mountains a range of mountains rising to 1813 m (5948 ft) which line the coast of CAMBODIA and separate the interior from the Gulf of THAILAND.

Cardiff (Caerdydd) the capital of WALES, situated in the southeast of the principality, in SOUTH GLAMORGAN. (Pop. 281,000)

Cardigan Bay the long, curving bay which, as part of the IRISH SEA, forms much of the west coast of WALES.

Cardiganshire *see* **Dyfed**.

Caribbean Sea a part of the western ATLANTIC OCEAN, bounded by the east coast of Central AMERICA, the north coast of South America and the WEST INDIES.

Caribbean, The a term that refers to the islands lying within the compass of the CARIBBEAN SEA.

Carinthia (Kärnten) the southern state of AUSTRIA, which borders ITALY and SLOVENIA. (9533 sq km/3681 sq miles; pop 536,730)

Carletonville a town on the west WITWATERSRAND in SOUTH AFRICA, formed by the amalgamation of several gold-mining settlements in the 1940s. Nearby is the Western Levels mine (3777 m/12,392 ft) below the surface)—the deepest in the world. (Pop. 100,200)

Carlisle a city 16 km (10 miles) south of the Scottish border in the northwestern English county of CUMBRIA, of which it is the administrative centre. It is situated near to the western end of Hadrian's Wall and has a castle and city wall, remnants of its past Border-fortress function. (Pop. 72,000)

Carlow a landlocked county in the southeast of the Republic of IRELAND. The county town is also called Carlow. (Pop. county 39,000)

Carlsbad *see* **Karlovy Vary**.

Carlsruhe *see* **Karlsruhe**.

Carmarthenshire *see* **Dyfed**.

Carmel, Mount a ridge of land rising to 528 m (1746 ft) in northern ISRAEL, mentioned in the Bible, and the place where the Carmelite Order of mendicant friars originated in the 12th century.

Caroline Islands a scattered group of islands in the western PACIFC OCEAN which now make up the Federated States of MICRONESIA and the separate state of BELAU.

Carpathian Mountains a broad sweep of mountains stretching for nearly 1000 km (625 miles) down the border between SLOVAKIA and POLAND and into central ROMANIA. They rise to 2663 m (8737 ft) at their highest point.

Carpatil Meridionali *see* **Transylvanian Alps.**

Carpentaria, Gulf of the broad gulf of shallow sea between the two hornlike peninsulas of northern AUSTRALIA.

Carrara a town 50 km (31 miles) north of PISA in ITALY, famous for centuries for its marble quarries. (Pop. 68,500)

Carrickfergus a town of historic 17th-century settlement of Scottish Protestants in the northeast of NORTHERN IRELAND, in County ANTRIM. (Pop. 17,633)

Carson City the state capital of NEVADA, USA (Pop. 35,900)

Cartagena (1) a major port on the CARIBBEAN coast of COLOMBIA. (Pop. 548,000). **(2)** a port of ancient origins on the MEDITERRANEAN coast of SPAIN. (Pop. 172,800)

Cartago a city and surrounding province that was the first settled part of COSTA RICA in 1563; until 1823 it was the national capital. (Pop. city 75,500/ province 270,000)

Carthage an ancient city state on the north AFRICAN coast near present-day TUNIS. Founded in 800BC by Phoenician traders, its power grew until finally crushed in the Punic Wars with Rome in the 3rd and 2nd centuries BC.

Casablanca (Dar el Beida) the main port and largest city of MOROCCO. (Pop. 2,140,000)

Cascade Range

Cascade Range a range of mountains stretching some 1125 km (700 miles) parallel to the coast of northern CALIFORNIA in the USA and into southern CANADA. The highest point is at Mount Rainier (4392 m/14,410 ft) in WASHINGTON State.

Caserta a city about 30 km (20 miles) north of NAPLES, famed for the sumptuous Palazzo Reale, built for Charles the Bourbon in 1752–54. (Pop. 66,800)

Cashel (Caiseal) a market town in County TIPPERARY, in south-central IRELAND, about 80 km (50 miles) northeast of Cork. The Rock of Cashel is a sacred and historic site where St Patrick was reputed to have blessed the shamrock to illustrate the Trinity; it was the seat of the kings of MUNSTER for over 700 years. (Pop. 2540)

Caspian Sea the largest inland (salt) sea in the world, supplied mainly by the River VOLGA. It lies to the north of IRAN, which shares its coasts with AZERBAIJAN, GEORGIA, KAZAKHSTAN and TURKMENISTAN.

Cassai *see* **Kasai**.

Cassel *see* **Kassel**.

Cassino a market town in central ITALY, halfway between ROME and NAPLES. It was the Roman *Casinum*. The Abbey of Monte Cassino, perched on a steep hill overlooking the town, was the scene of a famous six-month seige battle during World War II. (Pop. 31,000)

Castile (Castilla) a former kingdom of SPAIN, occupying most of the central area, now divided into two regions, Castilla-La Mancha and Castilla-León.

Castries the capital of ST LUCIA. (Pop. 45,000).

Catalonia (Cataluña) an autonomous region of SPAIN, in the northeast, centring on BARCELONA. (Pop. 5,958,000)

Catania a major port and the second largest city in SICILY. (Pop. 378,500)

Catskill Mountains a range of mountains in NEW YORK State, USA, famed for their scenic beauty. The highest peak is Slide Mountain (1281 m/4204 ft).

Caucasus (Kavkaz) the mountainous region between

the BLACK and CASPIAN SEAS, bounded by the RUSSIAN FEDERATION, GEORGIA, ARMENIA and AZERBAIJAN. It contains EUROPE's highest point, Mount ELBRUS (5642 m/ 18,510 ft).

Cauvery *see* **Kaveri**.

Cavan a county in the north of the Republic of IRELAND, part of the ancient province of ULSTER; Cavan is also the name of the county town. (1890 sq km/730 sq miles; pop. county 53,900)

Caveri *see* **Kaveri**.

Cawnpore *see* **Kanpur**.

Cayenne the capital of GUIANA (FRENCH). (Pop. 38,000)

Cayman Islands a group of three islands in the CARIBBEAN SEA 240 km (150 miles) northwest of Jamaica which form a British Crown colony. The capital is Georgetown, on Grand Cayman. (260 sq km/100 sq miles; pop. 19,100)

Cebu one of islands in the central PHILIPPINES, forming part of the VISAYAN group; also the name of its capital city. (5088 sq km/1964 sq miles; pop. island 2,092,000/city 490,231)

Celebes Sea a sea between the islands of eastern INDONESIA and the PHILIPPINES.

Celebes *see* **Sulawesi**.

Celle (Zelle) a picturesque old town, relatively unscathed during World War II, lies 35 km (22 miles) northeast of HANOVER, GERMANY. It is a major horse-breeding centre. (Pop. 75,000)

Celtic Sea a new name, given by politically sensitive oil prospectors, to the waters of the continental shelf area between southwestern ENGLAND, southern WALES and southern IRELAND.

Central African Federation a historical federation (1953–63) of NORTHERN RHODESIA, SOUTHERN RHODESIA, and NYASALAND, also known as the Federation of Rhodesia and Nyasaland.

Central African Republic is a landlocked country in central AFRICA bordered by CHAD in the north, CAMEROON in the west, SUDAN in the east and the CONGO and ZAÏRE in the south. The terrain consists of a 610–915 m (2000–3000 ft) high undulating plateau with dense tropical forest in the south and a semi-desert area in the east. The climate is tropical with little variation in temperature throughout the year. The wet months are May, June, October and November. Most of the population live in the west and in the hot, humid south and southwest. Over 86% of the working population are subsistence farmers, and the main crops grown are cassava, groundnuts, bananas, plantains, millet and maize. Livestock rearing is small-scale because of the prevalence of the tsetse fly. Gems and industrial diamonds are mined and vast deposits of uranium have been discovered.

Area : 622,984 sq km (240,534 sq miles)

Population : 2,900,000

Capital : Bangui

Form of government : Republic

Religions : Animism, RC

Currency : Franc CFA

Central Region a local government area of SCOTLAND formed in 1975 out of the old counties of Clackmannanshire and parts of Perthshire and Stirlingshire. (2590 sq km/1000 sq miles; pop. 273,000)

Central Russian Uplands (Srende Russkaya Vozvyshennost) a large hilly region in the west of the RUSSIAN FEDERATION, extending from just west of MOSCOW, southwards to the UKRAINE border; it never rises above 300 m (984 ft).

Central Siberian Plateau (Srende Sibirskoye Ploskogor'ye) *see* **Siberia.**

Centre a north-central region of FRANCE, to the south of PARIS and astride the LOIRE River, that includes the ancient province of Berry. The main towns are ORLÉANS and TOURS. (Pop. 2,264,000)

Cephalonia *see* **Ionian Islands**.

Ceram *see* **Seram.**

Ceské Budejovice (Budweiss) a historic town in the south of BOHEMIA, CZECH REPUBLIC, famous for its Budvar beer. (Pop. 92,800)

Ceuta a Spanish enclave in northern MOROCCO administered by SPAIN. (Pop. 80,000)

Cévennes the name given to the southern part of the MASSIF CENTRAL in FRANCE.

Ceylon *see* **Sri Lanka**.

Chad, a landlocked country in the centre of northern AFRICA, extends from the edge of the equatorial forests in the south to the middle of the SAHARA DESERT in the north. It lies more than 1600 km (944 miles) from the nearest coast. The climate is tropical with adequate rainfall in the south but the north experiences semi-desert conditions. In the far north of the country the Tibesti Mountains rise from the desert sand more than 3000 m (9843 ft). The southern part of Chad is the most densely populated and its relatively well-watered savanna has always been the country's most arable region. Recently, however, even here the rains have failed. Normally this area is farmed for cotton (the main cash crop), millet, sorghum, groundnuts, rice and vegetables. Fishing is carried out in the rivers and in Lake Chad. Cotton ginning is the principal industry.

Area : 1,284,000 sq km (495,752 sq miles)
Population : 5,540,000
Capital : Ndjamena (N'Djamena)
Other major cities : Sarh, Moundou
Form of government : Republic
Religions : Sunni Islam, Animism
Currency : Franc CFA

Chad, Lake a large lake in western CHAD, on the border with NIGER and NIGERIA. (26,000 sq km/10,000 sq miles)

Châlons-sur-Marne the capital of Marne départment, 150 km (93 miles) east of PARIS, FRANCE, on the plain of Champagne. (Pop. 54,400)

Chambéry the capital of Savoie départment, 45 km (28

miles) north of Grenoble, France; is dominated by a large 13th-century chateau, once the home of the dukes of Savoy. (Pop. 100,340)

Chamonix a winter sports resort in France, just to the north of Mont Blanc. (Pop. 11,000)

Champagne a region of northeastern France famous for the sparking wine called champagne. It now forms part of the administrative region called Champagne-Ardenne.

Chandannagar (Chandernagore) a town on the Hugli River on the northwest fringe of Calcutta. It was founded as a trading post of the French East India Company in 1688. (Pop. 101,900)

Chandigarh a modern city 230 km (143 miles) north of Delhi, India, planned by the French architect Le Corbusier (1887–1965). (Pop. 422,800)

Changchun the capital of Jilin province, China. (Pop. 1,604,000)

Chang-hua a historic city situated near the west coast of Taiwan. (Pop. 1,206,400)

Chang Jiang (Yangtze Kiang) the world's third longest river. It rises in Tibet and flows across central China into the East China Sea. (Length 6380 km/3965 miles)

Changsha the capital of Hunan province, China. (Pop. 2,638,000)

Channel Islands a group of islands in the English Channel, close to the coast of France, which are British Crown dependencies. The main islands are Jersey and Guernsey, but the group also includes the smaller inhabited islands of Alderney, Sark and Herm. (Pop. 134,700)

Chao Phrya, River a river running from north to south down the west side of Thailand and through its capital, Bangkok. (Length 100 km/620 miles)

Chapala, Lake the largest lake in Mexico, near Guadalajara. (2460 sq km/950 sq miles)

Charleroi an industrial city in central Belgium. (Pop. 213,000)

Charleston (1) the state capital of West Virginia, USA.

(Pop. city 59,400/metropolitan area 267,000) **(2)** An old port on the ATLANTIC coast of SOUTH CAROLINA, USA. (Pop. city 67,100/metropolitan area 472,500)

Charlestown the main town on the CARIBBEAN Island of NEVIS and linked to BASSETERRE on ST KITTS by ferry. (pop. 1800)

Charlotte Amalie the capital of the US VIRGIN ISLANDS, on St Thomas. (Pop. 11,800)

Charlottetown a port and the provincial capital of PRINCE EDWARD ISLAND, CANADA. (Pop. 45,000)

Chartres a market town, capital of the department of Eure-et-Loire, in northern FRANCE, 80 km (50 miles) west of PARIS. It is famous for its early 13th-century cathedral, with original stained-glass windows. (Pop. 80,340)

Chatham Islands a small group of Pacific islands about 850 km (530 miles) east of CHRISTCHURCH, NEW ZEALAND. (Pop. 750)

Chattanooga an industrial city and railway town in TENNESSEE, USA. (Pop. city 164,400/metropolitan area 422,500)

Chatham *see* **Medway Towns.**

Chechen-Ingush Republic one of the 16 autonomous republics of the RUSSIAN FEDERATION. (19,300 sq km/7450 sq miles; pop. 1,204,000)

Cheju Do an island belonging to South KOREA, lying some 90 km (56 miles) off its southern tip, and dominated by the sacred volcano, Mount Halla (1950 m/6398 ft). (1828 sq km/706 sq miles; pop. 463,000)

Chelyabinsk an industrial city in the RUSSIAN FEDERATION. (Pop. 1,086,000)

Chelyuskin, Cape (Mys Chelyuskin) the northernmost point of the EURASIA mainland (77° 44' N) at the tip of the TAIMYR PENINSULA in nothern SIBERIA, RUSSIAN FEDERATION.

Chemnitz an industrial city in southeast GERMANY, named Karl-Marx-Stadt during the period of Communist rule in former East Germany (until 1990). (Pop. 319,000)

Chengdu the capital of Sɪᴄʜᴜᴀɴ province, Cʜɪɴᴀ. (Pop. 2,470,000)

Chenstokhov *see* **Czestochowa.**

Cherbourg a port and naval dockyard on the north coast of the Cotentin peninsula of Nᴏʀᴍᴀɴᴅʏ, Fʀᴀɴᴄᴇ, on the Eɴɢʟɪsʜ Cʜᴀɴɴᴇʟ. (Pop. 89,200)

Chernigov an agricultural centre, industrial town and port on the Desna River, about 130 km (80 miles) northeast of Kɪᴇᴠ in the Uᴋʀᴀɪɴᴇ. (Pop. 270,000)

Chernobyl a city about 90 km (55 miles) north of Kɪᴇᴠ, in the Uᴋʀᴀɪɴᴇ. In April 1986 one of the reactors in its nuclear power station exploded, causing the world's worst nuclear accident.

Chernovtsy (Cernauti) an industrial city in the Uᴋʀᴀɪɴᴇ, near to the Romanian border, 225 km (140 miles) southeast of L'ᴠᴏᴠ. (Pop. 238,000)

Chesapeake Bay an inlet, 314 km (195 miles) long, on the east coast of the USA, shared by the states of Vɪʀɢɪɴɪᴀ and Mᴀʀʏʟᴀɴᴅ.

Cheshire a county in northwest Eɴɢʟᴀɴᴅ; the county town is Chester. (2322 sq km/897 sq miles; pop. 933,000)

Cheviot Hills a range of hills, 60 km (37 miles) long, which line the border between Sᴄᴏᴛʟᴀɴᴅ and the county of Nᴏʀᴛʜᴜᴍʙᴇʀʟᴀɴᴅ in Eɴɢʟᴀɴᴅ.

Cheyenne the state capital of Wʏᴏᴍɪɴɢ, USA. (Pop. 50,900)

Chiang Mai *see* **Chiengmai.**

Chianti the wine-making region of central Tᴜsᴄᴀɴʏ, Iᴛᴀʟʏ.

Chiba a large industrial city on Hᴏɴsʜᴜ Island, Jᴀᴘᴀɴ. (Pop. 788,900)

Chicago the largest city in the state of Iʟʟɪɴᴏɪs, and the third largest city in the USA (after Nᴇᴡ Yᴏʀᴋ and Lᴏs Aɴɢᴇʟᴇs). (Pop. city 2,992,500/metropolitan area 8,035,000)

Chichén Itzá a village in Yᴜᴄᴀᴛᴀɴ, Mᴇxɪᴄᴏ, the site of a complex of major ruins of the Mayans and Toltecs.

Chichester a cathedral city and county town of Wᴇsᴛ Sᴜssᴇx, about 90 km (55 miles) southwest of Lᴏɴᴅᴏɴ,

ENGLAND. Founded in the 1st century AD as Novioragus, it still retains its Roman plan, with an almost complete ring of medieval city walls. (Pop. 25,000)

Chiclayo a city in northwest PERU that is at the centre of the conurbation that includes Ferreñafe and Lambayeque. (Pop. 280,000)

Chiengmai (Chiang Mai) the second largest city in THAILAND, in the northwest of the country, famous for its temples and the crafts produced in the surrounding villages. (Pop. 200,700)

Chihuahua a city in northern central MEXICO, and the name of the surrounding province, of which it is the capital. (Pop. city 410,000)

Chile lies like a backbone down the PACIFIC coast of the South American continent. Its Pacific coastline is 4200 km (2610 miles) long. Because of its enormous range in latitude it has almost every kind of climate from desert conditions to icy wastes. The north, in which lies the ATACAMA DESERT, is extremely arid. The climate of the central region is Mediterranean and that of the south cool temperate. 60% of the population live in the central valley where the climate is similar to southern CALIFORNIA. The land here is fertile and the principal crops grown are wheat, sugar beet, maize and potatoes. It is also in the central valley that the vast copper mine of El Teniente is located. This is one of the largest copper mines in the world and accounts for Chile's most important source of foreign exchange.

Area : 756,945 sq km (292,256 sq miles)

Population : 12,960,000

Capital : Santiago

Other major cities : Arica, Talcahuano, Viña del Mar

Form of government : Republic

Religion : RC

Currency : Chilean peso

Chiltern Hills a range of hills to the northwest of LONDON, ENGLAND, rising to 260 m (850 ft).

Chi-lung (Keelung) a major seaport and industrial city at the north end of the island of TAIWAN, 30 km (20 miles) northeast of T'AIPEI.

Chimborazo an impressive snow-capped inactive volcano in the ANDES of ECUADOR, which at 6310 m (20,702 ft) is the highest point in the country; because of the bulge in the earth at the Equator it is 2150 m (7050 ft) farther from the centre of the earth than the summit of Mount EVEREST.

China, the third largest country in the world, covers a large area of East ASIA. In western China most of the terrain is very inhospitable—in the northwest there are deserts which extend into MONGOLIA and the RUSSIAN FEDERATION, and much of the southwest consists of the ice-capped peaks of TIBET. The southeast has a green and well-watered landscape comprising terraced hillsides and paddy fields. Most of China has a temperate climate but in such a large country wide ranges of latitude and altitudes produce local variations. China is an agricultural country, and intensive cultivation and horticulture are necessary to feed its population of over 1,000,000,000. Since the death of Mao in 1976, China has experienced a huge modernization of agriculture and industry by the supply of expertise, capital and technology from JAPAN and the West, and it has also been opened up to tourists.

Area : 9,596,961 sq km (3,705,387 sq miles)

Population : 1,114,000,000

Capital : Beijing (Peking)

Other major cities : Chengdu, Guangzhou, Shanghai, Tianjin, Wuhan

Form of government : People's Republic

Religions : Buddhism, Confucianism, Taoism

Currency : Yuan

China Sea a part of the PACIFIC OCEAN, off the east coast of CHINA.

Chindwin, River a river in BURMA, flowing parallel to the northwest border before joining the IRRAWADDY River in the centre of the country. (Length 1130 km/700 miles)

Chingola a commerical centre in the COPPERBELT of northern ZAMBIA. It was founded in 1943 to service the Nchanga copper mine. (Pop. 146,000)

Chin-men Tao (Quemoy) a group of two main islands and 12 islets in the TAIWAN STRAIT, belonging to Taiwan, but lying just off the coast of FUJIAN province of mainland CHINA close to the city of XIAMEN (AMOY). Like MA-TSU TAO they are heavily fortified and defended by Chinese Nationalist forces; they were shelled from the mainland in the 1950s.

Chios (Khios) an island in the AEGEAN SEA, belonging to GREECE but lying only 8 km (5 miles) from the coast of TURKEY. It is said to have been the home of the poet Homer (*c*.800BC). (904 sq km/349 sq miles; pop. 49,900)

Chisinau *see* **Kishinev**.

Chittagong the main port of BANGLADESH and its second largest city. (Pop. 1,392,000)

Cholon a component town of HO CHI MINH CITY, separated from the city proper by a narrow stream.

Cholula a town in southeast MEXICO famous for its extensive Toltec ruins dating from 500BC. (Pop. 160,000)

Chongqing (Chungking) an industrial city on the CHANG JIANG river, CHINA, and the largest city in SICHUAN province. (Pop. 2,650,000)

Chonju a historic city in the southwest of South KOREA. (Pop. 367,100)

Chonnam *see* **Kwangju**.

Christchurch the largest city on South Island, NEW ZEALAND. (Pop. 300,000)

Christiania *see* **Kristiansand**.

Christmas Island (1) an island in the eastern INDIAN OCEAN, 400 km (250 miles) to the south of JAVA, administered by AUSTRALIA since 1958. (142 sq km/55 sq miles; pop. 3500). **(2) (Kiritimati)** is the PACIFIC OCEAN's largest coral atoll, situated at the northeastern end of the KIRIBATI group. (432 sq km/167 sq miles; pop. 1300)

Chubu Sangaku

Chubu Sangaku *see* **Japan Alps.**

Chudskoye Ozero *see* **Peipus, Lake.**

Chukchi Peninsula (Chukotskiy Poluostrov) the easternmost part of the EURASIA continental landmass, in northeast SIBERIA of the RUSSIAN FEDERATION.

Chukchi Sea a part of the ARCTIC OCEAN, north of the BERING STRAIT, between ASIA and NORTH AMERICA.

Chungking *see* **Chongqing**.

Churchill a seaport and railhead on the west shore of HUDSON BAY, CANADA. It has one of the best harbours on the Bay and is the administrative and main tourist centre for this remote northern part of MANITOBA. (Pop. 1186)

Churchill, River a river which flows into the HUDSON BAY at the port of CHURCHILL after a journey through SASKATCHEWAN and MANITOBA. (Length 1610 km/1000 miles)

Chuvash Republic one of the 16 autonomous republics of the RUSSIAN FEDERATION. (18,300 sq km/7050 sq miles; pop. 1,314,000)

Cincinnati a city in the southwest of the state of OHIO, USA, on the OHIO River. (Pop. city 370,500/metropolitan area 1,673,500)

Cinque Ports a group of towns, originally five but later increased to seven, on the ENGLISH CHANNEL coast of KENT and SUSSEX, granted special privileges by King Edward the Confessor in the 11th century in return for defending the realm; they include DOVER, HASTINGS and Rye.

City, The *see* **London.**

C.I.S. *see* **Commonwealth of Independent States.**

Ciskei a Bantu homeland for the Xhosa people declared independent by the government of SOUTH AFRICA in 1981. (8300 sq km/3205 sq miles; pop. 728,400)

Citaltépetl a volcanic peak to the southeast of MEXICO CITY, and at 5699 m (18,697 ft) the highest point in MEXICO.

Clackmannanshire *see* **Central Region**.

Clare a county on the west coast of IRELAND; the county town is Ennis. (3188 sq km/1230 sq miles; pop. 87,500)

Clermont-Ferrand a city in the AUVERGNE region of central FRANCE. (Pop. 262,175)

Cleveland (1) a county of northeast ENGLAND created in 1974 out of Durham and Yorkshire to administer the industrial region along the River Tees, known as Teeside (583 sq km/225 sq miles; pop. 565,000). **(2)** a port and industrial city on the southern side of Lake ERIE, in OHIO, USA. (Pop. city 546,500/metropolitan area 1,867,000)

Cluj-Napoca a city of ancient origins in central ROMANIA. (Pop. 260,000)

Clwyd a county in northeast WALES created in 1974 out of the county of Flintshire and parts of Merionethshire and Denbighshire. (2425 sq km/936 sq miles; pop. 395,000)

Clyde, River a river in STRATHCLYDE region in southwest SCOTLAND which flows northwest to form an estuary 100 km (60 miles) long, called the Firth of Clyde, with GLASGOW at its head. (Length 170 km/105 miles)

Coast Mountains a mountain range in western CANADA that parallels the coast of BRITISH COLUMBIA; it contains the highest point in Canada, Mount Waddington, 4042 m (13,266 ft) high.

Coast Ranges a range of mountains lining the western coast of the USA, stetching 1600 km(1000 miles) from the borders with CANADA to LOS ANGELES. The highest point is in the San Jacinto Mountains (3301 m/10,831 ft).

Cobh a town and port in Cork Harbor on the south coast of IRELAND, some 10 km (6 miles) from the city of CORK. (Pop. 6600)

Coblenz *see* **Koblenz**.

Coburg a town in BAVARIA, 90 km (55 miles) north of NUREMBERG, and the former seat of the dukes of Saxe-Coburg-Gotha—one of whom was Prince Albert who married Victoria, queen of Britain, in 1840. (Pop. 45,000)

Cochin a port on the southwestern tip of INDIA. (Pop. 551,600)

Cochin China the name given to the region around the MEKONG delta during the French occupation of VIETNAM.

Cockburn Town

Cockburn Town the capital of Turks and Caicos. (Pop. 3200)

Cocos Islands (Keeling Islands) a cluster of 28 small coral islands in the eastern Indian Ocean, equidistant from Sumatra and Australia, and administered by Australia since 1955. (14 sq km/6 sq miles; pop. 700)

Cod, Cape a narrow, low-lying peninsula of sand dunes and marshland on the coast of Massachusetts, USA, where the Pilgrim Fathers landed in 1620.

Cognac a historic medieval town on the Charente river in west-central France, about 95 km (60 miles) north of Bordeaux. It is at the centre of the region famed for producing brandy, to which it gave its name. (Pop. 32,400)

Coll a low-lying, windswept island of the Inner Hebrides, off the west coast of Scotland. (72 sq km/45 sq miles; Pop. 131)

Cologne (Köln) a city and industrial centre on the River Rhine, Germany. (Pop. 932,400)

Colombia is situated in the north of South America, and most of the country lies between the Equator and 10° north. The Andes, which split into three ranges (the Cordilleras) in Colombia, run north along the west coast and gradually disappear towards the Caribbean Sea. Half of Colombia lies east of the Andes, and much of this region is covered in tropical grassland. Towards the Amazon Basin the vegetation changes to tropical forest. The climates in Colombia include equatorial and tropical, according to altitude. Very little of the country is under cultivation although much of the soil is fertile. The range of climates results in an extraordinary variety of crops of which coffee is the most important. Colombia is rich in minerals and produces about half of the world's emeralds. It is South America's leading producer of coal, and oil has recently been discovered.

Area : 1,138,914 sq km (439,735 sq miles)

Population : 33,000,000

Capital : Bogotá
Other major cities : Barranquilla, Cali, Cartagena,
  Medellin
Form of government : Republic
Religion : RC
Currency : Peso

Colombo a major port and the capital of SRI LANKA. (Pop.
600,000)

Colón the second largest city of PANAMA, lying at the
CARIBBEAN end of the Panama Canal. (Pop. 117,000)

Colonsay an isolated island of the Inner HEBRIDES, lying
13 km (8 miles) northwest of JURA, off the west coast of
SCOTLAND. (41 sq km/16 sq miles; Pop. 133)

Colorado an inland state of central western USA; the
state capital is DENVER. (270,000 sq km/104,247 sq miles;
pop. 3,231,000)

Colorado, River a river which rises in the ROCKY MOUN-
TAINS in the state of COLORADO, USA, and flows southwest
to the Gulf of CALIFORNIA, forming the GRAND CANYON on its
way. (Length 2330 km/1450 miles)

Colorado Springs a spa and resort city in the state of
COLORADO, USA. (Pop. city 247,700/metropolitan area
349,100)

Columbia the state capital of SOUTH CAROLINA. (Pop. city
98,600/metropolitan area 433,200)

Columbia, District of *see* **Washington D.C.**

Columbia, River a river which flows northwards from its
source in BRITISH COLUMBIA, CANADA, before turning south
into WASHINGTON STATE, USA and entering the PACIFIC
OCEAN at PORTLAND, OREGON. (Length 1950 km/1210 miles)

Columbus the state capital of OHIO, USA. (Pop. city
566,100/metropolitan area 1,279,000)

Common Market, The *see* **European Community.**

Commonwealth of Independent States (**C.I.S.**) an
organization created in 1991 to represent the common
interests of eleven independent states of the former
USSR. The name is a translation of *Sodruzhestvo Neza-*

visimikh Gosudarstv. The eleven member states are: ARMENIA, AZERBAIJAN, BELARUS, KAZAKHSTAN, KYRGYZSTAN, MOLDOVA, RUSSIAN FEDERATION, TAJIKISTAN, TURKMENISTAN, UKRAINE and UZBEKISTAN. The former Soviet republics of ESTONIA, LATVIA, LITHUANIA and GEORGIA did not join the CIS on gaining independence.

Como, Lake an Alpine lake about 35 km (22 miles) north of MILAN, ITALY, with the popular resorts of Bellagio, Como and Lecco.

Comorin, Cape the southern tip of INDIA.

Comoros, The consist of three volcanic islands in the INDIAN OCEAN situated between mainland AFRICA and MADAGASCAR. Physically, four islands make up the group, but the island of MAYOTTE remained a French dependency when the three western islands became a federal Islamic republic in 1975. The islands are mostly forested, and the tropical climate is affected by Indian monsoon winds from the north. There is a wet season from November to April. Only small areas of the islands are cultivated, and most of this land belongs to foreign plantation owners. The chief product was formerly sugar cane, but now vanilla, copra, maize, cloves and essential oils are the most important products. The forests provide timber for building and there is a small fishing industry.

Area : 2235 sq km (863 sq miles)

Population : 503,000

Capital : Moroni

Form of government : Federal Islamic Republic

Religion : Sunni Islam

Currency : Comorian franc

Conakry the capital of GUINEA, a port partly located on the island of Tumbo. (Pop. 763,000)

Concepción a city and surrounding province in the Bío-Bío region of central CHILE, about 420 km (260 miles) south of SANTIAGO; it is one of the country's most heavily industrialized areas. (Pop. city 210,000/province 762,800)

Concord the state capital of NEW HAMPSHIRE, USA. (Pop. 30,900)

Coney Island a former island, now attached to the south end of LONG ISLAND, NEW YORK, USA; it is the site of a long-established amusement park.

Congo formerly a French colony, the Republic of the Congo is situated in west-central AFRICA, where it straddles the Equator. The climate is equatorial, with a moderate rainfall and a small range of temperature. The Bateke Plateau has a long dry season, but the Congo Basin is more humid and rainfall approaches 2500 mm (98 inches) each year. About 62% of the total land area is covered with equatorial forest from which timbers such as okoume and sapele are produced. Valuable hardwoods such as mahogany are exported. Cash crops such as coffee and cocoa are mainly grown on large plantations, but food crops are grown on small farms, usually worked by the women. A manufacturing industry is now growing, and oil discovered offshore accounts for most of the Congo's revenues.

Area : 342,000 sq km (132,046 sq miles)
Population : 2,260,000
Capital : Brazzaville
Other major city : Pointe-Noire
Form of government : Republic
Religion : RC
Currency : Franc CFA

Congo, River *see* **Zaïre, River.**

Connaught (Connacht) one of the four old provinces into which IRELAND was divided.

Connecticut a state on the northeastern seaboard of the USA, in NEW ENGLAND; the capital is HARTFORD. (12,973 sq km/5009 sq miles; pop. 3,174,000)

Connemara a famously beautiful part of County GALWAY on the west coast of IRELAND centring upon the distinctive peaks of the Twelve Bens.

Constance, Lake (Bodensee) a lake in Europe surrounded by Germany to the north, Switzerland to the south and Austria to the east. (536 sq km/207 sq miles)

Constanta a major port on the Black Sea coast of Romania. (Pop. 283,600)

Constantine (Qacentina) an ancient walled city in the northeastern corner of Algeria. (Pop. 430,500)

Constantinople *see* **Istanbul**.

Cook Islands a group of 15 islands in the South Pacific, independent since 1965 but associated with New Zealand. The capital is Avarua. (240 sq km/93 sq miles; pop. 17,700; cur. Cook Islands dollar/ New Zealand dollar = 100 cents)

Cook, Mount the highest mountain in New Zealand, on South Island. (3753 m/12,313 ft)

Cook Strait the strait that separates North Island and South Island of New Zealand, 26 km (16 miles) across at its widest point.

Cooper Creek a river flowing into Lake Eyre in South Australia from its source in central Queensland. The upper stretch is known as the Barcoo River. (Length 1420 km/800 miles)

Copacabana a famous beachside suburb of Rio de Janeiro, Brazil.

Copán, a village in Honduras, is the site of a great Mayan city which flourished between AD450 and 800.

Copenhagen (København) a port and the capital of Denmark, located on the islands of Zealand and Amager. (Pop. 641,900)

Copperbelt the smallest province of Zambia, in the central part of the country about 225 km (140 miles) north of Lusaka. It is one of the world's largest copper reserves and has several mining towns, including Chingola, Kitwe, and Ndola. (31,328 sq km/12,096 sq miles; pop. 1,249,000)

Coral Sea a part of the Pacific Ocean, off the northeast coast of Australia.

Corcaigh *see* **Cork**.

Cordillera Cantabrica (Cantabrian Mountains) a

range of mountains in northern SPAIN, which extend westward from the PYRÉNÉES for about 480 km (300 miles), rising to the highest point in Peña Cerredo (2648 m/8685 ft).

Cordillera Central a major mountain range in northern LUZON, PHILIPPINES, running north to south for 320 km (200 miles) and with Mount Pulog (2928m/9606ft) as the highest peak.

Cordilleras Occidental-Central-Oriental the northern end of the ANDES, in western COLOMBIA, which takes the form of a three-pronged fork, with each of the three ranges running north and largely disappearing towards the CARIBBEAN; they rise to 5750 m (18,865 ft) in the central mountains.

Córdoba (Cordova) (1) a city in southern Spain, famous for its cathedral which was built originally as a mosque; also the name of the surrounding province. (Pop. city 284,700) **(2)** the second city of ARGENTINA, and the name of the surrounding province. (Pop. city 969,000)

Corfu (Kérkira) the most northerly of the IONIAN ISLANDS, in western GREECE; the capital is also called Corfu. (592 sq km/229 sq miles; pop. 97,100)

Corinth (Korinthos) a town in the PELOPONNESE in western GREECE, built near the Corinth Ship Canal. (Pop. 22,700)

Cork (Corcaigh) the second largest city in the Republic of IRELAND, at the head of a large natural harbour which cuts into the southern coast. Also the name of the county of which it is the county town. (County 7459 sq km/2880 sq miles; pop. county 402,300; pop. city 136,300)

Cornwall the county occupying the southwestern tip of ENGLAND; the county town is Truro. (3546 sq km/1369 sq miles; pop. 432,000)

Coromandel Coast the coast of southeastern INDIA around MADRAS.

Coromandel Peninsula the central peninsula reaching northwards from North Island, NEW ZEALAND.

Corpus Christi

Corpus Christi a port in Texas on the Gulf of Mexico. (Pop. city 258,100/metropolitan area 361,300)

Corsica (Corse) a large island in the Mediterranean Sea lying to the north of Sardinia, governed by France. (8680 sq km/3350 sq miles; pop. 240,000)

Corunna (La Coruña) a port and manufacturing town in northwest Spain, and also the name of the surrounding province. (Pop. town 232,400)

Costa Blanca a popular coastline along the southeast of Spain, centred on Alicante and including the specially created resort of Benidorm.

Costa Brava a strip of coastline to the northeast of Barcelona in Spain, famous for its beaches and its popular resorts.

Costa del Sol the extensive south Andalucian coast of Spain, stretching over 275 km (170 miles) from Gibraltar to Almeria; it includes many popular tourist resorts like Málaga, Marbella and Torremolinos.

Costa Rica with the Pacific Ocean to the south and west and the Caribbean Sea to the east, Costa Rica is sandwiched between the Central American countries of Nicaragua and Panama. Much of the country consists of volcanic mountain chains that run northwest to southeast. The climate is tropical with a small temperature range and abundant rain. The dry season is from December to April. The most populated area is the Valle Central, which was first settled by the Spanish in the 16th century. The upland areas have rich volcanic soils that are good for coffee growing, and the slopes provide lush pastures for cattle. Coffee and bananas are grown commercially and are the major agricultural exports. Costa Rica's mountainous terrain provides hydroelectric power, which makes it almost self-sufficient in electricity, and attractive scenery for its growing tourist industry.

Area : 51,100 sq km (19,730 sq miles)
Population : 2,910,000
Capital : San José

Other major city : Límon
Form of government : Republic
Religion : RC
Currency : Costa Rican colon

Costa Smeralda the "emerald coast" on the northeast side of the MEDITERRANEAN island of SARDINIA, famed for its watersports and its upmarket resorts.

Côte d'Azur the coast of southeast FRANCE, famous for its beaches and resorts such as ST TROPEZ, CANNES and NICE.

Côte d'Ivoire a former French colony in west AFRICA, Côte d'Ivoire is located on the Gulf of GUINEA with GHANA to the east and LIBERIA to the west. The southwest coast has rocky cliffs, but further east there are coastal plains which are the country's most prosperous region. The climate is tropical and affected by distance from the sea. The coastal area has two wet seasons, but in the north, there is only one. Côte d'Ivoire is basically an agricultural country which produces cocoa, coffee, rubber, bananas and pineapples. It is the world's largest producer of cocoa and the fourth largest producer of coffee. These two crops bring in half the country's export revenue. Since independence, industrialization has developed rapidly, particularly food processing, textiles and sawmills.

Area : 322,463 sq km (124,503 sq miles)
Population : 12,100,000
Capital : Yamoussoukro
Other major cities : Abidjan, Bouaké, Daloa
Form of government : Republic
Religions : Animism, Sunni Islam, RC
Currency : Franc CFA

Cotonou a port and the main business centre of BENIN. (Pop. 488,000)

Cotopaxi the world's highest active volcano (5896 m/ 19,344 ft) situated in the ANDES of ECUADOR. It last erupted in 1877.

Cotswold Hills a range of hills in western central ENGLAND, lying to the east of the River SEVERN.

Cottbus an industrial city on the Spree River, in BRANDENBURG state of eastern GERMANY. (Pop. 111,502)

Courtrai (Kortrijk) a long-established textile town in BELGIUM, near the French border. (Pop. 76,000)

Coventry an industrial city in the WEST MIDLANDS of ENGLAND. (Pop. 315,900)

Cowes a town in southern ENGLAND, at the north end of the Isle of WIGHT, famous for its annual yachting regatta. (Pop. 19,633)

Cozumel, Isla de a small CARIBBEAN island lying just off the northeast coast of the YUCATÁN peninsula, MEXICO. In Mayan legend it was the home of their sun god; today it is a tourist resort for the world's second largest coral reef, which is just offshore and extends over 400 km (250 miles) southwards to BELIZE.

Cracow (Krakow) the third largest city in POLAND, and the capital during medieval times. (Pop. 520,700)

Craiova an industrial city in southwest ROMANIA. (Pop. 228,000)

Crawley a designated "new town" in southern ENGLAND, in the northeastern part of WEST SUSSEX. Nearby, at Gatwick, is the site of LONDON'S second international airport. (Pop. 73,081)

Cremona a town on the River Po in central northern ITALY, famous for its violins, especially those of Antonio Stradivari (?1644–1737). (Pop. 80,800)

Crete (Krití) the largest and most southerly of the islands of GREECE, with important ruins of the Minoan civilization at KNOSSOS. The capital is HERAKLION. (8366 sq km/ 3229 sq miles; pop. 502,100)

Crewe a town in CHESHIRE, northwest ENGLAND, that was "put on the map" during the Industrial Revolution when, in 1840, it became a major railway junction and developed associated engineering workshops. (Pop. 48,000)

Crimea (Krym) a diamond-shaped peninsula jutting out into the northern part of the BLACK SEA and part of the UKRAINE. (25,900 sq km/10,000 sq miles; pop. 2,309,000)

Cristóbal the twin town of Colón in Panama, 80 km (50 miles) northwest of Panama City. Its name means "Christoper", and since Colón means "Columbus", America's discoverer is so commemorated.

Crna Gora *see* **Montenegro**.

Crnojevica *see* **Rijeka-Crnojevica**.

Croagh Patrick (Cruách Phádraig) a holy mountain just south of Clew Bay on the west coast of Ireland. It is the site of what is regarded as the oldest pilgrimage in the western world, commemorating St Patrick's fast on this mountain during Lent of AD441.

Croatia (Hrvatska), a republic of former Yugoslavia, declared itself independent in 1991 and was formally recognized by the EC and the UN in 1992. It is located in southeast Europe and is bounded to the west by the Adriatic Sea, to the north by Slovenia and Romania, and to the south by Bosnia-Herzegovina. Western Croatia lies in the Dinaric Alps. The eastern region, drained by the rivers Sava and Drava, is low-lying and agricultural. The chief farming region is the Pannonian Plain. Over one third of the country is forested and timber is a major export. Deposits of coal, bauxite, copper, oil and iron ore are substantial, and most of the republic's industry is based on the processing of these. In Istria in the northwest and on the Dalmatian coast tourism is a major industry.

Area : 56,538 sq km (21,824 sq miles)

Population : 4,601,500

Capital : Zagreb

Other major cities : Rijeka, Split

Form of government : Republic

Religions : RC, Eastern Orthodox

Currency : Dinar

Crocodile River *see* **Limpopo**.

Crocodilopolis *see* **El Faiyum**.

Crotone an industrial town with zinc works situated on the sole of the "boot" of Italy. Previously, it was the ancient Greek city of Croton, home of Pythagoras in the 6th century BC. (Pop. 26,700)

Crozet Islands a group of some 20 islands and islets in the SOUTHERN OCEAN, forming part of the FRENCH SOUTHERN AND ANTARCTIC TERRITORIES. (300 sq km/116 sq miles)

Cruách Phádraig *see* **Croach Patrick**.

Cuango, River *see* **Kwango, River.**

Cuanza, River a river that flows from the Bié Plateau of central ANGOLA almost 1000 km (600 miles) to reach the ATLANTIC just south of LUANDA. It is navigable for abut 200 km (120 miles) and was an important route into the interior for early explorers.

Cuba is the largest and most westerly of the Greater ANTILLES group of islands in the WEST INDIES. It is strategically positioned at the entrance to the Gulf of MEXICO and lies about 140 km (87 miles) south of the tip of FLORIDA. Cuba is as big as all other CARIBBEAN islands put together and is home to a third of the whole West Indian population. The climate is warm and generally rainy, and hurricanes are liable to occur between June and November. The island consists mainly of extensive plains, and the soil is fertile. The most important agricultural product is sugar and its by-products, and the processing of these is the most important industry. Most of Cuba's trade was with other communist countries, particularly the former USSR.

Area : 110,861 sq km (42,803 sq miles)

Population : 10,580,000

Capital : Havana (La Habana)

Other major cities : Camaguey, Holguin, Santiago de Cuba

Form of government : Socialist Republic

Religion : RC

Currency : Cuban peso

Cubango, River *see* **Kavango, River.**

Cúcuta a city in northern COLOMBIA on the border with VENEZUELA. (Pop. 516,000)

Cuenca a city in southern ECUADOR, founded by the Spanish in 1557, but also the site of a number of important Inca ruins. (Pop. 272,500)

Cuernavaca an old resort town in the mountains 80 km (50 miles) to the south of MEXICO CITY. (Pop. 557,000)

Culiacán a mining and agricultural centre, and capital of Sinaloa state in northwest MEXICO. (Pop. 358,000)

Culloden an area of moorland about 8 km (5 miles) to the east of INVERNESS in SCOTLAND, the scene of a bloody battle in 1746 in which the forces of the Young Pretender, Bonnie Prince Charlie, were defeated by the English under the Duke of Cumberland.

Cumaná a port on the north coast of VENEZUELA, 320 km (200 miles) east of CARACAS. It is the oldest Hispanic city in South AMERICA, founded by the Spaniards in 1520.

Cumberland *see* **Cumbria**.

Cumbernauld a new town, designated in 1955, 20 km (12 miles) northeast of GLASGOW, in central SCOTLAND. (Pop. 47,702)

Cumbria a county in northwest ENGLAND, created in 1974 from the old counties of Cumberland, Westmorland and a part of LANCASHIRE. (6809 sq km/2629 sq miles; pop. 483,000)

Cumbrian Mountains a dome-like range of mountains that forms the core of the LAKE DISTRICT in northwest ENGLAND, and includes the country's highest peak, Scafell Pike (978 m/3210 ft)

Curaçao an island in the CARIBBEAN lying just off the coast of VENEZUELA but a part of the NETHERLANDS ANTILLES. (444 sq km/171 sq miles; pop. 170,000)

Curitaba an industrial city in southern BRAZIL. (Pop. 1,442,000)

Cuttack a city in northeast INDIA about 320 km (200 miles) southwest of CALCUTTA. It is situated between two distributaries of the Mahanadi river, and is subject to floods. (Pop. 327,400)

Cuxhaven a busy seaport, fishing town and resort at the

mouth of the River ELBE in northwest GERMANY (Pop. 47,600)

Cuzco a city set in the ANDES mountains in PERU, and the name of the surrounding province. It was a centre of the Inca empire, and there are numerous Inca remains in the region, including MACHU PICCHU. (Pop. city 184,600)

Cwmbran a "new town" in central GWENT, southeast WALES, developed in the 1950s. (44,900)

Cyclades (Kikládhes) a group of some 220 islands in the middle of the AEGEAN SEA and belonging to GREECE. The best known are Tínos, Andros, Mílos, Míkonos, DELOS, Náxos, Paros, Kithnos, Serifos, Ios and Síros. (Pop. 88,400)

Cymru the Welsh name for WALES.

Cyprus is an island which lies in the eastern MEDITERRA-NEAN, about 85 km (53 miles) south of TURKEY. It has a long thin panhandle and is divided from west to east by two parallel ranges of mountains which are separated by a wide central plain open to the sea at either end. The highest point is Mount OLYMPUS (1951 m/6401 ft) in the southwest. The climate is Mediterranean with very hot dry summers and warm damp winters. This contributes towards the great variety of crops grown, eg early potatoes, vegetables, cereals, tobacco, olives, bananas, and grapes. The grapes are used for the strong wines and sherries for which Cyprus is famous. Fishing is a significant industry, but above all the island depends on visitors and it is the tourist industry which has led to a recovery in the economy since 1974.

Area : 9251 sq km (3572 sq miles)

Population : 698,800

Capital : Nicosia

Other major cities : Limassol, Larnaca

Form of government : Republic

Religions : Greek Orthodox, Sunni Islam

Currency : Cyprus pound

Cyrenaica one of the three historical regions of LIBYA,

occupying the eastern half of the country, with BENGHAZI as its principal city. (855,000 sq km (330,110 sq miles; pop. 979,800)

Cyrene an ancient ruined city, 225 km (140 miles) east and slightly north of BENGHAZI, in northeast LIBYA. Founded by the Greeks in 630BC, it flourished as one of the great classical cities for 1000 years before being destroyed by an earthquake in AD364. (Pop. 100,000 at its height)

Czech Republic, The, was newly constituted on January 1,1993, with the dissolution of the 74-year-old federal republic of Czechoslovakia. It is landlocked at the heart of central EUROPE, bounded by SLOVAKIA, GERMANY, POLAND and AUSTRIA. Natural boundaries are formed by the Sudeten Mountains in the north, the Erzgebirge, or Ore Mountains, to the northwest, and the Bohemian Forest in the southwest. The climate is humid continental with warm summers and cold winters. Most rain falls in summer and thunderstorms are frequent. Agriculture, although accounting for only a small percentage of the national income, is highly developed and efficient. Major crops are sugar beet, wheat and potatoes. Over a third of the labour force is employed in industry, the most important being iron and steel, coal, machinery, cement and paper. Recently investment has gone into electronic factories and research establishments.

Area : 78,864 sq km (30,449 sq miles)

Population : 10,291,900

Capital : Prague (Praha)

Other major cities : Brno, Ostrava, Plzen

Form of government : Republic

Religions : RC, Protestantism

Currency : Koruna

Czechoslovakia *see* **Czech Republic; Slovakia.**

Czestochowa (Chenstokhov) an industrial city in southern POLAND. Its Jasna Gora Monastery is a national shrine and pilgrimage centre. (Pop. 244,100)

D

Dabrowa Gornicza (Dombrau) a coal-mining and steel town near KATOWICE in southern POLAND. Its first mine was opened in 1796 to work the world's thickest coal seam at 20 m (66 ft); now preserved as a geological site of special interest. (Pop. 141,600)

Dacca (Dhaka) the capital of Bangladesh, on the delta of the Rivers GANGES and BRAHMAPUTRA. (Pop. 3,458,600)

Dachau a market town in BAVARIA, GERMANY, and the site of the first concentration camp to be built by the Nazis, in 1935. (Pop. 35,000)

Dagenham a motor-vehicle manufacturing town on the north shore of the THAMES Estuary, at the eastern end of GREATER LONDON, ENGLAND. (Pop. 149,132—Barking and Dagenham Borough)

Dagestan an autonomous republic of the RUSSIAN FEDERATION lying to the west of the CASPIAN SEA. The capital is MAKHACHKALA. (50,300 sq km/19,400 sq miles; pop. 709,000)

Dakar the main port and capital of SENEGAL. (Pop. 1,000,000).

Dakota *see* **North Dakota**; **South Dakota**.

Dal, Lake the most famous of the lakes of KASHMIR, INDIA, by SRINAGAR.

Dales, The *see* **Yorkshire Dales**.

Dalian *see* **Lüda**.

Dallas a city in northeast TEXAS, USA. (Pop. city 974,200/ metropolitan area 2,203,700)

Dalmatia (Dalmacija) the coast of CROATIA, on the ADRIATIC SEA. The main islands of the coast are Krk, Rab,

Losinj, Brac, Hvar, Korcula and Mljet. The principal tourist centre is DUBROVNIK.

Damanhur a town at the centre of the cotton-growing region on EGYPT's NILE delta, 60 km (38 miles) southeast of ALEXANDRIA. (Pop. 175,000)

Damaraland a plateau region of central NAMIBIA, and homeland of the Damara, or Bergdama, people; the capital is Khorixas. (46,560 sq km/17,977 sq miles; pop. 12,400)

Damascus (Dimashq) the capital of SYRIA, an oasis town. (Pop. 1,042,000)

Damavand, Mount an extinct volcano, and the highest peak in the ELBURZ MOUNTAINS, IRAN. (5670 m/18,600 ft)

Damietta *see* **Dumyat**.

Damman (Ad Dammán) a major oil centre and capital of the Eastern Province of SAUDI ARABIA; it is situated on the Gulf coast, 400 km (250 miles) east and slightly north of RIYADH, and with a large volume of oil exports it is the country's second port after JEDDA. (Pop. 150,000)

Damodar Valley the industrial heartland of WEST BENGAL, INDIA, located in the lower reaches of a tributary of the HUGLI river, northwest of CALCUTTA.

Da Nang (Tourane) the chief port of central VIETNAM on the SOUTH CHINA SEA, 600 km (375 miles) northeast of HO CHI MINH CITY. A former US military base during the Vietnam War (1965–75) it is now the site of an international airport. (Pop. 365,200)

Danelaw (Danelagh) the northern, central and eastern parts of Anglo-Saxon ENGLAND in which Danish law and custom were observed.

Danube, River (Donau) the longest river in Western EUROPE, rising in the BLACK FOREST in GERMANY, and passing through AUSTRIA, SLOVAKIA, HUNGARY and SERBIA of former YUGOSLAVIA, forming much of the border between BULGARIA and ROMANIA before turning north and forming a delta on the BLACK SEA. (Length 2850 km/1770 miles)

Danzig *see* **Gdansk**.

Dar'a (Deraa) a major rail and road junction town in the centre of a noted cereal-growing area of southern SYRIA, 8 km (5 miles) north of the Jordanian border. (Pop. 282,000)

Dardanelles the narrow ribbon of water, some 80 km (50 miles) long, in TURKEY which connects the AEGEAN SEA to the Sea of MARMARA (and from thence the BLACK SEA). GALLIPOLI is on the peninsula to the north. The Dardanelles were known as the Hellespont to the ancient Greeks.

Dar el Beida *see* **Casablanca**.

Dar es Salaam the largest town and main port of TANZANIA. It was the national capital until 1974 when the seat of government was transferred to DODOMA. (Pop. 757,346)

Darfur a large region of savannah-covered plateaux and the volcanic Marra Mountains, rising to 3022 m (9915 ft), that extends the length of western SUDAN's border with CHAD. (317,809 sq km/122,706 sq miles; pop. 3,094,000)

Darhan the second largest city of MONGOLIA, and a major coal-mining and industrial centre, situated 188 km (117 miles) north of ULAN BATOR on the trans-Mongolian railway. (Pop. 52,000)

Darién the eastern province of PANAMA, a narrow neck of land on the border with COLOMBIA, and the only gap in the Pan-American Highway, which otherwise runs from ALASKA to CHILE.

Darjiling (Darjeeling) a town in WEST BENGAL, INDIA near the border with NEPAL, famous for its tea. (Pop. 282,200)

Darling, River a river flowing from southern QUEENSLAND through NEW SOUTH WALES in AUSTRALIA before converging with the MURRAY RIVER. (Length 3057 km/1900 miles)

Darlington an industrial town in south DURHAM county of northeast ENGLAND; it is regarded as one of the birthplaces of the Industrial Revolution, with the opening of the world's first passenger railway line in 1825, developed by George Stephenson between Darlington and STOCKTON-ON-TEES. (Pop. 85,519)

Darmstadt an industrial town in HESSE, central GERMANY, and former capital of the Grand Duchy of Hesse-Dermstadt (1567–1945). (Pop. 138,200)

Darnah *see* **Derna**.

Dartmoor an area of remote moorland in the county of DEVON, ENGLAND. (945 sq km/365 sq miles)

Darwin the capital of the NORTHERN TERRITORY, AUSTRALIA. (Pop. 50,000)

Dasht-e Kavir (Salt Desert) *see* **Iranian Plateau.**

Dasht-e Lut (Barren Desert) *see* **Iranian Plateau.**

Datong (Tatung) an industrial city in SHANXI province, CHINA. (Pop. 800,000)

Daugavpils a major trading centre of southeast LATVIA, on the West Dvina river, 220 km (138 miles) inland from RIGA. It was founded as a city in 1274 by the Teutonic Knights. (Pop. 119.000)

Dauphiné *see* **Rhône-Alpes**.

Davao a city in the southern part of the island of MINDANAO, PHILIPPINES, and now that country's second largest city. It is also the name of the surrounding region. (Pop. city 540,000)

Davis Strait the broad strait, some 290 km (180 miles) across at its narrowest, separating BAFFIN ISLAND in CANADA and GREENLAND.

Davos one of the largest mountain resorts of SWITZERLAND, 1500m (4920ft) up in the GRAUBÜNDEN, southeast of ZÜRICH. (Pop. 12,500)

Dawson a settlement in the YUKON, northwest CANADA, at the confluence of the Yukon and Klondike rivers; it was a boom town of the Klondike gold rush of 1896. (Pop. 1320)

Dawson Creek a town in northeast BRITISH COLUMBIA, in western CANADA, that is the southeastern terminus of the ALASKA HIGHWAY. (Pop. 11,373)

Dayr az Zawr the largest town in eastern SYRIA, on the River EUPHRATES. (Pop. 332,000)

Dayton

Dayton an industrial city in southwest Ohio, USA, 64 km (40 miles) north of Cincinatti. (Pop. city 181,000/metropolitan area 930,000)

Daytona Beach a resort in northeast Florida, USA, on its sun-soaked Atlantic coast. (Pop. city 56,000/metropolitan area 300,000)

Dead Sea a small sea on the border between Israel and Jordan into which the River Jordan flows and does not exit. It is one of the lowest places on earth, at 396 m (1299 ft) below normal sea level, and is the body of water with the world's highest salt content. (1049 sq km/395 sq miles)

Death Valley a low-lying area of desert and salt beds in eastern California, USA.

Deauville an elegant resort on the Normandy coast of France, which was developed in the mid-19th century when rail access made seaside excursions fashionable. (Pop. 4770)

Debrecen an agricultural and industrial centre in eastern Hungary, which has grown up around the original medieval town. (Pop. 207,000)

Deccan the broad, triangular plateau which forms much of the southern part of India.

Dehra Dun a town in northern India, in the foothills of the Himalayas. It is famous as the supposed home of the Hindu god Shiva, and also for the military academy established by the British in the 1930s. (Pop. 293,000)

Delaware a state on the east coast of the USA, and the second smallest in the USA after Rhode Island. The capital is Dover. (5328 sq km/2057 sq miles; pop. 622,000)

Delft a small city in central western Netherlands, famous since the 16th century for its distinctive blue and white pottery. (Pop. 86,300)

Delhi, including New Delhi the capital of India, in the north of the country, on the Yamuna River. (Pop. 5,729,300)

Delos the smallest of the islands in the Cyclades group, Greece, said to be the birthplace of the god Apollo.

Delphi the ruins of the Temple of Apollo on Mount Parnassos, 166 km (102 miles) northwest of ATHENS, GREECE. It was the seat of the most important oracle of Ancient Greece

Demerara, River a river in central GUYANA which flows through the capital, GEORGETOWN. It has given its name to the type of brown sugar which is grown in the region. (Length 320 km/200 miles)

Denbighshire *see* **Clwyd**; **Gwynedd**.

Den Haag *see* **Hague, The**.

Denmark is a small European state lying between the NORTH SEA and the entrance to the BALTIC. It consists of a western peninsula and an eastern archipelago of 406 islands, only 89 of which are populated. The country is very low-lying, and the proximity of the sea combined with the effect of the Gulf Stream results in warm sunny summers and cold cloudy winters. The scenery is very flat and monotonous, but the soils are good and a wide variety of crops can be grown. It is an agricultural country, and three-quarters of the land is cultivated, mostly by the rotation of grass, barley, oats and sugar beet. Animal husbandry is, however, the most important activity, its produce including the famous Danish bacon and butter. Despite Denmark's limited range of raw materials, it produces a wide range of manufactured goods and is famous for its imaginative design of furniture, silverware and porcelain.

Area : 43,077 sq km (16,632 sq miles)

Population : 5,140,000

Capital : Copenhagen (København)

Other major cities : Ålborg, Århus, Odense

Form of government : Constitutional Monarchy

Religion : Lutheranism

Currency : Danish krone

Denmark Strait the arm of the North ATLANTIC OCEAN which separates ICELAND from GREENLAND, some 290 km (80 miles) apart.

Denpasar the capital of the island of BALI, INDONESIA. (Pop. 82,140)

Denver the state capital of COLORADO, USA. (Pop. city 504,600/metropolitan area 1,582,500)

Dera Ismail Khan a trading centre at a strategic crossing point of the INDUS River, in the NORTH WEST FRONTIER PROVINCE of PAKISTAN. (Pop. 116,000)

Derby a city of Saxon and Danish origins in the county of DERBYSHIRE, ENGLAND. (Pop. 215,000)

Derbyshire a county in north central ENGLAND; the county town is MATLOCK. (2631 sq km/1016 sq miles; pop. 911,000)

Derna (Darnah) the second most important port of CYRENAICA, LIBYA, after BENGHAZI. (Pop. 37,716)

Derry *see* **Londonderry**.

Des Moines the state capital of IOWA, USA. (Pop. city 190,800/metropolitan area 377,100)

Dessau an industrial town in eastern GERMANY, 100 km (60 miles) southwest of BERLIN, which was devastated by Allied bombing in World War II (Pop. 103,800)

Detroit a major industrial city and GREAT LAKES port in the state of MICHIGAN, USA. (Pop. city 1,089,000/metropolitan area 4,315,800)

Deutsche Bucht *see* **German Bight.**

Deva a metal-working town and important rail and road communications centre in the Mures valley of west-central ROMANIA. (Pop. 71,000)

Deventer a textile town founded in the 8th century on the IJssel river in east-central Netherlands; it is famed for *Deventerkoek* (honey gingerbread). (Pop. 64,500)

Devon a county in southwest ENGLAND; the county town is EXETER. (6715 sq km/2593 sq miles; pop. 980,000)

Dezhnev, Cape (Mys Dezhneva) the easternmost point of EURASIA, at the tip of the CHUKCHI PENINSULA in northeast SIBERIA of the RUSSIAN FEDERATION, and at the narrowest part of the BERING STRAIT; formerly called East Cape.

Dhahran (Az Zahran) a commercial centre with an important international airport in eastern SAUDI ARABIA.

It is also a centre for petroleum extraction business; the site of the country's original oil find in 1938. (Pop. 25,000)

Dhaka *see* **Dacca.**

Dhanbad a city in northeast INDIA and a centre for the coal mining industry of the DAMODAR VALLEY. (Pop. 433,100)

Dhaulagiri, Mount a mountain peak of the Great HIMALAYAS in NEPAL. (8167 m/26,795 ft)

Dhodhekanisos *see* **Dodecanese**.

Dien Bien Phu a small town in northwest VIETNAM where the French army was decisively defeated by the Communist and Nationalist Vietminh forces in 1954, effectively forcing the French to leave Vietnam.

Dieppe a resort, fishing and ferry port, town on the ENGLISH CHANNEL coast of NORMANDY, FRANCE. (Pop. 42,300)

Dijon the historic capital of the Bourgogne region (BURGUNDY) in western central FRANCE, famous in particular for its mustard. (Pop. 221,900)

Dimashq *see* **Damascus**.

Dinajpur the chief town of Dinajpur district in the north of BANGLADESH, and at the foot of the HIMALAYAS. (Pop. town 96,300/district 3,200,000)

Dinaric Alps (Dinara Planina) a series of fold mountain ranges that parallel the coast of DALMATIA and form at their highest ridges, 1500-2000 m (4920-6560 ft), the southwestern boundary between CROATIA and BOSNIA-HERZEGOVINA

Diourbel (Djourbel) a market town at the centre of a groundnut-growing area of SENEGAL, 140 km (88 miles) east of DAKAR. (Pop. 50,600)

Dire Dawa a modern industrial city 350 km (220 miles) east of ADDIS ABABA, ETHIOPIA, and on the railway line to DJIBOUTI. (Pop. 85,000)

Disko (Qeqertarsuaq) a large island in the DAVIS STRAIT, off the west coast of GREENLAND; it has extensive coal deposits. (8580 sq km/3310 sq miles)

Disneyland a popular theme park in ANAHEIM, near LOS ANGELES, CALIFORNIA, USA, opened in 1955 by Walt Disney, the film animator of *Mickey Mouse* and other famous cartoon characters.

Disney World, Walt the second Disney theme park, opened in 1971 on a site 25 km (16 miles) southwest of ORLANDO, FLORIDA, USA.

Diyarbakir a city on the River TIGRIS in southeastern TURKEY, and the name of the province of which it is the capital. (Pop. city 305,300)

Djelalabad *see* **Jalalabad.**

Djelfa (El-Djelfa) an important communications centre at the southern end of the 250-km (155-mile) railway from Algiers, and at the start of the middle trans-Saharan route of ALGERIA to TAMANRASSET. (Pop. 55,000)

Djenne an old town, thought to have been founded in the 8th century, today 380 km (240 miles) northeast of BAMAKO, MALI; it has always been an important centre for Islamic teaching. (Pop. 7000)

Djerba *see* **Jerba**.

Djibouti is situated in northeast AFRICA and is bounded almost entirely by ETHIOPIA, except in the southeast where it shares a border with SOMALIA. Its coastline is on the Gulf of ADEN. The land, which is mainly basalt plains, has some mountains rising to over 1500 m (4922 ft). The climate is hot, among the world's hottest, and extremely dry. Only a tenth of the land can be farmed even for grazing, so it has great difficulty supporting its modest population. The native population are mostly nomadic, moving from oasis to oasis or across the border to Ethiopia in search of grazing land. Most foodstuffs for the urban population in Djibouti city are imported. Cattle, hides and skins are the main exports.

Area : 23,200 sq km (8958 sq miles)

Population : 484,000

Capital : Djibouti

Form of government : Republic

Religion : Sunni Islam

Currency : Djibouti franc

Dnepr, River *see* **Dnieper, River.**

Dnepropetrovsk an industrial and agricultural city on the River DNIEPER in the UKRAINE. It was formerly (1787–96 and 1802–1920) known as Ekaterinoslav. (Pop. 1,140,000)

Dnestr, River *see* **Dniester, River.**

Dnieper (Dnepr), River the third longest river in EUROPE after the VOLGA and the DANUBE, flowing south through the RUSSIAN FEDERATION and the UKRAINE to the BLACK SEA via KIEV. (Length 2285 km/1420 miles)

Dniester (Dnestr), River a river flowing through the UKRAINE and MOLDOVA to the BLACK SEA. (Length 1411 km/877 miles)

Dobreta-Turnu-Severin an industrial city of southwest ROMANIA on the DANUBE, where it borders northeast SERBIA. Nearby is the Iron Gate, a spectacular gorge through which the river passes in a series of surging rapids. (Pop. 83,000)

Dobruja (Dobrogea) a fertile region between the DANUBE and the BLACK SEA, centred on CONSTANTA, ROMANIA (23,258 sq km/8980 sq miles)

Docklands a large area of east LONDON, ENGLAND, centred on the former Port of London on the north bank of the River THAMES. Transformed by a huge redevelopment, begun in the 1980s, it has much post-modern and futuristic architecture, including Britain's tallest building at Canary Wharf, standing 240 m (787 ft) high.

Dodecanese (Dhodhekanisos) a group of twelve islands belonging to GREECE in the eastern AEGEAN SEA near the coast of TURKEY. They are scattered between Samos in the north and Karpathos in the south and include Patmos, Kalimnos, KOS and RHODES, the largest in the group. They are also called the Southern Sporades. (Pop. 145,000)

Dodoma the capital (since 1974) of TANZANIA, in the centre of the country. (Pop. 45,700)

Dogger Bank a large submerged sandbank in the centre of the NORTH SEA, about 180 km (110 miles) off the northeast coast of ENGLAND; it is a famous fishing area, especially for cod, which is what *dogger* means in Dutch.

Doha (Ad Dawhah) the capital of QATAR. (Pop. 180,000)

Dolomites a range of mountains in northeastern ITALY, near the border with AUSTRIA. The highest point is Mount Marmolada (3342 m/10,964 ft)

Dominica, discovered by Columbus, is the most northerly of the WINDWARD ISLANDS in the WEST INDIES. It is situated between the islands of MARTINIQUE and GUADELOUPE. The island is very rugged, and, with the exception of 225 sq km (87 sq miles) of flat land, it consists of three inactive volcanoes, the highest of which is 1447 m (4747 ft). The climate is tropical and even on the leeward coast it rains two days out of three. The wettest season is from June to October when hurricanes often occur. The steep slopes are difficult to farm, but agriculture provides almost all Dominica's exports. Bananas are the main agricultural export, but copra, citrus fruits, cocoa, bay leaves and vanilla are also revenue earners for the country. Industry is mostly based on the processing of the agricultural products.

Area : 751 sq km (290 sq miles)

Population : 81,200

Capital : Roseau

Form of government : Republic

Religion : RC

Currency : Franc

Dominican Republic forms the eastern portion of the island of HISPANIOLA in the WEST INDIES. It covers two-thirds of the island, the smaller portion consisting of HAITI. The west of the country is made up of four almost parallel mountain ranges, and between the two most northerly is the fertile Cibao valley. The southeast is made up of fertile plains. Although well endowed with fertile land, only about 30% is cultivated. Sugar is the main crop and mainstay of the country's economy. It is grown mainly on plantations in the southeast plains.

Other crops grown are coffee, cocoa and tobacco. Some mining of gold, silver, platinum, nickel and aluminium is carried out, but the main industries are food processing and making consumer goods. The island has fine beaches and tourism is developing fast.

Area : 48,734 sq km (18,816 sq miles)
Population : 7,200,000
Capital : Santo Domingo
Other major city : Santiago de los Caballeros
Form of government : Republic
Currency : Dominican peso

Don, River a river flowing southwards into the Sea of Azov from its source to the south of Moscow. (Length 1870 km/1165 miles)

Donau *see* **Danube, River.**

Donbass *see* **Donets Basin.**

Donegal the northern-most county of the Republic of Ireland, on the west coast. The county town is also called Donegal. (Pop. county 125,100)

Donets Basin (Donbass) a coal mining region and major industrial area in the eastern Ukraine.

Donetsk the main industrial centre of the Donets Basin. (Pop. 1,064,000)

Dongbei (Manchuria) the northeastern region of China, covering part of the Nei Mongol Autonomous Region and the three provinces, Heilongjiang, Jilin and Liaoning. (1,300,000 sq km/502,000 sq miles; pop. 87,962,000)

Dorchester a market town in southern England, and administrative centre of Dorset county; associated with the author Thomas Hardy, especially as the "Casterbridge" of his novels. (Pop. 15,000)

Dordogne, River a river of southwestern France which rises in the Massif Central and flows west to the Gironde estuary. (Length 475 km/295 miles)

Dordrecht a river port and industrial city of medieval origin 19 km (12 miles) southeast of Rotterdam in the Netherlands. (Pop. 199,200)

Dorset

Dorset a county of southwest ENGLAND; the county town is Dorchester. (2654 sq km/1025 sq miles; pop. 618,000)

Dortmund a major city in the industrial RUHR region of western GERMANY. (Pop. 620,000)

Douai an industrial city in northern FRANCE, near LILLE, which was the political and religious centre for exiled English Roman Catholics in the 16th and 17th centuries; the *Douay Bible* was published here in 1610. (Pop. 44,738)

Douala the main port of CAMEROON, on the Gulf of GUINEA. (Pop. 800,000)

Dougga (Thugga) one of the best-preserved Roman cities in North AFRICA, about 110 km (70 miles) southwest of TUNIS; it lies on a much older site founded by native Berbers and later occupied by Phoenician colonists.

Douro (Duero), River a river flowing west from its source in northern central SPAIN and across northern PORTUGAL to the ATLANTIC OCEAN near OPORTO. (Length 895 km/555 miles)

Dover (1) a port in the county of KENT, ENGLAND, overlooking the ENGLISH CHANNEL at its narrowest point, opposite CALAIS, FRANCE. (Pop. 33,000). **(2)** The state capital of DELAWARE, USA. (Pop. 22,500)

Dover, Strait of the stretch of water separating ENGLAND and FRANCE, where the ENGLISH CHANNEL meets the NORTH SEA. The ports of DOVER and CALAIS are situated on either side of its narrowest point, 34 km (21 miles) across.

Down a county of NORTHERN IRELAND, on the east coast; the county town is Downpatrick. (2448 sq km/945 sq miles; pop. 362,100)

Downs, The two almost parallel ranges of low chalk hills—less than 300 m (1000 ft) high—in southeast ENGLAND, with The WEALD between. Both have spectacular cliffs at their southeastern ends at the ENGLISH CHANNEL: the North Downs with the famous White Cliffs of DOVER, and the South Downs finishing with the Seven Sisters at Beachy Head.

Drake Passage the broad strait, some 640 km (400 miles) wide, which separates Cape HORN on the southern tip of South AMERICA and ANTARCTICA.

Drakensberg Mountains a range of mountains which stretch 1125 km (700 miles) across LESOTHO and neighboring regions of SOUTH AFRICA. The highest point is Thabana Ntlenyana (3482 m/11,424 ft).

Drammen a port at the head of the Dramsfjorden, 40 km (25 miles) southwest of OSLO, in southern NORWAY. (Pop. 49,512)

Drava (Drau), River a river flowing from eastern AUSTRIA to CROATIA and SERBIA, where it forms much of the border with HUNGARY before joining the DANUBE. (Length 718 km/447 miles)

Dresden a historic city on the River ELBE in the south of eastern GERMANY. Formerly the capital of SAXONY, it was noted particularly for its fine porcelain. (Pop. 522,500)

Drogheda (Droichead Átha) a port on the BOYNE estuary about 40 km (25 miles) north of DUBLIN. It was the meeting place of IRELAND'S medieval parliaments. (Pop. 22,200)

Drvar a small timber-processing town in west BOSNIA-HERZEGOVINA; its full name is Titov Drvar, commemorating the former YUGOSLAVIA'S Communist leader, Marshal Tito (1892–1980). (Pop. 6417)

Dry Valleys (McMurdo Oasis) a name commonly applied to an ice-free area of ANTARCTICA, comprising extremely arid valleys near MCMURDO SOUND, where no rain has fallen for at least two million years. (3000 sq km/ 1160 sq miles).

Duarte, Pico a mountain peak in central DOMINICAN REPUBLIC which is the highest point in the WEST INDIES. (3175 m/10,417 ft)

Dubai (Dubayy) the second largest of the UNITED ARAB EMIRATES, at the eastern end of The GULF. Most of the population lives in the capital, also called Dubai. (3900 sq km/1506 sq miles; pop. emirate 296,000/city 265,700)

Dublin

Dublin (Baile Atha Cliath) the capital of the Republic of IRELAND, on the River LIFFEY, and also the name of the surrounding county. Its main port area is at Dun Laoghaire. (Pop. county 1,002,000/city 525,400)

Dubrovnik (Ragusa) a pretty medieval port on the ADRIATIC coast of CROATIA, for long a popular tourist destination. (Pop. 31,200)

Duero, River *see* **Douro, River**.

Duisburg a major inland port situated at the confluence of the Rivers RHINE and RUHR in GERMANY. (Pop. 541,800)

Dukhan an oil town 80 km (50 miles) west of DOHA, QATAR, on an oilfield that produces about half the country's output.

Duluth a port and industrial centre on Lake SUPERIOR, in the state of MICHIGAN, USA. (Pop. city 85,600/ metropolitan area 253,800)

Dumfries and Galloway a region of southwest SCOTLAND created out of the old counties of Dumfriesshire, Kirkudbrightshire and Wigtownshire. The regional capital is Dumfries. (6370 sq km/2459 sq miles; pop. 145,200)

Dumyat (Damietta) a textile town and port near the mouth of the Dumyat river, the main eastern branch of the NILE delta, in northern EGYPT. (Pop. 110,000)

Dun Laoghaire *see* **Dublin**.

Dunbartonshire *see* **Strathclyde**.

Dundalk (Dún Dealgan) a market town and port 77 km (48 miles) north of DUBLIN, Republic of IRELAND, and just south of the border with NORTHERN IRELAND. (Pop. 25,600)

Dundee a port on the east coast of SCOTLAND, on the north side of the Firth of Tay, and the administrative centre of TAYSIDE region. (Pop. 180,000)

Dunedin a port and industrial town on the SOUTH ISLAND, NEW ZEALAND, 300 km (190 miles) southwest of CHRISTCHURCH. It was founded by Scottish Presbyterians in 1848 and prospered from the discovery of gold nearby in 1861. (Pop. 110,000)

Dunfermline an industrial town in southwest FIFE, central SCOTLAND; former residence of Scottish kings, and burial place of many, including Robert the Bruce. Birthplace of Andrew Carnegie (1835). (Pop. 52,057)

Dunkirk (Dunkerque) a port and industrial town in northeastern FRANCE, close to the border with BELGIUM. It was virtually destroyed in 1940 when British, French and Belgian forces were trapped by the advancing German army, but were successfully evacuated to Britain in a fleet of small boats. (Pop. 196,600)

Durango a mineral-rich state in northern MEXICO, with a capital called (Victoria de) Durango. (Pop. state 1,200,000/ city 209,000)

Durban a port on the east coast of SOUTH AFRICA, and the largest city of the province of NATAL. (Pop. 960,800)

Durham a city of northeast ENGLAND, and the name of the county of which it is the county town. (County 2436 sq km/940 sq miles; pop. county 607,000/city 26,000)

Durrës the chief port of ALBANIA, founded by the Greeks in the 7th century BC, on a sheltered ADRIATIC bay. It is a very historic place, having been occupied by successive invaders; its old medieval town walls and towers remain intact. (Pop. 75,900)

Dushanbe an industrial city and the capital of TAJIKISTAN. (Pop. 539,000)

Düsseldorf a major commercial and industrial centre in the RUHR region of western GERMANY, situated on the River RHINE 34 km (21 miles) north of COLOGNE. (Pop. 579,800)

Dvina, River the name of two quite separate rivers. The West (Zapadnaya) Dvina flows from its source to the west of MOSCOW into the BALTIC SEA at RIGA in LATVIA. The North (Severnaya) Dvina flows through the northwest of the RUSSIAN FEDERATION to the WHITE SEA at ARCHANGEL. (Length West Dvina 1020 km/635 miles; North Dvina 1320 km/820 miles)

Dwarka one of the seven holy cities of the Hindus, situated on the tip of the peninsula to the south of the

Gulf of KUTCH, in northwest INDIA. It is said to be the capital of the god Krishna. (Pop. 21,400)

Dyfed a county in southwest WALES, created in 1974 out of the old counties of Cardiganshire, Carmarthenshire and Pembrokeshire. Carmarthen is the county town. (5765 sq km/2226 sq miles; pop. 377,000)

Dzerzhinsk a Russian chemical-industry town developed in the 1940s as an overflow for NIZHNIY NOVGOROD (GOR'KIY), which is only 30 km (18 miles) to the east. (Pop. 272,000)

Dzhambul an industrial town in southern KAZAKHSTAN, 250 km (155 miles) northeast of TASHKENT. (Pop. 298,000)

Dzierzoniow a textile town in southwest POLAND, 48 km (30 miles) from WROCLAW. It was an established linen-making town by 1500 and became Lower SILESIA'S main textile centre from 1700. (Pop. 37,600)

Dzungaria *see* **Xinjiang Uygur Autonomous Region.**

E

East Anglia an old Anglo-Saxon kingdom occupying the bulge of the east coast of ENGLAND between the THAMES estuary and The WASH, and now covered by the counties of NORFOLK, SUFFOLK, and parts of CAMBRIDGESHIRE and ESSEX.

Eastbourne a resort in southeast ENGLAND, in EAST SUSSEX, on the ENGLISH CHANNEL coast. (Pop. 77,608)

East Cape (1) the easternmost point of NEW GUINEA. **(2)** the easternmost point of NORTH ISLAND, NEW ZEALAND. **(3)** the former name for Cape DEZHNEV.

East China Sea a part of the North PACIFIC OCEAN between the east-central coast of CHINA and the RYUKYU ISLANDS.

East End, The a general term for the densely populated part of east LONDON, ENGLAND, containing former industrial and dockland areas.

Easter Island (Isla de Pascua) a remote and tiny island in the South PACIFIC OCEAN annexed by CHILE in 1888. About 1000 years ago it was settled by Polynesians who set up over 600 huge stone statues of heads on the island. (120 sq km/46 sq miles; pop. 1300)

Eastern Desert the smaller of EGYPT's two main deserts, is a bare broken plateau that slopes upwards on the east side of the NILE valley to a 2000 m (6500 ft) high mountainous rim overlooking the RED SEA.

Eastern Ghats a mountain range in southern INDIA, parallel to the coast along the Bay of BENGAL, and rising to about 600 m (2000 ft) as they provide the eastern rim of the DECCAN Plateau.

Eastern Townships an area of south-central Canada, in

southern QUEBEC, consisting of eleven townships south of the ST LAWRENCE river.

East Flanders *see* **Flanders**.

East Indies a regional term for the whole Malay-Indonesian archipelago, including or excluding the PHILIPPINES.

East Kilbride the first post-war designated "new town" in SCOTLAND, developed in 1947 11 km (7 miles) south of GLASGOW, STRATHCLYDE. It is now Scotland's sixth largest town. (Pop. 70,259)

East London a port on the INDIAN OCEAN coast of southeast CAPE PROVINCE, SOUTH AFRICA. (Pop. 160,582)

East Lothian *see* **Lothian**.

East Pakistan (Eastern Province of Pakistan) *see* **Bangladesh**.

East Prussia a former province of prewar Germany on the BALTIC SEA, centred on its capital Konigsberg (now KALININGRAD); it was separated from the rest of Germany in 1919 by the "Polish Corridor" and DANZIG city state.

East Siberian Sea a part of the ARCTIC OCEAN lying between the coast of northeastern SIBERIA, the NEW SIBERIAN ISLANDS and WRANGEL ISLAND; its northern limit is the edge of the Eurasian continental shelf. It is ice-free in August and September.

East Sussex a county in southeast ENGLAND; the county town is LEWES, and the largest urban area is the BRIGHTON-Hove coastal strip. (1795 sq km/693 sq miles; pop. 655,000)

Ebbw Vale a coal-mining and steel town in one of the many steep-sided valleys of south WALES, in the west of GWENT. (Pop. 22,422)

Ebolowa a timber and cocoa export-collection centre in southern CAMEROON, 110 km (70 miles) south of YAOUNDÉ. (Pop. 30,000)

Ebro, River a river flowing across northeastern SPAIN, from its source near the north coast to the MEDITERRANEAN SEA south of TARRAGONA. (Length 909 km/565 miles)

EC *see* **European Community**.

Echmiadzin an ancient town founded in the 6th century BC and a Christian religious centre in ARMENIA that attracts many pilgrims. (Pop. 37,000)

Ecuador is an Andean country situated in the northwest of the South American continent. It is bounded to the north by COLOMBIA and to the east and south by PERU. The country contains over thirty active volcanos. Running down the middle of Ecuador are two ranges of the ANDES which are divided by a central plateau. The coastal area consists of plains, and the eastern area is made up of tropical jungles. The climate varies from equatorial through warm temperate to mountain conditions, according to altitude. It is in the coastal plains that plantations of bananas, cocoa, coffee and sugar cane are found. In contrast to this, the highland areas are adapted to grazing, dairying and cereal growing. The fishing industry is important on the PACIFIC Coast, and processed fish is one of the main exports. Oil is produced in the eastern region, and crude oil is Ecuador's most important export.

Area : 283,561 sq km (109,483 sq miles)
Population : 10,490,000
Capital : Quito
Other major cities : Guayaquil, Cuenca
Form of government : Republic
Religion : RC
Currency : Sucre

Edam a small, mainly 16th and 17th-century town 40 km (25 miles) northeast of AMSTERDAM in the NETHERLANDS; it is famous for its round, red-skinned mild cheeses. (Pop. 21,000)

Edinburgh the capital of SCOTLAND, a university city and commercial centre, on the Firth of Forth (the estuary of the River Forth). (Pop. 439,000)

Edmonton the capital of ALBERTA, CANADA. (Pop. 657,000)

Edo *see* **Tokyo**.

Edrine (Adrianpole) an industrial border town in the European part of TURKEY. Until the 1930s, its old name commemorated the Roman Emperor Hadrian (AD76–138). (Pop. 86,700)

Edward (Rutanzige), Lake a lake in the GREAT RIFT VALLEY, on the border between UGANDA and ZAÏRE. (2135 sq km/820 sq miles)

Eger a Baroque spa town in northeast HUNGARY, 40 km (25 miles) southwest of MISKOLC; it is the centre of the wine-making district that produces *Egri Bikaver* (Bull's Blood) red wine. (Pop. 63,600)

Egmont, Mount (Taranaki) a beautiful, nearly symmetrical, dormant volcano in the TARANKI Peninsula in the southwest of NORTH ISLAND, NEW ZEALAND; the cone rises in splendid isolation to 2518 m (8261 ft).

Egypt is situated in northeast AFRICA, acting as the doorway between Africa and ASIA. Its outstanding physical feature is the river NILE, the valley and delta of which cover about 35,580 sq km (13,737 sq miles). The climate is mainly dry, but there are winter rains along the MEDITERRANEAN coast. The temperatures are comfortable in winter but summer temperatures are extremely high, particularly in the south. The rich soils deposited by floodwaters along the banks of the Nile can support a large population, and the delta is one of the world's most fertile agricultural regions. Some 96% of the population live in the delta and Nile valley, where the main crops are rice, cotton, sugar cane, maize, tomatoes and wheat. The main industries are food processing and textiles. The economy has been boosted by the discovery of oil, and although not in large quantities it is enough to supply Egypt's needs and to leave surplus for export. Suez Canal shipping and tourism connected with the ancient sites are also important revenue earners.

Area : 1,001,449 sq km (386,659 sq miles)

Population : 50,740,000

Capital : Cairo (El Qahira)

Other major cities : Alexandria, El Gîza

Form of government : Republic

Religions : Sunni Islam, Christianity

Currency : Egyptian pound

Eifel an upland area of western GERMANY between the MOSELLE River and the border with BELGIUM.

Eiger, The a mountain in southern central SWITZERLAND, renowned among climbers for its daunting north face. (3970 m/13,025 ft)

Eigg one of the Small Isles of the Inner HEBRIDES, lying off the west coast of Scotland; it rises to 393 m (1291 ft) in the cliff-shaped Sgurr of Eigg. (23 sq km/9 sq miles; pop. 78)

Eilat *see* **Elat**.

Eindhoven an industrial city in the southern central part of the NETHERLANDS. (Pop. 194,600)

Eire the Irish Gaelic name for IRELAND, and a former name for the Republic of Ireland (1937–49), and still often informally used to mean the same.

Eisenach a resort town in the west of the THÜRINGEN state in east-central GERMANY, associated with the religious reformer, Martin Luther (1483–1546) and the composer Johann Sebastian Bach (1685–1750). (Pop. 51,000)

Eisleben an industrial town in southern SACHSEN-ANHALT state of east-central GERMANY, and birthplace of Martin Luther (1483–1546).

Ekaterinburg *see* **Yekaterinburg**.

Ekaterinoslav *see* **Dnepropetrovsk**.

Ekofisk a large oilfield in the centre of the NORTH SEA, at the southern end of the Norwegian sector. The North Sea oil industry began here, with the first find in 1970. Later, an oil pipeline was laid to TEESSIDE, ENGLAND.

El Alamein a village on the MEDITERRANEAN coast of EGYPT, to the southwest of ALEXANDRIA, which gave its name to the battle fought between Allied troops under General Montgomery and German troops under General Rommel in 1942.

Elat (Eilat) a port and tourist resort in the very south of ISRAEL at the tip of the Gulf of AQABA, an arm of the RED SEA. (Pop. 18,800)

Elba an island lying about 10 km (6 miles) off the coast of TUSCANY, ITALY. (223 sq km/86 sq miles; pop. 28,400)

Elbe, River a largely navigable river flowing northward from the CZECH REPUBLIC through GERMANY to HAMBURG, and then into the NORTH SEA. (Length 1160 km/720 miles)

El Boulaida *see* **Blida**.

Elbrus, Mount the highest mountain in EUROPE, in the western CAUCASUS, RUSSIAN FEDERATION. (5642 m/18,510 ft)

Elburz Mountains a range of mountains in northern IRAN, between TEHRAN and the CASPIAN SEA. The highest peak is the extinct volcano, DAMAVAND (5670 m/18,600 ft).

El Djazair *see* **Algiers**.

El Djelfa *see* **Djelfa**.

Eldoret one of KENYA'S largest towns, lying on the main road and rail route to UGANDA some 260 km (160 miles) northwest of NAIROBI. (Pop. 70,000)

Eleuthera *see* **Bahamas**.

El Faiyum (Fayum) a large and fertile oasis to the west of the River NILE in EGYPT. Nearby is Crocodipolis, the ancient centre for worship of the crocodile god, Sebek. El Faiyum was a seat of the Middle Kingdom pharaohs (*c.* 1990–1785 BC). (Pop. 167,080)

El Gezira a major irrigation scheme in SUDAN between the Blue NILE and the White Nile.

El Gîza a sprawling suburb of CAIRO, EGYPT, at the edge of which stand the three most famous pyramids of the Ancient Egyptians. (Pop. 1,230,500)

Elgon, Mount (Wagagai) an extinct volcano on the border betweeen KENYA and UGANDA, about 100 km (62 miles) northwest of ELDORET; it rises to 4321 m (14,176 ft)

Elisabethville *see* **Lubumbashi**.

El Iskandarîya *see* **Alexandria**.

El Khartum *see* **Khartoum**.

Ellesmere Island a mountainous snow and ice-covered island in CANADA'S ARCTIC archipelago, separated from GREENLAND by the narrow Nares Strait. (197,000 sq km/ 75,780 sq miles)

Ellesmere Port a port in north CHESHIRE, northwest ENGLAND, situated on the MANCHESTER Ship Canal. (Pop. 63,134)

Ellis Island a small islet in NEW YORK harbour, near the Statue of Liberty, that housed the buildings of the US Immigration Office through which passed many millions of immigrants during its 62 years of operation. It is now a memorial centre to the different peoples and cultures who made AMERICA.

El Mansura a city in the delta of the River NILE in northern EGYPT. (Pop. 323,000)

El Paso a city in western TEXAS, USA, close to the border with MEXICO. (Pop. city 463,000/metropolitan area 526,500)

El Qahira *see* **Cairo**.

El Salvador is the smallest and most densely populated state in Central AMERICA. It is bounded north and east by HONDURAS and has a PACIFIC coast to the south. Two volcanic ranges run from east to west across the country. The Lempa river cuts the southern ranges in the centre of the country and opens as a large sandy delta to the Pacific Ocean. Although fairly near the Equator, the climate tends to be warm rather than hot, and the highlands have a cooler temperate climate. The country is predominantly agricultural, and 32% of the land is used for crops such as coffee, cotton, maize, beans, rice and sorghum, and a slightly smaller area is used for grazing cattle, pigs, sheep and goats. A few industries, such as food processing, textiles and chemicals, are found in the major towns.

Area : 21,041 sq km (8123 sq miles)
Population : 5,220,000
Capital : San Salvador
Other major cities : Santa Ana, San Miguel
Form of government : Republic
Religion : RC
Currency : Colón

Elsinore (Helsingør) a town of medieval origins on the island of ZEALAND, DENMARK, to the north of COPENHAGEN. Kronborg Castle, which dominates the town, is the setting for Shakespeare's play *Hamlet*. (Pop. 65,200)

Elvas a fortified hilltop town in southern Portugal, due east from LISBON and on the border with SPAIN, in an area noted for its plums. (Pop. 12,700)

Ely an English cathedral city in CAMBRIDGESHIRE, that used to stand on an island—the Isle of Ely—in the centre of The FENS; when the Fens where drained the island disappeared. (Pop. 10,000)

Emilia-Romagna a region on the east coast of northern central ITALY; the capital is BOLOGNA. (22,123 sq km/8542 sq miles; pop. 3,943,000)

Emmenthal the valley of the River Emme, in SWITZERLAND, famous for its distinctive cheese.

Empty Quarter *see* **Rub al-Khali.**

Enewetak *see* **Marshall Islands.**

Engadine the Swiss part of the Valley of the River Inn, which flows into AUSTRIA. The Upper Engadine is noted for its fashionable Alpine resorts, especially ST MORITZ.

Engel's an industrial town on the River VOLGA, in the RUSSIAN FEDERATION. (Pop. 175,000)

England the country occupying the greater part of the island of GREAT BRITAIN, and the largest of the countries that make up the UNITED KINGDOM. SCOTLAND lies to the north and WALES to the west. The capital is LONDON. (130,357 sq km/50,331 sq miles; pop. 46,795,000)

English Channel the arm of the eastern ATLANTIC OCEAN which separates the south coast of ENGLAND from FRANCE.

Enna a historic city at the centre of SICILY, ITALY; it has one of the island's most outstanding medieval castles. (pop. 28,900)

Enniskillen a town in southwestern NORTHERN IRELAND, and county administrative centre of FERMANAGH, situated on an island in the River Erne; scene of the defeat of King James II's forces in 1689. (Pop. 10,429)

Enschede an industrial town in the eastern part of the NETHERLANDS, close to the border with GERMANY. (Pop. 144,900)

Entebbe a town with an international airport on Lake VICTORIA, UGANDA. It was the capital until 1962. (Pop. 30,000)

Enugu a coal-mining centre in southern central NIGERIA, the capital of Biafra (IBOLAND) during the Civil War (1967–70). (Pop. 222,600)

Eolian (Lipari) Islands a group of small volcanic islands which lie between the north coast of SICILY and mainland ITALY. The main islands are STROMBOLI, LIPARI, Salina, Panarea and Vulcano. (Pop. 12,500)

Ephesus the ruins of an Ancient Greek city on the east coast of TURKEY, overlooking the AEGEAN SEA. Its Temple of Diana (or Artemis) was one of the Seven Wonders of the Ancient World.

Epirus (Ipiros) the region of northwest GREECE centred on YANNINA (IOANNINA), its chief town, and bordering ALBANIA and the IONIAN SEA, but cut off from the rest of the country by the PINDHOS MOUNTAINS. It is a hilly region, and the wettest in Greece. In 278BC, its king, Pyrrhus (319–272BC), won a battle against the Romans so costly to his troops that it gave rise to the expression "Pyrrhic victory". (9203 sq km/3553 sq miles; pop. 324,500)

Eptanisos *see* **Ionian Islands**.

Equateurville *see* **Mbandaka**.

Equatorial Guinea lies about 200 km (124 miles) north of the Equator on the hot humid coast of West AFRICA. The country consists of a square-shaped mainland area (Mbini), with its few small offshore islets, and the islands of Bioko and Pagalu. The climate is tropical and the wet season in Bioko and Pegalu lasts from December to February. Bioko is a very fertile volcanic island, and it is here that the capital, Malabo, is sited beside a volcanic crater flooded by the sea. It is also the centre of the country's cocoa production. The country now relies heavily on foreign aid. There is, however, much potential for a tourist industry.

Area : 28,051 sq km (10,830 sq miles)

Population : 417,000

Capital : Malabo

Other major city : Bata

Form of government : Republic

Religion : RC

Currency : Franc CFA

Ercolano *see* **Herculaneum.**

Erebus, Mount an active volcano on Ross Island, ANTARCTICA, rising to 3794 m (12,447 ft).

Erfurt a historic town and tourist centre in central GERMANY. (Pop. 215,000)

Erie, Lake one of the five GREAT LAKES (the second smallest after Lake ONTARIO), on the border between CANADA and the USA. (25,670 sq km/9910 sq miles)

Eriskay a small island in the WESTERN ISLES off the west coast of SCOTLAND, lying between BARRA and SOUTH UIST. It was here that Prince Charles Edward first landed on Scottish soil in 1744. (8 sq km/3 sq miles; pop. 201)

Eritrea an autonomous province of northern ETHIOPIA, bordering the RED SEA. The capital is ASMARA. (117,400 sq km/45,316 sq miles; pop. 3,000,000)

Erzebirge *see* **Ore Mountains**.

Erzurum a market town in western TURKEY, and the name of the surrounding province. (Pop. town 252,700)

Esbjerg a port on the west coast of JUTLAND, DENMARK. It is the world's largest exporter of butter and bacon, and Denmark's biggest fishing port. (Pop. 80,300)

Escorial, El (San Lorenzo del Escorial) a small town 40 km (25 miles) northwest of MADRID, famous for its splendid royal palace built (1563–84) for Philip II. (Pop. 9500)

Esfahan (Isfahan) a city in central IRAN noted for its magnificent blue-tiled mosques and other Islamic buildings. (Pop. 926,700)

Eskisehir a spa town in western TURKEY and the name of the surrounding province. (Pop. town 367,300)

Esmeraldas a northwestern province and regional capital of ECUADOR (Pop. province 248,000/city 141,000)

Espiritu Santo *see* **Vanuatu**.

Esseg *see* **Osijek**.

Essen an industrial city in western GERMANY, and the largest in the RUHR region. (Pop. 635,200)

Essex a county in southeast ENGLAND; the county town is Chelmsford. (3674 sq km/1419 sq miles; pop. 1,492,000)

Estonia lies to the northwest of the RUSSIAN FEDERATION and is bounded to the north by the Gulf of FINLAND, to the west by the BALTIC SEA and to the south by LATVIA. It is the smallest of the three previous Soviet Baltic Republics. Agriculture and dairy farming are the chief occupations, and there are nearly three hundred agricultural collectives and state farms. The main products are grain, potatoes, vegetables, meat, milk and eggs. Livestock includes cattle, sheep, goats and pigs. Almost 22% of Estonia is forested, and this provides material for sawmills, furniture, match and pulp industries. The country has rich, high-quality shale deposits, and phosphorous has been found near TALLINN. Peat deposits are substantial and supply some of the electric power stations.

Area : 45,100 sq km (17,413 sq miles)

Population : 1,573,000

Capital : Tallinn

Other major cities : Tartu, Narva

Form of government : Republic

Religion : Eastern Orthodox, Lutheranism

Currency : Rouble

Estremadura (Extremadura) a region of western SPAIN, arid and sparsely populated except in the valleys of the TAGUS and Guadiana rivers. (41,593 sq km/16,059 sq miles)

Ethiopia, one of AFRICA's largest countries, stretches from the shores of the RED SEA to the north of KENYA. Most of the country consists of highlands, which drop sharply towards SUDAN in the west and the Red Sea in the northeast. Because of the wide range of latitudes, Ethiopia has many climatic variations between the high temperate plateau and the hot humid lowlands. The country is very vulnerable to drought, but in some areas thunderstorms can erode soil from the slopes, reducing the area available for crop planting. Coffee is the main source of rural income, and teff is the main food grain. Droughts have brought much famine. Employment outside agriculture is confined to a small manufacturing sector in ADDIS ABABA and ASMARA. The country is wracked by environmental, economic and political problems, and many of the population have trekked to Sudan as refugees.

Area : 1,221,900 sq km (471,776 sq miles)

Population : 50,000,000

Capital : Addis Ababa (Adis Abeba)

Other major cities : Asmara, Dire Dawa

Form of government : People's Republic

Religion : Ethiopian Orthodox, Sunni Islam

Currency : Ethiopian birr

Ethiopian Highlands a highland region that covers more than half of EHTIOPIA and rises in the north to 4620 m (15,158 ft) at Ras Dashen. The Highlands are divided by the northern end of the GREAT RIFT VALLEY, in which a series of lakes has formed.

Etna, Mount the largest volcano in EUROPE, situated near the east coast of SICILY, ITALY, and still highly active. (3323 m/10,902 ft)

Etosha Pan a large shallow intermittent lake in the northern interior of NAMIBIA; it is dry for most of the year. Its many waterholes attract vast numbers of wild animals, now protected, since the creation of the Etosha National Park in 1958.

Euboea (Evvoia) a large island in the AEGEAN SEA, lying close to the east coast of mainland GREECE and joined to it by a bridge. (3655 sq km/1411 sq miles; pop. 188,400)

Euphrates, River (Al Furat) one of the great rivers of

the MIDDLE EAST, flowing from its source in eastern TURKEY, across SYRIA and central IRAQ to The GULF. (Length 2815 km/1750 miles)

Eurasia a general term applied to the continents of EUROPE and ASIA as a whole landmass.

Euro Disney a theme park opened in 1992 some 30 km (20 miles) to the east of PARIS, FRANCE, on a 1943-hectare (4801-acre) site.

Europe a continent that is divided from ASIA by a border that runs down the URAL Mountains to the CASPIAN SEA and then west to the BLACK SEA. For convenience it is commonly divided into two areas: Eastern Europe (the countries that have or had Communist governments since the Second World War) and Western Europe. (10,498,000 sq km/4,052,000 sq miles; pop. 682,000,000)

European Community (EC; The Common Market) the name for the association of European countries pursuing political and economic union; originally composed of the Treaty of Rome (1958) of BELGIUM, FRANCE, GERMANY, ITALY, LUXEMBOURG and the NETHERLANDS; joined in 1973 by the UNITED KINGDOM, REPUBLIC OF IRELAND and DENMARK, in 1981 by GREECE, and in 1986 by SPAIN and PORTUGAL. Several other countries have applied to join.

Europoort (Europort) a port and industrial complex, developed in the 1960's at the NORTH SEA end of the Nieuw Waterweg (New Waterway), 28 km (17 miles) west of the centre of ROTTERDAM, NETHERLANDS; it chiefly handles oil, and can take the world's largest tankers.

Everest, Mount the highest mountain in the world, situated on the border between NEPAL and CHINA in the eastern HIMALAYAS. (8848 m/29,028 ft)

Everglades a vast area of subtropical swampland on the western side of southern FLORIDA, USA.

Evvoia *see* **Euboea**.

Extremadura *see* **Estremadura**.

Eyre, Lake a large salt lake in SOUTH AUSTRALIA. (8900 sq km/3400 sq miles)

F

Fada an oasis settlement on the Ennedi plateau, about 900 km (560 miles) northeast of CHAD's capital, NDJAMENA; it was an anti-government stronghold in the civil war of the 1980s.

Faeroe (Faroe) Islands (Føroyar) a group of 18 islands in the North ATLANTIC OCEAN belonging to DENMARK, which lie approximately halfway between ICELAND and SCOTLAND. (1399 sq km/540 sq miles; pop. 44,500)

Fagatogo *see* **Pago Pago**.

Fairbanks a trade, tourist and university centre, and the largest inland town in ALASKA, USA; it lies in the centre of the state, 190 km (120 miles) south of the ARCTIC CIRCLE, on the Trans-Alaska Pipeline (oil). (Pop. 26,600)

Fair Isle a small island situated between the ORKNEY and SHETLAND ISLANDS to the north of SCOTLAND, famous for the distinctive, patterned sweaters made there. (Pop. 75)

Faisalabad (Lyallpur) an industrial city and agricultural centre in northeast PAKISTAN. (Pop. 1,092,000)

Faiyum *see* **El Faiyum**.

Falkirk an industrial town in CENTRAL REGION, SCOTLAND; scene of Edward I's defeat of Wallace (1298) and Prince Charles Edward's defeat of General Hawley (1746).

Falkland Islands (Islas Malvinas) a British Crown Colony consisting of two large islands and some 200 smaller ones lying about 650 km (410 miles) east of southern ARGENTINA. The capital is PORT STANLEY. (12,173 sq km/4700 sq miles; pop. 1800)

False Bay (Valsbaai) an inlet of the south ATLANTIC OCEAN, east of the Cape of GOOD HOPE, and so named as

early navigators often mistook it for TABLE BAY in SOUTH
AFRICA. False Bay was first explored in 1488 by the
Portuguese navigator Bartholomeu Dias (c. 1450–1500),
who was seeking a sea route to INDIA.

Falster an island linked to the main Danish island of
Zealand to its north by Europe's second longest bridge
(after the bridge to ÖLAND) until an even longer bridge is
soon opened across the nearby STORE BAELT. (514 sq km/
198 sq miles; pop. 45,900)

Famagusta a resort and port on the east coast of CYPRUS;
since 1974 it has been under Turkish occupation. (Pop.
39,500)

Fanling one of several new towns in the NEW TERRITORIES,
HONG KONG, created to relieve pressure of population on
the main built-up areas. It is 35 km (22 miles) north of
Kowloon, and close to the existing Chinese border; it has
a target population of 220,000. (Pop. 87,900)

Fao (Al Faw) a port and oil tanker terminal in IRAQ, at the
mouth of the SHATT AL ARAB waterway.

Farafangana a port on the INDIAN OCEAN side of MADAGAS-
CAR, 430 km (265 miles) south of ANTANANARIVO. (Pop.
136,000)

Far East, The a non-specific term used to describe the
countries of East and Southeast ASIA, including CHINA,
JAPAN, North and South KOREA, INDOCHINA, eastern SIBE-
RIA and adjacent islands.

Farewell, Cape (Kap Farvel) the southernmost tip of
GREENLAND, known to the local Eskimo population as
Uummannarsuaq.

Faro the capital of the ALGARVE province of PORTUGAL. (Pop.
28,200)

Faroe Islands *see* **Faeroe Islands**.

Fatehpur Sikri a magnificent deserted palace complex
some 150 km (93 miles) south of DELHI, INDIA, built as a
capital by the Moghul Emperor Akbar in 1580 but abandoned in 1605.

Fátima a village about 105 km (65 miles) north of LISBON,

PORTUGAL, which has been a place of pilgrimage since 1917, when the Virgin Mary is said to have appeared there, calling for world peace. (Pop. 6500)

Faya-Largeau (Faya Abouchar) an oasis and nomadic trading centre in north-central CHAD, 780 km (485 miles) north and slightly east of NJAMENA. It is the main administrative town of the northern half of the country. In the civil war of the 1980s it was a main stronghold of the Libyan-backed anti-government forces.

Fayum *see* **El Faiyum**.

Fens, The a flat low-lying area of eastern ENGLAND, west and south of The WASH; it consisted of salt marshes until it was dyked, drained and reclaimed in the 17th to 19th centuries.

Fergana an industrial city, in an irrigated farming region of the same name, 235 km (145 miles) east of TASHKENT, UZBEKISTAN. (Pop. city 180,000/region 1,944,000)

Fermanagh a lakeland county in the southwest of NORTH-ERN IRELAND; the county town is ENNISKILLEN. (1676 sq km/ 647 sq miles; pop. 51,400)

Fernando Póo *see* **Bioko**.

Ferrara a historic city in northeastern ITALY in the Po Valley. (Pop. 150,300)

Fertile Crescent a historical area of fertile land in the MIDDLE EAST, extending in a broad arc of territory curving from the head of The GULF, up the TIGRIS valley, around the northern edge of the Syrian Desert, and down through PALESTINE to the borders of EGYPT. It was gradually cultivated in an organized way from about 9000BC onwards.

Fès (Fez) a city in northern MOROCCO, the oldest of that country's four imperial cities. (Pop. 448,823)

Fezzan a historical region in the southwest of LIBYA, which is sparsely populated by oasis-dwellers. The chief town is Sebha. (725,000 sq km/279,000 sq miles; pop. 85,200)

Fife an ancient kingdom, and present-day region of eastern SCOTLAND. The administrative centre is Glenrothes. (1308 sq km/505 sq miles; pop. 344,000)

Figuig an oasis settlement at the edge of a vast stretch of barren Saharan desert in the extreme east of MOROCCO, on the border with ALGERIA and linked to major caravan routes. (Pop. 14,480)

Fiji is one of the largest nations in the western PACIFIC and consists of some 320 islands and atolls, but only 150 are inhabited. It is situated around the 180° International Date Line and lies about 17° south of the Equator. Fiji has high rainfall, high temperatures and plenty of sunshine all year round. The two main islands, Viti Levu and Vanua Levu, are extinct volcanoes, and most of the islands in the group are fringed with coral reefs. The southeastern islands have tropical rain forests, but a lot of timber has been felled, and soil erosion is a growing problem. The main cash crop is sugar cane, although copra, ginger and fish are also exported. Tourism is now a major industry.

Area : 18,274 sq km (7056 sq miles)
Population : 727,104
Capital : Suva
Form of government : Republic
Religions : Christianity, Hinduism
Currency : Fiji dollar

Finistère the department of FRANCE occupying the tip of the BRITTANY peninsula. (Pop. 828,000)

Finisterre, Cape the northwest corner of SPAIN.

Finland lies at the eastern limit of western EUROPE, with the RUSSIAN FEDERATION to the east and the Gulf of BOTHNIA to the west. Most of the country is low-lying except for the north, which rises to over 1000 m (3281 ft) in LAPPLAND. It is covered with extensive forests and thousands of lakes. The climate has great extremes between summer and winter. Winter is very severe and lasts about six months. Even in the south, snow covers the ground for three months in winter. Summers are short but quite warm, with light rain throughout the country. Finland is largely self-sufficient in food and produces great surpluses of dairy produce. Most crops are grown in the southwest. In the north, reindeer are herded and forests yield great quantities of timber for export. Major industries are timber products, wood pulp and paper, and machinery and shipbuilding, which has developed because of the country's great need for an efficient fleet of ice breakers.

Area : 338,127 sq km (130,551 sq miles)

Population : 4,970,000

Capital : Helsinki (Helsingfors)

Other major cities : Turku, Tampere

Form of government : Republic

Religion : Lutheranism

Currency : Markka

Finland, Gulf of the easternmost arm of the Baltic Sea, with the southern coast of Finland to the north, St Petersburg in the Russian Federation at its eastern end, and Estonia to the south.

Finnmark (Finmarken) the northernmost county of Norway and an area that was strategically important to the North Atlantic Treaty Organization (NATO), which has military installations here, because of the past Cold War with the former USSR and its satellite partners in the Warsaw Pact. (Pop. 77,400)

Fiordland a remote, sparsely populated area along the southwest coast of South Island, New Zealand, consisting of rugged mountains, precipitous valleys, fiords, and waterfalls, resembling the Norwegian coastal landscape. Most of the area is conserved as national park. (12,000 sq km/4635 sq miles)

Firenze *see* **Florence**.

Flanders (Vlaanderen, Flandre) a Flemish-speaking coastal region of northern Belgium, now divided into two provinces, East and West Flanders. (6115 sq km/2361 sq miles; pop. 2,400,000)

Fleetwood a fishing and ferry port, and industrial town at the north end of the FYLDE Peninsula, in LANCASHIRE, in northwest ENGLAND. (Pop. 28,467)

Flensburg a Baltic port in SCHLESWIG-HOLSTEIN, and the most northerly city in GERMANY, barely 2 km (1 mile) south of the border with DENMARK. (Pop. 87,900)

Flinders Island an island off the northeast coast of TASMANIA, AUSTRALIA; it is the largest island in the Furneaux Group (2077 sq km/802 sq miles; pop. 967)

Flinders Range mountains in the eastern part of SOUTH AUSTRALIA, stretching over 400 km (250 miles). St Mary Peak is the highest point (1188 m/3898 ft).

Flintshire *see* **Clwyd**.

Flodden a hillside in NORTHUMBRIA where, in 1513, invading Scots were defeated by the English, and King James IV of Scotland was killed.

Florence (Firenze) one of the great Renaissance cities of ITALY, straddling the River ARNO, and the capital of the region of TUSCANY. (Pop. 453,300)

Flores a volcanic island in the SUNDA group in INDONESIA, lying in the chain which stretches due east of JAVA. (14,250 sq km/550 sq miles; pop. 803,000)

Flores Sea a stretch of the PACIFIC OCEAN between FLORES and SULAWESI.

Florianópolis a port in southern BRAZIL, capital of Santa Caterina state, lying on the west coast of the offshore Santa Caterina Island. (Pop. 153,547)

Florida a state occupying the peninsula in the southeastern corner of the USA. The state capital is TALLAHASSEE. (151,670 sq km/58,560 sq miles; pop. 11,366,000)

Florida, Straits of the waterway which separates the southern tip of FLORIDA, USA from CUBA, some 145 km (90 miles) to the south.

Flotta a small low-lying island on the south side of SCAPA FLOW, in the ORKNEY ISLANDS off northern SCOTLAND. It is the site of a large oil pipeline terminal connected to the Piper, Claymore and Tartan fields in the NORTH SEA.

Flushing (Vlissingen) a port on the southwest coast of the NETHERLANDS. (Pop. 46,400)

Fly, **River** a largely navigable river flowing from the central mountains in western PAPUA NEW GUINEA to its broad estuary on the Gulf of PAPUA to the south. (Length 1200 km/750 miles)

Foggia a city in the PUGLIA region of southeastern ITALY. (Pop. 158,400)

Fontainebleau a town 55 km (35 miles) southeast of PARIS, FRANCE, with a 16th-century royal château and a famous forest. (Pop. 39,400)

Formosa *see* **Taiwan**.

Fortaleza a major port on the northeastern coast of BRAZIL. (Pop. 1,309,000)

Fort-de-France a port and the capital of the island of MARTINIQUE. (Pop. 100,000)

Forties a large underwater oilfield in the central NORTH SEA, lying in the British sector about 180 km (112 miles) east and slightly north of ABERDEEN. Britain's first North Sea oil find was made here in 1970, and by 1975, 400,000 barrels a day were flowing in a pipeline laid to the Grangemouth oil refinery in central SCOTLAND.

Fort Knox a military reservation in KENTUCKY, USA, 40 km (25 miles) southwest of LOUISVILLE; also the site of the principal depository of the country's gold bullion. (Pop. 37,600)

Fort Lamy see **Ndjamena**.

Fort Lauderdale a city and resort on the east coast of FLORIDA, USA, 40 km (25 miles) north of MIAMI. (Pop. city 149,900/metropolitan area 1,093,300)

Fort McMurray a town in northeast ALBERTA, CANADA, situated at the junction of the River Clearwater and the ATHABASCA, which is the terminus of a water transport system through to the ARCTIC. It also stands amid vast oil-sand deposits. (Pop. 31,000)

Fort Worth a city in north-east TEXAS, USA, just to the west of DALLAS and part of a Dallas-Fort Worth conurbation (the Southwest Metroplex). (Pop. city 414,600/metropolitan area 1,144,400)

Foshan an industrial city in GUANGDONG province, CHINA. (Pop. 500,000)

Fouta Djallon (Futa Jallon) a deeply dissected plateau in GUINEA, rising to over 900 m (3000 ft). The region contains large deposits of bauxite.

Foveaux Strait the narrow stretch of the SOUTHERN OCEAN that separates SOUTH ISLAND, from STEWART ISLAND, NEW ZEALAND. (24-34 km/15-21 miles wide)

France is the largest country in western EUROPE and has a coastline on the ENGLISH CHANNEL, the MEDITERRANEAN SEA and on the ATLANTIC OCEAN. The lowest parts of the country are the great basins of the north and southwest from which it rises to the MASSIF CENTRAL and the higher ALPS, JURA and PYRÉNÉES. Climate ranges from moderate maritime in the northwest to Medierannean in the south. Farming is possible in all parts of France. The western shores are ideal for rearing livestock, while the PARIS Basin is good arable land. It is in the southwest around BORDEAUX that the vineyards produce some of the world's best wines. The main industrial area of France is in the north and east, and the main industries are iron and steel, engineering, chemicals, textiles and electrical goods.

Area : 551,500 sq km (212,934 sq miles)

Population : 56,180,000

Capital : Paris

Other major cities : Bordeaux, Lyon, Marseille, Toulouse

Form of government : Republic

Religion : RC

Currency : Franc

Franceville the main town and trading centre for the southeastern region of GABON, which is rich in manganese and uranium (Pop. 35,000)

Franche-Comté a region of eastern FRANCE, covering the

JURA and the low country east of the River Saône. (Pop. 1,084,000)

Francistown the centre of trade, industry and tourism in the northeast of BOTSWANA; a former boom town of the 1890s gold rush. (Pop. 36,000)

Frankfort the state capital of KENTUCKY, USA. (Pop. 26,800)

Frankfurt (Frankfurt am Main) a major financial, trade and communications centre in central western GERMANY, on the River MAIN. (Pop. 614,700)

Frankfurt an der Oder a town on the River ODER in eastern GERMANY, on the border with POLAND. (Pop. 84,800)

Franz Josef Land (Zemlya Frantsa Iosita) a group of over 100 small Arctic islands, north of NOVAYA ZEMLYA, of the RUSSIAN FEDERATION. They are the most northerly pieces of land in the Eastern Hemisphere; they were discovered by Austrian explorers in 1873 and claimed by the Russians in the 1920s (20,700 sq km/8000 sq miles)

Fraser, River a river flowing through southern BRITISH COLUMBIA, CANADA, from its source in the ROCKY MOUNTAINS to the Strait of GEORGIA by VANCOUVER. (Length 1370 km/850 miles)

Fredericton the capital of NEW BRUNSWICK, CANADA. (Pop. 43,750)

Freemantle *see* **Perth** (Australia).

Freeport City the main port, industrial town and tourist centre of Grand Bahama island in the northwest of the BAHAMAS archipelago. (Pop. 17,000)

Freetown the main port and capital of SIERRA LEONE. (Pop. 316,300)

Freiburg (Freiburg im Breisgau) the largest city in the BLACK FOREST in south-west GERMANY, close to the border with FRANCE. (Pop. 175,000)

French Guiana (Guyane) *see* **Guiana (French)**.

French Polynesia a total of about 130 islands in the South PACIFIC OCEAN administered as overseas territories by FRANCE.

French Southern and Antarctic Territories a set of remote and widely scattered territories in ANTARCTICA and the ANTARCTIC OCEAN administered by FRANCE. They include the Crozet Islands and KERGUELEN.

Fresno a city in central eastern CALIFORNIA. (Pop. city 267,400/metropolitan area 564,900)

Friesian (Frisian) Islands a string of sandy, low-lying islands that line the coasts in the south-eastern corner of the NORTH SEA. The West Friesians (including Terchelling and Texel) belong to the NETHERLANDS; the East Friesians (including Borkum and Norderney) belong to GERMANY; and the North Friesians are divided between Germany and DENMARK.

Friuli-Venezia Giulia the region of Italy in the northeast corner bordering SLOVENIA and AUSTRIA, and centred on its capital TRIESTE. (7846 sq km/3029 sq miles; pop. 1,229,000)

Frunze *see* **Bishkek**.

Fuji, **Mount (Fujiyama)** the highest peak in JAPAN, a distinctive volcanic cone 100 km (62 miles) to the south-west of TOKYO. (3776 m/12,388 ft)

Fujian (Fukien) a coastal province in southeast China. The capital is FUZHOU. (120,000 sq km/46,350 sq miles; pop. 24,800,000)

Fukui a market town near the north coast of central HONSHU Island, JAPAN. (Pop. 250,300)

Fukuoka a port and the largest city on the island of KYUSHU, JAPAN. (Pop. 1,160,400)

Funafuti the capital of TUVALU, and the name of the atoll on which it is sited. (2.4 sq km/0.9 sq miles; pop. 2600)

Funchal the capital of MADEIRA. (Pop. 45,600)

Fundy, Bay of lies between NOVA SCOTIA and NEW BRUNSWICK, CANADA. It has the world's largest tidal range—15m (50 ft) between low and high tide.

Fünen (Fyn) the second largest of the islands of DENMARK, in the centre of the country. (2976 sq km/1048 sq miles; pop. 433,800)

Fushun a mining city in Liaoning province, China, situated on one of the largest coalfields in the world. (Pop. 1,800,000)

Fuzhou an important port and the capital of Fujian province, China. (Pop. 1,050,000)

Fylde a peninsula between the Wyre and Ribble rivers in Lancashire, in northwest England; its chief town is Blackpool.

Fyn *see* **Fünen**

Føroyar *see* **Faeroe Islands**.

G

Gabès a seaport and oasis town on the Gulf of Gabès, in southern Tunisia, 320 km (200 miles) south of Tunis. (Pop. 64,500)

Gabès, Gulf of a branch of the Mediterranean Sea which, with the Gulf of Sirte to the east, makes a deep indent in the coast of north Africa.

Gabon is a small country in west-central Africa, which straddles the Equator. It has a low narrow coastal plain, and the rest of the country comprises a low plateau. Three-quarters of Gabon is covered with dense tropical forest. The climate is hot, humid and typically equatorial, with little or no seasonal variations. Until the 1960s timber was virtually Gabon's only resource and then oil was discovered. By the mid 1980s it was Africa's sixth largest oil producer, and other minerals such as manganese, uranium and iron ore were being exploited. Much of the earnings from these resources were squandered, and most of the Gabonese people remain subsistence farmers. The country has great tourist potential, but because of the dense hardwood forests transport links with the interior are very difficult.

Area : 267,667 sq km (103,346 sq miles)
Population : 1,220,000
Capital : Libreville
Other major city : Port Gentile
Form of government : Republic
Religion : RC, Animism
Currency : Franc CFA

Gaborone the capital of Botswana, in the southeast of the country. (Pop. 79,000)

Gabrovo an industrial town and capital of the surrounding region of the same name, in north-central BULGARIA, immediately north of the BALKAN MOUNTAINS. (Pop. 83,000)

Gaeltacht (Gaedhealtacht) a term applied to any of the regions, mainly in western IRELAND and the WESTERN ISLES of SCOTLAND, where Gaelic is the venacular speech.

Gaeseong *see* **Kaesong**.

Gafsa an oasis town and major road and rail junction in central TUNISIA, 185 km (115 miles) west of SFAX; it is the centre of an important phosphate-mining region. (Pop. 61,000)

Galapagos Islands a group of 15 islands on the Equator administered by ECUADOR, but located some 1100 km (680 miles) to the west of that country. (7812 sq km/3016 sq miles; pop. 6200)

Galashiels a main centre of the BORDERS woollen textiles industry, in southeastern SCOTLAND, 56 km (35 miles) southeast of EDINBURGH. (Pop. 12,294)

Galati an inland port on the River DANUBE in eastern ROMANIA, close to the border with the MOLDOVA. (Pop. 261,000)

Galicia a region in the very northwest corner of SPAIN. (Pop. 2,754,000)

Galilee the most northerly region of ISRAEL, bordering LEBANON and SYRIA, with the Sea of Galilee (Lake TIBERIAS) on its eastern side.

Galle an old colonial city on a rocky headland at the southwestern corner of SRI LANKA. (Pop. 77,200)

Gallipoli (Gelibolu) the peninsula which marks the northern side of the DARDANELLES in TURKEY, and also the name of a port on the peninsula. In World War I, Allied troops (particularly Australians and New Zealanders) suffered heavy losses here in an unsuccessful attempt to take control of the Dardanelles.

Gällivare an iron-mining centre, 40 km (25 miles) within the ARCTIC CIRCLE, northern SWEDEN. (Pop. 25,417)

Galloway *see* **Dumfries and Galloway**.

Galveston a port in TEXAS, USA, sited on an island in the Gulf of MEXICO. (Pop. city 62,400/metropolitan area 215,400)

Galway a county in the central part of the west coast of IRELAND. The county town is also called Galway, or Galway City. (5940 sq km/2293 sq miles; pop. county 171,800/city 37,700)

Gambia, the smallest country in AFRICA, pokes like a crooked finger into SENEGAL. The country is divided along its entire length by the River Gambia, which can be crossed only at two main ferry crossings. Gambia has two very different seasons. In the dry season there is little rainfall, then the southwest monsoon sets in, with spectacular storms producing heavy rain for four months. Most Gambians live in villages with a few animals, and grow enough millet and sorghum to feed themselves. Groundnuts are the main and only export crop of any significance. The river provides a thriving local fishing industry, and the white sandy beaches on the coast are becoming increasingly popular with foreign tourists.

Area : 11,295 sq km (4361 sq miles)

Population : 875,000

Capital : Banjul

Form of government : Republic

Religion : Sunni Islam

Currency : Dalasi

Gambia, River a major river of West AFRICA, flowing into the ATLANTIC OCEAN from its source in GUINEA, through SENEGAL and then through GAMBIA, for which it provides a central and vital focus. (Length 483 km/300 miles)

Gambier Islands (Îles Gambier) a small group of PACIFIC islands in FRENCH POLYNESIA, some 1600 km (1000 miles) southeast of TAHITI; they are enclosed by a reef forming a large lagoon some 26 km (16 miles) wide.

Gand *see* **Ghent**.

Gander a town in eastern NEWFOUNDLAND, CANADA, with a major airport that used to be a busy refuelling stop for transatlantic airliners; although this need no longer exists, it is still the centre for North ATLANTIC air traffic control. (Pop. 10,405)

Ganges, River (Ganga) the holy river of the Hindus, flowing from its source in the HIMALAYAS, across northern INDIA and forming a delta in BANGLADESH as it flows into the Bay of BENGAL. (Length 2525 km/1568 miles)

Gangtok the capital of the former HIMALAYAN kingdom of SIKKIM, a state of northeast INDIA since 1975. (Pop. 37,800)

Gansu a mountainous province in northern central CHINA. The capital is LANZHOU. (450,000 sq km/170,000 sq miles; pop. 19,600,000)

Gao an historic town in central MALI, about 960 km (600 miles) down the NIGER river from the captial, BAMAKO. It was once the capital of the Songhai Empire but declined after the Moors occupied it in 1591. (Pop. 50,000)

Garda, Lake (Lago di Garda) the largest of the Alpine lakes of ITALY, lying in the north of the country, halfway between MILAN and VENICE (370 sq km/143 sq miles)

Gargano a mountainous promontory extending into the ADRIATIC SEA about 300 km (190 miles) northwest of the heel of ITALY; it rises to 1056 m (3465 ft)

Garmisch-Partenkirchen twin towns, about 75 km (45 miles) southwest of MUNICH, GERMANY, at the foot of the Bavarian Alps, which are one of the country's leading winter-sports resorts. (Pop. 28,000)

Garonne, River a major river of southwestern FRANCE, flowing north from its source in the central PYRÉNÉES in SPAIN to BORDEAUX, where it contributes to the GIRONDE estuary. (Length 575 km/355 miles)

Gascony (Gascogne) the historic name of an area in the southwestern corner of FRANCE bordering SPAIN.

Gaspé (1) a peninsula in southeast QUEBEC, CANADA, between the ST LAWRENCE estuary and NEW BRUNSWICK. **(2)** an industrial railway terminus town at the eastern end of the Gaspé Peninsula. (Pop. town 17,260)

Gauhati a tea-industry town in northeastern ASSAM,

INDIA, on the BRAHMAPUTRA River, about 70 km (43 miles) south of the border with BHUTAN. (Pop. 123,000)

Gaul an ancient region of western EUROPE, corresponding to northen ITALY, FRANCE, BELGIUM, and parts of GERMANY and the NETHERLANDS; it became a Roman province in the 2nd and 1st centuries BC.

Gävle a seaport and industrial city on the BALTIC coast of SWEDEN, 180 km (112 miles) north of STOCKHOLM; it exports softwoods and iron ore. (Pop. 87,700)

Gazankulu a former Bantu homeland in northeast TRANSVAAL, SOUTH AFRICA, which became a self-governing, but not independent, state in 1973. (7410 sq km/2860 sq miles; pop. 582,500)

Gaza Strip a finger of coastal land stretching from the Egyptian border to the MEDITERRANEAN port of Gaza. It borders with ISRAEL to its east and north. It was administered by EGYPT after the creation of Israel in 1948, and became home to numerous Palestinian refugees. It was taken over by Israel in the Six-Day War of 1967. (Pop. 510,000)

Gaziantep a town in southern central TURKEY, close to the border with SYRIA, and also the name of the surrounding province. (Pop. town 466,300)

Gdansk (Danzig) The main port of POLAND, on the BALTIC SEA. (Pop. 464,500)

Gdansk, Gulf of (Gulf of Danzig) a cup-shaped inlet of the BALTIC SEA in northeastern POLAND; it contains Poland's two most important ports, GDANSK and GDYNIA, sheltered by a long sand spit.

Gdynia (Gdingen) a port on the BALTIC coast of POLAND 16 km (10 miles) northwest of GDANSK. (Pop. 240,200)

Gêba a West African river that rises in the FOUTA DJALLON in GUINEA, flows through SENEGAL, then, as the country's main transportation artery, through GUINEA-BISSAU to the ATLANTIC OCEAN. (Length: 190 km/120 miles)

Geelong a port and the second largest city of VICTORIA, AUSTRALIA. (Pop. 142,000)

Geirangerfjord a 15-km (9-mile) long branch of Storfjord in west NORWAY, claimed to be the nation's most beautiful stretch of water, backed by spectacular 400-m ((1310-ft) high cliff walls in places. It is a favourite tourist haunt.

Gela a historical town, originally the ancient Greek city of Gelon, on the south coast of SICILY, ITALY; it has expanded since a petrochemical plant opened in th 1960's. (Pop. 74,800)

Gelibolu *see* **Gallipoli**.

Gelsenkirchen an industrial and coal mining town in the RUHR region of GERMANY. (Pop. 290,000)

General Santos (Dadiangas) a port and administrative centre in southern MINDANAO, PHILIPPINES. (Pop. 149,396)

Geneva (Genève; Genf) a city in the extreme southwest of SWITZERLAND, at the western end of Lake Geneva, and close to the border with FRANCE. It is also the name of the surrounding canton. (Pop. city 165,000)

Genk (Genck) an industrial town 30km (19 miles) north of LIÈGE, BELGIUM. Formerly a coal-mining centre, it is now involved in steel and car production. (Pop. 62,000)

Genoa (Genova) the major seaport of northwest ITALY, and the capital of LIGURIA. (Pop. 760,300)

Genoa, Gulf of (Golfo di Genova) the northern part of the LIGURIAN SEA, washing the shores of northwestern ITALY; GENOA lies at its head, and it is flanked by Riviera coasts dotted with resorts.

Gent *see* **Ghent**.

Georgetown (1) the main port and capital of GUYANA. (Pop. 200,000) **(2)** the capital and main port of the CAYMAN ISLANDS. (Pop. 12,970)

George Town a port and the main city of PENANG Island, MALAYSIA. (Pop. 250,600)

Georgia (1) a state in the southeast of the USA, named after George II by English colonists in 1733; the state capital is ATLANTA. (152,490 sq km/58,876 sq miles; pop. 5,837,000). **(2)** a republic in the southwest of the former USSR, occupying the central and western parts of the

CAUCASUS. It shares borders with TURKEY, ARMENIA, AZERBAIJAN and the RUSSIAN FEDERATION. It is bounded to the west by the BLACK SEA. Almost 40% of the country is covered with forests. Agriculture, which is the main occupation of the population, includes tea cultivation and fruit growing, especially citrus fruits and viticulture. The republic is rich in minerals, especially manganese. Industries include coal, timber, machinery, chemicals, silk, food processing and furniture. Georgia declared itself independent in 1991.

Area : 69,700 sq km (26,900 sq miles)
Population : 5,976,000
Capital : Tbilisi
Other major cities : Kutaisi, Rustavi, Batumi
Form of government : Republic
Religion : Russian Orthodox
Currency : Rouble

Georgia, Strait of the southern part of the stretch of water which separates VANCOUVER ISLAND from the coast of BRITISH COLUMBIA in CANADA.

Gerlach Peak (Gerlachovka)*see* **Tatra Mountains**.

German Bight (Deutsche Bucht) the part of the NORTH SEA, lying off the northwestern coast of GERMANY. It is also sometimes called the Helgoländer Bucht, after the island of HELGOLAND in the middle of the bight.

Germany is a large country in northern central EUROPE, which comprises the former East and West German Republics, reunified in 1990. In the north is the North German Plain, which merges with the North Rhinelands in the west. Further south, a plateau that stretches across the country from east to west is divided by the River RHINE. In the southwest, the BLACK FOREST separates the Rhine Valley from the fertile valleys and scarplands of Swabia. The Bohemian Uplands and Erz Mountains mark the border with the CZECH REPUBLIC. Generally, the country has warm summers and cold winters. Agricultural products include wheat, rye, barley, oats, potatoes and sugar beet. The main industrial and most densely populated areas are in the RHUR Valley. Principal industries are mechanical and electrical engineering. Chemical and textile industries are found in the cities along the Rhine, and motor vehicle industry in the large provincial cities. The country depends heavily on imports.

Area : 356,910 sq km (137,803 sq miles)
Population : 79,070,000
Capital : Berlin, Bonn (Seat of government)
Other major cities : Cologne, Frankfurt, Hamburg, Leipzig, Munich, Stuttgart
Form of government : Republic
Religions : Lutheranism, RC
Currency : Deutsche Mark

Germiston a gold-mining city in the eastern WITWATERSRAND, SOUTH AFRICA; it has the world's largest ore refinery, handling about 70 per cent of the Western world's gold bullion (Pop. 166,400)

Gerona an industrial city 88 km (55 miles) northeast of BARCELONA, SPAIN; it has a fine 14th-century cathedral. (Pop. 87,600)

Gettysburg a small town in southern PENNSYLVANIA, USA, about 105 km (65 miles) north and slightly west of WASHINGTON DC; it was the scene of a crucial battle (1863) during the American Civil War, in which Union forces decisively defeated the Confederate army. (Pop. 7194)

Gezira *see* **El Gezira**.

Ghadames (Ghadámis) a Saharan route centre in the extreme west of LIBYA, by the borders of ALGERIA and TUNISIA. Known as the "pearl of the desert," it is one of the oldest Berber oases. (Pop. 6300)

Ghana is located on the southern coast of West AFRICA between CÔTE D'IVOIRE and TOGO. In 1957, as the former British GOLD COAST, it became the first black African state to achieve independence from European colonial rule. It has palm-fringed beaches of white sand along the

Gulf of GUINEA, and where the great River VOLTA meets the sea there are peaceful blue lagoons. The climate on the coast is equatorial, and towards the north there are steamy tropical evergreen forests that give way in the far north to tropical savanna. The landscape becomes harsh and barren near the border with BURKINA FASO. Most Ghanaians are village dwellers whose homes are made of locally available materials. The south of the country has been most exposed to European influence, and it is here that cocoa, rubber, palm oil and coffee are grown. Ghana has important mineral resources, such as manganese and bauxite. Most of Ghana's towns are in the south, but rapid growth has turned many of them into unplanned sprawls.

Area : 238,533 sq km (92,098 sq miles)

Population : 14,900,000

Capital : Accra

Other major cities : Kumasi, Tamale, Sekondi-Takoradi

Form of government : Republic

Religions : Protestant, Animism, RC

Currency : Cedi

Ghardaïa an impressive 11th-century town 500 km (310 miles) south of ALGIERS, ALGERIA, on the Route du HOGGAR across the SAHARA. (pop. 65,000)

Ghats *see* **Eastern Ghats; Western Ghats.**

Ghawar the world's largest oilfield, lying inland along the GULF coast of SAUDI ARABIA to the west of QATAR. It can produce up to 5 million barrels of oil a day.

Ghazni a trading centre with a famous bazaar, 120 km (74 miles) southwest of KABUL, AFGHANISTAN; it has been a special Muslim town since the 9th century AD. (Pop. 32,000)

Ghent (Gent; Gand) a medieval city spanning the Rivers Lys and SCHELDE and the capital of the province of East FLANDERS, BELGIUM. (Pop. city 235,000/metropolitan area 490,000)

Giant's Causeway a promontory of columnar basalt on the ANTRIM coast of NORTHERN IRELAND, consisting of several thousand pillars, mainly hexagonal, that were formed by rapid cooling of lava. It is a World Heritage Site and a major tourist attraction.

Gibraltar a self-governing British Crown Colony on the southwestern tip of SPAIN, where a limestone hill called the Rock of Gibraltar rises to 425 m (1394 ft). Its commanding view over the Strait of Gibraltar has made the territory strategically significant. Spain lays claim to Gibraltar, but the UK is reluctant to relinquish it. English is the official language, although Spanish is also spoken. The capital is Gibraltar Town. (6.5 sq km/2.5 sq miles; pop. 32,200; cur. Gibraltar pound = 100 pence)

Gibraltar, Strait of the narrow waterway, 13 km (8 miles) at its narrowest, which connects the MEDITERRANEAN SEA to the ATLANTIC OCEAN, with SPAIN to the north and MOROCCO to the south.

Gibson Desert a desert of sand and salt marshes in central western AUSTRALIA, with the GREAT SANDY DESERT to the north and the GREAT VICTORIA DESERT to the south.

Gifu a town in central HONSHU Island, JAPAN. (Pop. 411,700)

Gijón a port and industrial town in AUSTURIAS, in the centre of the north coast of SPAIN. (Pop.256,000)

Gilbert Islands *see* **Kiribati**.

Gilgit a mountain district in northern PAKISTAN, noted for its great beauty. The small town of Gilgit perches startlingly beneath a dramatic rockface.

Gillingham *see* **Medway Towns**.

Gippsland a region of southeastern VICTORIA, AUSTRALIA, stretching from MELBOURNE to the NEW SOUTH WALES state boundary; it includes the famous Ninety Mile Beach.

Gironde the long, thin estuary stretching some 80 km (50 miles) which connects the Rivers DORDOGNE and GARONNE to the Atlantic coast of southwest FRANCE.

Gisborne a port and resort on the east coast of NORTH

ISLAND, NEW ZEALAND, 320 km (200 miles) southeast of AUCKLAND. The town is a centre for tourists exploring the whole EAST CAPE area. (Pop. 32,000)

Giuba, River *see* **Jubba, River**.

Giza *see* **El Gîza.**

Glamorgan a former county of south WALES, which was divided into three administrative regions in the 1970s: MID GLAMORGAN, WEST GLAMORGAN and SOUTH GLAMORGAN.

Glasgow a port on the River CLYDE, a major industrial centre and the largest city in SCOTLAND. (Pop. 751,000)

Glencoe a dramatically beautiful valley in western HIGHLANDS of SCOTLAND; it was the site of a massacre of the local MacDonald clan by members of the Campbell clan and English troops (1692).

Glen Mòr (Glen More) *see* **Great Glen, The.**

Glenrothes a new town founded in 1948 in east-central SCOTLAND; it is the administrative centre for FIFE region. (Pop. 32,700)

Gliwice (Gleiwitz) an industrial city in southern POLAND. (Pop. 211,000)

Gloucestershire a county in western ENGLAND; the county town is Gloucester. (2638 sq km/1019 sq miles; pop. 508,000)

Gniezno an ancient town in central POLAND, 45 km (28 miles) northeast of POZNAN; it was the country's first capital, in the 11th century. (Pop. 66,100)

Goa a territory on the west coast of INDIA, 400 km (250 miles) south of BOMBAY, which was captured by the Portuguese in 1510 and remained under the control of PORTUGAL until it was annexed by India in 1961. (3702 sq km/1429 sq miles; pop. 1,007,800)

Gobi Desert a vast expanse of arid land which occupies much of MONGOLIA and central northern CHINA. Temperatures range from very hot to extremely cold over the year. (1,295,000 sq km/500,000 sq miles)

Godavari, River a river which runs across the middle of the DECCAN peninsula in INDIA from its source in the

Western GHATS near BOMBAY to its delta on the central east coast. (Length 1465 km/910 miles)

Godthåb (Nuuk) The capital of GREENLAND. (Pop. 10,500)

Godwin Austen *see* **K2**.

Golan Heights an area of high ground in southwest SYRIA on the border with northern ISRAEL. The Heights were captured by Israel in the Arab-Israeli War of 1967 and annexed by Israel in 1981. (2225 m/7300 ft)

Gold Coast (1) the name given to a string of beach resorts on the east coast of QUEENSLAND, AUSTRALIA, to the south of BRISBANE. **(2)** *See* **Ghana**.

Golden Triangle the remote and mountainous region where the borders of THAILAND, BURMA and LAOS meet, noted in particular for its opium cultivation and as one of the world's main sources of the drug heroin.

Gomel an industrial city in southeastern BELARUS. (Pop. 452,000)

Gomera *see* **Canary Islands**.

Gonder a historic city about 400 km (250 miles) north and slightly west of ADDIS ABABA, ETHIOPIA. It was the royal town of the Abyssinian Empire from about 1700 to 1855. (Pop. 80,000)

Gondwanaland the southernmost of the two ancient continents into which Pangaea, an earlier supercontinent, divided and drifted apart about 180 million years ago. The northernmost was Laurasia.

Good Hope, Cape of the tip of the narrow Cape Peninsula which extends from the southwestern corner of SOUTH AFRICA.

Goodwin Sands a stretch of sandbanks and shoals in the ENGLISH CHANNEL, off the coast of KENT in southeast ENGLAND. Numerous ships have got into difficulty here.

Gor'kiy (Gorky) *see* **Nizhniy Novgorod**.

Gorakhpur a city in the north of INDIA, about 65 km (40 miles) south of the Nepalese border. Traditionally, it is the place of Buddha's death and cremation in about 483BC.

Görlitz an industrial city on the Neisse River (which forms the Polish border) in the easternmost corner of SACHSEN, GERMANY. (Pop. 80,200)

Goslar a former imperial seat of the Holy Roman Emperors at the foot of the HARZ MOUNTAINS in central GERMANY. It is now a popular resort town. (Pop. 54,000)

Göta Kanal a 610-km (380-mile) long waterway system that, by using rivers, lakes and canals, links GOTHENBURG with the BALTIC on the east coast of SWEDEN near Söderköping.

Gotham (1) a village in NOTTINGHAMSHIRE, in east-central ENGLAND, renowned for its legend of men feigning stupidity to prevent King John residing with them. **(2)** a nickname for the city of NEW YORK—and associated with the *Batman* comic strip.

Gothenburg (Göteborg) a major port on the KATTEGAT and the second largest city in SWEDEN. (Pop. 425,500)

Gotland an island in the BALTIC SEA which forms a county of SWEDEN. (3140 sq km/1210 sq miles; pop. 56,100)

Göttingen a university town in central GERMANY and an important trading centre in medieval times. (Pop. 138,000)

Gouda a historic town in eastern NETHERLANDS, famous for its cheese. (Pop. 59,200)

Governador Valadares a mining town 240 km (150 miles) northeast of BELO HORIZONTE; it produces gemstones. (Pop. 197,000)

Gozo *see* **Malta**.

Graaff-Reinet a well-preserved old market town founded in 1786 on the GREAT KAROO plateau about 190 km (120 miles) north of PORT ELIZABETH, SOUTH AFRICA. (Pop. 29.800)

Graham Land *see* **Antarctic Peninsula.**

Grahamstown a cathedral and university town in eastern CAPE PROVINCE, about 135 km (85 miles) southwest of EAST LONDON. (Pop. 25,100)

Grampian an administrative region of northeastern SCOTLAND created in 1975 out of the former counties of Aberdeenshire, Kincardineshire, Banffshire and part of Morayshire. The capital is ABERDEEN. (8550 sq km/3301 sq miles; pop. 497,000)

Grampian Mountains a range of mountains that stretch across northern SCOTLAND to the south of Loch NESS. The mountains rise to their highest point at BEN NEVIS (1344 m/4409 ft), the highest peak in the UK.

Granada a city in the SIERRA NEVADA of central southern SPAIN. An administrative centre during the Moorish occupation of Spain, during which its famous Alhambra Palace was built (1248-1345). Granada is also the name of the surrounding province. (Pop. city 262,200)

Granada the oldest Spanish settlement in NICARAGUA, founded in 1523, at the northern end of Lake Nicaragua. (Pop. 60,500)

Gran Canaria *see* **Canary Islands**.

Gran Chaco a large wilderness area—about the size of BRITAIN—that extends from northeastern ARGENTINA, through western PARAGUAY to the border area of BOLIVIA. (240,000 sq km/92,660 sq miles; pop. 100,000)

Grand Bahama *see* **Bahamas**.

Grand Banks a part of the continental shelf off southeastern NEWFOUNDLAND, which is one of the world's leading fishing grounds.

Grand Canyon the dramatic gorge of the COLORADO RIVER, in places over 1.5 km (1 mile) deep, in northwestern ARIZONA.

Grand Rapids a city 40 km (14 miles) to the east of Lake Michigan in the state of MICHIGAN, USA. (Pop. city 183,000/metropolitan area 626,500)

Grasse a town in the CÔTE D'AZUR, FRANCE, 12 km (7.5 miles) inland from CANNES, associated with the extraction of flower essences for the French perfume industry. (Pop. 38,400)

Graz the second largest city in AUSTRIA, in the southeast of the country. (Pop. 243,000)

Great Alföld (Nagyalföld) the monotonously flat "Great

Plain" of HUNGARY, east of the Danube and covering more than half the country; its fertile black earth soils have given rise to intensive cultivation and many villages and market towns. (51,800 sq km?19,995 sq miles)

Great Artesian Basin a vast area of east-central AUS-TRALIA, and part of the desert interior(bush country—outback) falling mainly in QUEENSLAND west of the GREAT DIVIDING RANGE. The main source of water in this region is underground and tapped by drilling artesian wells.

Great Australian Bight the arm of the SOUTHERN OCEAN which forms the deep indentation in the centre of the southern coastline of AUSTRALIA.

Great Australian Desert the collective word for the deserts that occupy much of the centre of AUSTRALIA. (3,830,000 sq km/1,480,000 sq miles)

Great Barrier Reef the world's most extensive coral reef which lines the coast of QUEENSLAND, AUSTRALIA, stretching some 2000 km (1250 miles).

Great Bear Lake the fourth largest lake in North AMERICA, in the remote northwest of CANADA. It drains into the MACKENZIE RIVER. (31,153 sq km/12,028 sq miles)

Great Belt *see* **Store Baelt**.

Great Bitter Lake *see* **Bitter Lakes**.

Great Britain the island shared by ENGLAND, SCOTLAND and WALES, and which forms the principal part of the UNITED KINGDOM OF GREAT BRITAIN AND NORTHERN IRELAND.

Great Dividing Range a range of mountains which runs down the east coast of AUSTRALIA, from QUEENSLAND in the north, across NEW SOUTH WALES to VICTORIA in the south, some 3600 km (2250 miles) in all. The highest point is Mount KOSCIUSKO. (2230 m/7316 ft)

Greater Antilles *see* **Antilles**.

Greater London *see* **London**.

Greater Manchester *see* **Manchester**.

Greater Sunda Islands *see* **Lesser Sunda Islands**.

Great Glen, The (Glen Mòr, Glen More) a major fault valley across the whole of SCOTLAND, extending 105 km

(65 miles) southwest from the MORAY FIRTH in the east to Loch Linnhe, an arm of the ATLANTIC OCEAN; it contains LOCH NESS, Loch Oich, Loch Lochy and the connecting CALEDONIAN CANAL.

Great Karoo (Central Karoo) an arid plateau in south-central CAPE PROVINCE, SOUTH AFRICA; it is separated from the Little Karoo by the Swartberg Mountains. (Average height 750 m/2500 ft)

Great Lakes the largest group of freshwater lakes in the world, drained by the ST LAWRENCE RIVER. There are five lakes, four of which (Lakes HURON, SUPERIOR, ERIE and ONTARIO) are on the border of CANADA and the USA; the fifth (Lake MICHIGAN) is in the USA.

Great Plains a vast area in North AMERICA of flat and undulating grassland east of the ROCKY MOUNTAINS and stretching from northern CANADA to TEXAS, USA. It includes the PRAIRIES, most of which are now ploughed for cereal and fodder crops.

Great Rift Valley a series of geological faults which has created a depression stretching 6400 km (4000 miles) from the valley of the River JORDAN across the RED SEA and down East AFRICA to MOZAMBIQUE.

Great Salt Lake a salt lake in northwest UTAH, USA, lying just to the northwest of SALT LAKE CITY. (5200 sq km/ 2000 sq miles)

Great Sand Sea *see* **Libyan Desert**.

Great Sandy Desert (1) the desert region in the northern part of WESTERN AUSTRALIA. **(2)** *see* **An Nafud**.

Great Slave Lake a lake drained by the MACKENZIE RIVER in the southern part of the NORTHWEST TERRITORIES of CANADA. (28,570 sq km/11,030 sq miles)

Great Smoky Mountains part of the APPALACHIAN MOUNTAINS, running along the border between TENNESSEE and NORTH CAROLINA. The highest point is Clingmans Dome (2025 m/6643 ft).

Great Victoria Desert a vast area of sand dunes straddling the border between WESTERN and SOUTH AUSTRALIA.

Great Wall of China the longest fortification in the world, winding a total of over 3400 km (2100 miles) from west GANSU to the BO HAI gulf, constructed in the 3rd century and largely rebuilt in the 15th century. It is clearly visible from space.

Great Yarmouth a port and resort at the mouth of the River Yare on the east coast of NORFOLK, in southeastern ENGLAND. It is also an important centre for servicing the southern NORTH SEA natural gas fields. (Pop. 48,000)

Great Zimbabwe an important historic site in central ZIMBABWE, about 300 km (185 miles) south of HARARE; it is associated with the Shona-Karanga civilization, which flourished between about AD1200 and 1450.

Greece is a peninsular-shaped country that is the most southeasterly extension of Western EUROPE. The Pindus Mountains divide Greece from the Albanian border in the north to the Gulf of CORINTH in the south. About 70% of the land is hilly, with harsh mountain climates and poor soils. The Greek islands and coastal regions have a typical MEDITERRANEAN climate, with mild rainy winters and hot dry summers. Winter in the northern mountains is severe, with deep snow and heavy precipitation. Agriculture is the chief activity, and large-scale farming is concentrated on the east coasts. The main industries are small processing plants for tobacco, food and leather. Fishing is an important activity around the 2000 islands that lie off the mainland. Tourists visit the country in the summer for the sun and in winter for its spectacular ancient ruins.

Area : 131,990 sq km (50,961 sq miles)
Population : 10,140,000
Capital : Athens (Athinai)
Other major cities : Patras, Piraeus, Thessaloníki
Form of government : Republic
Religion : Greek Orthodox
Currency : Drachma

Greenland a huge island to the northeast of North

Greenock

AMERICA, most of which lies within the ARCTIC CIRCLE. A province of DENMARK, the island was granted home rule in 1979. The economy is heavily reliant on fishing and most of the population is Eskimo. The capital is GODTHÅB (Nuuk). (2,175,600 sq km/840,000 sq miles; pop. 54,600; cur. Danish Krone = 100øre)

Greenock a port and former major shipbuilding town on the Firth of CLYDE, STRATHCLYDE, SCOTLAND. (Pop.57,324)

Greenwich a borough of east LONDON, ENGLAND, on the south bank of the River THAMES. It was the site of the Royal Observatory, and since 1884 has been accepted to be on 0° meridian from which all lines of longitude are measured. Greenwich Mean Time is the time at 0° longitude, against which all world time differences are measured.

Grenada is the most southerly of the Windward Island chain in the CARIBBEAN. Its territory includes the southern GRENADINE Islands to the north. The main island consists of the remains of extinct volcanoes and has an attractive wooded landscape. In the dry season its typical climate is very pleasant, with warm days and cool nights, but in the wet season it is hot day and night. Agriculture is the island's main industry, and the chief crops grown for export are cocoa, nutmegs, bananas and mace. Apart from the processing of its crops, Grenada has little manufacturing industry, although tourism is an important source of foreign revenue. It is a popular port of call for cruise ships.

Area : 344 sq km (133 sq miles)

Population : 110,000

Capital : St. Georges

Form of government : Constitutional Monarchy

Religions : RC, Anglicanism, Methodism

Currency : East Caribbean dollar

Grenadines a string of some 600 small islands that lie between ST VINCENT to the north and GRENADA to the south. Most of them belong to St Vincent, but the largest,

Carriacou, is divided between St Vincent and Grenada. Other islands include Union, Mustique and Bequia.

Grenoble a manufacturing city in southeast France, in the foothills of the Alps. (Pop. 396,800)

Gretna Green a village in the Dumfries and Galloway region of southern Scotland on the border with England; it is famous for the marrying of eloping couples at the blacksmith's "smiddy". (Pop. 5519)

Grimsby a fishing port in south Humberside in eastern England. (Pop. 92,147)

Grodno an industrial city on the lowlands of Belarus, beside the border with Poland; it was a former capital of Lithuania in the 13th century. (Pop. 239,000)

Groningen the largest city in the northeast of the Netherlands, and also the name of the surrounding province. (Pop. city 205,700)

Groznyy an oil city in the north Caucasus foothills, 145 km (90 miles) west of the Caspian Sea. It is capital of the autonomous Chechen-Ingush Republic of the Russian Federation. (Pop. 398,000)

Guadalajara a major city of central western Mexico. (Pop. 2,300,000)

Guadalcanal an island at the southern end of the archipelago where Honiara, capital of the Solomon Islands, is located. The bitterly contested battle in 1942–3 here between US forces and the occupying Japanese marked a turning point in the US Pacific campaign which eventually led to the defeat of the Japanese in 1945.

Guadalquivir a major river of Spain, flowing 580 km (360 miles) southwest into the Gulf of Cádiz on the southern Atlantic Coast.

Guadeloupe a group of islands in the Leeward Islands in the eastern Caribbean which since 1946 has been an overseas department of France. The principal island is Guadeloupe (divided into two parts, Basse Terre and Grande Terre). The other islands include Marie Galante, La Désirade, Iles des Saintes, St Barthélémy and St

Martin. The capital is Basse Terre. (1779 sq km/687 sq miles; pop. 328,400)

Guam the largest of the Mariana Islands in the western Pacific Ocean. (549 sq km/212 sq miles; pop. 112,000)

Guangdong a province of southeast China. The capital is Guangzhou (Canton). (210,000 sq km/81,000 sq miles; pop. 56,810,000)

Guangxi-Zhuang an autonomous region of southern China on the border with Vietnam. To the south of the city of Guilin, around the Gui Jiang River, is a famous landscape of towering rock hills which rise up from the watery plains. The regional capital is Nanning. (230,000 sq km/890,000 sq miles; pop. 34,700,000)

Guangzhou (Canton) a major port in southeast China, the country's sixth largest city and the capital of Guangdong province. (Pop. 5,350,000)

Guantanamo a city in the southeast of Cuba, and also the name of the surrounding province. The USA has a naval base at nearby Guantanamo Bay. (Pop. city 205,000)

Guatemala City the capital of Guatemala, in the southeast of the country. (Pop. 1,329,600)

Guatemala is situated between the Pacific Ocean and the Caribbean Sea, where North America meets Central America. It is a mountainous country with a ridge of volcanoes running parallel to the Pacific coast. It has a tropical climate, with little or no variation in temperature and a distinctive wet season. The Pacific slopes of the mountains are exceptionally well watered and fertile, and it is here that most of the population are settled. Coffee growing on the lower slopes dominates the economy. A small strip on the coast produces sugar, cotton and bananas. Industry is mainly restricted to the processing of the agricultural products. Guatemala is politically a very unstable country, and civil conflict has practically destroyed tourism.
Area : 108,889 sq km (42,042 sq miles)
Population : 9,000,000

Capital : Guatemala City
Other major cities : Puerto Barrios, Quezaltenango
Form of government : Republic
Religion : RC
Currency : Quetzal

Guayaquil the main port and the largest city of ECUADOR. (Pop. 1,223,500)

Guernica a small town in the BASQUE country of northeast SPAIN where the Basque parliament used to assemble. In 1937, during the Spanish Civil War, it was heavy bombed from the air by German forces. (Pop. 17,836)

Guernsey one of the CHANNEL ISLANDS, lying in the centre of the group and some 50 km (30 miles) off the coast of FRANCE. The capital is St Peter Port. (78 sq km/30 sq miles; pop. 55,000)

Guiana (French) *or* **Guyane** is situated on the northeast coast of South AMERICA and is still an overseas department of FRANCE. It is bounded to the south and east by BRAZIL and to the west by SURINAME. The climate is tropical with heavy rainfall. Guiana's economy relies almost completely on subsidies from France. It has little to export apart from shrimps, and the small area of land that is cultivated produces rice, manioc and sugar cane. Recently the French have tried to develop the tourist industry and to exploit the extensive reserves of hardwood in the jungle interior.

Area : 90,000 sq km (34,749 sq miles)
Population : 73,800
Capital : Cayenne
Form of government : French overseas department
Religion : RC
Currency : Franc

Guiana Highlands a vast, sparsely populated area of heavily forested hills, south of the ORINOCO river, extending eastwards from eastern VENEZUELA, across northern BRAZIL, GUYANA, SURINAM and GUYANE; it rises to Roraima, a flat-topped mountain, 2810 m (8565 ft) high.

Guilin *see* **Guangxi-Zhuang**.

Guinea, formerly a French West African territory, is located on the coast at the "bulge" in AFRICA. It is a lush, green, beautiful country about the same size as the UNITED KINGDOM. It has a tropical climate with constant heat and a high rainfall near the coast. Guinea has great agricultural potential, and many of the coastal swamps and forested plains have been cleared for the cultivation of rice, cassava, yams, maize and vegetables. Further inland, on the plateau of FOUTA DJALLON, dwarf cattle are raised, and in the valleys bananas and pineapples are grown. Coffee and kola nuts are important cash crops grown in the Guinea Highlands to the southwest. Minerals such as bauxite, iron ore and diamonds are mined, but development is hampered by lack of transport.

Area : 245,857 sq km (94,925 sq miles)

Population : 6,710,000

Capital : Conakry

Other major cities : Kankan, Labé

Form of government : Republic

Religion :Sunni Islam

Currency : Guinea franc

Guinea Bissau formerly a Portuguese territory, Guinea Bissau is located south of SENEGAL on the ATLANTIC coast of West AFRICA. It is a country of stunning scenery and rises from a deeply indented and island-fringed coastline to a low inland plateau. The adjacent Bijagos archipelago forms part of its territory. The climate is tropical, with abundant rain from June to November but hot dry conditions for the rest of the year. Years of Portuguese rule and civil war have left Guinea Bissau impoverished, and it is one of the poorest West African states. The country's main aim is to become self-sufficient in food, and the main crops grown are groundnuts, sugar cane, plantains, coconuts and rice. Fishing is an important export industry.

Area : 36,125 sq km (13,948 sq miles)

Population : 966,000
Capital : Bissau
Form of government : Republic
Religion : Animism, Sunni Islam
Currency : Peso

Guinea, Equatorial *see* **Equatorial Guinea.**

Guinea, Gulf of the arm of the ATLANTIC OCEAN which creates the deep, right-angled indent in the west coast of AFRICA.

Guiyang an industrial city in central southern CHINA, and capital of GUIZHOU province. (Pop. 1,260,000)

Guizhou a province of central southern CHINA. The capital is GUIYANG. (170,000 sq km/65,600 sq miles; pop. 27,310,000)

Gujarat a state lining the northwest coast of INDIA, on the border with PAKISTAN. The capital is Gandinagar. Gujarat was the home state of the "father of modern India"—Mahatma Gandhi (1869–1948). (196,024 sq km/75,665 sq miles; pop. 34,085,800)

Gujranwala a textile city in the province of PUNJAB, PAKISTAN, some 65 km (40 miles) north of LAHORE. (Pop. 658,753)

Gulf, The the huge inlet to the south of IRAN which is connected to the ARABIAN SEA by the Strait of HORMUZ. It is often referred to as the Persian Gulf, or the Arabian Gulf.

Guyana, the only English-speaking country in South AMERICA, is situated on the northeast coast of the continent, on the ATLANTIC OCEAN. The country is intersected by many rivers, and the coastal area comprises tidal marshes and mangrove swamps. It is on this coastal area that rice is grown, and vast plantations produce sugar. The jungle in the southwest has potential for the production of minerals, hardwood and hydroelectric power, but 90% of the population live in the coastal area, where the climate is moderated by sea breezes. The country is deeply divided politically, and nothing has been done to improve productivity, with the result that today the country is in an economic crisis.

Area : 214,969 sq km (83,000 sq miles)

Population : 990,000

Capital : Georgetown

Other major city : New Amsterdam

Form of government : Cooperative Republic

Religions : Hinduism, Protestantism, RC

Currency : Guyana dollar

Guyane *see* **Guiana (French)**.

Gwalior a city in central INDIA, 280 km (174 miles) southeast of DELHI. (Pop. 555,900)

Gwangju *see* **Kwangju**.

Gwent a county in southeast WALES, bordering the SEVERN estuary just to the east of CARDIFF. The county was created in 1974 and more or less coincides with the old county of Monmouthshire. The county town is Cwmbran. (1376 sq km/532 sq miles; pop. 440,000)

Gwynedd a county in northwest WALES which includes the island of ANGLESEY. It was created in 1974 out of the former county of Caernarfonshire, and parts of Denbighshire and Merionethshire. The administrative centre is Caernarfon. (3868 sq km/1493 sq miles; pop. 232,000)

H

Haarlem a city in central western NETHERLANDS, 18 km (11 miles) from AMSTERDAM. (Pop. 154,300)

Hachinohe a large fishing port and processing centre on the PACIFIC coast of northern HONSHU Island, JAPAN (Pop. 241,000)

Hadhramaut a 560-km (350-mile) long, and wide, inland valley, running parallel to the Gulf of ADEN in central YEMEN.

Hadrian's Wall a fortified Roman wall across northern ENGLAND, of which substantial parts remain, extending from the SOLWAY FIRTH in the west to Wallsend at the mouth of the River Tyne in the east. It was built in 120-123AD on the orders of Emperor Hadrian as a defence against the tribes of northern Britain. (Length 117 km/ 73 miles)

Hagen a steel town in the industrial RUHR region of western GERMANY. (Pop. 210,000)

Hague, The (Den Haag; 's-Gravenhage) the administrative centre of the NETHERLANDS, on the west coast. (Pop. 449,300)

Haifa the main port of ISRAEL. (Pop. 224,700)

Hä'il an oasis town in north-central SAUDI ARABIA, on the old caravan route from IRAQ to MECCA and MEDINA. (Pop. 45,000)

Hainan Island a large tropical island in the SOUTH CHINA SEA belonging to CHINA, and the southern-most extremity of that country. (33,670 sq km/13,000 sq miles; pop. 5,400,000)

Hainaut (Hainault; Henegouwen) the industrial province of south BELGIUM, along the border with FRANCE, and centred on a former coalfield. The main towns are CHARLEROI, MONS and TOURNAI. (3787 sq km/1462 sq miles; pop. 313,000)

Haiphong a port in the north of VIETNAM, 90 km (55 miles) east of the capital, HANOI. It is Vietnam's third largest city after HO CHI MINH CITY and Hanoi. (Pop. 1,379,000)

Haiti occupies the western third of the large island of HISPANIOLA in the CARIBBEAN. It is a mountainous country, the highest point reaching 2680 m (8793 ft) at La Selle. The mountain ranges are separated by deep valleys and plains. The climate is tropical but semi-arid conditions can occur in the lee of the central mountains. Hurricanes and severe thunderstorms are a common occurrence. Only a third of the country is arable, yet agriculture is the chief occupation. Many farmers grow only enough to feed their own families, and the export crops, coffee, sugar and sisal, are grown on large estates. Severe soil erosion caused by extensive forest clearance has resulted in a decline in crop yields. Haiti is the poorest country in the Americas and has experienced many uprisings and attempted coups, the most recent being in January 1991.

Area : 27,750 sq km (10,714 sq miles)

Population : 5,700,000

Capital : Port-au-Prince

Other major cities : Les Cayes, Gonaïves, Jérémie

Form of government : Republic

Religions : RC, Voodooism

Currency : Gourde

Hajar Mountains a range running parallel to the Gulf of OMAN in northeastern OMAN; they rise to 3018 m (9000 ft) in the Jebel Akhar (Green Mountains)

Hakodate a port at the southern tip of HOKKAIDO Island, JAPAN. (Pop. 319,200)

Halab *see* **Aleppo**.

Halicarnassus *see* **Bodrum**.

Halifax (1) the capital of NOVA SCOTIA, CANADA. (Pop. city 114,595/metropolitan area 278,000) **(2)** a town in West

YORKSHIRE, ENGLAND. (Pop. 88,000)

Halle an industrial town and inland port served by the Saale River in central GERMANY. (Pop. 236,500)

Halmahera *see* **Maluku**.

Halmstad a seaport and industrial city on the KATTEGAT coast of southwestern SWEDEN, 150 km (93 miles) southeast of GOTHENBURG. (Pop. 76,600)

Hälsingborg *see* **Helsingborg**.

Hamadan (Hamedan) an ancient carpet-making and major trading bazaar town in west-central IRAN, 300 km (185 miles) southwest of TEHRAN. (Pop. 234,500)

Hamah an industrial city in eastern SYRIA, on the River ORONTES. (Pop. 514,750)

Hamamatsu a city in southern HONSHU Island, JAPAN. (Pop. 514,100)

Hamar a market town on the west shore of Lake Mjøsa in south-central NORWAY, 100 km (63 miles) north of OSLO (Pop. 27,000)

Hamburg the main port of GERMANY, situated on the River ELBE. (Pop. 1,617,800)

Hamelin (Hameln) a town in northern GERMANY. It is famous for its legendary Pied Piper, who in 1284 is said to have rid the town of a plague of rats by playing his pipe to them and luring them to their deaths in the River WESER. (Pop. 56,300)

Hamersley Range part of the PILBARA RANGE in WESTERN AUSTRALIA. The highest peak is Mount BRUCE (1235 m/ 4052 ft).

Hamhung (Hamheung) a port and industrial city on the east coast of North KOREA. (Pop. 420,000)

Hamilton (1) the capital of BERMUDA. (Pop. 3000) **(2)** a port and industrial city at the western end of Lake ONTARIO, CANADA. (Pop. city 306,430/metropolitan area 542,090). **(3)** a town in the north-western part of NORTH ISLAND, NEW ZEALAND. (Pop. 97,900). **(4)** a town in the STRATH-CLYDE region of SCOTLAND, 17 km (10 miles) southeast of GLASGOW. (Pop. 51,700)

Hammamet a popular beach resort town on the southern coast of the peninsula immediately east of TUNIS, in northern TUNISIA. (Pop. 30,500)

Hammerfest a town in the very north of NORWAY, and one of the world's most northerly settlements. (Pop. 7400)

Hampshire a county of central southern ENGLAND; the county town is WINCHESTER. (3773 sq km/1456 sq miles; pop. 1,500,000)

Hangzhou (Hangchow) a port and industrial city on the east coast of central CHINA, at the head of an estuary called Hangzhou Wan. Hangzhou is at the southern end of the Grand Canal, which links it to BEIJING, 1100 km (690 miles) to the north. (Pop. 1,105,000)

Hankow *see* **Wuhan**.

Hannover *see* **Hanover**.

Hanoi the capital of VIETNAM, in the north of the country. (Pop. 2,570,900)

Hanover (Hannover) a historic city in central northern GERMANY. (Pop. 514,000)

Haora (Howrah) an industrial city in WEST BENGAL, INDIA, on the HUGLI River, facing CALCUTTA. (Pop. 744,400)

Harare the capital of ZIMBABWE; it was formerly called Salisbury (until 1982). (Pop. 656,000)

Harbin the largest city of northern CHINA, situated in central DONGBEI (Manchuria), and capital of HEILONGJIANG province. (Pop. 2,100,000)

Hardangerfjord one of the longest fiords in NORWAY—running 145 km (90 miles) east and southeast of BERGEN; it is the site of several hydroelectric plants and popular tourist resorts.

Hargeysa a market town in northern SOMALIA, about 130 km (80 miles) inland to the southwest of the port of BERBERA. It was the capital of British Somaliland from 1941 to 1960. (Pop. 50,000–80,000)

Haridwar (Hardwar) a holy town of Hinduism on the

GANGES about 165 km (102 miles) northeast of DEHLI; over 2 million Hindu pilgrims come here each year. (Pop. 145,900)

Hari Rud a river which flows westwards from central AFGHANISTAN, through the city of HERAT before turning north to form part of the border with IRAN, ending in TURKMENISTAN. (Length 1125 km/700 miles)

Harlem a district of MANHATTAN, NEW YORK City, USA; it is on the Upper East Side and had its heyday in the jazz era of the 1920s and 1930s.

Harlow a new town in west ESSEX, designated in 1947 with a planned population of 80,000. (Pop. 79,276)

Harris the southern and more mountainous part of the Isle of LEWIS, which is the largest and northernmost of the WESTERN ISLES off SCOTLAND. (500 sq km/193 sq miles; pop. 2879)

Harrisburg the state capital of PENNSYLVANIA, USA. (Pop. city 52,100/metropolitan area 570,200)

Harrogate an attractive town in NORTH YORKSHIRE, 30 km (18 miles) west of YORK, which became one of ENGLAND's most fashionable spas in the 19th century. (Pop. 66,000)

Hartford the state capital of CONNECTICUT, USA. (Pop. city 136,400/metropolitan area 1,030,400)

Hartlepool an industrial town and seaport on the NORTH SEA, in CLEVELAND, northeast ENGLAND; it was greatly enlarged in 1967 by its amalgamation with West Hartlepool. (Pop. 94,359)

Harwich a major NORTH SEA ferry port in northeast ESSEX, southeast ENGLAND. (Pop. 15,076)

Haryana a state in northwest India, formed in 1966. (44,212 sq km/17,066 sq miles; pop. 12,922,600)

Harz Mountains a range of mountains, noted for their forests, old mining towns and tourist resorts, in central GERMANY. The highest peak is the Brocken (1142 m/ 3747 ft).

Hastings (1) a historic port and resort on the south coast of ENGLAND, in the county of East SUSSEX. The Battle of

Hastings of 1066, in which the English were defeated by the Normans, was fought nearby. (Pop. 77,000) **(2)** a town on NORTH ISLAND, NEW ZEALAND, about 250 km (155 miles) northeast of the capital, WELLINGTON; it lies inland from Hawke Bay, at the centre of a fruit-growing and pastoral area. (Pop. 52,600)

Hat Yai a rubber-processing town and popular resort in the far south of THAILAND, about 40 km (25 miles) from the Malaysian border. (Pop. 261,400)

Hatteras, Cape the tip of a chain of islands lining the coast of NORTH CAROLINA, USA, notorious for its violent weather.

Hausaland the northern region of NIGERIA, inhabited by the Hausa peoples, and centred on the SOKOTO River basin in the northwest and the great plateaux to the east. It consists mainly of dry savanna given over to one of the country's main cattle-producing areas. The main towns are KANO, SOKOTO and KADUNA.

Haute Normandie *see* **Normandy.**

Hautes Fagnes *see* **Hohes Venn**.

Havana (La Habana) the capital of CUBA, a port on the northwest coast of the island. It is also the name of the surrounding province. (Pop. 1,925,000)

Hawaii a group of 122 islands just to the south of the Tropic of Cancer, some 3700 km (2300 miles) from the coast of CALIFORNIA. Since 1959 they have formed a state of the USA. The main islands are OAHU, MAUI and Hawaii Island, which at 10,488 sq km (4049 sq miles) is by far the largest. HONOLULU, the state capital, is on Oahu. (16,705 sq km/6450 sq miles; pop. 1,054,000)

Hawke's Bay a rich farming district of NORTH ISLAND, NEW ZEALAND, centred on Hawke Bay on the east coast. (11,289 sq km/4358 sq miles; pop. 148,400)

Heard Island a remote and uninhabited island in the INDIAN OCEAN, about 4000 km (2500 miles) southwest of WESTERN AUSTRALIA's capital, PERTH; at its centre is the active volcano Mawson Peak. (2745 m/9006 ft)

Hebei a province in northern CHINA which surrounds (but does not include) BEIJING. The capital is SHIJIAZHUANG. (180,000 sq km/70,000 sq miles; pop. 51,046,400)

Hebrides some 500 islands lying off the west coast of SCOTLAND, consisting of the Inner Hebrides to the southeast, whose main islands are TIREE, JURA, COLL, MULL, EIGG and SKYE, and the Outer Hebrides to the northwest, whose islands include LEWIS and HARRIS, the UISTS, BENBECULA and BARRA.

Hebron an ancient biblical town on the WEST BANK, lying 35 km (21 miles) southwest of JERUSALEM. It is the traditional burial place of Abraham—the father of the Hebrew people. (Pop. 38,000)

Hefei an industrial city in central eastern CHINA, capital of ANHUI province. (Pop. 1,484,000)

Heidelberg a university town in southwest GERMANY on the NECKAR RIVER. (Pop. 130,000)

Heilongjiang a province of DONGBEI (Manchuria) in northern CHINA; the capital is HARBIN. (464,000 sq km/179,000 sq miles; pop. 32,700,000)

Heilong Jiang, River *see* **Amur, River.**

Hejaz (Hijaz) a mountainous region which lines the RED SEA, formerly an independent kingdom but since 1932 a part of SAUDI ARABIA.

Hekla an active volcano in the south of ICELAND, about 112 km (75 miles) east of REYKJAVIK. Its crater is 5 km (3 miles) wide, and the rim reaches a height of 1491 m (4892 ft). It last erupted in 1970.

Helena the state capital of MONTANA, USA. (Pop. 24,600)

Heligoland (Helgoland) a small island and former naval base in the NORTH SEA off the coast of GERMANY. (2.1 sq km/0.5 sq miles; pop. 2000)

Hellespont *see* **Dardanelles.**

Helsingborg the main Swedish ferry port to DENMARK, at the narrowest part of the ØRESUND, opposite the Danish town of HELSINGØR (ELSINORE). (Pop. 105,500)

Helsingfors *see* **Helsinki.**

Helsingør *see* **Elsinore**.

Helsinki (Helsingfors) the capital and chief industrial centre and port of FINLAND. (Pop. 482,900)

Henan a province of central CHINA; the capital is ZHENGZHOU. (160,000 sq km/62,000 sq miles; pop. 71,890,000)

Henzada an important rice-trading centre on the IRRAWADDY delta in the south of BURMA, 125 km (78 miles) northwest of YANGON (RANGOON).

Heraklion (Iraklion) the capital and main port of the island of CRETE. (Pop. 111,000)

Herat a city in western AFGHANISTAN on the HARI RUD River. (Pop. 150,500)

Hercegovina *see* **Bosnia-Herzegovina**.

Herculaneum (Ercolano) an excavated Graeco-Roman town on the Bay of NAPLES, which was buried by the eruption of the volcano, Mount VESUVIUS, along with POMPEII, in AD79.

Hereford and Worcester a county in the west of ENGLAND, on the border with WALES, which was created in 1974 when the old counties of Herefordshire and Worcestershire were combined. The county town is Worcester. (3927 sq km/1516 sq miles; pop. 648,000)

Herefordshire *see* **Hereford and Worcester.**

Hermon, Mount a mountain in southern LEBANON near the borders with SYRIA and ISRAEL. It is the source of the River JORDAN. (2814 m/9332 ft)

Hertfordshire a county in southeast ENGLAND, to the north of LONDON. The county town is Hertford. (1634 sq km/631 sq miles; pop. 980,000)

Herzegovina *see* **Bosnia-Herzegovina**.

Hessen (Hesse) a state in central western GERMANY. The capital is WIESBADEN. (21,112 sq km/8151 sq miles; pop. 5,500,000)

Highland Region an administrative region in northern SCOTLAND comprising the most northerly part of the mainland and many of the Inner HEBRIDES. It is the largest county in the UK. It was created in 1975 out of the old counties of Caithness, Nairnshire, Sutherland, most of Inverness-shire, Ross and Cromarty and parts of Argyll and Morayshire. The capital is INVERNESS. (26,136 sq km/10,091 sq miles; pop. 196,000)

Highlands the rugged region of northern SCOTLAND, which includes the GRAMPIAN mountains and the NORTH WEST HIGHLANDS.

Hildesheim a cathedral town in north-central GERMANY, 30 km (19 miles) south and slightly east of HANOVER. (Pop. 101,000)

Hilversum a garden-city satellite town for AMSTERDAM, 25 km (15 miles) to the southeast; it is also headquarters for the Dutch broadcasting service.

Himachal Pradesh a state in northern INDIA, in mountainous country bordering TIBET. (55,673 sq km/21,490 sq miles; pop. 4,280,000)

Himalayas the massive mountain range stretching some 2400 km (1500 miles) in a broad sweep from the northern tip of INDIA, across NEPAL, BHUTAN and southern TIBET to ASSAM in north-eastern India. The average height of the mountains is some 6100 m (20,000 ft), rising to the world's tallest peak, Mount EVEREST (8848 m/29,028 ft).

Himeji an industrial city and port in southern HONSHU Island, JAPAN. (Pop. 452,900)

Hims *see* **Homs**.

Hindu Kush a range of mountains which stretches some 600 km (370 miles) at the western end of the HIMALAYAS, straddling the web of borders where AFGHANISTAN, TAJIKISTAN, CHINA, INDIA and PAKISTAN meet. The highest peak is Tirich Mir (7690 m/25,229 ft) in Pakistan.

Hindustan (Hindoostan) a general term for the land of the Hindus, and especially INDIA north of the DECCAN, but excluding BENGAL.

Hiroshima an industrial city in southwestern HONSHU Island, JAPAN. Three quarters of the city was destroyed on August 6, 1945 when the world's first atomic bomb was dropped here, killing 78,000 people. (Pop. 899,400)

Hispaniola the name of the large CARIBBEAN island that is shared by HAITI and the DOMINICAN REPUBLIC. (76,200 sq km/29,400 sq miles)

Hitachi an industrial city on the east coast of HONSHU Island, JAPAN. (Pop. 206,100)

Hobart a port and capital of the island of TASMANIA, AUSTRALIA, on the southeast coast. (Pop. 173,700)

Ho Chi Minh City (Saigon) the largest city in VIETNAM, and the capital of former independent South Vietnam. (Pop. 3,500,000)

Hodeida (Al Hudaydah) the main industrial and commercial port of YEMEN after ADEN; it is situated 144 km (87 miles) southwest of SAN'A (Pop.128,000)

Hofuf (al Hufuf) the world's largest oasis, situated 112 km (70 miles) southwest of DHAHRAN, SAUDI ARABIA; it is an important trading and communications centre. (Pop. 102,000)

Hoggar (Ahaggar) a remote mountain range rising from the desert landscape of southern ALGERIA, and noted for the weathered shapes of its rock formations. The highest peak is Mount Tahat (2918 m/9573 ft).

Hohes Venn (Hautes Fagnes) a forested upland region in the easternmost part of BELGIUM, on the border with GERMANY and about 20 km (13 miles) south and slightly east of AACHEN. It is largely a nature reserve, with Botrange (at 694 m/2277 ft) as the country's highest point.

Hohe Tauern a part of eastern ALPS in southern AUSTRIA, rising to the highest point at Grossglockner (3797 m/12,460 ft), Austria's highest peak.

Hohhot an industrial city and the capital of the NEI MONGOL AUTONOMOUS REGION (Inner Mongolia), CHINA. (Pop. 1,130,000)

Hokkaido the most northerly of the main islands of JAPAN, and the second largest after HONSHU. The capital is SAPPORO. (78,509 sq km/30,312 sq miles; pop. 5,679,400)

Holguin an administrative and manufacturing centre in

the fertile region at the southeast end of CUBA. (Pop. 186,000)

Holland a name generally applied to the NETHERLANDS, but in fact the term really applies to the central coastal region which comprise the two provinces of Noord Holland and Zuid Holland.

Hollywood a suburb in the northern part of LOS ANGELES in CALIFORNIA, USA. It has long served as the base for the USA's powerful film industry.

Holyhead a ferry port on the west coast of ANGLESEY, northwest WALES, that makes for the most direct route between BRITAIN and the Republic of IRELAND. (Pop. 10,467)

Holy Island a small island off the northeastern coast of NORTHUMBRIA, ENGLAND; it is linked to the mainland by a tidal causeway. It is the site of a monastery founded by St Aidan in AD635.

Holy Land a general term referring to that area in the MIDDLE EAST that corresponds roughly to biblical PALESTINE and modern-day ISRAEL.

Homs (Hims) an industrial city of ancient origins on the River ORONTES in SYRIA. (Pop. 414,401)

Honduras is a fan-shaped country in Central AMERICA, which spreads out towards the CARIBBEAN SEA at the Gulf of HONDURAS. Four-fifths of the country is covered in mountains, which are indented with river valleys running towards the very short PACIFIC coast. There is little change in temperatures throughout the year, and rainfall is heavy, especially on the Caribbean coast where temperatures are also higher than inland. The country is sparsely populated, and, although agricultural, only about 25% of the land is cultivated. Honduras was once the world's leading banana exporter, but its main export agriculture is now more diverse. Grains, coffee and sugar are important crops, and these are grown mainly on the coastal plains of the Pacific and Caribbean. The forests are not effectively exploited, and industry is small-scale. *Area* : 112,088 sq km (43,277 sq miles)

Hong Kong

Population : 4,440,000
Capital : Tegucigalpa
Form of government : Republic
Religion : RC
Currency : Lempira

Hong Kong is a British Dependent Territory located in the SOUTH CHINA SEA and consists of Hong Kong Island (once a barren rock), the peninsula of KOWLOON and about 1000 sq km (386 sq miles) of adjacent land known as the New Territories. Hong Kong is situated at the mouth of the Pearl River, about 130 km (81 miles) southeast of GUANGZHOU (Canton). The climate is warm subtropical with cool dry winters and hot humid summers. Hong Kong has no natural resources, even its water comes from reservoirs across the Chinese border. Its main assets are its magnificent natural harbour and its position close to the main trading routes of the PACIFIC. Hong Kong's economy is based on free enterprise and trade, an industrious work force, and an efficient and aggressive commercial system. Hong Kong's main industry is textiles and clothing, which accounts for 38% of its domestic exports.

Area : 1045 sq km (403 sq miles)
Population : 5,760,000
Form of government : Colony under British administration until 1997 when China will take over.
Religions : Buddhism, Taoism, Christianity
Currency : Hong Kong dollar

Honiara the capital of the SOLOMON ISLANDS, situated on GUADALCANAL. (Pop. 23,500)

Honolulu the state capital of HAWAII, USA, on the south coast of the island of OAHU. (Pop. city 373,000/ metropolitan area 805,300)

Honshu the central and largest of the islands of JAPAN, which contains most of the country's large cities. (230,988 sq km/89,185 sq miles; pop. 96,685,000)

Hooghly, River *see* **Hugli, River.**

Hook of Holland (Hoek van Holland) the coastal port of ROTTERDAM, NETHERLANDS, at the mouth of the Nieuw Waterweg (New Waterway), about 25 km (15 miles) west of the city centre. It is the terminus for NORTH SEA ferries and boat-trains.

Hoorn a former ZUIDER ZEE seaport, now a town on the west side of the IJSSELMEER about 30 km (20 miles) northeast of AMSTERDAM. The 17th-century town centre remains largely intact and is a popular place for visitors. (Pop. 26,000)

Hormuz (Ormuz), Strait of the narrow strait at the mouth of The GULF between the horn-like protrusion of the MUSANDAM peninsula of OMAN to the south, and IRAN to the north.

Horn, Cape (Cabo de Hornos) The southern tip of South AMERICA, represented by a spattering of remote islands belonging to CHILE off TIERRA DEL FUEGO.

Houston the largest city in TEXAS, USA. (Pop. city 1,705,700/metropolitan area 3,164,400)

Howrah *see* **Haora**.

Hrvatska *see* **Croatia**.

Hua-lien the largest port and industrial town on the PACIFIC east coast of TAIWAN. (Pop. 359,000)

Huambo a railway town and provincial capital lying 520 km (320 miles) southeast of LUANDA, ANGOLA; it was formerly known as Nova Lisboa. (Pop. 61,900)

Huang He (Hwang Ho; Yellow River) the second longest river in CHINA after the CHANG JIANG (Yangtze), flowing from the QINGHAI mountains across northern central China to the YELLOW SEA, south of BEIJING. (Length 5464 km/3395 miles)

Huascaran a peak in the ANDES in central PERU, and that country's highest mountain. (6768 m/22,205 ft)

Hubei a landlocked province of central CHINA. (180,000 sq km/69,500 sq miles; pop. 46,320,000)

Huddersfield a wool-textile town in WEST YORKSHIRE, 24 km (15 miles) southwest of LEEDS (Pop. 124,000)

Hudson Bay a huge bay in northeastern CANADA, hemmed in to the north by BAFFIN ISLAND, and connected to the ATLANTIC OCEAN by the Hudson Strait.

Hudson River a river flowing from its source in the ADIRONDACK MOUNTAINS in NEW YORK State, USA, to the ATLANTIC OCEAN at New York City. The ERIE Canal joins the Hudson River to link New York to the GREAT LAKES. (Length 492 km/306 miles)

Hué the capital and powerbase of the rulers of VIETNAM from 200BC to the 19th century, located in the central coastal region of the country. (Pop. 190,100)

Huelva an ore-exporting port and fishing centre about 95 km (60 miles) northwest of CÁDIZ on the south ATLANTIC coast of SPAIN. (Pop. 127,800)

Hugli (Hoogly) a major branch of the River GANGES which forms at its delta and flows through CALCUTTA and the surrounding industrial conurbations into the Bay of BENGAL. (Length 193 km/120 miles)

Hull *see* **Kingston upon Hull**.

Humber the estuary of the Rivers OUSE and TRENT which cuts deep into the east coast of ENGLAND to the north of the WASH. (Length 60 km/35 miles)

Humberside a county on the northeast coast of ENGLAND, centring upon the HUMBER estuary. It was created in 1974 out of parts of the East and West Ridings of YORKSHIRE and LINCOLNSHIRE. The county town is Beverley. (3512 sq km/1356 sq miles; pop. 854,000)

Hunan an inland province of southeast CHINA. The capital is CHANGSHA. (210,000 sq km/81,000 sq miles; pop. 52,320,000)

Hungary landlocked in the heartland of EUROPE, Hungary is dominated by the great plain to the east of the River DANUBE, which runs north-south across the country. In the west lies the largest lake in Central Europe, Lake BALATON. Winters are severe, but the summers are warm and, although wet in the west, summer droughts often occur in the east. Hungary experienced a modest boom in its economy in the 1970s and 1980s. The government invested money in improving agriculture by mechanizing farms, using fertilizers and bringing new land under cultivation. Yields of cereals for breadmaking and rice have since soared, and large areas between the Danube and Tisza Rivers are now used to grow vegetables. Industries have been carefully developed where adequate natural resources exist. New industries, like the manufacturing of electrical and electronic equipment, are now being promoted, and tourism is fast developing around Lake Balaton.

Area : 93,032 sq km (35,920 sq miles)

Population : 10,590,000

Capital : Budapest

Other major cities : Debrecen, Miskolc, Pécs, Szeged

Form of government : Republic

Religions : RC, Calvinism, Lutheranism

Currency : Forint

Hungnam a fishing port and industrial centre on the east coast of North Korea, about 200 km (125 miles) northeast of Pyongyang. (Pop. 260,000)

Hunter Valley the valley of the Hunter River, lying 100 km (60 miles) north-west of Sydney, Australia. It is particularly noted for its wine.

Huntingdonshire *see* **Cambridgeshire**.

Huntsville an old agricultural town with textile industries in northern Alabama, about 30 km (20 miles) from the Tenessee border. It also has space-rocket manufacturing plants. (Pop. city 149,500/metropolitan area 210,000)

Huron, Lake one of the Great Lakes, lying at the centre of the group on the border between Canada and the state of Michigan in the USA. (59,570 sq km/23,000 sq miles)

Hwange (Wankie) a coal-mining town near Zimbabwe's extreme western tip, over 500 sq km (310 miles) west and slightly south of Harare. (Pop. 39,000)

Hwang Ho *see* **Huang He.**

Hyderabad (1) the capital of the state of ANDHRA PRADESH in eastern south INDIA. (Pop. 2,093,500). **(2)** a city on the INDUS delta 160 km (100 miles) northeast of KARACHI, PAKISTAN. (Pop. 795,000)

Hydra (Idhra) a small island in the AEGEAN SEA, off the east coast of the PELOPONNESE, GREECE, noted as a haven for tourists where motor traffic is prohibited.

I

Iasi a historic city in northeastern ROMANIA, near the border with MOLDOVA. (Pop. 271,400)

Ibadan the second largest city in NIGERIA, some 120 km (75 miles) north of LAGOS. It is a busy market town, and noted for its university. (Pop. 1,009,000)

Ibagué a major market town in the centre of a cattle-rearing and coffee-growing region of west-central COLOMBIA, about 140km (85 miles) west of BOGOTÁ. It is famed as the musical capital of Colombia, with renowned orchestras, choirs, and annual folk festivals. (Pop. 361,000)

Ibarra a market and tourist centre in north-central EQUADOR on the PAN AMERICAN HIGHWAY, 90km (55 miles) northeast of QUITO (Pop. 59,000)

Ibb a small inland town in southwest YEMEN, 150 km (94 miles) south of SAN'A; it is the chief town of the "Green Valley", an area noted for its superb scenery of contrasting mountains and valleys. (Pop. 19,700)

Iberia (Iberian Peninsula) the major square-shaped penisula of southwest EUROPE, occupied by SPAIN and PORTUGAL.

Ibiza (Iviza) *see* **Balearic Islands.**

Iboland a densely populated region of southeastern NIGERIA inhabited by the Ibo people. The attempt by the region to break away from Nigeria (1967-70) under the name of Biafra caused a civil war that led to a famine which killed over a million people. (Pop. 10,000,000)

Ica, River *see* **Putumayo, River**.

Icarian Sea the part of the AEGEAN SEA between the islands of Patmos and Leros, and the coast of ASIA MINOR, where, according to legend, Icarus fell into the sea.

Içel *see* **Mersin**.

Iceland is a large island situated in a tectonically unstable part of the North ATLANTIC OCEAN, just south of the ARCTIC CIRCLE. The island has over 100 volcanoes, at least one of which erupts every five years. One-ninth of the country is covered with ice and snowfields, and there are about seven hundred hot springs, which are an important source of central heating. The climate is cool temperate, but because of the effect of the North Atlantic Drift it is mild for its latitude. The southwest corner is the most densely populated area as the coast here is generally free from ice. Only 1% of the land is cultivated, mostly for fodder and root crops to feed sheep and cattle. The island's economy is based on its sea-fishing industry, which accounts for 70% of exports. Wool sweaters and sheepskin coats are also exported.

Area : 103,000 sq km (39,768 sq miles)

Population : 253,500

Capital : Reykjavík

Form of government : Republic

Religion : Lutheranism

Currency : Icelandic króna

Idaho a inland state in the northwest of the USA. The state capital is BOISE. (216,413 sq km/83,557 sq miles; pop. 1,005,000)

Idfu a trading centre on the NILE, 123 km (76 miles) north of ASWAN. It was an important city of ancient UPPER EGYPT and has one of the best-preserved antiquities in a 250BC temple to the falcon-headed god Horus. (Pop. 27,000)

Idhra *see* **Hydra**.

Idi Amin Dada, Lake *see* **Edward (Rutanzige), Lake**.

Idlib a large commercial and agricultural centre in northwestern SYRIA. (Pop. 428,000)

Ieper *see* **Ypres.**

Ife a major cultural and religious centre in southwestern NIGERIA, 170 km (105 miles) northeast of LAGOS. It is probably the oldest town of the Yoruba people, having its origins in the 7th century AD. (Pop. 209.100)

Ifni a former Spanish provincial enclave on the ATLANTIC coast of southern MOROCCO, which was returned to the latter in 1969. The local population is mainly Berber, many living in the old colonial capital, Sidi Ifni. (Pop. town 16,300)

Iguaçu Falls a spectacular waterfall on the border between BRAZIL and the extreme northeast of ARGENTIA, and 19 km (12 miles) from PARAQUAY on the Iguaçu River, which divides into hundreds of falls separated by forested rocky islands. (Width 4 km/2.5 miles; height 82 m/269 ft)

Ijebu Ode a market town in southwest NIGERIA, lying 75 km (47 miles) northeast of LAGOS. It handles the many tropical products grown in this fertile region of YORUBALAND. (Pop. 110,300)

IJsselmeer formerly a large inlet of the NORTH SEA known as the Zuiderzee on the northeastern coast of the NETHERLANDS, but after the creation of the dam called the Afsluitdijk across its mouth, it has filled with water from the River IJssel and is now a freshwater lake, bordered by fertile areas of reclaimed land (polders).

Ilebo an important transportation centre, formerly called Port Francqui, in central ZAÏRE, 580 km (360 miles) due east of KINSHASA. Lying on the KASAI River, it is the terminus of the railway from the mineral-rich SHABA region, the products of which are then transported downstream by river to Kinshasa. (Pop. 40,000)

Ile de France a region and former province of FRANCE with PARIS at its centre, now consisting of eight separate departments. (12,012 sq km/4638 sq miles; pop. 10,073,000)

Illinois a state in the MIDWEST of the USA, bordering Lake MICHIGAN to the north. The capital is SPRINGFIELD, but CHICAGO is its main city. (146,075 sq km/56,400 sq miles; pop. 11,535,000)

Iloili the regional centre and main port of the western VISAYAN ISLANDS of the PHILIPPINES, situated on the southwest coast of Panay. (Pop. city 244,800/province 1,300,000)

Ilorin the capital of Kwara state in west-central NIGERIA, 260 km (160 miles) northeast of LAGOS. It is a meeting place of Hausa, Fulani, Yoruba and European cultures. (Pop. 335,400)

Imjin River a river which flows from its source in southern North KOREA across the border into SOUTH KOREA and to the YELLOW SEA. In 1951, during the Korean War, it was the scene of a heroic stand by the British 1st Gloster Regiment. (Length 160 km/100 miles)

Impfondo an important trading and transport centre for the forested region of northern CONGO; formerly Desbordesville, it is a landing point for boat passengers on the UBANGI River. (Pop. 30,000)

Imphal a city and capital of MANIPUR state, in the far east of INDIA. Formerly the seat of the Manipur Kings, it was the site of a major Anglo-Indian victory over the Japanese in 1944, which was a turning point in the British recovery of BURMA. (Pop. 156,600)

Inagua *see* **Bahamas.**

Inch'on (Incheon) a port and industrial city on the western (YELLOW SEA) coast of South KOREA, 39 km (24 miles) west of SEOUL. (Pop. 1,083,900)

India is a vast country in South ASIA, which is dominated in the extreme north by the world's youngest and highest mountains, the HIMALAYAS. At the foot of the Himalayas, a huge plain, drained by the INDUS and GANGES rivers, is one of the most fertile areas in the world and the most densely populated part of India. Further south, the ancient DECCAN plateau extends to the southern tip of the country. India generally has four seasons, the cool, the hot, the rainy, and the dry. Rainfall varies from 100 mm (3.94 inches) in the northwest desert to 10,000 mm (394 inches) in ASSAM. About 70% of the population depend on agriculture for their living, and the lower slopes of the Himalayas represent one of the world's best tea-growing areas. Rice, sugar cane and wheat are grown in the

Ganges plain. An increase in the production of food is needed to support the rapidly growing population.

Area : 3,287,590 sq km (1,269,338 sq miles)

Population : 843,930,000

Capital : New Delhi

Other major cities : Bangalore, Bombay, Calcutta, Delhi, Hyderabad, Madras

Form of government : Federal Republic

Religions : Hinduism, Sunni Islam, Christianity

Currency : Rupee

Indiana a state in the MIDWEST of the USA to the southeast of Lake MICHIGAN. The state capital is INDIANAPOLIS. (93,994 sq km/36,291 sq miles; pop. 5,499,000)

Indianapolis the state capital of INDIANA and venue of the famous annual *Indianapolis 500* car race. (Pop. city 710,300/metropolitan area 1,194,600)

Indian Desert *see* **Thar Desert.**

Indian Ocean the third largest ocean, bounded by ASIA to the north, AFRICA to the west and AUSTRALIA to the east. The southern waters merge with the ANTARCTIC OCEAN. (73,481,000 sq km/28,364,000 sq miles)

Indian Subcontinent a regional term that refers to the whole of the Indian peninsula as being a distinct part of the Asian landmass; as such, it generally includes INDIA, PAKISTAN, NEPAL, BHUTAN, BANGLADESH and the outlier of SRI LANKA.

Indo-Gangetic Plain a term used to describe the vast combined lowland area of the INDUS and GANGES river basins, that sweeps in a broad cresent across eastern PAKISTAN, northern INDIA and BANGLADESH, with an almost imperceptible watershed, in the PUNJAB. It is one of the world's most fertile areas.

Indonesia is made up of 13,667 islands that are scattered across the INDIAN and PACIFIC OCEANS in a huge crescent. Its largest landmass is the province of KALIMANTAN, which is part of the island of BORNEO. SUMATRA is the largest individual island. JAVA, however, is the dominant and most densely populated island. The climate is generally tropical monsoon, and temperatures are high all year round. The country has one hundred volcanoes, and earthquakes are frequent in the southern islands. Overpopulation is a big problem, especially in Java where its fertile rust-coloured soil is in danger of becoming exhausted. Rice, maize and cassava are the main crops grown. Indonesia has the largest reserves of tin in the world and is one of the world's leading rubber producers. Indonesia's resources are not as yet fully developed, but there is great potential for economic development.

Area : 1,904,569 sq km (735,354 sq miles)

Population : 179,100,000

Capital : Jakarta

Other major cities : Badung, Medan, Semarang, Surabaya

Form of government : Republic

Religions : Sunni Islam, Christianity, Hinduism

Currency : Rupiah

Indore a textile-manufacturing city, and once the capital of the princely state of Indore, in western MADHYA PRADESH, central INDIA. (Pop. 829,300)

Indus, River one of the great rivers of ASIA, whose valleys supported some of the world's earliest civilizations, notably at MOHENJO DARO. It flows from its source in TIBET and across the northern tip of INDIA before turning south to run through the entire length of PAKISTAN to its estuary on the ARABIAN SEA, south of KARACHI. (Length 3180 km/1975 miles)

Inhambane a seaport on the site of an ancient Arab settlement on the INDIAN OCEAN coast of southern MOZAMBIQUE; it is the capital of the large province of the same name. (Pop. town 27,000/province 1,037,500)

Inland Sea (Seto Naikai) the almost enclosed area of sea between the islands of HONSHU, SHIKOKU and KYUSHU in JAPAN. It extends for almost 500 km (310 miles) and contains hundreds of islands and islets.

Inner Hebrides *see* **Hebrides**.

Inner Mongolia *see* **Nei Mongol Autonomous Region.**

Innsbruck a tourist resort, manufacturing town and capital of the TYROL in west-central AUSTRIA, lying on the Inn River 140 km (87 miles) southwest of SALZBURG (Pop. 116110)

In Salah (Ain Salah) a Saharan junction post on the "Route du HOGGAR", in the centre of ALGERIA. (Pop. 9300)

Inuvik a fur-trading, transport and administrative centre on the eastern side of the MACKENZIE River delta in the NORTHWEST TERRITORIES of CANADA. It was inaugurated as a model Inuit (Eskimo) community in 1954. (Pop. 3145)

Invercargill a sheep and dairy farming centre on the FOVEAUX STRAIT in the extreme south of SOUTH ISLAND, NEW ZEALAND. (Pop. 54,000)

Inverness a town in northeastern SCOTLAND at the head of the MORAY FIRTH and at the eastern end of Loch NESS. (Pop. 40,000)

Ioannina *see* **Yannina**.

Iona a small island off the southwestern tip of MULL in western SCOTLAND where the Irish monk St Columba founded a monastery in AD563. (8 sq km/3 sq miles)

Ionian Islands (Eptanisos) the seven largest of the islands which lie scattered along the west coast of GREECE in the IONIAN SEA. They are CORFU, Paxoí, Cephalonia, Levkás, ITHACA, Zákinthos and Kíthira. (Pop. 182,700)

Ionian Sea that part of the MEDITERRANEAN SEA which lies between southern ITALY and GREECE. It is named after Io, a mistress of the Ancient Greek god Zeus.

Ios (Nios) *see* **Cyclades.**

Iowa a state in the MIDWEST of the USA bounded on the east and west by the upper reaches of the MISSISSIPPI and MISSOURI rivers. The capital is DES MOINES. (145,791 sq km/56,290 sq miles; pop. 2,884,000)

Ipiros *see* **Epirus**.

Ipswich an important NORTH SEA port, and county town of

SUFFOLK in eastern ENGLAND, 110 km (68 miles) northeast of LONDON. (Pop. 120,000)

Iquique the most important fishing port of CHILE, lying on the PACIFIC coast of the far northern province of Tarapacá, of which it is the capital city. (Pop. 113,000)

Iquitos a cultural, religious and tourist centre in the interior of eastern PERU, lying on the far western upper reaches of the AMAZON. (Pop. 178,000)

Iráklion *see* **Heraklion**.

Iran lies across The GULF from the Arabian peninsula and stretches from the CASPIAN SEA to the ARABIAN SEA. It is a land dominated by mountains in the north and west, with a huge expanse of desert in its centre. The climate is mainly hot and dry, although more temperate conditions are found on the shores of the Caspian Sea. In winter, terrible dust storms sweep the deserts and almost no life can survive. Most of the population live in the north and west, where TEHRAN is situated. The only good agricultural land is on the Caspian coastal plains, and here rice is grown. About 5% of the population are nomadic herdsmen who wander in the mountains. Most of Iran's oil is in the southwest, and other valuable minerals include coal, iron ore, copper and lead. Precious stones are found in the northeast. The main exports are petrochemicals, carpets and rugs, textiles, raw cotton and leather goods.

Area : 1,648,000 sq km (636,293,sq miles)

Population : 53,920,000

Capital : Tehran

Other major cities : Esfahan, Mashhad, Tabriz

Form of government : Islamic Republic

Religion : Shia Islam

Currency : Rial

Iranian Plateau the high desert plateau that covers most of east central IRAN at between 1500–3000 m (4920–9840 ft). It includes the Dasht-e Kavir (Salt Desert) and the Dasht-e Lut (Barren Desert).

Irapuato an expanding market town in the central state of Guanajuato, MEXICO. Heavy industries are being developed under the federal government's decentralization plans. (Pop. 300,000)

Iraq is located in southwest ASIA, wedged between The GULF and SYRIA. It is almost landlocked except for its outlet to The Gulf at SHATT AL ARAB. Its two great rivers, the TIGRIS and the EUPHRATES, flow from the northwest into The Gulf at this point. The climate is arid with very hot summers and cold winters. The high mountains on the border with TURKEY are snow covered for six months of the year, and desert in the southwest covers nearly half the country. The only fertile land in Iraq is in the basins of the Tigris and Euphrates, where wheat, barley, rice, tobacco and cotton are grown. The world's largest production of dates also comes from this area. Iraq profited from the great oil boom of the 1970s, but during the war with Iran, oil terminals in The Gulf were destroyed and the Trans-Syrian Pipeline closed. Iraq is now wholly reliant on the pipeline from KIRKUK to the MEDITERRANEAN.

Area : 438,317 sq km (169,234 sq miles)
Population : 17,060,000
Capital : Baghdad
Other major cities : Al-Basrah, Al Mawsil
Form of government : Republic
Religion : Shia Islam, Sunni Islam
Currency : Iraqi dinar

Irbid an ancient city and grain-trading centre in the north of JORDAN, 70 km (43 miles) from AMMAN, and set 529 m (1735 ft) above sea level. (Pop. 150,000)

Ireland an island off the west coast of GREAT BRITAIN, almost four-fifths of which is the independent Republic of IRELAND, while the remainder is NORTHERN IRELAND, which is a province of the UK. (80,400 sq km/32,588 sq miles, pop. 5,202,000)

Ireland, Republic of is one of Europe's most westerly countries, situated in the ATLANTIC OCEAN and separated from GREAT BRITAIN by the IRISH SEA. It has an equable climate, with mild southwest winds, which makes temperatures uniform over most of the country. The Republic extends over four-fifths of the island of Ireland, and the west and southwest are mountainous, with the highest peak reaching 1041 m (3416 ft) at Carrauntoohil. The central plain is largely limestone covered in boulder clay which provides good farmland and pasture. Despite the fertile land, the Republic of Ireland remains one of the poorest countries in western Europe. The rural population tend to migrate to the cities, mainly DUBLIN, which is the main industrial centre and the focus of radio, television, publishing and communications. Lack of energy resources and remoteness from major markets has slowed industrial development.

Area : 70,284 sq km (27,137 sq miles)

Population : 3,540,000

Capital : Dublin (Baile Atha Cliath)

Other major cities : Cork, Galway, Limerick, Waterford

Form of government : Republic

Religion : RC

Currency : Punt = 100 pighne

Irian Jaya the western half of the island of NEW GUINEA, which has been part of INDONESIA since 1963. (410,660 sq km/158,556 sq miles; pop. 2,584,000)

Iringa a regional capital and maize-growing market centre in east-central TANZANIA, 420 km (260 miles) southwest of DAR ES SALAAM. (Pop. 57,182)

Irish Sea the arm of the ATLANTIC that separates the islands of IRELAND and GREAT BRITAIN.

Irkutsk an industrial city on the Trans-Siberian Railway lying near the southern end of Lake BAIKAL in the RUSSIAN FEDERATION. (Pop. 590,000)

Ironbridge (Coalbrookdale) a historic town in a gorge of the River SEVERN in central SHROPSHIRE, some 40 km (25 miles) northwest of BIRMINGHAM; it is widely regarded as an important early cradle, if not birthplace, of the Industrial Revolution. It is conserved as a World Heritage Site.

Irrawaddy, River the central focus of BURMA (Myanmar), flowing from its two primary sources in the north of the country to MANDALAY and then south to its delta in the Bay of BENGAL. (Length 2150 km/1335 miles)

Irtysh, River a largely navigable river flowing northwards from its source near the border between northwest CHINA and MONGOLIA across the centre of KAZAKHSTAN and through OMSK to join the River OB' on its journey to the ARCTIC OCEAN. (Length 4440 km/2760 miles)

Irún a Basque industrial town on the Spanish side of the border with FRANCE adjoining the BAY OF BISCAY. (Pop. 53,500)

Irvine a new town on the Firth of CLYDE, in west-central SCOTLAND; it was designated in 1966. (Pop. 32,852)

Ischia a beautiful volcanic island at the northern end of the Bay of NAPLES. (46 sq km/18 sq miles; pop. 43,900)

Iseyin a textile town on the northwestern edge of YORUBALAND, about 175 km (110 miles) north of LAGOS. (Pop. 153,100)

Isfahan *see* **Esfahan**.

Ishinomaki a fishing port on the northeastern coast of HONSHU Island; it is a base for JAPAN's deep-sea fishing fleet. (Pop. 122,700)

Iskenderun a port of ancient origin in southern TURKEY, in the northeastern corner of the MEDITERRANEAN SEA. (Pop. 173,600)

Isla(s) for features whose names begin "Isla" or "Islas", see main part of name.

Islamabad the capital of PAKISTAN since 1967, in the north of the country. (Pop. 201,000)

Islands, Bay of a small inlet on the northeast coast of NORTH ISLAND, NEW ZEALAND. It was here that the first major contacts between Maoris and Europeans took place, including the signing of the Treaty of Waitangi in 1840, and the subsequent wars, until an uneasy peace was established in 1847.

Islay the southernmost and third largest of the Inner HEBRIDES, off the west coast of SCOTLAND. It is renowned for its distilling of malt whisky. (606 sq km. 234 sq miles; pop. 3792)

Isles(s) for features whose names begin "Isle" or "Isles", see main part of name.

Ismâ'ilîya a town orginally set up in 1863 as a construction camp for the SUEZ CANAL at its midpoint; it has become established again after being devastated by Israeli troops in the October War of 1973. (Pop. 146,000)

Israel occupies a long narrow stretch of land in the southeast of the MEDITERRANEAN. Its eastern boundary is formed by the GREAT RIFT VALLEY, through which the River JORDAN flows to the DEAD SEA. The south of the country is made up of a triangular wedge of the NEGEV Desert which ends at the Gulf of AQABA. The climate in summer is hot and dry, in winter it is mild with some rain. The south of the country is arid and barren. Most of the population live on the coastal plain bordering the Mediterranean, where TEL AVIV-JAFFA is the main commercial city. Israel's agriculture is based on collective settlements known as *Kibbutz*. It is virtually self-sufficient in foodstuffs and a major exporter of its produce. Jaffa oranges are famous throughout EUROPE. A wide range of products is processed or finished in the country, and main exports include finished diamonds, textiles, fruit, vegetables, chemicals, machinery and fertilizers.

Area : 20,770 sq km (8019 sq miles)

Population : 4,820,000

Capital : Jerusalem (Yerushalayim)

Other major cities : Tel Aviv-Jaffa, Haifa

Form of government : Republic

Religion : Judaism, Sunni Islam, Christianity

Currency : Shekel

Issyk-Kul' a lake in southern central KAZAKHSTAN, set in the high mountains that line the border with CHINA. (6280 sq km/2424 sq miles)

Istanbul the largest city in Turkey, built mainly on the western bank of the Bosphorous, with a commanding view of shipping entering the Black Sea. It was founded by the Greeks in 660BC and was known as Byzantium; between AD330 and 1930 it was called Constantinople. (Pop. 5,858,600)

Istra (Istria) an arrowhead-shaped peninsula on the north Adriatic coast of Croatia, stretching 97 km (60 miles) south from Trieste, Italy, on the west of its isthmus. Most of the peninsula was ceded by Italy to the former Yugoslavia in 1946.

Italy is a republic in southern Europe, which comprises a large peninsula and the two main islands of Sicily and Sardinia. The Alps form a natural boundary with its northern and western European neighbours, and the Adriatic Sea to the east separates it from the countries of former Yugoslavia. The Apennine Mountains form the backbone of Italy and extend the full length of the peninsula. Between the Alps and the Apennines lies the Po Valley, a great fertile lowland. Sicily and Sardinia are largely mountainous. Much of Italy is geologically unstable, and it has four active volcanoes, including Etna and Vesuvius. Italy enjoys warm dry summers and mild winters. The north is the main industrial centre, and agriculture there is well mechanized. In the south farms are small and traditional. Industries in the north include motor vehicles, textiles, clothing, leather goods, glass and ceramics. Tourism is an important source of foreign currency.

Area : 301,268 sq km (116,320 sq miles)
Population : 57,600,000
Capital : Rome (Roma)
Other major cities : Milan, Naples, Turin, Genoa, Palermo
Form of government : Republic
Religion : RC
Currency : Lira

Ithaca (Ithaki) the smallest of the IONIAN ISLANDS, situated off the west coast of GREECE. Odysseus (Ulysses), the hero of Homer's *Odyssey*, was a son of the royal house of Ithaca. (93 sq km/36 sq miles; pop. 3650)

Ivanovo a textile manufacturing city in the RUSSIAN FEDERATION, 240 km (150 miles) northeast of MOSCOW. (Pop. 476,000)

Iviza *see* **Balearic Islands.**

Ivory Coast *see* **Côte d'Ivoire.**

Iwaki a major chemical industry town on the east coast of HONSHU Island, JAPAN, 175 km (110 miles) northeast of Tokyo, established in 1966 on a former coalfield. (Pop. 350,600)

Iwo Jima the largest in the group of islands called the Volcano Islands belonging to JAPAN, which lie some 1200 km (745 miles) south of TOKYO in the PACIFIC OCEAN. It was the scene of bitter fighting in 1945 at the end of World War II, when US troops took the island from the Japanese. (21 sq km/8 sq miles)

Ixtacihuatl a volcanic peak south of MEXICO CITY, which is twinned with neighbouring POPOCATÉPETL. (5286 m/17,342 ft)

Izmir (Smyrna) a port of ancient Greek origin on the AEGEAN coast of TURKEY, to the south of ISTANBUL. (Pop. 1,489,800)

Izmit (Kocaeli) a port and naval base on the Sea of MARMARA, 90 km (55 miles) southeast of ISTANBUL. (Pop. 236,100)

Izumo a town near the north coast of western HONSHU Island, north of HIROSHIMA; it is the site of JAPAN's oldest Shinto shrine, dating from the 1st century AD. (Pop. 80,700)

J

Jabalpur (Jubbulpore) a city in central Madhya Pradesh state of central India, lying on the banks of the upper Narmada river. (Pop. 614,879)

Jackson the state capital of Mississippi. (Pop. city 208,800/metropolitan area 382,400)

Jacksonville a port on the northeast coast of Florida, USA. (Pop. city 578,000/metropolitan area 795,300)

Jadotville *see* **Likasi**.

Jaén a medieval castellated cathedral town in central Andalusia, southern Spain, 290 km (180 miles) south of Madrid; it manufactures chemicals, brandy and leather goods. (Pop. 96,400)

Jaeren a peninsula in the extreme southwest of Norway, to the south of Stravanger. Often seen as "as little bit of Denmark attached to Norway" because of its absence of hills and its intensive agriculture. (1700 sq km/656 sq miles)

Jaffna a port on the tip of the northern peninsula of Sri Lanka, and the main centre for the Tamil population of the island. (Pop. 118,200)

Jaipur the capital of the state of Rajasthan, India. (Pop. 1,015,200)

Jajce a former capital of Bosnia, 53 km (35 miles) south of the city of Banja Luka. Marshal Tito proclaimed Yugoslavia a federal socialist republic at Jajce on 29 November 1943. (Pop. 9100)

Jakarta the capital of Indonesia, a port on the northwestern tip of Java. (Pop. 6,503,000)

Jalalabad (Djelalabad) a trading town in eastern Afghanistan, 120 km (74 miles) east of Kabul, commanding the head of the KHYBER PASS. It is capital of Nangarhar, the country's most densely populated province. (Pop. 57,800)

Jalapa an old colonial town and capital of Veracruz state in south central MEXICO, lying 130 km (80 miles) inland from the Gulf of MEXICO, in the Sierra Madre Oriental mountains. Food processing is the main industry. (Pop. 212,800)

Jamaica is an island state in the CARIBBEAN SEA about 150 km (93 miles) south of CUBA. The centre of the island comprises a limestone plateau, and this is surrounded by narrow coastal flatlands and palm-fringed beaches. The highest mountains, the BLUE MOUNTAINS, are in the east of the island. The climate is tropical with high temperatures at the coast, with slightly cooler and less humid conditions in the highlands. The island lies right in the middle of the hurricane zone. The traditional crops grown are sugar cane, bananas, peppers, ginger, cocoa and coffee, and new crops such as winter vegetables, fruit and honey are being developed for export. Despite this, the decline in the principal export products, bauxite and alumina, has resulted in near economic stagnation. Tourism is an important industry, as is the illegal trade in cannabis.

Area : 10,990 sq km (4243 sq miles)

Population : 2,400,000

Capital : Kingston

Other major cities : Montego Bay, Spanish Town

Form of government : Constitutional Monarchy

Religion : Anglicanism, RC, other Protestantism

Currency : Jamaican dollar

James Bay the southern arm of the HUDSON BAY, CANADA, which extends 440 km (273 miles) into ONTARIO and QUEBEC.

Jammu and Kashmir the state in the very north of INDIA, bordering CHINA and PAKISTAN. The total size of the state is 222,236 sq km (85,783 sq miles), but its borders are disputed, and following wars with Pakistan (1947–49, 1967 and 1971) and annexation by China in the 1950s, India occupies only about a half of what it claims. (Pop. 5,987,400)

Jamshedpur an industrial city in northeast INDIA which grew up around steel foundries set up by Jamshedi Tata in 1907–11. (Pop. 669,600)

Jamuna, River the name given to the river formed by the BRAHMAPUTRA and the Tista as it flows through BANGLA-DESH to join the GANGES.

Janakpur a lowland town and Hindu pilgrimage centre in the southeast of NEPAL, 10 km (6 miles) from the border with INDIA to the south. (Pop. 143,000)

Jan Mayen an island in the ARCTIC OCEAN, 540 km (335 miles) northeast of ICELAND, annexed by NORWAY in 1929; it is dominated by Beerenberg, an extinct volcano 2277 m (7470 ft) high. Weather station personnel are its only inhabitants. (380 sq km/146 sq miles)

Japan is located on the eastern margin of ASIA and consists of four major islands, HONSHU, HOKKAIDO, KYUSHU and SHIKOKU, and many small islands. It is separated from the mainland of Asia by the Sea of Japan. The country is made up of six chains of steep, serrated mountains, which contain about 60 active volcanoes. Earthquakes are frequent and widespread, and often accompanied by giant tidal waves (tsunami). Summers are warm and humid, and winters mild, except on Hokkaido, which is covered in snow in winter. Japan's agriculture is highly advanced, with extensive use made of fertilizers and miniature machinery for the small fields. Fishing is important. Japan is the second largest industrial economy in the world. It is very dependent on imported raw materials, and its success is based on manufacturing industry, which employs about one-third of the work force.

Area : 377,801 sq km (145,869 sq miles)

Population : 123,260,000

Capital : Tokyo
Other major cities : Osaka, Nagoya, Sapporo, Kobe,
Kyoto, Yokohama
Form of government : Constitutional Monarchy
Religion : Shintoism, Buddhism, Christianity
Currency : Yen

Japan Alps (Chubu Sangaku) a mountainous area of
central HONSHU Island, about 200 km (125 miles) northwest of TOKYO; it is similar in appearance to the European ALPS, and includes two of the highest peaks in
JAPAN, Mount Hotaka (3190 m/10,466 ft) and Mount Yari
(3180 m/10,434 ft).

Japan, Sea of a part of the PACIFIC OCEAN that lies
between JAPAN and the Korean peninsula.

Jarash (Jerash) a town 38 km (24 miles) north of AMMAN,
JORDAN, containing well-preserved remains of an ancient
Roman city. (Pop. 29.000)

Jaroslaw (Jaroslau; Yaroslav) an agricultural town in
the southeast corner of POLAND, 30 km (18 miles) from the
border with UKRAINE. It was an important medieval
marketplace, at the crossroads of the Rhineland-Russia
and Baltic-Black Sea trade routes. (Pop. 38,600)

Java (Jawa) the central island in the southern chain of
islands of INDONESIA. The capital is JAKARTA. (130,987 sq
km/50,574 sq miles; pop. 91,269,600)

Java Sea an arm of the PACIFIC OCEAN that separates JAVA
and BORNEO.

Jaworzno a coal-mining, metal-processing and electric-
ity-generating town in southeastern POLAND, 25 km (15
miles) east of KATOWICE. (Pop. 93,900)

Jayapura the administrative centre for IRIAN JAYA, situated on the north coast of NEW GUINEA; it was formerly
known as Hollandia, Kota Baru, and Sukarnapura. (Pop.
45,800)

Jbail a historic seaport 29 km (18 miles) north of BEIRUT,
LEBANON. It is the site of the biblical "Gebal", the place
claimed to be the oldest continuously inhabited town in

the world; there are many remains from successive civilizations going back to 9000BC. (Pop. 1200)

Jedda *see* **Jiddah.**

Jefferson City the state capital of MISSOURI, USA. (Pop. 35,000)

Jena a university town in southern central GERMANY, 80 km (50 miles) south-west of LEIPZIG. The Prussian army was defeated by the French under Napoleon here in 1806. (Pop. 107,700)

Jerba (Djerba) an island in the Gulf of GABES belonging to TUNISIA. It has become a popular tourist resort in recent years. (67 sq km/42 sq miles; pop. 92,300)

Jerez de la Frontera (Jerez) a town in southwest SPAIN, just inland from CADIZ, famous for the sweet wine to which it has given its name, sherry. (Pop. 176,200)

Jericho a town in the WEST BANK area occupied by ISRAEL since 1967, on the site of a city that dates back to about 7000BC. (Pop. 15,000)

Jersey the largest of the British CHANNEL ISLANDS. The capital is St Helier. (117 sq km/45 sq miles; pop. 77,000)

Jerusalem (Yerushalayim, El Quds esh Sherif) the capital of ISRAEL, and a historic city considered holy by Muslims, Christians and Jews. (Pop. 446,500)

Jessore an agricultural town in the centre of the flood plains of southwest BANGLADESH; it trades in rice, jute, tamarind, tobacco, and sugar cane. (Pop. 149,400)

Jhansi a railway-engineering town in central INDIA, 380 km (236 miles) southeast of DEHLI.

Jiangsu a heavily populated but highly productive province on the central east coast of CHINA. The capital is NANJING. (100,000 sq km/38,600 sq miles; pop. 60,521,000)

Jiangxi an inland province of southeastern CHINA. Its capital is NANCHANG. (160,000 sq km/39,000 sq miles; pop. 32,290,000)

Jiddah (Jedda) a port on the RED SEA coast of SAUDI ARABIA, and one of the country's main centres of population. (Pop. 750,000)

Jilin (Kirin) a province of central DONGBEI (Manchuria) in northern CHINA. The capital is CHANGCHUN. (180,000 sq km/69,500 sq miles; pop. 22,502,000)

Jima a market town and centre in a coffee-growing area of southwest ETHIOPIA, 230 km (145 miles) from ADDIS ABABA. (Pop. 70,000)

Jinan the capital of SHANDONG province, situated close to the HUANG HE River, 360 km (225 miles) to the south of BEIJING. (Pop. 3,200,000)

Jodhpur a city in central RAJASTHAN, INDIA, on the perimeter of the THAR DESERT. The city has given its name to the riding breeches that first became popular here. (Pop. 506,300)

Jogjakarta *see* **Yogyakarta.**

Johannesburg the centre of the RAND gold-mining area of SOUTH AFRICA and now that country's largest town. (Pop. 1,536,500)

John o'Groats the village traditionally held to be on the most northerly point of mainland SCOTLAND and GREAT BRITAIN.

Johor Bahru (Johore) a port and growing city in MALAYSIA situated on the southern tip of the MALAY PENINSULA opposite SINGAPORE, to which it is connected by a causeway. It is also the capital of the state of Johor. (Pop. city 246,400)

Jönköping an industrial city, dating from the 13th century, at the south end of Lake VÄTTERN, in south-central SWEDEN; it is famed for the mechanized production of safety matches, which was first developed here in 1845. (Pop. 107,362)

Jordan is almost landlocked except for a short coastline on the Gulf of AQABA. It is bounded by SAUDI ARABIA, SYRIA, IRAQ and ISRAEL. Almost 80% of the country is desert, and the rest comprises the East Bank Uplands and Jordan Valley. In general, summers are hot and dry, and winters cool and wet, with variations related to altitude. The east has a desert climate. Only one-fifth of the country is fertile enough to be farmed, but the country is self-sufficient in potatoes, onions and poultry meat. The agricultural system is intensive and efficient. AMMAN is the main industrial centre of the country, and the industries include phosphates, petroleum products, cement, iron and fertilizers. The rich Arab states, such as Saudi Arabia, give Jordan substantial economic aid.

Area : 97,740 sq km (37,737 sq miles)
Population : 3,170,000
Capital : Amman
Other major cities : Irbid, Zarga
Form of government : Constitutional Monarchy
Religion : Sunni Islam
Currency : Jordan dinar

Jordan, River a river flowing southwards from Mount HERMON in southern LEBANON, through northern ISRAEL to Lake TIBERIAS (Sea of Galilee) and then on through Jordan into the DEAD SEA, where it evaporates. The WEST BANK to the north of the Dead Sea is disputed territory which has been occupied by Israel since the Six Day War in 1967. (Length 256 km/159 miles)

Jos Plateau an upland area in the centre of NIGERIA, rising to an average height of 1250 m (4100 ft). Striking scenery makes it a popular resort area. It is also a source of tin, and the town of Jos is the centre for the mining industry.

Juan de Fuca Strait the channel to the south of VANCOUVER ISLAND on the border between CANADA and the USA, through which ships from VICTORIA, VANCOUVER and SEATTLE can pass to reach the PACIFIC OCEAN.

Juan Fernández Islands a group of three remote islands in the PACIFIC OCEAN belonging to CHILE and some 650 km (400 miles) due west of SANTIAGO. (181 sq km/62 sq miles; pop. 550)

Jubbulpore *see* **Jabalpur**.

Judaea the southern part of ancient PALESTINE, occupying the area of modern ISRAEL between the MEDITERRANEAN coast to the west and the DEAD SEA and River JORDAN to the east.

Julian Alps (Alpi Giulie; Julijske Alpe) a mountain range in northwest SLOVENIA; it has over 200 peaks exceeding 2000 m (6550 ft) including Triglav, at 2863 m (9393 ft) the highest point in all former YUGOSLAVIA.

Jumna, River *see* **Yamuna, River.**

Juneau the state capital of ALASKA. (Pop. 23,800)

Jungfrau a famous peak in the Bernese Oberland range in the Swiss ALPS, popular with climbers but now also ascended by cable car. (4158 m/13,642 ft)

Jura (1) a large upland band of limestone in eastern central FRANCE which lines the border with SWITZERLAND, giving its name to a department in France and a canton in Switzerland. A further extension continues across southern GERMANY as far as NUREMBERG (the Swabian and Franconian Jura). **(2)** the fourth in size of the Inner Hebrides group of islands, off the west coast of Scotland; it is mountainous and sparsely populated. (381 sq km/ 147 sq miles; pop. 228)

Jutland (Jylland) a large peninsula stretching some 400 km (250 miles) northwards from GERMANY to separate the NORTH SEA from the BALTIC SEA. Most of it is occupied by the mainland part of DENMARK, which calls it Jylland, while the southern part belongs to the German state of SCHLESWIG-HOLSTEIN.

Jylland *see* **Jutland**.

K

K2 (Godwin Austen) the second highest mountain in the world after Mount EVEREST, situated in the KARAKORAM mountain range on the disputed border between PAKISTAN and CHINA. (8611 m/28,250 ft)

Kabardino-Balkar Republic one of the 16 autonomous republics of the RUSSIAN FEDERATION, lying on the north side of the CAUCASUS; the capital is Nalchik. (12,500 sq km/4825 sq miles; pop. 695,000)

Kabul the capital and main city of AFGHANISTAN, in the northeast of the country on the Kabul River. (Pop. 1,036,400)

Kabwe (Broken Hill) the oldest mining town of ZAMBIA, developed in the early 1900s to extract the lead, zinc and vanadium deposits found about 100 km (60 miles) north of LUSAKA, in the centre of the country. (Pop. 143,600)

Kachchh *see* **Kutch.**

Kaduna the capital of the province of the same name, situated in central NIGERIA. Lying at the heart of the country's cotton-growing area, it was the capital of the vast Northern Region during British colonial rule. (Pop. town 202,000/province 4,500,000)

Kaesong (Gaeseong) an industrial city, about 150 km (93 miles) southeast of PYONGYANG, NORTH KOREA; it was the capital of Korea during the Koryo dynasty (AD918-1392). (Pop. 140,000)

Kagoshima a port on the south coast of KYUSHU Island, JAPAN. (Pop. 530,500)

Kaifeng a city of ancient origins in HENAN province, CHINA. (Pop. 500,000)

Kairouan a city in northern TUNISIA, to Muslims the most holy city of the MAGHREB. (Pop. 72,300)

Kajanni a wood-products and transport town in central FINLAND, lying just southeast of Oulu Lake (Pop. 35,900)

Kalahari a region of semi-desert occupying much of southern BOTSWANA and straddling the border with SOUTH AFRICA and NAMIBIA.

Kalamazoo a market and industrial town in southern MICHIGAN, USA. (Pop. city 77,200/metropolitan area 215,200)

Kalémié a town founded in 1891, as Albertville; it is an important inland port on the ZAÏRE west shore of Lake TANGANYIKA, which provides a vital ferry link in the rail system from the interior to DAR ES SALAAM on the INDIAN OCEAN. (Pop. 61,000)

Kalgoorlie a town in southern WESTERN AUSTRALIA which has grown up around its gold and nickel reserves. (Pop. 19,800)

Kalimantan the greater part of BORNEO, which is governed by INDONESIA. (538,718 sq km/208,000 sq miles; pop. 6,724,000)

Kalimnos (Calino) *see* **Dodecanese.**

Kalinin *see* **Tver**.

Kaliningrad (Königsberg) a port and industrial city on the BALTIC coast belonging to the RUSSIAN FEDERATION, in an enclave between LITHUANIA and POLAND. Founded in the 13th century, it was called Königsberg and was the capital of EAST PRUSSIA, but was ceded to the former USSR in 1945 and renamed after Mikhail Kalinin, the Soviet President 1937–46. (Pop. 380,000)

Kalisz (Kalisch) an industrial city in south-central POLAND, 105 km (65 miles) southeast of POZNAN. (Pop. 102,900)

Kalmar a seaport in southeast SWEDEN opposite the isle of ÖLAND to which it is linked by a 6-km (4-mile) long bridge. (Pop. 54,165)

Kalmyk (Kalmuck) Republic an autonomous republic of the RUSSIAN FEDERATION, lying to the northwest of the CASPIAN SEA. (75,900 sq km/29,300 sq miles; pop. 315,000)

Kaluga an industrial city and railway junction in the west-central RUSSIAN FEDERATION, lying on the Oka River 160 km (100 miles) southwest of Moscow. (Pop. 291,000)

Kamchatka a peninsula, some 1200 km (750 miles) long, which drops south from eastern SIBERIA into the north PACIFIC OCEAN. (Pop. 422,000)

Kamina an important transport centre in the SHABA region of southern ZAÏRE, on the ILEBO-LUBMUMBASHI railway. (Pop. 57,000)

Kamloops a city at the confluence of the North and South Thompson rivers, in south-central BRITISH COLUMBIA, western CANADA, 260 km (163 miles) northeast of VANCOUVER; it is a centre for gold and copper mining, and cattle rearing. (Pop. 65,000)

Kampala the capital and main city of UGANDA, situated on Lake VICTORIA. (Pop. 500,000)

Kampuchea *see* **Cambodia.**

Kananga a city in central southern ZAÏRE, founded in 1894 as Luluabourg. (Pop. 704,000)

Kanazawa a historic port on the central northern coast of HONSHU Island, JAPAN. (Pop. 430,500)

Kanchanaburi a sugar cane-growing centre, 120 km (75 miles) west of BANGKOK near the river KWAI in southern THAILAND. (Pop. 139,100)

Kandahar the second largest city in AFGHANISTAN, situated in the southeastern part of the country, near the border with PAKISTAN. (Pop. 191,400)

Kandy a town in the central mountains of SRI LANKA, which was once the capital of the Sinhalese kings and is sacred to Buddhists. (Pop. 101,300)

Kangaroo Island a mineral-rich island off the coast of SOUTH AUSTRALIA, about 100 km (63 miles) southwest of ADELAIDE. (Pop. 3300)

Kangchenjunga the world's third highest mountain (after Mount EVEREST and K2), situated in the eastern HIMALAYAS, on the borders between NEPAL, CHINA and the Indian state of SIKKIM. (8586 m/28,170 ft)

Ka-Ngwane a small state, formerly a Bantu homeland, in east TRANSVAAL, SOUTH AFRICA, bordering SWAZILAND. (3910 sq km/1510 sq miles; pop. 458,000)

Kankan the main town of upper GUINEA and an important communications centre, being the terminus of the 485-km (300-mile) long railway from CONAKRY and a focus of roads linking Guinea with MALI, LIBERIA and CÔTE D'IVOIRE

Kano a historic trading city of the Hausa people of northern NIGERIA, the third largest city in Nigeria after LAGOS and IBADAN. (Pop. city 475,000)

Kanpur (Cawnpore) an industrial city in northern central INDIA. (Pop. 1,639,100)

Kansas a state in the GREAT PLAINS of the USA. The state capital is TOPEKA. (213,064 sq km/82,264 sq miles; pop. 2,450,000)

Kansas City an industrial city on the MISSOURI RIVER which straddles the border between the states of MISSOURI and KANSAS. (Pop. city 603,600/metropolitan area 1,476,700)

Kansk an industrial city in central SIBERIA of the RUSSIAN FEDERATION, about 800 km (500 miles) east of NOVOSIBIRSK along the TRANS-SIBERIAN-RAILWAY. (Pop. 103,000)

Kao-hsiung the second largest city in TAIWAN and a major port, situated in the southwest of the island. (Pop. 1,269,000)

Kap Farvel *see* **Farewell, Cape**.

Karachi a port and industrial centre, and the largest city in PAKISTAN. (Pop. 5,103,000)

Karaganda an industrial city in the mining region of KAZAKHSTAN. (Pop. 608,000)

Karakoram a range of mountains at the western end of the HIMALAYAS on the borders between PAKISTAN, CHINA and INDIA.

Kara Kum (Karakumy) a sand desert in southern TURKMENISTAN, to the east of the CASPIAN SEA, and on the borders with IRAN and AFGHANISTAN.

Kara Sea a branch of the ARCTIC OCEAN off the central

northern coast of the RUSSIAN FEDERATION.

Karawanke Alps (Karawanken; Caravanche) an east-west mountain range that forms the border between AUSTRIA and SLOVENIA; its highest point at Grintavec is 2558 m (8392 ft)

Karbala a town in central IRAQ, 90 km (55 miles) south of BAGHDAD. As the site of the tomb of Hussein bin Ali and his brother Abbas, grandsons of the prophet Mohammed, it is held sacred by the Shia Muslims. (Pop. 107,500)

Karelia a region which straddles the border between FINLAND and the RUSSIAN FEDERATION.

Karelia (Karjala) Republic one of the 16 autonomous republics of the RUSSIAN FEDERATION, lying just south of the ARCTIC CIRCLE between FINLAND, the WHITE SEA and Lake LAGODA. The capital is PETROZAVODSK. (172,400 sq km/66,500 sq miles: pop. 769,000)

Kariba Dam a hydroelectric dam on the River ZAMBEZI on the border between ZAMBIA and ZIMBABWE.

Karl-Marx-Stadt *see* **Chemnitz.**

Karlovy Vary (Carlsbad; Karlsbad) a spa town in the CZECH REPUBLIC. (Pop. 59,200)

Karlskrona the main naval base of SWEDEN, lying on the BALTIC coast in the southeastern corner of the country; it was founded in the 17th century. (Pop. 59,393)

Karlsruhe (Carlsruhe) an industrial city in the valley of the River RHINE, in southwestern GERMANY. (Pop. 275,000)

Karnak the site of the extensive ruins of a temple complex dating from about 1560-1090BC, on the eastern bank of the River NILE in central EGYPT.

Karnataka a state in southwest INDIA. The capital is BANGALORE. (191,791 sq km/74,031 sq miles; pop. 37,135,700)

Kärnten *see* **Carinthia.**

Karoo (Karroo) two separate regions of semi-desert, the GREAT KAROO and the Little Karoo, lying between the mountain ranges of southern CAPE PROVINCE, SOUTH AF-RICA.

Kasai (Cassai), River a major river of ZAÏRE. (Length 2150 km/1350 miles)

Kashmir a mountainous region straddling the border between INDIA and PAKISTAN and subject to dispute since the partition of India and Pakistan in 1947. About half of the former princely state of JAMMU AND KASHMIR is now ruled by Pakistan and is known as AZAD KASHMIR.

Kassala a market town in the centre of a cotton-growing province of the same name, 400 km (250 miles) east of KHARTOUM, SUDAN (Pop. town 143,000)

Kassel (Cassel) an industrial city in central GERMANY. (Pop. 190,400)

Kasvin *see* **Qazvin.**

Katanga *see* **Shaba**.

Kathmandu (Katmandu) the capital and principal city of NEPAL. (Pop. 195,260)

Katowice (Kattowitz) an industrial city in central southern POLAND. (Pop. 361,300)

Katsina the northernmost town in HAUSALAND, northern NIGERIA; it is also the market centre for the Katsina state. (Pop. 145,500)

Kattegat (Cattegat) the strait, 34 km (21 miles) at its narrowest, at the entrance to the BALTIC SEA, that separates SWEDEN from the JUTLAND peninsula of DENMARK.

Kaunas (Kovno) an industrial city and former capital of LITHUANIA. (Pop. 400,000)

Kaválla a city and port of MACEDONIA, GREECE, 160 km (100 miles) east of SALONIKI. Nearby is Philippi, scene of the battle in which Mark Antony and Octavian defeated Brutus and Cassius in 42BC, and where St Paul first preached in Europe, and wrote his epistle to the Philippians. (Pop. 56,400)

Kavango (Cubango), River a river, known formerly as the Okavango, which flows southeast from central ANGOLA to form the border with NAMIBIA before petering out in the swampy inland Okavango Delta in northern BOTSWANA. (Length 1600 km/1000 miles)

Kaveri (Caveri, Cauvery), River a holy river of southern India, flowing southeast from the Deccan plateau to the coast on the Bay of Bengal. (Length 800 km/497 miles)

Kavkaz *see* **Caucasus.**

Kawasaki an industrial city on the east coast of Honshu Island, Japan, forming part of the Tokyo-Yokohama conurbation. (Pop. 1,088,600)

Kayes a market town in the extreme west of Mali, about 100 km (60 miles) from the border with Senegal. It lies on the Dakar-Bamako railway. (Pop. 45,000)

Kayseri a textile town in the centre of Turkey, 230 km (140 miles) southeast of Ankara; it lies at the foot of an extinct volcano, Erciyas Dagi, 3916 m (12,048 ft) high. (Pop. 378,500)

Kazakhstan, the second largest republic of the former USSR, extends approximately 3000 km (1864 miles) from the coast of the Caspian Sea to the northwest corner of Mongolia. The west of the country is low-lying, the east hilly, and in the southeast mountainous areas include parts of the Tian Shan and Altai ranges. The climate is continental and very dry with great extremes of temperature. Much of the country is semi-desert. Crops can only be grown in the wetter northwest regions or on land irrigated by the Syrdar'ya river. Extensive pastoral farming is carried out in most of the country, and cattle, sheep and goats are the main livestock reared. The country is rich in minerals, particularly copper, lead, zinc, coal, tungsten, iron ore, oil and gas. Kazakhstan declared itself independent in 1991.

Area : 2,717,000 sq km (1,050,000 sq miles)

Population : 15,654,000

Capital : Alma Ata (Almaty)

Other major city : Karaganda

Form of government : Republic

Religion : Sunni Islam

Currency : Rouble

Kazan' an industrial city and capital of the TATAR REPUBLIC in central RUSSIAN FEDERATION. (Pop. 1,039,000)

Kazanluk a town in central BULGARIA, lying in the "Valley of Roses" between the BALKAN MOUNTAINS and SREDNA GORA, and centre of the attar of roses perfume industry. (Pop. 61,000)

Kazan-rettó (Volcano Islands) a group of three volcanic islands in the west PACIFIC OCEAN, about 1100 km (700 miles) to the south of JAPAN, to whom they belong. The largest is IWO JIMA. (28 sq km/11 sq miles)

Kecskemét a city at the centre of HUNGARY, on the GREAT ALFÖLD (plain), 80 km (50 miles) southeast of BUDAPEST; it is the market centre of a rich agricultural area, specializing in vineyards and fruit farms. (Pop. 101,300)

Kediri the main centre of a rice-growing region of southeast JAVA, which is famous for its handicrafts, including silverwork and batik. (Pop. 200,000)

Keeling Islands *see* **Cocos Islands.**

Keelung see Chi-lung.

Kefallinia *see* **Ionian Islands.**

Keflavík a town and ICELAND'S main civil airport, part of which is a US military base, about 32 km (20 miles) southwest of REYKJAVIK. (Pop. 6700)

Kelang a river rising in central Peninsular MALAYSIA and flowing through KUALA LUMPUR into the Strait of MALACCA at Port Kelang (formerly Port Swettenham); this port has been developed to reduce the country's need to use SINGAPORE. Upstream, the town of Kelang is a southwestern dormitory for the capital. (Pop. town 192,000)

Kells a market town in County MEATH, IRELAND. It was the site of a monastery founded in the 6th century by St Columba, which was the source of the illuminated Book of Kells.

Kelsty *see* **Kielce.**

Kemerovo an industrial city in the KUZNETSK coal mining region of southern SIBERIA. (Pop. 505,000)

Kengtung a town in the GOLDEN TRIANGLE of far eastern

BURMA, reputed to be the centre of the illegal growing of and trade in the opium poppy. (Pop. 174,000)

Kénitra (Mina Hassan Tani) a port on the ATLANTIC coast of MOROCCO, 40 km (25 miles) north of RABAT; it is the main outlet for produce from the coastal plain and around FÉS and MEKNES. (Pop. 189,000)

Kennedy, Cape *see* **Canaveral, Cape.**

Kent a county in the extreme southeast of ENGLAND. The county town is Maidstone. (3732 sq km/1441 sq miles; pop. 1,494,000)

Kentucky a state in east central USA. The state capital is FRANKFORT. (104,623 sq km/40,395 sq miles; pop. 3,726,000)

Kenya located in east AFRICA, Kenya straddles the Equator and extends from Lake VICTORIA in the southwest to the INDIAN OCEAN in the southeast. Highlands run north to south through central Kenya and are divided by the steep-sided GREAT RIFT VALLEY. The coastal lowlands have a hot humid climate, but in the highlands it is cooler and rainfall heavier. In the east it is very arid. The southwestern region is well watered with huge areas of fertile soil, and this accounts for the bulk of the population and almost all its economic production being there. The main crops grown for domestic consumption are wheat and maize. Tea, coffee, sisal, sugar cane and cotton are grown for export. Oil refining at MOMBASA is the country's largest single factory, and other industry includes food processing and textiles. Tourism is an important source of foreign revenue.

Area : 580,367 sq km (224,080 sq miles)

Population : 24,080,000

Capital : Nairobi

Other major cities : Mombasa, Kisumu

Form of government : Republic

Religions : RC, Protestantism, other Christianity, Animism

Currency : Kenya shilling

Kenya, Mount a towering extinct volcano in central Kenya, the second highest mountain in AFRICA after Mount KILIMANJARO. (5200 m/17,058 ft)

Kerala a state occupying the western coast of the southern tip of INDIA. The capital is TRIVANDRUM. (38,863 sq km/ 15,005 sq miles; pop. 25,453,000)

Kerch' a Crimean port and major fishing base on the narrows between the BLACK SEA and the Sea of AZOV; an ancient city founded by the Greeks in the 6th century BC and later ruled by Rome, Genoa, Turkey, Russia, and now by the Ukraine. (Pop. 166,000)

Kerguelen the largest in a remote group of some 300 islands in the southern INDIAN OCEAN forming part of the FRENCH SOUTHERN AND ANTARCTIC TERRITORIES, now occupied only by the staff of a scientific base. (3414 sq km/ 1318 sq miles)

Kérkira *see* **Corfu.**

Kermanshah *see* **Bakhtaran.**

Kerry a county in the southwest of the Republic of IRELAND, noted for the rugged beauty of its peninsulas and its green dairy pastures. The county town is Tralee. (4701 sq km/1815 sq miles; pop. 122,800)

Key West a port and resort at the southern end of Florida Keys, a chain of coral islands off the southern tip of FLORIDA, USA. (Pop. 24,900)

Khabarovsk a major industrial city in southeastern SIBERIA, lying just 35 km(22 miles) north of the border with CHINA. (Pop. 569,000)

Khajuraho a town in northern MADYA PRADESH, INDIA, noted in particular for its Hindu and Jain temples which are famed for their intricate and erotic sculpture.

Khaniá (Chania) a port on the northwest coast of CRETE, GREECE; it was known in ancient times as Cydonia and later was occupied by the Venetians (1252-1645) and Turks (1645-1898). (Pop. 62,000)

Khar'kov a major industrial and commercial centre of the UKRAINE. (Pop. 1,536,000)

Kharg Island a small island in the northern GULF where IRAN has constructed a major oil terminal.

Khartoum (El Khartum) the capital of SUDAN, situated at the confluence of the Blue NILE and White Nile. (Pop. 561,000)

Khios *see* **Chios.**

Khone Falls a massive set of waterfalls on the River MEKONG in southern LAOS, which prevents the river from being navigable beyond this point. With a maximum width of 10.8 km (6.7 miles), these are the widest in the world.

Khorasan the northeastern province of IRAN, bordering AFGHANISTAN and TURKMENISTAN. The capital is MASHHAD. (Pop. 3,267,000)

Khudzhand one of central ASIA's oldest cities, originally called Khodzhent, and, until 1992, as Leninabad. It lies in TDJIKISTAN, about 145 km (90 miles) south of TASHKENT. It was founded by Alexander the Great (356-323BC). (Pop. 147,000)

Khulna a port and district in southwest BANGLADESH. (Pop. town 646,400)

Khuzestan (Khuzistan) a province in southwestern IRAN, and the country's main oil-producing area. The capital is AHVAZ. (Pop. 2,177,000)

Khyber Pass a high pass (1072 m/3518 ft) over the Safed Koh mountains connecting PESHAWAR in PAKISTAN with KABUL in AFGHANISTAN. It has been of great strategic importance throughout history.

Kiel a port and shipbuilding city on the BALTIC coast of northern GERMANY. It stands at the mouth of the Kiel Ship Canal which permits ocean-going ships to cross the JUTLAND peninsula from the BALTIC to HAMBURG and the NORTH SEA. (Pop. 248,400)

Kielce (Kelsty) an industrial city in central southern POLAND. (Pop. 197,000)

Kiev (Kiyev) the capital of the UKRAINE, situated on the DNIEPER River. Founded in the 6th century, it is now a major industrial city. (Pop. 2,411,000)

Kigali the capital of RWANDA. (Pop. 170,000)

Kigoma an inland port on the east shore of Lake TANGAN-YIKA; it is the rail terminus of the line from DAR ES SALAAM and main transit port for BURUNDI. Nearby is the old fishing village of Ujiji, where Henry Morton Stanley found the missing explorer David Livingstone in 1871. (Pop. 50,000)

Kikládhes *see* **Cyclades**.

Kildare a county in the southeast of the Republic of IRELAND, famous for its racehorses and the racecourse, The Curragh. The county town is Naas. (1694 sq km/654 sq miles; pop. 104,100)

Kilimanjaro, Mount Africa's highest mountain, in north-eastern TANZANIA. (5895 m/19,340 ft)

Kilkenny a county in the southeast of the Republic of IRELAND, and also the name of its capital city. (2062 sq km/769 sq miles; pop. county 70,800/city 10,100)

Killarney a market town in county KERRY, in the Republic of IRELAND, which is at the centre of a landscape of lakes and mountains much admired and visited for its beauty. (Pop. 7700)

Kimberley a town in the north of CAPE PROVINCE, SOUTH AFRICA, which is at the centre of South Africa's diamond mining industry. (Pop. 153,900)

Kimberleys, The a vast plateau of hills and gorges in the north of WESTERN AUSTRALIA. (420,000 sq km/162,000 sq miles)

Kincardineshire *see* **Grampian**.

Kindia an old colonial hill station at the edge of the FOUTA DJALLON in western GUINEA; it now markets fruit, especially bananas. (Pop. 79,900)

Kindu a river port in east-central ZAÏRE, the terminus of the interior railway system that extends southwards to the SHABA mining region, and a branch line to KALÉMIÉ on Lake TANGANYIKA. (Pop. 50,000)

Kingston (1) the capital and main port of JAMAICA. (Pop. 700,000) **(2)** an industrial and university city on the northeast shore of Lake ONTARIO; it was a former capital of CANADA (1841–1844). (Pop. 52,600)

Kingston upon Hull (Hull) a port in the county of HUMBERSIDE in eastern ENGLAND, situated on the north side of the HUMBER estuary. (Pop. 270,000)

Kingstown the capital of ST VINCENT and a port, famed for its botanical gardens. (Pop. 22,800)

Kinross-shire *see* **Tayside**.

Kinshasa the capital of ZAÏRE, on the banks of the River ZAÏRE. It is the largest city in Central AFRICA. (Pop. 2,444,000)

Kintyre a narrow 64-km (40-mile) long peninsula on the west coast of SCOTLAND that protrudes southwards, ending at the Mull of Kintyre headland; it is the country's closest point to IRELAND, only 20 km (12 miles) across the NORTH CHANNEL.

Kircudbrightshire *see* **Dumfries and Galloway.**

Kirghizia (Kirgizia) *see* **Kyrgyzstan.**

Kirghiz Steppe (Kirgiziya Step) the vast treeless grassland plains, sometimes simply known as "The Steppes", that stretch uninterrupted across most of central KAZAKHSTAN. They are extremely fertile, and good yields of grain crops are cultivated on their rich black earth (chernozem) and chestnut steppe soils.

Kiribati comprises three groups of coral atolls and one isolated volcanic island spread over a large expanse of the central PACIFIC. The group includes Banaba Island, the Phoenix Islands, and some of the Line Islands. The climate is maritime equatorial with a high rainfall. Most islanders are involved in subsistence agriculture. The principal tree is the coconut, which grows well on all the islands. Palm and breadfruit trees are also found. Soil is negligible, and the only vegetable that can be grown is calladium. Tuna fishing is an important industry, and Kiribati had granted licences to the former USSR to fish its waters. Phosphate sources have now been exhausted, and the country is heavily dependent on overseas aid. *Area* : 726 sq km (280 sq miles)

Population : 66,250
Capital : Tarawa
Form of government : Republic
Religions : RC, Protestantism
Currency : Australian dollar

Kirin *see* **Jilin.**

Kiritimati *see* **Christmas Island.**

Kirkcaldy a port, resort and industrial town in south FIFE, east-central SCOTLAND, 17 km (11 miles) north of EDINBURGH, across the Firth of FORTH; it was the birthplace of Adam Smith (1723) and Robert Adam (1728); it was famed for the development of linoleum products. (Pop. 46,314)

Kirkuk an industrial city and regional capital in the Kurdish north of IRAQ. (Pop. 650,000)

Kirov an industrial city in east central RUSSIAN FEDERATION, founded in the 12th century. (Pop. 407,000)

Kiruna a major iron-mining centre in the far north of SWEDEN, from which the ore is taken across to the ice-free port of NARVIK on the Norwegian ATLANTIC coast. (Pop. 30,534)

Kisalföld *see* **Little Alföld.**

Kisangani a commercial centre and regional capital in northern ZAÏRE, on the River ZAÏRE. It was originally called Stanleyville. (Pop. 339,000)

Kishinev (Chisinau) the capital of MOLDOVA. (Pop. 605,000)

Kismaayo (Kismayu) a port in southern SOMALIA; it exports bananas. (Pop. 40,000-70,000)

Kistna, River *see* **Krishna, River.**

Kisumu one of the largest towns in KENYA, at the head of the Gulf of Winam on the east side of Lake VICTORIA. It was the original terminus of the UGANDA railway and busiest port on the lake, but since the break-up of the East African Community in the 1970s, trade has declined. (Pop. 200,000)

Kita-Kyushu a major industrial city situated in the north of KYUSHU Island, JAPAN. (Pop. 1,056,400)

Kitchener-Waterloo two towns in southern ONTARIO, CANADA, which have become twin cities, 100 km (62 miles) west of TORONTO. (Pop. 288,000)

Kíthira (Cerigo) *see* **Ionian Islands.**

Kitwe a mining town and commercial centre of the COPPERBELT, ZAMBIA, about 290 km (180 miles) north of LUSAKA. (Pop. 314,800)

Kivu, Lake a lake in the GREAT RIFT VALLEY on the border between RWANDA and ZAÏRE. (2850 sq km/1100 sq miles)

Kiyev *see* **Kiev.**

Kizil Irmak the longest river in TURKEY, flowing westwards from the centre of the country near SIVAS, before curling north to the BLACK SEA. (Length 1130 km/700 miles)

Kladno a coal-mining and steel-making town of the CZECH REPUBLIC, in BOHEMIA, 25 km (15 miles) northwest of PRAGUE. (Pop. 72,700)

Klagenfurt the capital of CARINTHIA, AUSTRIA, 100 km (63 miles) southwest of GRAZ; most of its old buildings are 16th century in origin, following a major fire in 1514. (Pop. 86,000)

Klaipeda a major port and shipbuilding centre on the BALTIC coast of LITHUANIA. (Pop. 181,000)

Klondike, River a short river flowing through YUKON TERRITORY in northwestern CANADA to meet the Yukon River at Dawson. Gold was discovered in the region in 1896, causing the subsequent goldrush. (Length 160 km/ 100 miles)

Knock (Cnoc) a village in County MAYO, in the west of the Republic of IRELAND, where a group of villagers witnessed a vision of the Virgin Mary and other saints in 1879. It has now become a Marian shrine of world importance. (Pop. 1400)

Knossos the site of an excavated royal palace of the Minoan civilization, 5 km (3 miles) southeast of HERAKLION, the capital of CRETE. The palace was built in about 1950BC and destroyed in 1380BC.

Knoxville an industrial city in eastern TENNESSEE, USA, and a port on the TENNESSEE RIVER. (Pop. city 174,000/ metropolitan area 589,400)

Kobe a major container port and shipbuilding centre at the southern end of HONSHU Island, JAPAN. (Pop. 1,410,800)

København *see* **Copenhagen.**

Koblenz (Coblenz) a city at the confluence of the Rivers RHINE and MOSELLE in western GERMANY, and a centre for the German winemaking industry. (Pop. 113,000)

Kodiak Island an island in the Gulf of ALASKA and site of the first European settlement in Alaska, made by Russians in 1784; it is renowned for its large brown bears, known as "Kodiaks". (8974 sq km/3465 sq miles; pop. 9409)

Kofu a silk-producing and wine-making town in the mountains of central HONSHU Island, 105 km (65 miles) west of TOKYO, JAPAN. (Pop. 202,400)

Kola Peninsula (Kol'skiy Poluostrov) a bulging peninsula in the BARENTS SEA in the extreme northwest of the RUSSIAN FEDERATION, to the east of MURMANSK.

Kolding a long-established market town in east JUTLAND, at the crossroads of DENMARK's main east-west and north-south communication routes. The town's Geographical Garden contains over 2000 varieties of plants from all over the world. (Pop. 56,300)

Kolhãpur a university town in southern MAHARASHTRA state in southwest INDIA, about 320 km (200 miles) southeast of BOMBAY. (Pop. 346,306)

Köln *see* **Cologne.**

Kolonia the capital of the Federated States of MICRONESIA, on the island of POHNPEI. (Pop. 22,000).

Kolwezi a leading mining and processing centre for copper and cobalt in the mineral-rich region of SHABA, in southern ZAÏRE. (Pop. 80,000)

Kolyma, River a river in northeastern SIBERIA, flowing north from the gold-rich Kolyma mountains into the East Siberian Sea. (Length 2600 km/1600 miles)

Komi Republic an autonomous republic in the north of the RUSSIAN FEDERATION, which produces timber, coal, oil and natural gas. (415,900 sq km/160,600 sq miles; pop. 1,197,000)

Komodo a small island of Indonesia in the Lesser SUNDA group, between SUMBAWA and FLORES, noted above all as the home of the giant monitor lizard, the Komodo Dragon. (520 sq km/200 sq miles)

Kompong Som the main seaport of CAMBODIA, lying on the Gulf of THAILAND, in the southwest of the country. It has grown rapidly since the 1960s, when road and rail links were opened through the Elephant Mountains to PHNOM PENH, 160 km (100 miles) to the northeast. (Pop. 53,000)

Komsomol'sk na-Amure one of the largest industrial cities in the far east of the RUSSIAN FEDERATION; it is a port on the AMUR River, some 880 km (550 miles) northeast of VALDIVOSTOK. It was founded by members of the *Komosomol* (Young Communist League) in 1932. (Pop. 291,000)

Königsberg *see* **Kaliningrad.**

Konin a coal-mining and aluminium-smelting town in west-central POLAND, 88 km (55 miles) east of POZNAN. (Pop. 73,000)

Konya a carpet-making town and capital of the province of the same name in central southern TURKEY, 235 km (14 miles) south of ANKARA. (Pop. town 438,900)

Kópavogur the second largest town of ICELAND, situated in the favoured southwest corner of the island, just southeast of the capital, REYKJAVIK. (pop. 14,400)

Korcë the main centre for a large wheat and sugar beet-growing basin in the highland southeast of ALBANIA; it stands at 855 m (2805 ft) above sea level. (Pop. 63,600)

Korcula *see* **Dalmatia.**

Korea, North occupies just over half the Korean peninsula in east ASIA. The Yala and Tumen Rivers form its northern border with CHINA and the RUSSIAN FEDERATION. Its southern border with South KOREA is just north of the 38th parallel. It is a mountainous country, three-quarters of which is forested highland or scrubland. The climate is warm temperate, although winters can be cold in the north. Most rain falls during the summer. Nearly 90% of its arable land is farmed by cooperatives, which employ over 40% of the labour force, and rice is the main crop grown. North Korea is quite well endowed with fuel and minerals. Deposits of coal and hydroelectric power generate electricity, and substantial deposits of iron ore are found near PYONGYANG and Musan. Some 60% of the labour force are employed in industry, the most important of which are metallurgical, building, cement and chemicals.

Area : 120,538 sq km (46,540 sq miles)

Population : 22,420,000

Capital : Pyongyang

Other major cities : Chongjin, Nampo

Form of government : Socialist Republic

Religions : Chondoism, Buddhism

Currency : North Korean won

Korea, South occupies the southern half of the Korean peninsula and stretches about 400 km (249 miles), from the Korea Strait to the demilitarized zone bordering North KOREA. It is predominantly mountainous with the highest ranges running north to south along the east coast. The west is lowland, which is extremely densely populated. The extreme south has a humid warm temperate climate, while farther north it is more continental. Most rain falls in summer. Cultivated land represents only 23% of the country's total area, and the main crop is rice. The country has few natural resources but has a flourishing manufacturing industry and is the world's leading supplier of ships and footwear. Other important industries are electronic equipment, electrical goods, steel, petrochemicals, motor vehicles and toys. Its people enjoy a reasonably high standard of living brought about by hard work and determination.

Area : 99,016 sq km (38,230 sq miles)

Population : 42,800,000
Capital : Seoul (Soul)
Other major cities : Pusan, Taegu, Inch'on
Form of government : Republic
Religions : Buddhism, Christianity
Currency : South Korean won

Korea Strait the stretch of water, 64 km (40 miles) at its narrowest), which separates the southern tip of South KOREA from JAPAN. It is also sometimes known as the Tsushima Strait, after the island of that name.

Korinthos *see* **Corinth.**

Koror the capital of BELAU. (Pop. 8000)

Kortrijk *see* **Courtrai**.

Kos (Cos) one of the DODECANESE ISLANDS, belonging to GREECE, in the AEGEAN SEA, noted as the birthplace (*c*.460BC) of Hippocrates, the father of medicine. (290 sq km/112 sq miles; pop. 20,300)

Kosciusko, Mount the highest mountain in AUSTRALIA, a peak in the SNOWY MOUNTAINS range in southern NEW SOUTH WALES. (2230 m/7316 ft)

Kosice a rapidly growing industrial city, and the regional capital of eastern SLOVAKIA. (Pop. 214,300)

Kosovo an autonomous province in the southwest of SERBIA. About 75% of the population are ethnic Albanians. The capital is PRISTINA. (10,887 sq km/4202 sq miles; pop. 1,584,000)

Kosrae the most easterly of the Federated States of MICRONESIA, consisting of a single atoll lying about 500 km (310 miles) southeast of POHNPEI, in the west-central PACIFIC OCEAN. (Pop. 5600)

Kostroma one of the oldest cities in the RUSSIAN FEDERATION, lying in the west of the country, 315 km (195 miles) northeast of MOSCOW. It was founded in the 12th century as a fortress town to guard the north-south trade routes along the Kostroma and VOLGA rivers. Today it is a textile centre. (Pop. 267,000)

Kota Baharu a port and capital of Kelantan state on the

northeast coast of Peninsular MALAYSIA, just south of the border with THAILAND. (Pop. 176,000)

Kota Kinabalu the capital of SABAH state on the north-west coast of BORNEO; it was formerly known as Jesselton in the colonial days of British North Borneo. Nearby is Mount Kinabalu, 4094 m (13,432 ft) high. (Pop. 108,800)

Kotka the second busiest port of FINLAND, after HELSINKI; it lies in the southeast of the country, on the Gulf of Finland, 50 km (30 miles) west of the Russian border. (Pop. 59,400)

Kotor a small medieval seaport on the fiord-like coast of MONTENEGRO; it lies on the south side of the spectacular Gulf of Kotor, which is one of the world's finest natural harbours. (Pop. 20,400)

Kourou a small coastal town of GUYANE, 55 km (35 miles) west of the capital, CAYENNE. It has been the site of European Space Agency rocket launches since 1968. (Pop. 7000)

Kovno *see* **Kaunas.**

Kowloon a mainland territory of HONG KONG, lying opposite and to the north of Hong Kong Island. (Pop. 800,000)

Kra, Isthmus of the narrow neck of land, only some 50 km (30 miles) wide and shared by BURMA and THAILAND, which joins Peninsular MALAYSIA to the mainland of South-East ASIA.

Kragujevac a commerical town in central SERBIA, 97 km (60 miles) southeast of BELGRADE. It was a former Serbian capital (1818-39). (Pop. 164,800)

Krajina the region of southwest CROATIA occupying the narrow neck of the country, lying to the east of DALMATIA; it has assumed major strategic importance in the conflicts resulting from the break-up of the former YUGOSLAVIA in the 1990s. The capital is Knin.

Krakatau (Krakatoa) a volcano which erupted out of the sea between JAVA and SUMATRA in INDONESIA in 1883 in an explosion that was heard 5000 km (3100 miles) away, and which killed 36,000 people. Today the site is marked by a more recent volcano called Anak Krakatau (Son of Krakatau).

Krakow *see* **Cracow.**

Krasnodar an agricultural centre and industrial city in the RUSSIAN FEDERATION near the BLACK SEA. (Pop. 604,000)

Krasnoyarsk a mining city on the Trans-Siberian Railway in central southern SIBERIA. (Pop. 860,000)

Krefeld a textile town specializing in silk in western GERMANY, near the border with the NETHERLANDS. (Pop. 224,000)

Krishna (Kistna), River a river that flows through southern INDIA from its source in the Western GHATS to the Bay of BENGAL. (Length 1401 km/871 miles)

Kristiania *see* **Oslo.**

Kristiansand (Christiansand) the main port of southern Norway, on the SKAGERRAK, founded in 1624 by King Christian of Denmark. Today, it is an industrial town with ferry connections to DENMARK and ENGLAND. (Pop. 61,800)

Krití *see* **Crete**.

Krivoy Rog a city in the DONETS BASIN mining region of the UKRAINE. (Pop. 680,000)

Krk (Veglia) a richly fertile island belonging to CROATIA, in the northern ADRIATIC SEA. (408 sq km/158 sq miles; pop. 1500)

Krung Thep *see* **Bangkok.**

Krym *see* **Crimea.**

Kuala Lumpur the capital of MALAYSIA, sited on the banks of the Kelang and Gombak Rivers. (Pop. 937,900)

Kuala Terengganu the capital of Terengganu state on Peninsular MALAYSIA's remote east coast, about 140 km (85 miles) south of the border with THAILAND. (Pop. 186,700)

Kuantan the capital of Pahang State on the east coast of Peninsular MALAYSIA linked to the capital, KUALA LUMPUR, by a new trans-peninsula highway. (136,700)

Kuanza, River *see* **Cuanza, River.**

Kuching a major town and riverside port in the extreme southwest of the state of Savawak, in East Malaysia; it was the seat of Sarawak's former ruling family of white rajahs. (Pop. 120,000)

Kumamoto a city in the west of Kyushu Island, Japan, noted for its electronics industries. (Pop. 555,700)

Kumasi a town in central southern Ghana, and the capital of the Ashanti people. (Pop. 415,300)

Kumayri a city in Armenia, originally called Aleksandropol, and, until 1992, as Leninakan; it lies on the side of Mount Aragats, 4090 m (13,418 ft), close to the Turkish border. It was founded in 1837 by Armenian refugees fleeing Turkish persecution. (Pop. 220,000)

Kunlun Shan a mountain range with peaks in excess of 7000 m (23,000 ft), extending eastwards from the Karakoram Range to form the northern flank of the Tibetan Plateau in Central Asia.

Kunming an industrial and trading city, and capital of Yunnan province in southern, central China. (Pop. 1,930,000)

Kuopio a resort and religious centre for the Orthodox Church in Finland, founded in 1782 in the centre of the country. (Pop. 77,300)

Kurashiki a city in southwestern Honshu Island, Japan. Although now a major industrial centre, it still preserves much of its medieval heritage. (Pop. 411,400)

Kurdistan a region of the Middle East occupied by the Kurdish people spanning the borders of Iraq, Iran and Turkey. Although proposals for an independent Kurdistan were agreed in 1920 between World War I Allies and Turkey, this plan has never been realized. Greater autonomy was in principle granted to the Kurdish people in Iraq after the Gulf War of 1991.

Kure a major shipbuilding and steel-making town on the Inland Sea shore of Honshu Island, Japan. (Pop. 226,500)

Kuril (Kurile) Islands (Kuril'skiye Ostrova) a long chain of some 56 volcanic islands stretching between the southern coast of the KAMCHATKA peninsula in eastern RUSSIAN FEDERATION and HOKKAIDO Island, northern JAPAN. The archipelago was taken from Japan by the former USSR in 1945; this remains an issue of contention between the Russian Federation and Japan. (15,600 sq km/6020 sq miles)

Kursk a major industrial city in the RUSSIAN FEDERATION, 450 km (280 miles) south of MOSCOW. It was the scene of a devastating tank battle in 1943 which left the city in ruins. (Pop. 423,000)

Kurukshetra a sacred Hindu city in northern INDIA, 140 km (87 miles) north of DELHI. (Pop. 186,100)

Kushiro a fishing port and pulp and paper-making town on the southeast coast of HOKKAIDO Island, JAPAN. (Pop. 214,500)

Kutaisi the second largest city of GEORGIA after TBILISI, lying 85 km (53 miles) east of the BLACK SEA, in the southwest of the country. (Pop. 210,000)

Kutch (Kachchh) an inhospitable coastal region on the border between PAKISTAN and INDIA, which floods in the monsoon season and then dries out into a baking, salty desert. (44,185 sq km/17,060 sq miles)

Kuwait is a tiny Arab state on The GULF, which comprises the city of Kuwait at the southern entrance of Kuwait Bay and a small undulating desert wedged between IRAQ and SAUDI ARABIA. It has nine small offshore islands. It has a dry desert climate that is cool in winter but very hot and humid in summer. There is little agriculture because of lack of water, and major crops produced are melons, tomatoes, onions and dates. Shrimp fishing is becoming an important industry. Large reserves of petroleum and natural gas are the mainstay of the economy. It has about 950 oil wells, but 600 were fired during the Iraqi occupation in 1991 and are unlikely to resume production for several years. Apart from oil, industry includes boat building, food production, petrochemicals, gases and construction.

Kuybyshev

Area : 17,818 sq km (6880 sq miles)
Population : 2,040,000
Capital : Kuwait (Al Kuwayt)
Form of government : Constitutional Monarchy
Religion : Sunni Islam, Shia Islam
Currency : Kuwait dinar

Kuybyshev *see* **Samara**.

Kuzbass *see* **Kuznetsk Basin.**

Kuznetsk *see* **Novokuznetsk.**

Kuznetsk Basin (Kuzbass) a major industrial region of southern SIBERIA, lying on the richest coalfield in the RUSSIAN FEDERATION. Its many cities include NOVOKUZNETSK and KEMEROVO. (69,900 sq km/27,000 sq miles)

Kwai, River two tributaries of the Mae Khlong River in western THAILAND, the Kwai Yai (Big Kwai) and the Kwai Noi (Little Kwai). During World War II, Allied prisoners of war were forced by their Japanese captors to build a railroad line and a bridge over the Kwai Yai at the cost of some 110,000 lives.

Kwajalein one of the largest atolls in the world, with a lagoon covering some 2800 sq km (1100 sq miles). The island forms part of the MARSHALL ISLANDS in the PACIFIC OCEAN, and is leased to the USA as a missile target.

KwaNdebele a semi-autonomus black homeland in central TRANSVAAL province, northeastern SOUTH AFRICA. (3410 sq km/1317 sq miles)

Kwangju (Gwangju; Chonnam) an industrial city and regional capital in the southwestern corner of South KOREA. (Pop. 727,600)

Kwango (Cuango), River a river which rises in northern ANGOLA and flows northwards to join the River KASAI in ZAÏRE. (Length 110 km/680 miles)

KwaZulu a self-governing black homeland consisting of 10 separate territories in NATAL, SOUTH AFRICA. (32,390 sq km/12,503 sq miles; pop. 4,186,000)

Kyoga, Lake an area of shallow water and swamps fed by the NILE, 110 km (70 miles) north of Lake VICTORIA; it extends over 200 km (125 miles) east to west, forming a barrier to communications.

Kyongju an ancient city in the southeast of South KOREA which was the capital of the Silla kingdom from 57BC to AD935. (Pop. 108,000)

Kyoto situated in central southern HONSHU Island, this was the old imperial capital of JAPAN from AD794 to 1868. (Pop. 1,479,100)

Kyrenia (Kirínia) the main north-coast port, resort and market town of CYPRUS; it has been under Turkish occupation since the invasion of 1974. (Pop. 23,000)

Kyrgyzstan, a central Asian republic of the former USSR, declared itself independent in 1991. It is located on the border with northwest CHINA. Much of the country is occupied by the TIAN SHAN Mountains which rise to spectacular peaks. The highest is Pik Pobedy, 7439 m (24,406 ft), which lies on the border with China. In the northeast of the country is Issyk-Kul', a large lake that is heated by volcanic action and never freezes. Most of the country is semi-arid or desert, but climate is greatly influenced by altitude. In general, soils are badly leached except in the valleys, where wheat and other grains can be grown. Grazing of sheep, horses and cattle is carried out extensively. In the west the raising of silkworms is important to the economy. Other industries include non-ferrous metallurgy, machine building, coal mining, tobacco, food processing, textiles and gold mining.

Area : 198,500 sq km (76,600 sq miles)

Population : 3,886,000

Capital : Bishkek (formerly Frunze)

Form of government : Republic

Religion : Sunni Islam

Currency : Rouble

Kyushu the most southerly of JAPAN's main islands, and the third largest after HONSHU and HOKKAIDO. (43,065 sq km/16,627 sq miles; pop. 13,276,000)

L

Laatokka, Lake *see* **Ladoga, Lake.**

Laâyoune (El Aaiún) the capital city of the disputed territory of WESTERN SAHARA, lying in the northwest of the country, 20 km (12 miles) from the ATLANTIC coast. Its Arabic name means "the springs", signifying its oasis orgins. It is controlled by MOROCCO.

Labé a market town in the cooler FOUTA DJALLON mountain region of west-central GUINEA, some 260 km (260 miles) northeast of CONAKRY. (Pop. 79,700)

Labrador the mainland part of the province of NEWFOUNDLAND, on the east coast of CANADA. (295,800 sq km/112,826 sq miles)

Laccadive Islands *see* **Lakshadweep.**

La Coruña *see* **Corunna**.

Ladakh a remote and mountainous district in the northeastern part of the state of JAMMU AND KASHMIR, INDIA, noted for its numerous monasteries which preserve the traditions of Tibetan-style Buddhism. The capital is LEH. (Pop. 70,000)

Ladoga (Ladozhskoye; Laatokka), Lake Europe's largest lake, in western RUSSIAN FEDERATION, to the northeast of ST PETERSBURG. (18,390 sq km/7100 sq miles)

Ladysmith a city in Western NATAL, eastern SOUTH AFRICA; it was beseiged by the Boers for four months (1899-1900) during the Boer War. (Pop. 37,700)

Lae the second largest and fastest-growing town of PAPUA NEW GUINEA, lying on the north coast, 320 km (200 miles) north of PORT MORESBY. (pop. 62,000)

Laghouat an administrative centre and staging post on the Route du HOGGAR, 400 km (250 miles) south of ALGIERS, ALGERIA.

Lagos the principal port and former capital (until 1992) of NIGERIA, situated on the Bight of BENIN. (Pop. 1,477,000)

Lahore a city in eastern central PAKISTAN, close to the border with INDIA. (Pop. 2,922,000)

Lahti a modern industrial town some 100 km (60 miles) north and slightly east of HELSINKI; it is principally involved in wood-based industry, but is also the venue of FINLAND's annual winter-sports competitions. (Pop. 94,100)

Lake District a region of lakes and mountains in the county of CUMBRIA, in northwest ENGLAND. It includes England's highest peak, Scafell Pike (978 m/3208 ft), and a series of lakes famed for their beauty, notably Windermere, Coniston and Ullswater.

Lake of the Woods a lake spattered with some 17,000 islands in southwestern ONTARIO, CANADA, on the border with the USA. (4390 sq km/1695 sq miles)

Lakshadweep a territory of INDIA consisting of 27 small islands (the Amindivi Islands, Laccadive Islands and Minicoy Islands) lying 300 km (186 miles) off the southwest coast of mainland India. (32 sq km/12 sq miles; pop. 40,250)

La Mancha a high, arid plateau in central SPAIN, some 160 km (100 miles) south of MADRID, the setting for *Don Quixote*, a 17th-century novel by Miguel de Cervantes.

La Manche the French name for the ENGLISH CHANNEL; it means "the sleeve", reflecting the shape of this stretch of water that narrows towards the east.

Lambaréné a provincial capital in eastern central GABON, famous as the site of the hospital founded by Albert Schweitzer (1875–1965). (Pop. 28,000)

Lambert Glacier the world's largest known glacier, discovered in 1956, lies near the Davis Base in the Australian Antarctic Territory. It flows 400 km (250 miles) through the Prince Charles Mountains to the Amery Ice Shelf, at which point it is 200 km (125 miles) wide. It is moving forward at about 750 m (2460 ft) per year.

Lampang a rice-growing and teak timber-trade centre about 530 km (330 miles) north of BANGKOK in northwestern THAILAND. (Pop. 215,800)

Lanarkshire *see* **Strathclyde.**

Lancashire a county of northwest ENGLAND, once the heart of industrial Britain. The county town is Preston. (3043 sq km/1175 sq miles; pop. 1,378,000)

Land's End the tip of the peninsula formed by CORNWALL in southwest ENGLAND, and the most westerly point of mainland England.

Landes a department of the AQUITAINE region on the coast of southwest FRANCE. (Pop. 297,400)

Langeland an island in the FUNEN group in central DENMARK. It is linked by a bridge to Funen. It has popular beaches; its main town is Rudkøbing. (283 sq km/109 sq miles; pop. 17,700)

Languedoc-Rousillon a region of FRANCE which lines the MEDITERRANEAN coast from the River RHONE to the border with SPAIN. (27,376 sq km/10,567 sq miles; pop. 1,927,000)

Lansing the state capital of MICHIGAN, USA. (Pop. city 128,000/metropolitan area 416,200)

L'Anse-au-Meadow a historic site in northern NEW-FOUNDLAND, CANADA, where Vikings from GREENLAND landed in the 10th century, forming possibly the first European settlement in North AMERICA. The remains of their colony were discovered in the 1960s and are open to view.

Lantau the largest of the islands which form part of the New Territories of HONG KONG. A new international airport for Hong Kong is being developed on the island, with connecting bridges to the mainland New Territories in prospect.(150 sq km/58 sq miles; pop. 17,000)

Lanzarote *see* **Canary Islands.**

Lanzhou a major industrial city and the capital of GANSU province, central CHINA. (Pop. 2,260,000)

Laois a county in the centre of the Republic of IRELAND. The county town is Portlaoise. (1718 sq km/664 sq miles; pop. 51,200)

Laos is a landlocked country in South-East ASIA, which is ruggedly mountainous apart from the MEKONG River plains along its border with THAILAND. The ANNAM Mountains, which reach 2500 m (8203 ft), form a natural border with VIETNAM. It has a tropical monsoon climate with high temperatures throughout the year and heavy rains in summer. Laos is one of the poorest countries in the world, and its development has been retarded by war, drought and floods. The principal crop is rice, grown on small peasant plots. There is some export of timber, coffee and electricity. All manufactured goods must be imported. The capital and largest city, VIENTIANE, is the country's main trade outlet via Thailand.

Area : 236,800 sq km (91,428 sq miles)

Population : 4,050,000

Capital : Vientiane

Form of government : People's Republic

Religion : Buddhism

Currency : Kip

La Paz a city set high in the ANDES of BOLIVIA, and the capital and seat of government. (Pop. 900,000)

Lapland *see* **Lappland**.

La Plata a port on the estuary of the River PLATE (Rio de la Plata) in northeastern ARGENTINA, 56 km (35 miles) southeast of BUENOS AIRES. (Pop. 455,000)

Lappeenranta (Villmanstrand) one of FINLAND's largest softwood-processing centres, founded in 1649 as a port on the south shore of Lake Saimaa in the southeast of the country, 25 km (15 miles) from the Russian border. (Pop. 54,000)

Lappland (Lapland) the region of northern SCANDINAVIA and the adjoining territory of the RUSSIAN FEDERATION, traditionally inhabited by the nomadic Lapp people; also a province of northern FINLAND, called Lappi.

Laptev Sea part of the ARCTIC OCEAN bordering central northern SIBERIA.

Laramie a market town in a stock-raising and mining

area on the high plateau plains of southeast WYOMING, USA; it was founded in 1868 as a Union Pacific Railroad depot. (Pop. 25,300)

La Rioja *see* **Rioja**.

Larnaca a port, with an international airport, on the southeast coast of CYPRUS. (Pop. 48,400)

La Rochelle an ATLANTIC seaport, tourist centre and capital of Charente-Maritime départment in western FRANCE. It played a leading part in the 16th-century Wars of Religion, between Protestant Hugenots and Catholic forces. (Pop. 104,700)

Lascaux a set of caves in the DORDOGNE department of southwest FRANCE where (in 1940) Paleolithic wall paintings dating back to about 15,000BC were discovered.

Las Palmas de Gran Canaria the main port and largest city of the CANARY ISLANDS, on the island of Gran Canaria. (Pop. 366,500)

La Spezia a major naval base and port about 75 km (47 miles) southeast of GENOA. (Pop. 115,200)

Las Vegas a city in the southeast of the state of NEVADA, USA. This state's liberal gaming laws has allowed Las Vegas to develop as an internationally famous centre for gambling and entertainment. (Pop. city 183,200/metropolitan area 536,500)

Latakia (Al Ladhiqiyah) a city on the MEDITERRANEAN coast of SYRIA, founded by the Romans, and now that country's main port. (Pop. 204,000)

Latium *see* **Lazio.**

Latvia is a BALTIC state that regained its independence in 1991 with the break-up of the USSR. It is located in northeast EUROPE, on the BALTIC SEA, and is sandwiched between ESTONIA and LITHUANIA. Latvians traditionally lived by forestry, fishing and livestock rearing. The chief agricultural occupations are cattle and dairy farming, and the main crops grown are oats, barley, rye, potatoes and flax. Latvia's population is now 70% urban, and agriculture is no longer the mainstay of the economy.

Cities such as Riga, the capital, Daugavpils, Ventspils and Liepaja now produce high-quality textiles, machinery, electrical appliances, paper, chemicals, furniture and foodstuffs. Latvia has extensive deposits of peat, which is used to manufacture briquettes. It also has deposits of gypsum, and in the coastal areas amber is frequently found.

Area : 63,700 sq km (24,595 sq miles)

Population : 2,681,000

Capital : Riga

Other major cities : Daugavpils, Jurmala, Liepaja

Form of government : Republic

Religion : Lutheranism

Currency : Rouble

Launceston the second city and port of TASMANIA, AUSTRALIA, situated at the head of the Tamar river estuary, about 160 km (100 miles) north of HOBART. It exports agricultural and timber products. (Pop. 65,000)

Laurasia *see* **Gondwanaland**.

Lausanne a city on the north shore of Lake GENEVA, SWITZERLAND, and capital of the French-speaking canton of Vaud. (Pop. 140,000)

Laval a city in QUEBEC province of CANADA which effectively forms a northern surburb of MONTREAL. (Pop. 238,300)

Lazio (Latium) a region occupying the central western coast of ITALY around ROME, the regional capital. (17,203 sq km/6642 sq miles; pop. 3,076,000)

Lebanon is a mountainous country in the eastern MEDITERRANEAN. A narrow coastal plain runs parallel to its 240-km (149-mile) Mediterranean coast and gradually rises to the spectacular Lebanon Mountains, which are snow covered in winter. The Anti Lebanon Mountains form the border with SYRIA, and between the two ranges lies the BEQA'A Valley. The climate is Mediterranean with short warm winters and long hot and rainless summers. Rainfall can be torrential in winter and snow falls on high ground. Lebanon is an agricultural country, the main regions of production being the Beqa'a Valley and the coastal plain. Main products include olives, grapes, citrus fruit, apples, cotton, tobacco and sugar beet. Industry is small scale and includes cement, fertilizers and jewellery. There are oil refineries at Tripoli and Sɪᴅᴏɴ.

Area : 10,400 sq km (4015 sq miles)

Population : 2,800,000

Capital : Beirut (Beyrouth)

Other important cities : Tripoli, Zahle

Form of government : Republic

Religions : Shia Islam, Sunni Islam, Christianity

Currency : Lebanese pound

Lebowa a self-governing homeland created for the North Sotho people, made up of several unconnected areas, in the north of the province of Tʀᴀɴsᴠᴀᴀʟ, Sᴏᴜᴛʜ Aғʀɪᴄᴀ. (Pop. 2,246,000)

Le Cap *see* **Cap-Haitien**.

Lecce a historic city in the Pᴜɢʟɪᴀ region of Iᴛᴀʟʏ. (Pop. 97,200)

Leeds an important industrial town on the River Aire in West Yᴏʀᴋsʜɪʀᴇ, in northern Eɴɢʟᴀɴᴅ. (Pop. 450,000)

Leeuwarden the provincial capital of Friesland, in the north of the Nᴇᴛʜᴇʀʟᴀɴᴅs, and a dairying and textile centre. (Pop. 85,100)

Leeward and Windward Islands (1) the Lesser Aɴᴛɪʟʟᴇs in the southern Cᴀʀɪʙʙᴇᴀɴ are divided into two groups. The northern islands in the chain, from the Vɪʀɢɪɴ Isʟᴀɴᴅs to Gᴜᴀᴅᴇʟᴏᴜᴘᴇ are the Leeward Islands; the islands further south, from Dᴏᴍɪɴɪᴄᴀ to Gʀᴇɴᴀᴅᴀ, form the Windward Islands. **(2)** the Sᴏᴄɪᴇᴛʏ Isʟᴀɴᴅs of Fʀᴇɴᴄʜ Pᴏʟʏɴᴇsɪᴀ are also divided into Leeward and Windward Islands.

Leghorn *see* **Livorno.**

Legoland *see* **Billund**.

Le Havre the largest port on the north coast of Fʀᴀɴᴄᴇ. (Pop. 255,900)

Leicester a historic cathedral city, and the county town of LEICESTERSHIRE. (Pop. 280,000)

Leicestershire a county in central ENGLAND. Since 1974 it has also incorporated the former county of Rutland. The county town is LEICESTER. (2553 sq km/986 sq miles; pop. 864,000)

Leiden (Leyden) a university city in western NETHERLANDS on the River Oude RIJN. (Pop. 103,800)

Leinster one of the four ancient provinces into which IRELAND was divided, covering the southeastern quarter of the country.

Leipzig an industrial city and important cultural centre in southeastern GERMANY. (Pop. 559,000)

Leitrim a county in the northwest of the Republic of IRELAND, with a small strip of coast and a northern border with FERMANAGH in NORTHERN IRELAND. The county town is Carrick-on-Shannon. (1525 sq km/589 sq miles; pop. 27,600)

Lelystad a new town about 40 km (25 miles) north and slightly east of AMSTERDAM on the East Flevoland polder, an area of low-lying land reclaimed from the IJSSELMEER in 1957. It is named after Cornelius Lely, the statesman-engineer who first pioneered the polder project in the 1920s. (Pop. 52,300)

Léman, Lake another name for Lake GENEVA.

Le Mans a university city in north western FRANCE, famous for the 24-hour car race held annually at a circuit nearby. (Pop. 194,000)

Lemberg *see* **L'vov.**

Lena, River a river, navigable for much of its length, which flows across eastern SIBERIA, from its source close to Lake BAIKAL to the LAPTEV SEA in the north. (Length 4400 km/2730 miles)

Leninabad *see* **Khudzhand.**

Leninakan *see* **Kumayri.**

Leningrad *see* **St Petersburg.**

Lens a sprawling industrial city in the coal-mining region of northern FRANCE. (Pop. 327,400)

Léon (1) a major manufacturing city in central MEXICO. (Pop. 675,000) **(2)** a historic city, founded by the Romans, in northwest SPAIN, and capital of the province of the same name. (Pop. city 131,200) **(3)** the second largest city of NICARAGUA, after MANAGUA, lying near the northern PACIFIC coast. It has the country's oldest university—founded in 1804—and Central AMERICA's largest cathedral (1746–1846). (Pop. 158,600)

Léopoldville *see* **Kinshasa.**

Leptis Magna the well-preserved ruins of an ancient Roman port on the MEDITERRANEAN coast of LIBYA.

Lérida a textile, leather and paper-manufacturing town in western CATALONIA, SPAIN. It was the scene of a nine-month battle in 1937-8, during the Spanish Civil War. (Pop. 109,600)

Lesbos a large, fertile island in the eastern AEGEAN SEA, belonging to GREECE, but only 10 km (6 miles) from the coast of TURKEY. It was the birthplace of the poet Sappho (*c*.612–580BC) whose love for other women gave rise to the term lesbian. (1630 sq km/630 sq miles; pop. 41,900)

Lesotho is a small landlocked kingdom entirely surrounded by the Republic of SOUTH AFRICA. Snow-capped mountains and treeless uplands, cut by spectacular gorges, cover two-thirds of the country. The climate is pleasant with variable rainfall. Winters are generally dry, with heavy frosts in lowland areas and frequent snow in the highlands. Due to the mountainous terrain, only one-eighth of the land can be cultivated, and the main crop is maize. Yields are low because of soil erosion on the steep slopes and over-grazing by herds of sheep and cattle. Wool, mohair and diamonds are exported, but most foreign exchange comes from money sent home by Lesotho workers in South Africa. Tourism is beginning to flourish, the main attraction to South Africans being the casinos in the capital MASERU, as gambling is prohibited in their own country.

Area : 30,355 sq km (11,720 sq miles)

Population : 1,720,000
Capital : Maseru
Form of government : Monarchy
Religions : RC, other Christianity
Currency : Loti

Lesser Antilles *see* **Antilles**.

Lesser Sunda Islands (Nusa Tenggara) a chain of islands to the east of JAVA, INDONESIA, stretching from BALI to TIMOR. (The Greater Sunda Islands comprise BORNEO, SUMATRA, JAVA and SULAWESI.)

Leszno (Lissa) a beer-brewing and china-making town in southwestern POLAND. It was settled by Czech Protestants in the 16th century and became a centre for Polish Calvinism. (Pop. 52,900)

Lethbridge a city in southern ALBERTA, CANADA; it was established in 1870 as a coal-mining camp but now is the centre of a large ranching and irrigated farming region, whose products it processes,. (Pop. 54,070)

Levant, The a former name for the area of the eastern MEDITERRANEAN now occupied by LEBANON, SYRIA and ISRAEL.

Levkas *see* **Ionian Islands**

Lewes a market town in southeast ENGLAND, and administrative centre for EAST SUSSEX county. It was the site of a battle in 1264 in which King Henry III was defeated by Simon de Montfort. (Pop. 13,770)

Lewis the northern part of the island of Lewis with HARRIS, which is the largest and by far the most populated of the Outer HEBRIDES. The chief town, and capital of the WESTERN ISLES authority, is Stornoway. (1634 sq km/631 sq miles; pop. 21,252)

Lexington a city in central KENTUCKY, USA, named after the Battle of Lexington in MASSACHUSETTS (1775) which marked the beginning of the American Revolutionary War. (Pop. city 210,200/metropolitan area 327,200)

Leyden *see* **Leiden**

Leyte an island of the VISAYAN group in the central

PHILIPPINES. The main town is Tacloban. (7213 sq km/ 2785 sq miles; pop. 1,480,000)

Lhasa the capital of TIBET, an autonomous region of CHINA. It lies 3606 m (11,830 ft) above sea level. (Pop. 120,000)

Liaoning a coastal province of DONGBEI (Manchuria), northeast CHINA, bordering North KOREA. The capital is SHENYANG. (140,000 sq km/540 sq miles; pop. 34,426,000)

Liberec an industrial town in the north of the CZECH REPUBLIC, close to the borders with both POLAND and GERMANY. It manufactures vehicles, textile machinery, clothing, furniture and foodstuffs. Nearby is the Bohemian glass-making area. (Pop. 99,600)

Liberia is located in West AFRICA and has a 560-km (348-mile) coast stretching from SIERRA LEONE to CÔTE D'IVOIRE. It is the only African country never to be ruled by a foreign power. It has a treacherous coast with rocky cliffs and lagoons enclosed by sand bars. Inland the land rises to a densely forested plateau dissected by deep, narrow valleys. Farther inland still, there are beautiful waterfalls, and the Nimba Mountains rise to over 1700 m (5577 ft). Agriculture employs three-quarters of the labour force and produces cassava and rice as subsistence crops and rubber, coffee and cocoa for export. The Nimba Mountains are rich in iron ore, which accounts for 70% of export earnings. There is potential for tourism to develop. Forest and animal reserves are magnificent, and the beaches and lagoons are beautiful, but so far the facilities are very average.

Area : 111,369 sq km (43,000 sq miles)

Population : 2,440,000

Capital : Monrovia

Form of government : Republic

Religion : Animism, Sunni Islam, Christianity

Currency : Liberian dollar

Libreville the capital and main port of GABON. It is so called ("Freetown") because it was originally a settlement for freed slaves. (Pop. 308,000)

Libya is a large north African country that stretches from the south coast of the MEDITERRANEAN to, and in some parts beyond, the Tropic of Cancer. The SAHARA DESERT covers much of the country, extending right to the Mediterranean coast at the Gulf of SIRTE. The only green areas are the scrublands found in the northwest and the forested hills near BENGHAZI. The coastal area has mild wet winters and hot dry summers, but the interior has had some of the highest recorded temperatures of anywhere in the world. Only 14% of the people work on the land, the main agricultural region being in the northwest, near TRIPOLI. Many sheep, goats and cattle are reared, and there is an export trade in skins, hides and hairs. Libya is one of the world's largest producers of oil and natural gas. Other industries include food processing, textiles, cement and handicrafts.

Area : 1,759,540 sq km (679,358 sq miles)

Population : 4,000,000

Capital : Tripoli (Tarabulus)

Other major cities : Benghazi, Misurata

Form of government : Socialist People's Republic

Religion : Sunni Islam

Currency : Libyan dinar

Libyan Desert a notably sandy part of the SAHARA DESERT, which stretches over eastern LIBYA, western EGYPT and northwestern SUDAN, and includes the Great Sand Sea.

Liechtenstein the principality of Liechtenstein is a tiny central European state situated on the east bank of the River RHINE and is bounded by AUSTRIA to the east and SWITZERLAND to the west. In the east of the principality the ALPS rise to 2599 m (8527 ft) at Grauspitze. The climate is mild alpine. Once an agricultural country, Liechtenstein has rapidly moved into industry in the last thirty years. It has a great variety of light industries, such as textiles, high-quality metal goods, precision instruments, pharmaceuticals and ceramics. It is a popular location for foreign companies to have their headquarters in order that they can benefit from the country's lenient tax laws. Tourism is also big business, beautiful scenery and good skiing being the main attractions.

Area : 160 sq km (62 sq miles)

Population : 28,181

Capital : Vaduz

Form of government : Constitutional Monarchy

Religion : RC

Currency : Swiss franc

Liège (Luik) a historic city in eastern BELGIUM, and capital of the province of Liège, built on the confluence of the Rivers MEUSE and Ourthe. (Pop. city 203,000/metropolitan area 609,000)

Liepája an all-year ice-free BALTIC port, industrial city and former Soviet naval base in the southwest of LATVIA. (Pop. 110,000)

Liffey, River the river upon which DUBLIN, the capital of the Republic of IRELAND, is set. (Length 80 km/49 miles)

Liguria the region of northwestern ITALY which fronts the Gulf of GENOA; it has a border with FRANCE. (5415 sq km/ 2091 sq miles; pop. 1,772,000)

Ligurian Sea the northern arm of the MEDITERRANEAN SEA to the west of ITALY, which includes the Gulf of GENOA.

Likasi (Jadotville) a mining, industrial and commercial city in the mineral-rich SHABA region in the southeast of ZAÏRE; it lies on the LUBUMBASHI-ILEBO railway line. (Pop. 190,000)

Lille Bælt (Little Belt) the channel between the Danish peninsula of JUTLAND and the island of FUNEN. It was bridged (road/rail) in 1935 at its narrowest point (600 m/ 666 yds)

Lille-Roubaix-Tourcoing a conurbation of industrial towns in northeastern FRANCE. (Pop. 945,600)

Lilongwe the capital of MALAWI, and the second largest city in the country after BLANTYRE. (Pop. 172,000)

Lima the capital of PERU, situated on the River Rimac, 13 km (8 miles) from the coast. (Pop. 5,500,000)

Limassol the main port of CYPRUS in the southern part of the island. (Pop. 107,200)

Limburg (1) (Limbourg) a Flemish-speaking province in northeast BELGIUM. The capital is Hasselt. (2422 sq km/935 sq miles: pop. 727,000) **(2)** a hilly province in the extreme southeast of the NETHERLANDS, including the "panhandle" section in which the capital, MAASTRICHT, is located.

Limerick a city and port on the River SHANNON, and the county town of the county of Limerick, in the southwest of the Republic of IRELAND. (County 2686 sq km/1037 sq miles; pop. county 161,700; pop. city 60,700)

Limfjorden a broad sea channel that cuts across north JUTLAND from the KATTEGAT in the east to the NORTH SEA in the west; the last kilometre (0.6 mile) is being canalized.

Limoges a city in eastern central FRANCE, famous for its richly decorated porcelain. It is the capital of the LIMOUSIN region. (Pop. 144,100)

Limousin a region of east-central FRANCE in the foothills of the MASSIF CENTRAL, famous in particular for its Limousin cattle. (Pop. 737,000)

Limpopo, River a river which flows northwards from its source in the TRANSVAAL to form part of the border between SOUTH AFRICA and BOTSWANA before crossing southern MOZAMBIQUE to reach the INDIAN OCEAN. Also known as the Crocodile River in its upper reaches. (Length 1610 km/1000 miles)

Lincoln (1) a historic city, with a fine cathedral dating from the 11th century, and the county town of LINCOLN-SHIRE, ENGLAND. (Pop. 77,000). **(2)** The state capital of NEBRASKA, USA. (Pop. city 180,400/metropolitan area 203,000)

Lincolnshire a county on the east coast of central ENGLAND. The county town is LINCOLN. (5885 sq km/2272 sq miles; pop. 558,000)

Lindisfarne a small island, also known as Holy Island,

just off the east coast of NORTHUMBERLAND in northeast ENGLAND. It has an 11th-century priory built on the site of a monastery founded in the 7th century.

Linköping an industrial city in southeastern SWEDEN, 200 km (125 miles) southwest of STOCKHOLM. It was an important religious centre in the Middle Ages; today it manufactures cars, aircraft and railway rolling stock. (Pop. 40,000)

Linz a city and port on the River DANUBE in northern AUSTRIA. (Pop. 201,500)

Lion, Golfe de (Gulf of Lions) the arm of the MEDITER-RANEAN SEA which forms a deep indent in the southern coast of FRANCE, stretching from the border with SPAIN to TOULON, and centreing on the delta of the River RHONE.

Lipari the largest of the volcanic EOLIAN ISALNDS that lie off the north coast of SICILY, ITALY. (38 sq km/15 sq miles; pop. 10,700)

Lisbon (Lisboa) the capital and principal port of PORTU-GAL, situated on the broad River TAGUS, approximately 15 km (9 miles) from the ATLANTIC coast. (Pop. 817,600)

Lisburn a market town in NORTHERN IRELAND, 10 km (6 miles) southwest of BELFAST; it is the centre of the linen industry. (Pop. 40,000)

Lissa *see* **Leszno**.

Lithuania lies to the northwest of the RUSSIAN FEDERATION and BELARUS and is bounded to the north by LATVIA and west by POLAND. It is the largest of the three former Soviet Baltic Republics. Before 1940 Lithuania was a mainly agricultural country but has since been considerably industrialized. Most of the land is lowland covered by forest and swamp, and the main products are rye, barley, sugar beet, flax, meat, milk and potatoes. Industry includes heavy engineering, shipbuilding and building materials. Oil production has started from a small field at Kretinga. Amber is found along the BALTIC coast and is used by Lithuanian craftsmen for making jewellery. *Area* : 65,200 sq km (25,174 sq miles)

Population : 3,690,000
Capital : Vilnius
Other major cities : Kaunas, Klaipeda, Siauliai
Form of government : Republic
Religion : RC
Currency : Rouble

Little Alförd (Kisalförd) a triangular plain covering the northwest of HUNGARY, bounded in the southeast by the Bakony Hills. It is similar to the GREAT ALFÖLD.

Little Belt *see* **Lille Bælt**.

Little Karoo *see* **Karoo**.

Little Rock the state capital of ARKANSAS, USA. (Pop. city 170,100/metropolitan area 492,700)

Liverpool a major port on the estuary of the River MERSEY in northwest ENGLAND; it is the administrative centre of MERSEYSIDE. (Pop. 497,000)

Livingston a new town in west LOTHIAN, central SCOTLAND, 24 km (15 miles) west of EDINBURGH; it was designated in 1962. (Pop.38,594)

Livingstone Falls a series of 92 cataracts on the lower reaches of the ZAÏRE River, in the westernmost part of the country, between KINSHASA and MATADI. The total fall is 260 m (853 ft) in 354 km (220 miles).

Livingstone *see* **Maramba**.

Livingstonia a town in northern MALAWI, 400 km (250 miles) north of LILONGWE. It is named after the explorer David Livingstone. The town was founded as a mission in 1875.

Livorno (Leghorn) a port and industrial city on the coast of TUSCANY, northern ITALY. (Pop. 175,300)

Ljubljana an industrial city on the River Sava, and the capital of SLOVENIA. (Pop. 305,200)

Llanfairpwllgwyngyll (Llanfair P.G.) a village in southeast ANGLESEY, northwest WALES; its name, unabbreviated, is *Llanfairpwllgwyngyllgogerychwyrndrobwllllantysiliogogogoch*, reckoned to be the longest name in GREAT BRITAIN. Translated from Welsh, it means "St Mary's church in the hollow of the white hazel near the rapid whirlpool of Llandysilio of the red cave".

Llangollen a small town on the River Dee in the Welsh county of CLWYD, 50 km (30 miles) south of LIVERPOOL. Since 1947 it has become renowned for its annual international *eisteddfod*—a folk festival of music, poetry and dance. (Pop. 3200)

Llanos a large region of tropical grassland, or savannah, in the ORINOCO basin and GUIANA HIGHLANDS of northern South AMERICA, and, in particular, in central VENEZUELA.

Lobito an important seaport on the ATLANTIC OCEAN coast of ANGOLA, 390 km (240 miles) south of LUANDA. Founded in 1834, it grew rapidly on the opening up of the interior with the completion of the BENGUELA Railway in the 1920s. (Pop. 59,000)

Loch Lomond *see* **Lomond, Loch.**

Loch Ness *see* **Ness, Loch.**

Lod (Lydda) a modern industrial town based around ISRAEL's main international airport, located 15 km (10 miles) southeast of TEL AVIV.

Lodz an industrial city and the second largest city in POLAND, located in the centre of the country. It was rebuilt after being destroyed in World War II. (Pop. 848,500)

Lofoten an ARCTIC island group off the northwest coast of NORWAY, from which they are separated by the Vestfjorden channel. Their cod fisheries are amongst the richest in the world. (1667 sq km/644 sq miles; pop. 26,200)

Logan, Mount the highest mountain in CANADA, and the second highest in North America after Mount MCKINLEY. It is situated in southwest YUKON, on the border with ALASKA. (5951 m/19,524 ft)

Loire, River the longest river in FRANCE, flowing northwards from the southeastern MASSIF CENTRAL and then to the west to meet the ATLANTIC OCEAN just to the west of NANTES. Its middle reaches are famous for their spectacular châteaux, and for the fertile valley which produces fine white wines. (Length: 1012 km/629 miles)

Lolland the third largest Danish island, lying in the south of the archipelago, separated from GERMANY by the Fehmarn Belt. It is low-lying and mainly fertile. The chief towns are Nakskov, Maribo and Sakskøbing. (1234 sq km/476 sq miles; pop. 81,800)

Lombardy (Lombardia) the central northern region of ITALY, which drops down from the ALPS to the plain of the River Po, one of the country's most productive areas in both agriculture and industry. MILAN is the regional capital. (23,854 sq km/9210 sq miles; pop. 898,700)

Lombok an island of the LESSER SUNDA group, east of BALI. (5435 sq km/2098 sq miles; pop. 1,300,200)

Lomé the capital and main port of TOGO, situated close to the border with GHANA. (Pop. 283,000)

Lomond, Loch a scenic lake at the southern edge of the HIGHLANDS of SCOTLAND, whose "*bonnie banks*" are celebrated in song; it is the largest inland water in BRITAIN, only 28 km (18 miles) northwest of GLASGOW (Length: 34 km/21 miles; width: 8 km/5 miles max.)

London (1) the capital of the UNITED KINGDOM, which straddles both banks of the River THAMES near its estuary. The metropolitan area of GREATER LONDON consists of 33 boroughs, including the CITY, an international centre for trade and commerce. (Pop. 6,755,000). **(2)** an industrial city in southwestern ONTARIO, Canada. (Pop. 284,000)

Londonderry (Derry) the second largest city in NORTHERN IRELAND after BELFAST, and the county town of the county of Londonderry. (County 2076 sq km/801 sq miles; pop. county 84,000; pop. city 62,000)

Long Island an island off the coast of NEW YORY State, stretching some 190 km (118 miles) to the northeast away from the city of NEW YORK. Its western end forms part of the city of New York (the boroughs of Brooklyn and Queens) but the rest is a mixture of residential suburbs, farmland and resort beaches. (3685 sq km/1423 sq miles)

Longford a county in the centre of the Republic of IRE-

LAND, with a county town of the same name. (1044 sq km/ 403 sq miles; pop. 31,100)

Lord Howe Island a small island lying some 600 km (375 miles) to the east of the coast of NEW SOUTH WALES, AUSTRALIA, now a popular resort. (16 sq km/6 sq miles; pop. 300)

Lorraine a region of northeast FRANCE, with a border shared by BELGIUM, LUXEMBOURG and GERMANY. The regional capital is METZ. (Pop. 2,320,000)

Los Angeles a vast, sprawling city on the PACIFIC OCEAN in southern CALIFORNIA, USA, the second largest city in the USA after NEW YORK. (Pop. city 3,096,700/conurbation 12,372,600)

Lothian a local government region in southeast central SCOTLAND, with EDINBURGH as its administrative centre. It was created in 1975 out of the former counties of Midlothian, and East and West Lothian. (1756 sq km/678 sq miles; pop. 745,000)

Lough Neagh *see* **Neagh, Lough.**

Louisiana a state in central southern USA, on the lower reaches of the MISSISSIPPI River, and with a coastline on the Gulf of MEXICO. The state capital is BATON ROUGE. (125,675 sq km/48,523 sq miles; pop. 4,481,000)

Louisville a city and commercial centre, in northern KENTUCKY, USA, on the OHIO River. (Pop. city 289,800/ metropolitan area 962,600)

Lourdes one of the world's most important Marian shrines, in the foothills of the central PYRÉNÉES, FRANCE. It became a place of miraculous healing after a series of visions of the Virgin Mary witnessed by Bernadette Soubirous in 1858. (Pop. 17,600)

Lourenço Marques *see* **Maputo.**

Louth a county on the east coast of the Republic of IRELAND, bordering NORTHERN IRELAND. The county town is Dundalk. (823 sq km/318 sq miles; pop. 88,500)

Low Countries, The a lowland region of mainland western EUROPE, on the NORTH SEA, consisting principally of

BELGIUM and the NETHERLANDS, but sometimes taken to include LUXEMBOURG, and therefore the same as BENELUX.

Lower Egypt an ancient kingdom based on that part of EGYPT north of CAIRO, including the NILE delta and MEDITERANEAN coast. Union with the kingdom of UPPER EGYPT in 3100BC was followed by 30 dynasties of pharaohs who ruled Egypt until the Greek conquest in 332BC.

Lowlands, The the relatively low, but not flat, region of central SCOTLAND, around the FORTH and CLYDE valleys, and separating the HIGHLANDS from the SOUTHERN UPLANDS.

Loyalty Islands a major outlying group of three main islands, part of NEW CALEDONIA, which lie 100 km (60 miles) to the west. The main product is coconuts. (Pop. 15,500)

Lualaba, River a river that flows northwards across the eastern part of ZAÏRE from the border with ZAMBIA before joining the River Lomami to form the River ZAÏRE. (Length 1800 km/1120 miles)

Luanda The capital of ANGOLA, and a major port on the ATLANTIC OCEAN. (Pop. 700,000)

Lübeck a BALTIC port in northern GERMANY, lying some 20 km (12 miles) from the coast on the River Trave. (Pop. 80,000)

Lublin (Lyublin) a city and agricultural centre in southeastern POLAND. (Pop. 320,000)

Lubumbashi the principal mining town of ZAÏRE, and the capital of the Shaba region in the southeast of the country. It was founded in 1910 and known as Elisabethville until 1966. (Pop. 600,000)

Lucca a town in northwestern TUSCANY, ITALY. Surrounded by 16th-century fortifications, its medieval street plan incorporates the site of a Roman amphitheatre. (Pop. 89,100)

Lucerne (Luzern) a city set on the beautiful Lake Lucerne in central SWITZERLAND, retaining much of its medieval past; also the name of the surrounding canton. (Pop. city 67,500)

Lucknow the capital of the state of UTTAR PRADESH in central northern INDIA. (Pop. 1,007,600)

Lüda (Dalian) an industrial city and port in LIAONING province, northeastern CHINA. (Pop. 4,000,000)

Ludhiana a town in central PUNJAB, INDIA, home of the respected Punjab Agricultural University. (Pop. 607,000)

Ludwigshafen a town, industrial centre and river port on the River RHINE in southwestern GERMANY. (Pop. 163,000)

Lugansk a major industrial city of the eastern UKRAINE in the DONETS BASIN. Renamed Voroshilovgrad in 1970 after Kliment Voroshilov, president of the former USSR (1953–60). Its name reverted to Lugansk in 1990. (Pop. 491,000)

Luik *see* **Liège.**

Luluabourg *see* **Kananga.**

Lumbini the birthplace of Buddha (Prince Siddhartha Gautama, *c*.563–488BC), part of the village of Rummindei in central southern NEPAL.

Lund an old university town in the extreme southwestern SKÅNE province of SWEDEN, 16 km (10 miles) northeast of MALMÖ. It was founded in the 11th century by the Danish King Canute, who also ruled England.

Lüneburg a canal port in northwest GERMANY, 40 km (25 miles) southeast of HAMBURG. Nearby, on the Lüneburg Heath, the British Field Marshal Montgomery received the surrender of the German troops in May 1945, ending World War II in Europe. (Pop. 60,600)

Luoyang a city of ancient origins, founded in about 2100BC, in HENAN province in eastern central CHINA. As a principal centre of the Shang dynasty (18th-12th centuries BC), it is rich in archaeological remains. (Pop. 500,000)

Lusaka the capital of ZAMBIA, situated in the southeast of the country. (Pop. 538,500)

Luton an industrial town in BEDFORDSHIRE, ENGLAND, 50 km (30 miles) north of LONDON. It is a centre of the British car-manufacturing industry, and also has a busy international airport. (Pop. 165,000)

Luxembourg the grand duchy of Luxembourg is a small

independent country bounded by BELGIUM on the west, FRANCE on the south, and GERMANY on the east. In the north of the duchy, a wooded plateau, the Oesling, rises to 550 m (1804 ft), and in the south a lowland area of valleys and ridges is known as the Gutland. Northern winters are cold and raw, with snow covering the ground for almost a month, but in the south winters are mild and summers cool. In the south the land is fertile, and crops grown include maize, roots, tubers and potatoes. Dairy farming is also important. It is in the south, also, that beds of iron ore are found, and these form the basis of the country's iron and steel industry. In the east Luxembourg is bordered by the MOSELLE River, in whose valley wines are produced.

Area : 2586 sq km (998 sq miles)

Population : 378,400

Capital : Luxembourg

Form of government : Constitutional Monarchy

Religion : RC

Currency : Luxembourg franc

Luxor a town that has grown up around one of the great archaeological sites of ancient EGYPT, on the east bank of the River NILE in the centre of the country, just south of the ancient capital, THEBES, and 3 km (2 miles) from KARNAK. (Pop. 78,000)

Luzern *see* **Lucerne.**

Luzon the largest island of the PHILIPPINES, in the north of the group, with the nation's capital, MANILA, at its centre. (104,688 sq km/40,420 sq miles; pop. 29,400,000)

L'vov (Lemberg) a major industial city of medieval origins in the western UKRAINE. (Pop. 688,000)

Lyallpur *see* **Faisalabad.**

Lydda see Lod.

Lyons (Lyon) the second largest city in FRANCE after PARIS, situated at the confluence of the Rivers RHÔNE and SAONE in the southeast of the country. (Pop. 1,236,100)

Lyublin *see* **Lublin.**

M

Maas, River *see* **Meuse.**

Maastricht the capital of the southernmost Dutch province, LIMBURG, lying on the MAAS River, by the border with BELGIUM and only 24 km (15 miles) from AACHEN, GERMANY; it is a multilingual town. Appropriately at "the heart of EUROPE", it was in Maastricht, on 11 December 1991, that the leaders of the 12 EC countries reached a historic argeement on closer political and economic union. (Pop. city 112,600/Greater Maastricht 156,500)

Macáu (Macao) a tiny Portuguese province on the coast of south CHINA, opposite HONG KONG. Occupied by the Portuguese since 1557, the territory will be handed back to China in 1997. The vast majority of the population is Chinese, and the dominant language is Cantonese. Tourism and the handling of trade destined for China are major sources of income. The capital is Macau City. (15.5 sq km/6 sq miles; pop. 406,000; cur. Pataca = 100 avos)

Macdonnell Ranges the parallel ranges of mountains of central AUSTRALIA, in the southern part of the NORTHERN TERRITORY, near to ALICE SPRINGS. The highest peak is Mount Ziel (1510 m/4954 ft).

Macedonia (1) (Makedhonía) the largest region of GREECE, occupying most of the northern part of the mainland, and with northern borders with ALBANIA, former YUGOSLAVIA and BULGARIA. (Pop. 2,122,000). **(2) (Makedonija)** the most southerly of the republics of former Yugoslavia, with SKOPJE as its capital. (25,713 sq km/9928 sq miles; pop. 1,912,200)

Maceió a port on the central east coast of BRAZIL. (Pop. 401,000)

Macgillicuddy's Reeks a range of mountains in the southwest of the Republic of IRELAND which includes the country's highest peak at CARRAUNTOOHIL (1040 m/3414 ft).

Machu Picchu the ruins of a great Inca city, set spectacularly on a mountain ridge high in the ANDES near CUZCO, in south central PERU. It was abandoned in the 16th century and rediscovered only in 1911.

Mackay a port on the east coast of QUEENSLAND, AUSTRALIA, some 800 km (500 miles) northwest of BRISBANE. It is at the centre of a major sugar cane-growing area, and processes and exports about a third of the country's total production. (Pop. 31,600)

Mackenzie, River a river flowing northwards through the western part of the NORTHWEST TERRITORIES of CANADA from the GREAT SLAVE LAKE to the ARCTIC OCEAN. (Length 4250 km/2640 miles)

Mâcon a market centre of the Mâconnais wine area of the BURGUNDY region, lying on the river Saône, 60 km (37 miles) north of LYON. (Pop. 39,900)

Madagascar is an island state situated off the southeast coast of AFRICA, separated from the mainland by the MOZAMBIQUE Channel. Madagascar is the fourth largest island in the world and the centre of it is made up of high savanna-covered plateaux. In the east, forested mountains fall steeply to the coast and in the southwest, the land falls gradually through dry grassland and scrub. The staple food crop is rice and 80% of the population grow enough to feed themselves. Cassava is also grown but some 58% of the land is pasture and there are more cattle than people. The main export earners are coffee, vanilla, cloves and sugar. There is some mining for chromite and an oil refinery at Toamasina on the east coast. Upon independence in 1960, Madagascar became known as the Malagasy Republic, but was changed back by referendum in 1975.

Area : 587,041 sq km (226,657 sq miles)

Madang

Population : 11,440,000
Capital : Antananarivo
Other major cities : Fianarantsoa, Mahajanga, Toamasina
Form of government : Republic
Religions : Animism, RC, Protestantism
Currency : Malagasy franc

Madang a port on the north coast of PAPUA NEW GUINEA, which processes and exports many tropical foodstuffs and timber products. (Pop. 34,250)

Madeira the main island in a small group in the eastern ATLANTIC OCEAN which have belonged to PORTUGAL since the the the 16th century, lying some 1000 km (620 miles) due west of CASABLANCA in MOROCCO. The capital is FUNCHAL. (740 sq km/286 sq miles; pop. 248,500)

Madeira, River one the AMAZON's main tributaries, flowing northeast from the Bolivian ANDES; it joins the Amazon east of MANAUS. (Length 2013 km/1251 miles)

Madhya Pradesh the largest state in INDIA, in the centre of the country. The capital is BHOPAL. (443,446 sq km/171,170 sq miles; pop. 52,178,800)

Madison the state capital of WISCONSIN, USA. (Pop. city 170,700/metropolitan area 333,000)

Madras the main port on the east coast of INDIA, and the capital of the state of TAMIL NADU. (Pop. 4,289,300)

Madrid the capital of SPAIN, situated in the middle of the country, and also the name of the surrounding province. (Pop. city 3,188,300/province 4,727,000)

Madura an island off the northeastern coast of JAVA. (5290 sq km/2042 sq miles; pop. 1,860,000)

Madurai a textile city in TAMIL NADU, in the southern tip of INDIA. (Pop. 907,700)

Mae Nam Khong, River *see* **Salween, River.**

Mafikeng (Mafeking) a town in the black state of BOPHUTHATSWANA, SOUTH AFRICA, scene of the Relief of Mafeking in 1890, ending an eight-month siege of British troops by the Boers. (Pop. 29,400)

Magadan a port and industrial city on the north shore of the Sea of OKHOTSK in the far east of the RUSSIAN FEDERATION; founded in 1933, it is the administrative centre for a huge hinterland. (Pop. 138,000)

Magdalena, River a river which flows northwards through western COLOMBIA and into the CARIBBEAN at BARRANQUILA. (Length 1550 km/965 miles)

Magdeburg a city and inland port on the River ELBE in eastern GERMANY, 120 km (75 miles) southwest of BERLIN. (Pop. 289,000)

Magellan, Strait of the waterway, 3 km (2 miles) across at its narrowest, which separates the island of TIERRA DEL FUEGO from the southern tip of mainland South AMERICA. It was discovered by the Portuguese navigator Ferdinand Magellan (?1480–1521) in 1520.

Maggiore, Lake (Lago Maggiore) an Alpine lake straddling the border between ITALY and SWITZERLAND, and lying some 80 km (50 miles) northeast of MILAN; it is a popular tourist area, with resorts such as Verbania, Stresa and Locarno.

Maghreb (Maghrib) the name by which the countries of northwest AFRICA, MOROCCO, ALGERIA and TUNISIA are often called collectively.

Magnitogorsk an industrial city specializing in iron and steel, in the southern URAL MOUNTAINS in the RUSSIAN FEDERATION, founded in 1930. (Pop. 421,000)

Mahajanga a port on the northwest coast of MADAGASCAR, some 400 km (250 miles) from ANTANANARIVO; it was formerly Mujunga, founded in about 1700 by Arab traders. (Pop. 66,000)

Maharashtra a state in the centre of the west coast of INDIA, with BOMBAY as its capital. (307,690 sq km/118,768 sq miles; pop. 62,784,200)

Mahore *see* **Mayotte.**

Maidstone the administrative centre of KENT, southeast ENGLAND, which lies on the River Medway. (Pop. 72,311)

Maiduguri an industrial town and capital city of Borno

state in the northeast corner of Nigeria, lying on the Plain of Bornu, about 100 km (60 miles) southwest of Lake Chad. Since being connected to the south by rail in 1964, it has been an important meeting place of roads from neighbouring countries. (Pop. 225,100)

Main, River a river that snakes its way westwards from its source near Bayreuth in central Germany, passing through Frankfurt am Main before joining the River Rhine at Mainz. (Length 524 km/325 miles)

Maine a state in the northeastern corner of the USA, bordering Canada. The state capital is Augusta. (86,027 sq km/33,215 sq miles; pop. 1,164,000)

Mainz a city and inland port on the confluence of the Rivers Rhine and Main in western central Germany. (Pop. 185,000)

Majorca (Mallorca) the largest of the Balearic Islands, in the western Mediterranean. The capital is Palma. (3639 sq km/1405 sq miles; pop. 460,000)

Majuro an atoll of three islands (Dalap, Uliga and Darrit) which together form the capital of the Marshall Islands. (Pop. 8700)

Makassar *see* **Ujung Padang.**

Makassar Strait the broad stretch of water, 130 km(81 miles) across at its narrowest, which separates the islands of Borneo and Sulawesi in Indonesia.

Makedhonía *see* **Macedonia**.

Makedonija *see* **Macedonia**.

Makeyevka an industrial city in the Donets Basin in the southern Ukraine. (Pop. 448,000)

Makgadikgadi Pans *see* **Okavango Basin.**

Makhachkala a port and industrial city on the west coast of the Caspian Sea, and the capital of the republic of Dagestan. (Pop. 269,000)

Makkah *see* **Mecca.**

Makurdi the capital of Benue state in east-central Nigeria and an important communications centre connecting Benue river steamers with the Kaduna-Port Harcourt railway, as well as road and air links. (Pop. 86,800)

Malabar Coast the name given to the coastal region of the state of KERALA in southwestern INDIA.

Malabo a port and the capital of EQUATORIAL GUINEA, situated on the north coast of BIOKO Island. (Pop. 37,200)

Malacca *see* **Melaka.**

Malacca, Strait of the busy waterway, just 50 km (31 miles) wide at its narrowest, which separates the island of SUMATRA in INDONESIA from the southern tip of MALAYSIA, with SINGAPORE at its eastern end.

Málaga a port, manufacturing city, and tourist resort on the MEDITERRANEAN coast of ANDALUCIA, southern SPAIN. Also the name of the province of which it is the capital. (Pop. town 503,300)

Malagasy Republic *see* **Madagascar.**

Malawi (Nyasa), Lake a long, narrow lake which runs down most of the eastern side of Malawi and forms Malawi's border with TANZANIA and MOZAMBIQUE. (23,300 sq km/9000 sq miles)

Malawi lies along the southern and western shores of the third largest lake in AFRICA, Lake MALAWI. To the south of the lake the Shire river flows through a valley, overlooked by wooded, towering mountains. The tropical climate has a dry season from May to October and a wet season for the remaining months. Agriculture is the predominant occupation and many Malawians live on their own crops. Plantation farming is used for export crops. Tea is grown on the terraced hillsides in the south and tobacco on the central plateau. Malawi has bauxite and coal deposits but due to the inaccessibility of their locations, mining is limited. Hydroelectricity is now being used for the manufacturing industry but imports of manufactured goods remain high. Malawi was formerly the British colony of Nyasaland, a name meaning "Land of the Lake" given to it by the 19th-century explorer, David Livingstone.

Area : 118,484 sq km (45,747 sq miles)

Malay Peninsula

Population : 7,980,000
Capital : Lilongwe
Other major cities : Blantyre, Mzuzu, Zomba
Form of government : Republic
Religions : Animism, RC, Presbyterianism
Currency : Kwacha

Malay Peninsula *see* **Malaysia**.

Malaysia the Federation of Malaysia lies in the SOUTH CHINA SEA in southeast ASIA, and comprises Peninsular Malaysia on the Malay peninsula and the states of SABAH and SARAWAK on the island of BORNEO. Malaysia is affected by the monsoon climate. The northeast monsoon brings rain to the east coast of Peninsular Malaysia in winter, and the southwest monsoon brings rain to the west coast in summer. Throughout the country the climate is generally tropical and temperatures are uniformly hot throughout the year. Peninsular Malaysia has always had thriving rubber-growing and tin dredging industries and now oil palm growing is also important on the east coast. Sabah and Sarawak have grown rich by exploiting their natural resources, the forests. There is also some offshore oil and around the capital, KUALA LUMPUR, new industries such as electronics are expanding.

Area : 329,749 sq km (127,316 sq miles)
Population : 17,810,000
Capital : Kuala Lumpur
Other major cities : Ipoh, Georgetown, Johor Baharu
Form of government : Federal Constitutional Monarchy
Religion : Sunni Islam
Currency : Malaysian ringgit

Maldives the Republic of Maldives lies 640 km (398 miles) southwest of SRI LANKA in the INDIAN OCEAN and comprises 1200 low-lying coral islands grouped into 12 atolls. Only about 202 of the islands are inhabited, and the highest point is only 1.5 m (5 ft) above sea level. The climate is hot and humid and affected by monsoons between May and August. The islands are covered with coconut palms, and some millet, cassava, yams and tropical fruit are grown. Rice, however, the staple diet of its islanders, has to be imported. Fishing is an important occupation and the chief export is now canned or frozen tuna, most of which goes to JAPAN. Tourism is now developing fast and has taken over fishing as the major foreign currency earner.

Area : 298 sq km (115 sq miles)
Population : 214,139
Capital : Malé
Form of government : Republic
Religion : Sunni Islam
Currency : Rufiyaa

Malé the main atoll of the MALDIVES, and the town which is the country's capital. (2.6 sq km/1 sq mile; pop. 29,000)

Mali is a landlocked state in West AFRICA. The country mainly comprises vast and monotonous plains and pla-teaux. It rises to 1155 m (3790 ft) in the Adrar des Iforas range in the northeast. The SAHARA in the north of the country is encroaching southwards and the country is one of the poorest in the world. In the south there is some rain and plains are covered by grassy savanna and a few scattered trees. The river NIGER runs through the south of the country and small steamboats use it for shipping between Koulikoro and Gao. Only one fifth of the land can be cultivated. Rice, cassava and millet are grown for domestic consumption and cotton for export. Droughts in the early 1970s resulted in thousands of cattle dying, crop failure, famine and disease killing many of the population. Iron ore and bauxite have been discovered but as yet have not been mined.

Area : 1,240,192 sq km (478,838 sq miles)
Population : 9,090,000
Capital : Bamako
Other major cities : Segou, Mopti
Form of government : Republic

Religions : Sunni Islam, Animism
Currency : Franc CFA

Malines *see* **Mechelen**.

Mallorca *see* **Majorca**.

Malmö a port in southwest SWEDEN, on the narrow channel which separates Sweden from COPENHAGEN in DENMARK. (Pop. 229,900)

Malta, a small republic in the middle of the MEDITERRANEAN, lies just south of the island of SICILY. It comprises three islands, Malta, Gozo and Comino, which are made up of low limestone plateaux with little surface water. The climate is Mediterranean with hot, dry sunny summers and little rain. Winters are cooler and wetter. Malta is virtually self sufficient in agricultural products and exports potatoes, vegetables, wine and cut flowers. The British military base on Malta was once the mainstay of the economy but after the British withdrew in the late 1970s, the naval dockyard was converted for commercial shipbuilding and repairs, which is now one of the leading industries. Tourism has also boomed and the island has become popular for retirement in the sunshine with low taxes.

Area : 316 sq km (122 sq miles)
Population : 354,900
Capital : Valletta
Form of government : Republic
Religion : RC
Currency : Maltese pound

Maluku (Moluccas) a group of some 1000 islands in eastern INDONESIA. They are known as the Spice Islands, for they were once the only source of cloves and nutmegs in the world. The principal islands are Halmahera, Seram and Buru. The capital is AMBON. (74,505 sq km/ 28,766 sq miles; pop. 1,411,000)

Man the administrative and commercial capital of the western region of CÔTE D'IVOIRE.

Man, Isle of an island of the BRITISH ISLES, in the IRISH SEA, halfway between ENGLAND and IRELAND. It is a British Crown possession, not a part of the UK, and has its own parliament, the Court of Tynwald. The capital is Douglas. (585 sq km/226 sq miles; pop. 66,000)

Manado a fishing port and foodstuffs-processing centre, it is also the provincial capital of North SULAWESI, situated at the northeastern tip of the Indonesian island. (Pop. 129,910)

Managua the capital of NICARAGUA, situated on the edge of Lake Managua. (Pop. 630,000)

Manaus a major port on the River AMAZON in BRAZIL, lying 1600 km (1000 miles) from the sea. (Pop. 635,000)

Manchester a major industrial and commercial city in northwest ENGLAND, and the administrative centre for the metropolitan county of Greater Manchester. It is connected to the estuary of the River MERSEY by the Manchester Ship Canal. (County 1286 sq km/497 sq miles; pop. city 448,000/county 2,594,778)

Manchuria *see* **Dongbei.**

Mandalay the principal city of central BURMA, and a port on the River IRRAWADDY. (Pop. 417,300)

Mangalore a port on the MALABAR COAST of KARNATAKA state in southern INDIA. (Pop. 165,174)

Manhattan an island at the heart of NEW YORK City, USA, lying between the HUDSON, HARLEM and East Rivers, and at the north end of Upper Bay. New York was founded in the early 17th century when Dutch settlers purchased Manhattan from the Indians for 60 florins (*c.* $20), calling their colony New Amsterdam. Today, skyscraper-dominated Manhattan is the centre of a great world metropolis and is the home of the United Nations headquarters. (47 sq km/22 sq miles; pop. 1,428,285)

Manila the capital of the PHILIPPINES. The city is an important port and commercial centre, and is sited on LUZON island. The surrounding urban area is known as Metro Manila (Pop. city 6,000,000/Metro Manila 8,000,000)

Manipur

Manipur a small state of INDIA in the far northeast, on the border with BURMA. The capital is Imphal. (22,327 sq km/8618 sq miles; pop. 1,421,000)

Manitoba the most easterly of the prairie provinces of CANADA. The capital is WINNIPEG. (650,087 sq km/250,998 sq miles; pop. 1,026,000)

Manizales a city in the centre of a major coffee-growing region of west-central COLOMBIA; it straddles an Andean ridge at a height of 2126 m (6975 ft). (Pop. 259,000)

Mannheim an inland port and industrial city on the confluence of the Rivers RHINE and NECKAR. (Pop. 300,000)

Mansura *see* **El Mansura.**

Mantua (Mantova) a city in the valley of the River PO, in the LOMBARDY region of ITALY, retaining much of its medieval heritage. (Pop. 60,400)

Maoming a city in the GUANGDONG province of southern CHINA, close to oil shale deposits and emerging as an important mining centre. (Pop. 200,000)

Maputo the capital and main port of MOZAMBIQUE. It was formerly known as Lourenço Marques. (Pop. 785,500)

Maracaibo the second largest city in VENEZUELA, in the northwest. (Pop. 1,100,000)

Maracaibo, Lake a shallow lake in northwest VENEZUELA, linked to the CARIBBEAN SEA by a channel. It contains one of the richest oil fields in the world. (13,280 sq km/5127 sq miles)

Maracay an industrial city and capital of the Arugua state of northern VENEZUELA, 50 km (30 miles) to the west of CARACAS. (Pop. 387,700)

Maramba (Livingstone) a tourist town for visitors to the VICTORIA FALLS, lying on the ZAMBIA side of the border with ZIMBABWE. Formerly called Livingstone, after the famous Scottish missionary and explorer, Dr. David Livingstone (1813-73), it was the capital of the then Northern Rhodesia between 1911 and 1935. Today it is the capital of Zambia's Southern Province. (Pop. 72,000)

Marathón a small town in GREECE, near the site of a battle in 490BC in which the Athenians defeated the Persians, and from which a courier ran the 42 km (26 miles) southeastwards to break the news to the citizens of ATHENS—a feat that gave the name "marathon" to the long-distance race that remains the climax of the modern Olympic Games.

Marbella a popular resort on the MEDITERRANEAN coast of southern SPAIN, in the province of MALAGA. (Pop. 67,900)

Marburg *see* **Maribor.**

Marche (Marches) a region of central eastern ITALY, lining the ADRIATIC coast. The capital is ANCONA. (9694 sq km/3743 sq miles; pop. 1,424,000)

Mar del Plata a coastal city and beach resort on the northeast coast of ARGENTINA, 400 km (250 miles) south of BUENOS AIRES. (Pop. 424,000)

Margarita an island belonging to VENEZUELA, lying just off its northeastern coast, rapidly becoming a popular tourist destination. (929 sq km/355 sq miles; pop. 38,000)

Mariana Islands a chain of small volcanic islands about 2400 km (1500 miles) east of the northern PHILIPPINES, comprising the US territories of GUAM and NORTH MARIANA.

Marianas Trench a major curving trench on the seabed of the northwestern PACIFIC OCEAN, near GUAM, containing the Challenger Deep, which was confirmed in 1960 as being the world's deepest spot. (Depth 11,033 m/36,198 ft below sea level)

Marianske Lazne (Marienbad) a spa town in western Czech Republic. (Pop. 18,400)

Maribor (Marburg) an industrial city in SLOVENIA. (Pop. 185,700)

Marie Galante *see* **Guadeloupe.**

Marienbad *see* **Marianske Lazne.**

Marigot *see* **St Martin.**

Mari Republic one of the 16 autonomous republics of the RUSSIAN FEDERATION, situated in the west-central part of the country, in the middle of the VOLGA basin. The capital is Yoshkar-Ola. (22,300 sq km/8955 sq miles; pop. 713,000)

Maritime Provinces (Maritimes; Atlantic Provinces) a regional term for the Canadian provinces of NEW BRUNSWICK, NOVA SCOTIA, PRINCE EDWARD ISLAND and NEW-FOUNDLAND, although the latter may be excluded.

Marlborough Sounds the rugged coastline of the deeply indented peninsula at the northeastern tip of SOUTH ISLAND, NEW ZEALAND, lying across the COOK STRAIT from WELLINGTON.

Marmara, Sea of a small sea lying between the DARDA-NELLES and the BOSPHORUS, providing a vital link in the route between the MEDITERRANEAN SEA and the BLACK SEA. The surrounding coasts all belong to TURKEY.

Marmolada, Mount *see* **Dolomites.**

Marquesas Islands a group of a dozen or so fertile, volcanic islands in the northeastern sector of FRENCH POLYNESIA, lying about 1400 km (875 miles) northeast of TAHITI. (1189 sq km/459 sq miles; pop. 6500)

Marrakech (Marrakesh) a historic oasis city in central western MOROCCO, founded in the 11th century and formerly the country's capital. (Pop. 440,000)

Marsala a wine-making and fishing town at the western tip of SICILY, ITALY. (Pop. 79,900)

Marseilles (Marseille) the largest port in FRANCE, on the MEDITERRANEAN coast, and France's third largest city after PARIS and LYONS. (Pop. 1,110,500)

Marshall Islands a scattered group of some 1250 islands in MICRONESIA, in the western PACIFIC OCEAN. They form a self-governing republic which remains in free association with the USA Copra is the main export. The principal languages are Marshallese and English, and the capital is MAJURO. (181 sq km/70 sq miles; pop. 37,000; cur. U.S. dollar = 100cents)

Martinique one of the larger of the islands in the WIND-WARD ISLANDS group in the southern CARIBBEAN, lying between DOMINICA and ST LUCIA. It is administered as a department of FRANCE. FORT-DE-FRANCE is the capital. (1079 sq km/417 sq miles; pop. 330,000)

Maryland a state on the central east coast of the USA, virtually divided in two by CHESAPEAKE BAY. The state capital is ANNAPOLIS. (27,394 sq km/10,577 sq miles; pop. 4,392,000)

Masan an industrial city and port 60 km (35 miles) west of PUSAN in South KOREA; it developed under colonial Japanese rule (1940-45) and is now the centre of a free-trade zone. (Pop. 386,700)

Masbate *see* **Visayan Islands.**

Maseru the capital of LESOTHO. (Pop. 45,000)

Mashhad (Meshed) a major trading centre and the capital of KHORASAN province in northeastern IRAN. (Pop. 1,120,000)

Mashonaland the northern and eastern regions of ZIMBABWE, inhabited for over 2000 years by the Shona peoples, the country's largest language group, and today consisting of three provinces centred on HARARE.(112,089 sq km/43,278 sq miles: pop. 2,837,400)

Mason-Dixon Line the state boundary between PENNSYLVANIA and MARYLAND to its south, surveyed 1763–7 by Charles Mason and Jeremiah Dixon. It is considered to be the traditional border between the North and the South of the USA.

Masqat *see* **Muscat.**

Massa a town in northwestern TUSCANY, ITALY, at the foot of the Apuan Alps; the old medieval town was expanded by a new town in the 16th century, built by the dukes of Cybo-Malaspina, and in the 20th century by industrial development, particularly in the chemical industry. (Pop. 66,600)

Massachusetts one of the NEW ENGLAND states on the northeastern coast of the USA The capital is BOSTON. (21,386 sq km/8257 sq miles; pop. 5,822,000)

Massawa *see* **Mits'iwa**.

Massif Central the rugged upland region which occupies much of southern central FRANCE to the west of the River RHONE. The highest point is at Puy de Sancy (1885 m/6184 ft).

Masuria (Mazuria; Masuren; Pojezierze Mazurskie)
a lakeland district of northern POLAND, on the NORTH
EUROPEAN PLAIN, east of the VISTULA river. Its long winding lakes and intervening gravel hills and ridges were
formed by retreating glaciers at the end of the last Ice
Age.

Matabeleland (Ndebeleland) the southern and western regions of ZIMBABWE, the home of the Matabele (*or*
Ndebele) peoples who first settled here between 1820 and
1840; today it consists of two provinces centred on
BULAWAYO. (132,087 sq km/51,000 sq miles; pop. 1,379,400)

Matadi the capital of the Bas-Zaïre region at the narrow
seaward part of western ZAÏRE. It is a busy commercial
seaport on the Zaïre River estuary, at the upper limit of
navigation for ocean-going ships, and just downstream
from the LIVINGSTONE FALLS.(Pop. 162,000)

Matanzas a seaport centre of the sugar-cane industry and
capital of the fertile province of the same name, lying 90
km (55 miles) east of HAVANA, CUBA. (Pop. city 112,000/
province 568,000)

Mathura (Muttra) a city in northern INDIA, on the YAMUNA
River upstream of AGRA; it is revered by Hindus as the
birthplace of Krishna, a legendary hero and god of
Hinduism.

Mato Grosso a vast plateau region, in the south-central
part of BRAZIL bordering BOLIVIA and PARAQUAY, that takes
its name from its characteristic landscape: *mato grosso*
means "thick scrub". (1,232,000 sq km/475,700 sq miles)

Matopo Hills a granite range south of BULAWAYO, ZIMBA-
BWE, rising to 1554 m (5098 ft) and topped by character-
istically large rounded boulders, amongst which lies the
tomb of Cecil Rhodes (1853-1902), the South African
statesman and pioneer of former Rhodesia.

Ma-tsu Tao (Matsu Islands) a group of heavily fortified
islands belonging to TAIWAN, lying only 19 km (12 miles)
off the coast of FUJIAN province of mainland CHINA.

Matsuyama a port and industrial city on the north coast

of SHIKOKU Island, JAPAN. (Pop. 426,600)

Matterhorn (Monte Cervino) a distinctive, pyramid-shaped peak on the border between ITALY and SWITZERLAND, 5 km (3 miles) south of ZERMATT. (4477 m/14,690 ft)

Maui the second largest island of HAWAII, USA. (1885 sq km/727 sq miles; pop. 63,000)

Mauna Kea a dormant volcano in the north of the island of HAWAII, USA; it is the highest point in the island-state and used as one of the world's best astronomical observation sites. (4205 m/13,796 ft)

Mauna Loa an active volcano in the centre of the island of HAWAII. (4169 m/13,677 ft)

Mauritania, a country nearly twice the size of France, is located on the west coast of AFRICA. About 47% of the country is desert, the SAHARA covering much of the north. The only settlements found in this area are around oases, where a little millet, dates and vegetables can be grown. The main agricultural regions are in the Senegal river valley in the south. The rest of the country is made up of the drought-stricken SAHEL grasslands. The majority of the people are traditionally nomadic herdsmen but the severe droughts since the 1970s have killed about 70% of the nations animals and the population have settled along the Senegal river. As a result, vast shanty towns have sprung up around all the towns. Deposits of iron ore and copper provide the country's main exports and development of these and the fishing industry on the coast is the only hope for a brighter future.

Area : 1,025,520 sq km (395,953 sq miles)

Population : 1,970,000

Capital : Nouakchott

Form of government : Republic

Religion : Sunni Islam

Currency : Ouguiya

Mauritius is a beautiful island with tropical beaches which lies about 20° south in the INDIAN OCEAN, 800 km (497 miles) east of MADAGASCAR. The islands of Rodrigues and Agalepa are part of Mauritius. Mauritius is a volcanic island with many craters surrounded by lava flows. The central plateau rises to over 800 m (2625 ft), then drops sharply to the south and west coasts. The climate is hot and humid, and southwesterly winds bring heavy rain in the uplands. The island has well-watered fertile soil, ideal for the sugar plantations that cover 45% of the island. Although the export of sugar still dominates the economy, diversification is being encouraged. The clothing and electronic equipment industries are becoming increasingly important and tourism is now the third largest source of foreign exchange.

Area : 2040 sq km (788 sq miles)

Population : 1,081,669

Capital : Port Louis

Form of government : Constitutional Monarchy

Religions : Hinduism, RC, Sunni Islam

Currency : Mauritius rupee

Mayagüez a seaport, industrial city and cultural centre on the west coast of PUERTO RICO. (Pop. 101,000)

Maymyo a hill town near MANDALAY in central BURMA, developed by the British in 1886 as the colonial summer capital. (Pop. 100,800)

Mayo a county on the west coast of the Republic of IRELAND, noted for its rugged splendor. The county town is Castlebar. (4831 sq km/1865 sq miles; pop. 114,700)

Mayotte (Mahore) part of the COMOROS Island group, lying between MADAGASCAR and the mainland of AFRICA. Unlike the other three islands in the group, Mayotte voted to remain under the administration of France when the Comoros Islands became independent in 1974. (373 sq km/144 sq miles; pop. 60,000)

Mazar-e Sharif a manufacturing town in northern AFGHANISTAN, which contains the tomb of Ali, the son-in-law of Mohammed, and a place of pilgrimage for Shiite Muslims. (Pop. 110,400)

Mazatlán a fast-growing beach resort at the mouth of the

Gulf of CALIFORNIA in west-central MEXICO. (Pop. 202,000)

Mbabane the capital of SWAZILAND. (Pop. 36,000)

Mbale one of UGANDA's largest towns; lying in the southeast by the Kenyan border, it is the regional centre for the east of the country, especially the coffee-growing area on the slopes of Mount ELGON. (Pop. 40,000)

Mbandaka (Equateurville) a commercial and industrial city lying on the ZAÏRE River at the downstream point where it crosses the Equator for the second time. It serves an extensive region of ZAÏRE, producing tropical products. (Pop. 160,000)

Mbeya a regional capital in southwest TANZANIA, close to ZAMBIA and on the strategic links of road, rail (TanZam) and pipeline that were routed from DAR ES SALAAM in the 1960s and 1970s. (Pop. 100,000)

Mbuji-Mayi (Bakwanga) the capital of Kasai-Oriental in central ZAÏRE and centre of a major diamond-mining region that produces, by weight, about 75 per cent of the world's industrial diamonds. (Pop. 383,000)

McKinley, Mount the highest mountain in North AMERICA, located in the Denali National Park in southern ALASKA, USA. (6194 m/20,320 ft)

McMurdo Oasis *see* **Dry Valleys**.

McMurdo Sound an arm of the ROSS SEA on the International Date Line. The American MacMurdo Base on Ross Island is the largest scientific research station in ANTARCTICA.

Meath a county on the east coast of the Republic of IRELAND, to the north of DUBLIN. The county town is Navan. (2336 sq km/902 sq miles; pop. 95,400)

Meaux the chief town of the Brie cheese-making district on the Marne river, 40 km (25 miles) east of PARIS, FRANCE.

Mecca (Makkah) a city in central western SAUDI ARABIA, 64 km (40 miles) east of the RED SEA port of JIDDAH. An important trading city on caravan routes in ancient times, it was the birthplace of the Prophet Mohammed, and as such is the holiest city of Islam. (Pop. 375,000)

Mechelen (Malines) a cathedral city and BELGIUM's religious capital since the 15th century, situated halfway between BRUSSELS and ANTWERP. (Pop. 65,000)

Mecklenburg-Vorpommern the northeasternmost of the 16 states (*Länder*) of GERMANY; it was reinstated as a *Land* after reunification in 1990. Its chief city is ROSTOCK on its BALTIC coast. (23,838 sq km/9204 sq miles; pop. 2,100,000)

Medan a major city in northern SUMATRA, INDONESIA. (Pop. 2,378,000)

Medellín the second largest city in COLOMBIA after the capital BOGOTA, situated in the centre of the country, 240 km (150 miles) northwest of the capital. (Pop. 1,998,000)

Medicine Hat the main industrial and trading centre of southeastern ALBERTA, CANADA. It stands on a large natural gas field. (Pop. 40,385)

Medina (Al Madinah) the second holiest city of Islam after MECCA. The Prophet Mohammed fled from Mecca to Medina, 350 km (217 miles) to the north, to escape persecution in AD622 (year 0 in the Islamic lunar calendar). (Pop. 210,000)

Mediterranean Sea a large sea bounded by southern EUROPE, North AFRICA and southwest ASIA. It is connected to the ATLANTIC OCEAN by the Strait of GIBRALTAR.

Médoc one of the prime wine-producing regions of FRANCE, a flat, triangular-shaped piece of land between the GIRONDE estuary and the ATLANTIC OCEAN.

Medway Towns a conurbation on the lower Medway River in KENT, southeast ENGLAND, about 50 km (30 miles) east of LONDON, comprising Rochester, Gillingham and Chatham. Many historic buildings remain, including Roman city walls, a Norman castle, a medieval cathedral, and an Elizabethan 16th-century naval dockyard. (Pop. 210,000)

Meerut an industrial town of northern INDIA, 60 km (40 miles) northeast of DELHI. The Indian Mutiny began here in 1857. (Pop. 536,600)

Meghalaya a predominantly rural state in the hills of northeastern INDIA, with BANGLADESH to the south. (22,429 sq km/8658 sq miles; pop. 1,335,800)

Meiktila a textile town in central Burma, some 130 km (80 miles) south of MANDALAY, at the centre of a cotton-growing area. (Pop. 229,600)

Meissen a historic town on the River ELBE, 20 km (12 miles) to the northwest of DRESDEN, in southeastern GERMANY. It is famous above all for its fine porcelain, produced here since 1710. (Pop. 38,200)

Meknès a former capital, with a fine 17th-century royal palace, in northern MOROCCO. (Pop. 320,000)

Mekong, River the great river of South-East ASIA, flowing from TIBET, through southern CHINA, LAOS and CAMBODIA before forming a massive and highly fertile delta in southern VIETNAM and flowing into the SOUTH CHINA SEA. (Length 4425 km/2750 miles)

Melaka (Malacca) a port on the southwest coast of MALAYSIA, overlooking the Straits of MALACCA, once a key port in Far Eastern trade. (Pop. 87,500)

Melanesia the central and southern group of islands in the South PACIFIC OCEAN, including the SOLOMON ISLANDS, VANUATU, FIJI and NEW CALEDONIA.

Melbourne the second largest city in AUSTRALIA after SYDNEY and the capital of the state of VICTORIA. (Pop. 2,700,000)

Melilla a Spanish enclave on the MEDITERRANEAN coast of northern MOROCCO, about 225 km (140 miles) east of CEUTA.

Melos *see* **Cyclades.**

Memel *see* **Klaipeda.**

Memphis a city on the River MISSISSIPPI in the southwest corner of TENNESSEE, USA, on the border with and extending into ARKANSAS. (Pop. city 648,000/ metropolitan area 934,600)

Menai Strait the narrow strait, 180 m (590 ft) across at its narrowest, separating mainland WALES from the island of ANGLESEY, spanned by road and rail bridges.

Mendoza a trading, processing and wine-producing centre in the foothills of the ANDES, in western ARGENTINA. (Pop. 600,000)

Menorca *see* **Minorca.**

Mercia a historic kingdom of central and southern ENGLAND during the Anglo-Saxon period, which reached its height under King Offa (757-96)

Mérida (1) the historic capital of the YUCATAN province of eastern MEXICO. (Pop. 424,500) **(2)** a market town southwest of Madrid, Spain. (Pop. 41,800) **(3)** an administrative centre of a state of the same name, high in the Andes of Venezuela. (Pop. 110,000)

Merionethshire *see* **Gwynedd.**

Mersey, River a river in northwest ENGLAND. It forms an estuary to the south of LIVERPOOL which is deep and wide enough to permit access for ocean-going ships to Liverpool and MANCHESTER (via the Manchester Ship Canal. (Length 110 km/70 miles)

Merseyside a metropolitan county created in 1974 out of parts of LANCASHIRE and CHESHIRE, centring on River MERSEY, with LIVERPOOL as its administrative centre. (652 sq km/252 sq miles; pop. 1,501,000)

Mersin (İçel) the principal MEDITERRANEAN port of TURKEY, in the central south of the country, to the north of CYPRUS. (Pop. 314,100)

Merthyr Tydfil an industrial town at the head of one of the south WALES valleys, situated on a coalfield in MID GLAMORGAN. (Pop. 53,843)

Meseta the central plateau of SPAIN, covering about three quarters of the country. (Area 350,000 sq km/135,000 sq miles)

Meshed *see* **Mashhad.**

Mesolóngion (Missolonghi) a small town in southwestern GREECE, on the north coast of the Gulf of PATRAS. It is remembered for its heroic role in the Greek struggle for independence from TURKEY, when it held out against three sieges 1824–6. (Pop. 10,200)

Mesopotamia the "Fertile Crescent" of land lying between the Rivers TIGRIS and EUPHRATES, mainly in modern IRAQ, where some of the world's earliest civilizations arose (Sumer, ASSYRIA and BABYLON). The name means "land between the rivers."

Messina a historic port, founded in the 8th century BC, in northeast SICILY, overlooking the narrow Strait of Messina (6 km/4 miles wide at its narrowest) which separates Sicily from mainland ITALY. (Pop. 266,300)

Metz the capital of the industrial LORRAINE region in eastern FRANCE, situated on the River MOSELLE, close to the border with GERMANY. (Pop. 194,800)

Meuse (Maas), River a river which flows northwest from its source in the LORRAINE region of FRANCE, across central BELGIUM and into the NETHERLANDS, where it joins part of the delta of the River RHINE before entering the NORTH SEA. (Length 935 km/580 miles)

Mexico, the most southerly country in North AMERICA, has its longest border with the USA to the north, a long coast on the PACIFIC OCEAN and a smaller coast in the west of the Gulf of MEXICO. It is a land of volcanic mountain ranges and high plateaux. The highest peak is Citlaltepetl, 5699 m (18,697 ft), which is permanently snow capped. Coastal lowlands are found in the west and east. Its wide range of latitude and relief, produce a variety of climates. In the north there are arid and semi arid conditions while in the south there is a humid tropical climate. 30% of the labour force are involved in agriculture growing maize, wheat, kidney beans and rice for subsistence and coffee, cotton, fruit and vegetables for export. Mexico is the world's largest producer of silver and has large reserves of oil and natural gas. Developing industries are petrochemicals, textiles, motor vehicles and food processing.

Area : 1,958,201 sq km (756,061 sq miles)

Population : 81,140,000

México City

Capital : México City

Other major cities : Guadalajara, Monterrey, Puebla de Zaragoza

Form of government : Federal Republic

Religion : RC

Currency : Mexican peso

México City the capital of MEXICO, and the most populous city in the world. It lies to the south of the country on a high plateau 2200 m (7350 ft) above sea level. (Pop. 17,000,000)

Mexico, Gulf of an arm of the ATLANTIC OCEAN, bounded by the FLORIDA peninsula in the southeast USA and the YUCATAN peninsula in MEXICO, with the island of CUBA placed in the middle of its entrance.

Miami a major city and resort on the ATLANTIC coast of southeast FLORIDA, USA. (Pop. city 372,600/metropolitan area 1,706,000)

Michigan a state in north central USA, formed out of two peninsulas between the GREAT LAKES, with Lake MICHIGAN in the middle. The capital is LANSING. (150,780 sq km/ 58,216 sq miles; pop. 9,088,000)

Michigan, Lake one of the GREAT LAKES, and the only one to lie entirely within the USA. (57,750 sq km/22,300 sq miles)

Micronesia one of the three main groupings of islands of the PACIFIC OCEAN, lying to the northwest of the other two main groupings, MELANESIA and POLYNESIA. They stretch from BELAU to KIRIBATI.

Micronesia, Federated States of a group of some 600 tropical islands in the west PACIFIC, which became a self-governing republic in 1982 while remaining in free association with the USA, which considers it strategically important. Heavily dependent on US aid, the country exports copra and fish. The principal language is English, and the capital is KOLONIA. (701 sq km/271 sq miles; pop. 89,000; cur. U.S. dollar = 100cents)

Mid-Atlantic Ridge an S-shaped ridge of submarine

mountains that runs down the centre of the ATLANTIC OCEAN, the result of the continental plates of the sea floor drifting apart. Parts of the ridge reach the surface as volcanic islands, including ICELAND, the AZORES, ASCENSION, ST HELENA and TRISTAN DA CUNHA.

Middle East a non-specific term used to describe an area of southwest ASIA, which is mainly Islamic and/or Arabic-speaking. Countries included are: TURKEY, IRAN, IRAQ, SYRIA, JORDAN, ISRAEL, SAUDI ARABIA, LEBANON, YEMEN, OMAN, the UNITED ARAB EMIRATES, QATAR, BAHRAIN and KUWAIT.

Middlesbrough the county town of CLEVELAND, ENGLAND. (Pop. 149,800)

Middle West *see* **Midwest.**

Mid Glamorgan a county in central southern WALES, which was formed in 1974 out of part of the former counties of Breconshire, Glamorgan and Monmouthshire. The administrative centre is in CARDIFF. (1000 sq km/393 sq miles; pop. 538,000)

Midi-Pyrénées the largest region of FRANCE, in the southwest of the country, stretching from the MASSIF CENTRAL to the PYRÉNÉES and centred on its capital and chief city, TOULOUSE. (45,348 sq km/17,647 sq miles; pop. 2,326,000)

Midlands, The a term used to describe the central industrial counties of England: DEBYSHIRE, NORTHAMPTONSHIRE, NOTTINGHAMSHIRE, STAFFORDSHIRE, WARWICKSHIRE, LEICESTERSHIRE, and WEST MIDLANDS.

Midlothian *see* **Lothian.**

Midway Islands two atolls in the north PACIFIC OCEAN, some 2000 km (1242 miles) northwest of HAWAII. They have been possessions of the USA since 1867, and were the scene of a decisive US naval victory against the Japanese in 1942. (3 sq km/2 sq miles; pop. 2200)

Midwest (Middle West) a term used to describe the fertile north-central part of the USA. States in the Midwest include OHIO, MICHIGAN, INDIANA, ILLINOIS, WISCONSIN, MINNESOTA, IOWA and MISSOURI, but others, such as

KANSAS, are also often included.

Mien Bac the northern region of VIETNAM, called Tonkin (Tongking) when a part of French Indochina.

Mien Trung the central region of VIETNAM, called Annam when a part of French Indochina.

Mikinai *see* **Mycenae.**

Míkinos *see* **Cyclades.**

Milan (Milano) the major industrial and commercial centre of northern ITALY, and the country's second largest city after ROME, situated in central LOMBARDY. (Pop. 1,605,000)

Milos *see* **Cyclades.**

Milton-Keynes a new town in north BUCKINGHAMSHIRE, 56 km (35 miles) northwest of LONDON, ENGLAND; it was founded in 1967. (Pop. 106,974)

Milwaukee a port on the west side of Lake MICHIGAN, and the main industrial centre of WISCONSIN, USA. (Pop. city 620,800/metropolitan area 1,393,800)

Mina al-Ahmadi the main oil terminal of KUWAIT, lying on the GULF, 40 km (25 miles) south of Kuwait City.

Mina Hassan Tani *see* **Kénitra**

Minch, The the broad channel separating northwest SCOTLAND from the Outer HEBRIDES or WESTERN ISLES.

Mindanao the second largest island of the PHILIPPINES. (94,631 sq km/36,537 sq miles; pop. 11,100,000)

Mindoro an island in the western central PHILIPPINES. (9736 sq km/3759 sq miles)

Minicoy Islands *see* **Lakshadweep.**

Minneapolis a major agricultural and commercial centre in southeast MINNESOTA, USA, on the River MISSISSIPPI, and adjoining ST PAUL. (Pop. city 258,300/ metropolitan area 2,230,900)

Minnesota a state in north central USA. The state capital is ST PAUL. (217,736 sq km/84,068 sq miles; pop. 4,193,000)

Minorca (Menorca) the second largest of the BALEARIC ISLANDS (after MAJORCA). The capital is Mahon. (702 sq km/271 sq miles; pop. 50,200)

Minsk a major industrial city, and the capital of BELARUS. (Pop. 1,442,000)

Miquelon *see* **St Pierre and Miquelon.**

Miskolc a city in the northeast of HUNGARY, and the country's second largest city after BUDAPEST. (Pop. 210,000)

Misrátah an oasis town and seaport on the MEDITERRANEAN coast of LIBYA, 140 km (87 miles) east of TRIPOLI. (Pop. 103,400)

Mississippi a state in central southern USA with a small coastline on the Gulf of MEXICO. The state capital is JACKSON. (123,585 sq km/47,716 sq miles; pop. 2,613,000)

Mississippi, River the second longest river in the USA. It rises in MINNESOTA and runs south the length of the country to the Gulf of MEXICO. (Length 3779 km/2348 miles)

Missolonghi *see* **Mesolóngion.**

Missouri a state in the MIDWEST of the USA. The state capital is JEFFERSON CITY. (180,487 sq km/69,686 sq miles; pop. 5,029,000)

Missouri, River the main tributary of the MISSISSIPPI with which it is the longest river in North America. It rises in MONTANA, flows north, east and southeast to join the Mississippi at ST LOUIS. (Length 3969 km/2466 miles)

Mitchell, Mount *see* **Appalachian Mountains.**

Mits'iwa (Massawa) the main RED SEA port of ERITREA province in ETHIOPIA (Pop. 35,000)

Mittelland the northern region of SWITZERLAND, between the RHINE, JURA and ALPS, which is low-lying and subdued in comparison with the rest of the country. It is the most populated area, with more than half the people—living in a concentration of industrial towns, e.g. BASLE, ZÜRICH, WINTERTHUR, ST GALLEN.

Mizoram a union territory of INDIA, in the hilly northeast, on the border with BURMA. The capital is Aijal. (21,081 sq km/8137 sq miles; pop. 493,800)

Mobile a port on the coast of ALABAMA, USA, on the Gulf of MEXICO. (Pop. city 204,900/metropolitan area 465,700)

Mobutu Sese Seko, Lake *see* **Albert, Lake.**

Moçambique an ancient Arab port and later a Portuguese stronghold and colonial capital of MOZAMBIQUE until 1907; it lies on a small coral island off the northern coast of the country, and was visited by Vasco da Gama in 1498. (Pop. 12,200)

Modena an industrial city retaining many vestiges of its medieval past, in northeastern ITALY. (Pop. 178,300)

Mogadishu (Muqdisho; Mogadiscio) the capital and main port of of SOMALIA. (Pop. 400,000)

Mogilev an industrial city, largely rebuilt afer World War II, on the DNIEPER river in central BELARUS. (Pop. 334,000)

Mohammedia a fishing port and coastal resort 25 km (16 miles) northeast of CASABLANCA, MOROCCO (Pop. 105,100)

Mohave Desert *see* **Mojave Desert.**

Mohenjo Daro an ancient city in the valley of the River INDUS, in southern PAKISTAN. It was inhabited for about 1000 years from 2500BC.

Mojave (Mohave) Desert a desert in southern CALIFORNIA, stretching from DEATH VALLEY to LOS ANGELES. (38,850 sq km/15,000 sq miles)

Moldova (Moldavia) (1) the neighbouring region of northeast Romania. **(2)** was a Soviet socialist republic from 1940 until 1991 when it became independent of the former USSR. It is bounded to the west by ROMANIA and to the north, east and south by UKRAINE. The republic consists of a hilly plain that rises to 429 m (1408 ft) in the centre. Its main rivers are the Prut in the west and the DNIESTER in the north and east. Moldova's soils are fertile, and crops grown include wheat, corn, barley, tobacco, sugar beet, soybeans and sunflowers. There are also extensive fruit orchards, vineyards and walnut groves. Beekeeping and silkworm breeding are widespread throughout the country. Food processing is the main industry. Other industries include metal working, engineering and the manufacture of electrical equipment. *Area* : 33,700 sq km (13,000 sq miles)

Population : 4,052,000
Capital : Kishinev
Other major cities : Tiraspol, Bendery
Form of government : Republic
Religion : Russian Orthodox
Currency : Rouble

Molise a region of eastern ITALY, on the ADRIATIC coast, between ABRUZZI and PUGLIA. (4438 sq km/1714 sq miles; pop. 332,900)

Molotov *see* **Perm'.**

Molucca Sea an arm of the PACIFIC OCEAN between SULAWESI (Celebes) and the MALUKU islands of INDONESIA. It is linked in the south to the BANDA and SERAM Seas.

Moluccas *see* **Maluku.**

Mombasa the second city of KENYA and an important port on the INDIAN OCEAN. (Pop. 500,000)

Monaco is a tiny principality on the MEDITERRANEAN surrounded landwards by the Alpes Maritimes department of FRANCE. It comprises a rocky peninsula and a narrow stretch of coast. It has mild moist winters and hot dry summers. The old town of Monaco-Ville is situated on a rocky promontory and houses the royal palace and the cathedral. The Monte Carlo district has its world-famous casino and La Condamine has thriving businesses, shops, banks and attractive residential areas. Fontvieille is an area reclaimed from the sea where now marinas and light industry are located. Light industry includes chemicals, plastics, electronics, engineering and paper but it is tourism that is the main revenue earner.

Area : 195 hectares (48 acres)
Population : 29,876
Capital : Monaco-Ville
Form of government : Constitutional Monarchy
Religion : RC
Currency : Franc

Monaco-Ville the capital of MONACO, sited on a rocky headland that sticks out into the MEDITERRANEAN SEA. (Pop. 1250)

Monaghan a county in the central north of the Republic of IRELAND, with a county town of the same name. (1291 sq km/498 sq miles; pop. county 51,200)

Mönchengladbach an industrial city in the southwest of the RUHR region of western GERMANY, 25 km (16 miles) west of DUSSELDORF. (Pop. 257,000)

Moncton a city on the Petitcodiac River in southeast NEW BRUNSWICK, which acts as the transport hub for the MARITIME PROVINCES of CANADA. (Pop. 54,750)

Mongolia is a landlocked country in northeast Asia which is bounded to the north by the RUSSIAN FEDERATION and by CHINA to the south, west and east. Most of Mongolia is mountainous and over 1500 m (4922 ft) above sea level. In the northwest are the Hangayn Mountains and the ALTAI, rising to 4362 m (14,312 ft). In the south there are grass-covered steppes and desert wastes of the GOBI. The climate is very extreme and dry. For six months the temperatures are below freezing and the summers are mild. Mongolia has had a traditional nomadic pastoral economy for centuries and cereals including fodder crops are grown on a large scale on state farms. Industry is small scale and dominated by food processing. The mining industry has been developed at Darhan and Erdenet with aid from the former USSR and copper accounts for 40% of the country's exports.

Area : 1,566,500 sq km (604,826 sq miles)

Population : 2,095,000

Capital : Ulan Bator (Ulaanbaatar)

Other major cities : Darhan, Erdenet

Form of government : Republic

Religion : Previously Buddhism but religion is now suppressed

Currency : Tugrik

Monmouthshire see **Gwent.**

Monrovia the capital and principal port of LIBERIA. (Pop. 425,000)

Mons (Bergen) a town in southwest BELGIUM; it was the

scene of the first encounter between British and German troops in World War I. (Pop. 94,000)

Montana a state in the northwest of the USA, on the border with CANADA. The state capital is HELENA. (381,087 sq km/147,138 sq miles; pop. 826,000)

Monte Carlo an elegant coastal town and resort in MONACO, famed in particular for its casinos. (Pop. 13,200)

Montego Bay the second largest town and seaport of JAMAICA (after KINGSTON) lying on the northwest coast of the island; it is the site of the place Christopher Colombus visited in 1494. (Pop. 70,000)

Montenegro (Crna Gora) the smallest of the republics of former YUGOSLAVIA, in the southwest on the ADRIATIC SEA and bordering ALBANIA. The capital is TITOGRAD. (13,812 sq km/5331 sq miles; pop. 584,300)

Monterey a resort town on the Pacific coast of central CALIFORNIA, USA, 135 km (85 miles) southeast of SAN FRANCISCO. It is well known for its annual jazz festival. (Pop. 28,700)

Monterrey an industrial city in northeast MEXICO, the country's third largest city after MEXICO CITY and GUADALJARA. (Pop. 1,916,500)

Montevideo the capital of URUGUAY, and an important port on the River PLATE estuary. (Pop. 1,500,000)

Montgomery the state capital of ALABAMA, USA. (Pop. city 185,000/metropolitan area 284,800)

Montgomeryshire *see* **Powys.**

Montpelier the state capital of VERMONT, USA. (Pop. 8200)

Montpellier a university and trading city in central southern FRANCE, the capital of the LANGUEDOC-ROUSSILLON region. (Pop. 225,300)

Montreal the second largest city in CANADA after TORONTO, on the ST LAWRENCE RIVER, in the south of the province of QUEBEC. Two-thirds of the population are French-speaking Québecois. (Pop. 2,828,250)

Montserrat a British Crown colony in the LEEWARD IS-

LANDS, in the southeastern CARIBBEAN. The capital is called PLYMOUTH. (102 sq km/39 sq miles)

Monza a city in northern ITALY, 12 km (8 miles) northeast of MILAN. (Pop. 122,500)

Mopti a market town on the Bani River near its confluence with the NIGER in central MALI; it is a centre for the river trade with CÔTE D'IVOIRE and GHANA. (Pop. 54,000)

Moravia a historical region of the CZECH REPUBLIC, east of BOHEMIA, west of SLOVAKIA, with POLAND to the north and AUSTRIA to the south.

Moray Firth an inlet of the NORTH SEA cutting some 56 km (35 miles) into the eastern coast of northeast SCOTLAND, with INVERNESS at its head.

Morayshire *see* **Grampian.**

Mordovia Republic one of the 16 autonomous republics of the RUSSIAN FEDERATION, in the mid-VOLGA basin of the west-central part of the country. The capital is Saransk. (26,200 sq km/10,110 sq miles; pop. 984,000)

Morioka an industrial city in northeast HONSHU Island and northern terminus for JAPAN's famous "bullet train"— *shinkansen*. (Pop. 235,500)

Morocco, in northwest AFRICA, is strategically placed at the western entrance to the MEDITERRANEAN SEA. It is a land of great contrasts with high rugged mountains, the arid SAHARA and the green ATLANTIC and Mediterranean coasts. The country is split from southwest to northeast by the ATLAS mountains. The north has a pleasant Mediterranean climate with hot dry summers and mild moist winters. Farther south winters are warmer and summers even hotter. Snow often falls in winter on the Atlas mountains. Morocco is mainly a farming country, wheat, barley and maize are the main food crops and it is one of the world's chief exporters of citrus fruit. Morocco's main wealth comes from phosphates, reserves of which are the largest in the world. The economy is very mixed. Morocco is self sufficient in textiles, it has car assembly plants, soap and cement factories and a large sea fishing industry. Tourism is a major source of revenue.

Area : 446,550 sq km (172,413 sq miles)

Population : 24,500,000

Capital : Rabat

Other major cities : Casablanca, Fez, Marrakech

Form of government : Constitutional Monarchy

Religion : Sunni Islam

Currency : Dirham

Moroni the capital of the COMOROS islands. (Pop. 20,000)

Moscow (Moskva) the capital of the RUSSIAN FEDERATION, sited on the Moskva River. It is an ancient city with a rich heritage, and is the political, industrial and cultural focus of the country. (Pop. 8,600,000)

Moselle (Mosel), River a river which flows northwards from the southeastern LORRAINE region of eastern FRANCE to form part of the border between Luxembourg and GERMANY before flowing eastwards to meet the River RHINE at KOBLENZ. (Length 550 km/340 miles)

Mosi-oa-Toenga *see* **Victoria Falls**.

Moskva *see* **Moscow**.

Mostar a tourist centre and former capital of Herzegovina, now part of BOSNIA-HERZEGOVINA, lying 80 km (50 miles) southwest of SARAJEVO. The city, whose name means "old bridge", is famed for its 16th-century bridge with a high single span. (Pop. 110,400)

Mosul (Al Mawsil) a historic trading city on the banks of the River TIGRIS in northwest IRAQ, and an important centre for the surrounding oil-producing region. (Pop. 1,500,000)

Motherwell and Wishaw an industrial twin-town and former steelmaking centre in STRATHCLYDE region of west-central SCOTLAND. (Pop. 67,797)

Mount Isa a major mining centre in the remote and otherwise barren northeast part of QUEENSLAND, AUSTRALIA; it produces 70 per cent of the country's copper output. (Pop. 23,600)

Mourne Mountains a mountain range of noted scenic

beauty in the south of County Down, Northern Ireland. The highest point is Slieve Donard (852 m /2795 ft).

Mozambique is a republic located in southeast Africa. A coastal plain covers most of the southern and central territory, giving way to the western highlands and north to a plateau including the Nyasa Highlands. The Zambezi river separates the high plateaux in the north from the lowlands in the south. The country has a humid tropical climate with highest temperatures and rainfall in the north. Normally conditions are reasonably good for agriculture but a drought in the early 1980s, followed a few years later by severe flooding, resulted in famine and more than 100,000 deaths. A lot of industry was abandoned when the Portuguese left the country and, due to lack of expertise, was not taken over by the local people. There is little incentive to produce surplus produce for cash and food rationing has now been introduced. This also has led to a black market which now accounts for a sizable part of the economy.

Area : 801,590 sq km (309,494 sq miles)

Population : 14,900,000

Capital : Maputo

Other major cities : Beira, Nampula

Form of government : Republic

Religions : Animism, RC, Sunni Islam

Currency : Metical

Mozambique Channel the broad strait, some 400 km (250 miles) across at its narrowest, which separates the island of Madagascar from mainland Africa.

Mühlheim an der Ruhr an industrial city and port on the River Ruhr, in the Ruhr region of western Germany. (Pop. 174,000)

Mulhouse an industrial city in the Alsace region of eastern France. (Pop. 222,700)

Mull an island just off the central western coast of Scotland. (925 sq km/357 sq miles)

Multan an industrial city in Punjab province in eastern

central PAKISTAN. (Pop. 730,000)

Munich (München) a historic and industrial city in southern GERMANY, and capital of BAVARIA. (Pop. 1,300,000)

Münster an inland port and industrial centre on the DORTMUND-EMS Canal in northwestern GERMANY. (Pop. 260,000)

Munster one of the four historic provinces of IRELAND, covering the southwest quarter of the country.

Muqdisho *see* **Mogadishu**.

Murcia a trading and manufacturing city in southeastern SPAIN, and capital of the province of the same name. (Pop. city 288,600)

Murmansk the largest city north of the ARCTIC CIRCLE, a major port and industrial centre on the KOLA PENINSULA in the far northwestern corner of the RUSSIAN FEDERATION. (Pop. 412,000)

Murray, River a major river of southeast AUSTRALIA, which flows westwards from its source in the SNOWY MOUNTAINS to form much of the boundary between the states of NEW SOUTH WALES and VICTORIA. It is joined by the River DARLING before flowing across the southeastern corner of SOUTH AUSTRALIA and into the INDIAN OCEAN. (Length 2570 km/1600 miles)

Mururoa an atoll in the southeastern sector of FRENCH POLYNESIA, used by FRANCE since 1966 as a testing ground for nuclear weapons.

Musandam a rocky, horn-shaped peninsula which juts out into The GULF to form the southern side of the Strait of HORMUZ. It belongs to OMAN, but is separated from it by part of the UNITED ARAB EMIRATES.

Muscat (Masqat) the historic capital of OMAN. The neighbouring port of Muttrah has developed rapidly in recent decades to form the commercial centre of Muscat. (Pop. (with Muttrah) 80,000)

Muscovy a principality of RUSSIA from the 13th to 16th centuries, with MOSCOW as the capital.

Mustique a privately owned island in the GRENADINES, to

the south of ST VINCENT, in the southeastern CARIBBEAN. (Pop. 200)

Muttra *see* **Mathura**.

Muttrah *see* **Muscat**.

Myanmar *see* **Burma**.

Mycenae (Mikinai) an ancient city in the northeast of the PELOPONNESE, GREECE, inhabited from 1580 to 1100BC.

Mysore an industrial city in the state of KARNATAKA, southern INDIA. (Pop. 470,000)

N

Naberezhnyye Chelny an industrial town in the RUS-
SIAN FEDERATION. Renamed Brezhnev in 1984 after the
Soviet president Leonid Brezhnev (1906–82). Name re-
verted to Naberezhnyye Chelny in 1988. (Pop. 414,000)

Nablus the largest town on the Israeli-occupied WEST
BANK. (Pop. 44,000)

Nador a port on the northern MEDITERRANEAN coast of
MOROCCO, principally involved in processing and exporting iron ore. (Pop. 63,000)

Naesby a village in NORTHAMPTONSHIRE, south-central
ENGLAND, near to which is the site of the decisive battle of
the Civil War (1642-45) when the New Model Army of
Oliver Cromwell's Parliamentarians defeated the Royal-
ist forces of King Charles I.

Naga Hills a mountain range on the border between INDIA
and BURMA, rising to 3826 m (12,553 ft) through dense
stands of bamboo.

Nagaland a primarily agricultural state in the hilly far
northeastern corner of INDIA, bordering BURMA. (16,579
sq km/6399 sq miles; pop. 774,900)

Nagano a light-industrial town set deep in the JAPAN ALPS
of central HONSHU Island. (Pop. 337,000)

Nagasaki a port and industrial city on the west coast of
KYUSHU Island, JAPAN. Three days after the first atomic
bomb destroyed HIROSHIMA, a second was dropped on
Nagasaki (August 9, 1945), killing 40,000 people. (Pop.
446,300)

Nagorny Karabakh (Nagorno Karabakhskaya) a disputed autonomous enclave in AZERBAIJAN, which is claimed
by ARMENIA. Three quarters of the population are Armenian.

Nagoya a port and industrial centre on the southeastern coast of HONSHU, JAPAN. (Pop. 2,065,800)

Nagpur a commercial centre and textile manufacturing city on the DECCAN plateau of MAHARASHTRA state, central INDIA. (Pop. 1,302,100)

Nagyalföld *see* **Great Alföld**.

Nairobi the capital of KENYA and a commercial centre, in the southwest highland region. (Pop. 1,250,000)

Najd (Nejd) an extensive region of plateau ridges and shallow valleys, much covered by sandy desert, that occupies most of eastern and central SAUDI ARABIA.

Najran an oasis town in the extreme southwest of SAUDI ARABIA, close to the YEMEN border; it has remarkable five to eight-storey mud houses. (Pop. 53,000)

Nakhichevan an autonomous republic, enclaved by AR-MENIA, but a part of AZERBAIJAN. The capital is also called Nakhichevan. (5500 sq km/2120 sq miles; pop. republic 252,000/capital 37,000)

Nakhodka a port in the far east of the RUSSIAN FEDERATION that was built in the 1950s to relieve VLADIVOSTOK, some 90 km (55 miles) to the west; it is now the ocean terminal of the TRANS-SIBERIAN RAILWAY. (Pop. 148,000)

Nakhon Ratchasima an engineering and market town in south-central THAILAND; it is the gateway to the Khorat plateau of the northeast. (Pop. 366,200)

Nakhon Si Thammarat an ancient Buddhist centre and main trading town on the Isthmus of KRA, in the far south of THAILAND. (Pop. 277,400)

Nakuru one of KENYA's largest towns, developed in the early 20th century as the main business centre for the "White Highlands" European settlers who favoured the surrounding area of fertile land at this, the highest part of the GREAT RIFT VALLEY floor. The nearby soda-lake, Lake Nakuru, is famed for its vast flocks of flamingos. (Pop. 120,000)

Namaland (Namaqualand) an arid region along the ATLANTIC coast, astride the NAMIBIA-CAPE PROVINCE (SOUTH

AFRICA) border, which is the home of the Nama,or Namaqua, a Hottentot people; it is rich in diamonds and copper.

Namib Desert a sand desert lining the coast of NAMIBIA in southwestern AFRICA.

Namibe (Moçamedes) a port and capital of the surrounding province of the same name, in southern ANGOLA, developed by the Portuguese in the 1840s as a fishing centre. (Pop. city 52,200/province 233,145)

Namibia is situated on the Atlantic coast of southwest AFRICA. The present state, which gained full independence in 1990, was first created out of the 19th-century European colonial carve-up of African territory—as German South West Africa (1884–1915). During World War I it was occupied by SOUTH AFRICA, which afterwards administered it as the mandated South West Africa. There are three main regions in the country. Running down the entire Atlantic coastline is the NAMIB DESERT, east of which is the Central Plateau of mountains, rugged outcrops, sandy valleys and poor grasslands. East again and north is the KALAHARI DESERT. Namibia has a poor rainfall, the highest falling at Windhoek, the capital. Even here it only amounts to 200–250 mm (8–10 inches) per year. It is essentially a stock-rearing country with sheep and goats raised in the south and cattle in the central and northern areas. Diamonds are mined just north of the River ORANGE, and the largest open groove uranium mine in the world is located near Swakopmund. One of Africa's richest fishing grounds lies off the coast of Namibia, and mackerel, tuna and pilchards are an important export.

Area : 824,292 sq km (318,259 sq miles)
Population : 1,290,000
Capital : Windhoek
Form of government : Republic
Religions : Lutheranism, RC, other Christianity
Currency : Rand

Nampula a trading and administrative centre of northern Mozambique, 150 km (90 miles) inland on the Moçambique railway into the interior. (Pop. 126,100)

Nanchang an industrial city and commercial centre in central southeastern China, and the capital of Jiangxi province. (Pop. 2,390,000)

Nancy a manufacturing city in northeast France, and former capital of Lorraine. (Pop. 314,200)

Nanjing (Nanking) a major industrial and trading city built on the lower reaches of the Chang Jiang (Yangtze) river, and the capital of Jiangsu province, central eastern China. (Pop. 3,551,000)

Nanning the capital of the Guangxi-Zhuang autonomous region in the extreme southeast of China. (Pop. 607,000)

Nansei-shoto *see* **Ryukyu Islands.**

Nantes a port and commercial centre in northwestern France and capital of the Loire Atlantique department. (Pop. 474,100)

Naples (Napoli) the third largest city in Italy after Rome and Milan, is a port situated on the spectacular Bay of Naples. (Pop. 1,203,900)

Nara a historic city in south Honshu Island, Japan, the capital of Japan in the 8th century. (Pop. 327,000)

Narvik a port in northern Norway, east of the Lofoten and Vesterålen islands, which, being ice-free, exports iron ore from the Swedish mines near Kiruna, to which is linked by rail. (Pop. 15,000)

Nashville the state capital of Tennessee, USA, an industrial city famous as the traditional home of Country and Western music. (Pop. city 462,500/ metropolitan area 890,300)

Nassau the capital of the Bahamas, on the north side of New Providence Island. (Pop. 120,000)

Nasser, Lake a massive artificial lake on the River Nile in southern Egypt, created when the Aswan High Dam was completed in 1971. It was named after the former president (1956–70) of Egypt, Gamal Abdel Nasser (1918–

70). (5000 sq km/1930 sq miles)

Natal (1) a port city on the northeast tip of BRAZIL, and capital of the state of Rio Grande do Norte. (Pop. 417,000) **(2)** a province on the eastern coast of SOUTH AFRICA. The capital is PIETERMARITZBURG, but the main city is DURBAN. (86,976 sq km/33,573 sq miles; pop. 2,841,700)

Nauru is the world's smallest republic. It is an island situated just 40 km (25 miles) south of the Equator and is halfway between AUSTRALIA and HAWAII. It is an oval-shaped coral island only 20 km (12 miles) in diameter and is surrounded by a reef. The centre of the island comprises a plateau which rises to 60 m (197 ft) above sea level. The climate is tropical with a high and irregular rainfall. The country is rich, due entirely to the deposits of high quality phosphate rock in the central plateau. This is sold for fertilizer to AUSTRALIA, NEW ZEALAND, JAPAN and South KOREA. Phosphate deposits are likely to be exhausted by 1995 but the government is investing overseas.

Area : 21 sq km (8 sq miles)
Population : 8100
Capital : Yaren
Form of government : Republic
Religions : Protestantism, RC
Currency : Australian dollar

Navadwip a town in WEST BENGAL, INDIA, 95 km (60 miles) north of CALCUTTA, which is an important place of Hindu pilgrimage and a seat of Sanskrit learning. (Pop. 129,800)

Navan (An Uaimh) the county town and market centre for MEATH, Republic of IRELAND. Nearby is the Hill of Tara, the historic seat of the ancient Irish Kings. (Pop. 5000)

Navarra (Navarre) a province in the mountainous north-eastern part of SPAIN. The capital is PAMPLONA. (10,420 sq km/4023 sq miles; pop. 507,400)

Naxos a fertile island in the southern AEGEAN SEA, the largest of the CYCLADES. (428 sq km/165 sq miles)

Nazareth a town in northern ISRAEL, and the childhood

home of Jesus. (Pop. 46,300)

Ndebeleland *see* **Matebeleland**.

Ndjamena (N'Djamena) the capital of CHAD, in the southeast of the country. It was founded by the French in 1900 and named Fort Lamy. (Pop. 303,000)

Ndola a mining and ore-processing town founded in 1904, and now capital of ZAMBIA'S COPPERBELT province. (Pop. 282,400)

Neagh, Lough a lake in the centre of NORTHERN IRELAND; it is the largest inland water in the British Isles. (Area: 388 sq km/150 sq miles)

Near East, The an outdated term for what is currently referred to as the MIDDLE EAST and originally used to descibe the BALKAN states and the area of the former Ottoman Empire.

Nebraska a state in the MIDWEST of the USA, in the very centre of the country. The capital is LINCOLN. (200,018 sq km/77,227 sq miles; pop. 1,606,000)

Neckar, River a tributary of the River RHINE, rising in the BLACK FOREST in the southwest of GERMANY. (365 km/227 miles)

Needles, The *see* **Wight, Isle of**.

Nefud *see* **An Nafúd**.

Negembo a fishing port and tourist resort on the west coast of SRI LANKA, 30 km (19 miles) north of COLOMBO. (Pop. 61,400)

Negev a desert in southern ISRAEL.

Negro (1) a major tributary of the AMAZON river, which it joins at MANAUS, having flowed 2250 km (1400 miles) southeast from eastern COLOMBIA and through northern BRAZIL. **(2)** a river in south-central ARGENTINA, flowing 1014 km (630 miles) southeast to the ATLANTIC OCEAN south of BAHÍA BLANCA. **(3)** a river flowing 467 km (290 miles) southwest through central URUGUAY.

Negros the fourth largest island of the PHILIPPINES. (12,704 sq km/4905 sq miles; pop. 2,750,000)

Nei Mongol Autonomous Region (Inner Mongolia) a

region of northeastern CHINA, bordering MONGOLIA. The capital is HOHHOT. (1,200,000 sq km/460,000 sq miles; pop. 18,510,000)

Neisse, River a tributary of the ODER, which flows north from its source in the CZECH REPUBLIC to form part of the border between GERMANY and POLAND. (Length 256 km/ 159 miles)

Nejd *see* **Najd**.

Nelson a port at the north end of SOUTH ISLAND, NEW ZEALAND, situated at the head of TASMAN BAY. (Pop. 33,300)

Nepal is a long narrow rectangular country, landlocked between CHINA and INDIA on the flanks of the eastern HIMALAYAS. Its northern border runs along the mountain tops. In this border area is EVEREST (8848 m /29,028 ft), the highest mountain in the world. The climate is sub-tropical in the south, and all regions are affected by the monsoon. Nepal is one of the world's poorest and least developed countries, with most of the population trying to survive as peasant farmers. It has no significant minerals, however with Indian and Chinese aid roads have been built from the north and south to KATHMANDU. The construction of hydroelectric power schemes is now underway.

Area : 140,797 sq km (54,362 sq miles)

Population : 18,000,000

Capital : Kathmandu

Form of government : Constitutional Monarchy

Religion : Hinduism, Buddhism

Currency : Nepalese rupee

Ness, Loch a deep, 37-km (23-mile) long lake lying in the northeastern part of the GREAT GLEN in the HIGHLANDS of SCOTLAND. The loch is famous because of repeated claims that a monster inhabits its depths.

Netanya a resort on ISRAEL'S MEDITERRANEAN coast, about 30 kmm (19 miles) north of TEL AVIV. It is also the centre of the country's diamond-cutting and polishing industry.

Netherlands

(Pop. 107,200)

Netherlands, The situated in northwest EUROPE, the Netherlands is bounded to the north and west by the NORTH SEA. Over one-quarter of the Netherlands is below sea level and the Dutch have tackled some huge reclamation schemes to add some land area to the country. One such scheme is the IJSSELMEER, where four large areas (polders) reclaimed have added an extra 1650 sq km (637 sq miles) for cultivation and an overspill town for AMSTERDAM. The Netherlands has mild winters and cool summers. Agriculture and horticulture are highly mechanized, and the most notable feature is the sea of glass under which salad vegetables, fruit and flowers are grown. Manufacturing industries include chemicals, machinery, petroleum, refining, metallurgy and electrical engineering. The main port of the Netherlands, ROTTERDAM, is the largest in the world.

Area : 40,844 sq km (15,770 sq miles)

Population : 14,890,000

Capital : Amsterdam

Seat of government : The Hague (Den Haag, 's-Gravenhage)

Other major cities : Eindhoven, Rotterdam

Form of government : Constitutional Monarchy

Religions : RC, Dutch reformed, Calvinism

Currency : Guilder

Netherlands Antilles an overseas division of the NETHERLANDS, spread over the southern CARIBBEAN. The principal islands are: CURACAO, ST MARTIN, ST EUSTATIUS, and BONAIRE. ARUBA was part of the group until 1986.

Neusatz *see* **Novi Sad.**

Nevada a state in the west of the USA, consisting mostly of desert. The state capital is CARSON CITY. (286,298 sq km/110,540 sq miles; pop. 936,000)

Neva, River the river which flows through ST PETERSBURG. (Length 74 km/45 miles)

Nevers the historic capital city of Nièvre départment and of the former Duchy of NIVERNIAS, on the LOIRE river, in central FRANCE. (Pop. 61,250)

Nevis *see* **St Kitts and Nevis.**

New Amsterdam *see* **Guyana; Manhattan**.

Newark a major port city in NEW JERSEY. (Pop. 314,400/ metropolitan area 1,875,300)

New Britain the largest offshore island belonging to PAPUA NEW GUINEA, in the BISMARCK Archipelago. (36,500 sq km/11,125 sq miles; pop. 237,000)

New Brunswick a state on the coast in southeast CANADA, bordering the USA. The state capital is FREDERICTON. (73,436 sq km/28,354 sq miles; pop. 696,000)

New Caledonia the main island of a group called by the same name in the South PACIFIC, which form an overseas territory of FRANCE. The capital is NOUMEA. (19,103 sq km/ 7376 sq miles; pop. 155,000)

Newcastle (1) a port and industrial city in NEW SOUTH WALES, AUSTRALIA. (Pop. 259,000) **(2)** a coal-mining and steel-manufacturing town at the foot of the DRAKENSBERG in northwest NATAL, SOUTH AFRICA. (Pop. 55,700)

Newcastle-under-Lyme a town in the Potteries region of STAFFORDSHIRE, central ENGLAND. (Pop. 74,600)

Newcastle upon Tyne a historic and industrial city in the county of TYNE AND WEAR, northeast ENGLAND. (Pop. 280,000)

New Delhi became the official capital of INDIA in 1931. (Pop. 273,000)

New England the name given to northeastern states of the USA: MAINE, VERMONT, NEW HAMPSHIRE, CONNECTICUT, MASSACHUSETTS and RHODE ISLAND.

New Forest an ancient royal hunting forest, in southwest HAMPSHIRE, southern ENGLAND. Its woodlands and open heaths are now popular with tourists. (364 sq km/141 sq miles)

Newfoundland the province in the extreme east of CANADA. The capital is ST JOHN'S. (372,000 sq km/143,634 sq miles; pop. 568,000)

New Georgia an island, and its associated group, lying in the middle of the SOLOMON ISLANDS chain in the southwest PACIFIC OCEAN.(1300 sq km/500 sq miles)

New Guinea one of the world's largest islands, divided into two parts: independent PAPUA NEW GUINEA in the east and IRIAN JAYA, a state of INDONESIA, in the west.

New Hampshire a state of NEW ENGLAND, in the northwest of the USA. The state capital is CONCORD. (24,097 sq km/9304 sq miles; pop. 998,000)

New Haven a port in CONNECTICUT, USA. It is the home of Yale University, one of the oldest and most prestigious in AMERICA, dating from 1701.(Pop. city 124,200/metropolitan area 506,000)

New Hebrides *see* **Vanuatu.**

New Ireland a mountainous island that is a part of PAPUA NEW GUINEA, lying to the north in the BISMARCK Archipelago, to the northeast of NEW BRITAIN. (9850 sq km/3800 sq miles)

New Jersey a state on the ATLANTIC coast in the northeast of the USA. The state capital is TRENTON. (20,295 sq km/7836 sq miles; pop. 7,562,000)

New Mexico a state in the southwest of the USA, bordering MEXICO. The state capital is SANTA FE. (315,115 sq km/121,666 sq miles; pop. 1,450,000)

New Orleans an important and historic port in southern LOUISIANA, on the MISSISSIPPI delta. (Pop. city 559,100/metropolitan area 1,318,800)

New Plymouth the chief town of the rich dairying area of the TARANAKI peninsula of NORTH ISLAND, NEW ZEALAND; it was one of the country's earliest European settlements, being founded in 1841. (Pop. 36,100)

Newport (1) a port and naval base in RHODE ISLAND, USA. (Pop. 29,900) **(2)** a steel-making town and port on Usk river in GWENT, southeast WALES. (Pop. 105,374) **(3)** the administrative centre of the Isle of WIGHT, lying in centre-north of the island. (Pop. 23,570)

Newport News a major eastern seaboard port in VIR-

GINIA, USA. (Pop. city 154,600/metropolitan area (with NORFOLK) 1,261,200)

New Providence *see* **Bahamas.**

New Siberian Islands (Novosibiriskiye Ostrova) a group of ARCTIC islands belonging to the RUSSIAN FEDERATION and lying off the north coast of the mainland, and between the EAST SIBERIAN and LAPTEV seas. (37,555 sq km/14,500 sq miles)

New South Wales the most populous of the states of AUSTRALIA, situated in the southeast of the country. The capital is SYDNEY. (801,430 sq km/309,433 sq miles; pop. 5,379,000)

New Territories *see* **Hong Kong.**

New York (City) the most populous city in the USA, its most important port, and a major financial centre. It is sited on the mouth of the HUDSON River, and comprises five boroughs: MANHATTAN, the Bronx, Queens, Brooklyn and Staten Island. (Pop. city 7,322,600/metropolitan area 8,376,900)

New York (State) a populous state in the northeast of the USA, on the ATLANTIC coast. The state capital is ALBANY (128,402 sq km/49,576 sq miles; pop. 17,783,000)

New Zealand lies southeast of AUSTRALIA in the South PACIFIC. It comprises two large islands, NORTH ISLAND and SOUTH ISLAND, Stewart Island and the Chatham Islands. New Zealand enjoys very mild winters with regular rainfall and no extremes of heat or cold. North Island is hilly with isolated mountains and active volcanoes. On South Island the SOUTHERN ALPS run north to south, and the highest point is Mount COOK (3753 m/12,313 ft). The CANTERBURY PLAINS lie to the east of the mountains. Two-thirds of New Zealand is suitable for agriculture and grazing, meat, wool and dairy goods being the main products. Forestry supports the pulp and paper industry and a considerable source of hydroelectric power produces cheap electricity for the manufacturing industry which now accounts for 30% of New Zealand's exports.

Ngaliema

Area : 270,986 sq km (104,629 sq miles)
Population : 3,390,000
Capital : Wellington
Other major cities : Auckland, Christchurch, Dunedin, Hamilton
Form of government : Constitutional Monarchy
Religions : Anglicanism, RC, Presbyterianism
Currency : New Zealand dollar

Ngaliema, Mount *see* **Ruwenzori.**

Ngamiland a remote region of savanna and swamp grassland, centred on the OKAVANGO BASIN in BOTSWANA.

Ngorongoro Crater a large extinct volcanic crater in north-central TANZANIA. It is 18 km (11 miles) wide and accommodates communities of Masai normads, 100,000 of their cattle, and more than 30,000 big game—wild animals.

Nha Trang a market town, port and resort on the east coast of VIETNAM. (Pop. 197,900)

Niagara Falls spectacular waterfalls on the Niagara River, situated on the CANADA-USA border between Lakes ERIE and ONTARIO.

Niagara-on-the-Lake a well-conserved old colonial town and popular resort at the northern end of the Niagara River, where it enters Lake ONTARIO near the CANADA-USA border; it was the first capital of Upper Canada (1792-6), the present-day province of Ontario. (Pop. 12,180)

Niamey the capital of NIGER. (Pop. 400,000)

Nicaragua lies between the PACIFIC OCEAN and the CARIBBEAN SEA, on the isthmus of Central AMERICA, and is sandwiched between HONDURAS to the north and COSTA RICA to the south. The east coast contains forested lowland and is the wettest part of the island. Behind this is a range of volcanic mountains and the west coast is a belt of savanna lowland running parallel to the Pacific coast. The western region, which contains the two huge lakes, NICARAGUA and Managua, is where most of the population live. The whole country is subject to devastating earthquakes. Nicaragua is primarily an agricultural country and 65% of the labour force work on the land. The main export crops are coffee, cotton and sugar cane. All local industry is agriculture-related.

Area : 130,000 sq km (50,193 sq miles)

Population : 3,750,000

Capital : Managua

Form of government : Republic

Religion : RC

Currency : Córdoba

Nicaragua, Lake a large lake in the southwest of NICARAGUA. (8264 sq km/3191 sq miles)

Nice a city, harbour and famous resort town of the CÔTE D'AZUR, southeastern FRANCE. (Pop. 451,500)

Nicobar Islands *see* **Andaman and Nicobar Islands**.

Nicosia the capital of CYPRUS, situated in the centre of the island. (Pop. 161,100)

Nieder-Österreich *see* **Lower Austria**.

Niedersachsen *see* **Lower Saxony**.

Niger is a landlocked republic in west AFRICA, lying just south of the Tropic of Cancer. Over half of the country is covered by the encroaching SAHARA DESERT in the north, and the south lies in the drought-stricken SAHEL. In the extreme southwest corner, the river NIGER flows through the country, and in the extreme southeast lies Lake CHAD, but the rest of the country is extremely short of water. The people in the southwest fish and farm their own food, growing rice and vegetables on land flooded by the river. Farther from the river, crops have failed year after year as a result of successive droughts since 1968. Even in the north, where the population are traditionally herdsmen, drought has wiped out whole clans. Uranium mined in the Aïr mountains is Niger's main export.

Area : 1,267,000 sq km (489,189 sq miles)

Population : 7,450,000

Capital : Niamey

Niger

Form of government : Republic
Religion : Sunni Islam
Currency : Franc CFA

Niger, River a river in West AFRICA flowing through GUINEA, MALI, NIGER and NIGERIA to the Gulf of GUINEA. (Length 4170 km/2590 miles)

Nigeria is a large and populous country in west AFRICA, and from the Gulf of GUINEA it extends north to the border with NIGER. It has a variable landscape, from the swampy coastal areas and tropical forest belts of the interior, to the mountains and savanna of the north. The two main rivers are the NIGER and the BENUE, and just north of their confluence lies the Jos Plateau. The climate is hot and humid and rainfall, heavy at the coast, gradually decreases inland. The dry far north is affected by the Harmattan, a hot dry wind blowing from the SAHARA. The main agricultural products are cocoa, rubber, groundnuts and cotton. However, only cocoa is of any significance for export. The country depends on revenue from petroleum exports but fluctuations in the world oil market have left Nigeria with economic problems.

Area : 923,768 sq km (356,667 sq miles)
Population : 118,700,000
Capital : Abuja (New Federal Capital), Lagos (Capital until 1992)
Other major cities : Ibadan, Kano, Ogbomsho
Form of government : Federal republic
Religions : Sunni Islam, Christianity
Currency : Naira

Nijmegen a city of eastern central NETHERLANDS, close to the border with GERMANY. (Pop. 234,000)

Nikolayev a port and industrial city on the north coast of the BLACK SEA, in the UKRAINE. (Pop. 480,000)

Nile, River (An Nil) a river in AFRICA and, with the AMAZON, one of the two longest rivers in the world. It rises in BURUNDI, flows into Lake VICTORIA and then flows northwards through UGANDA, SUDAN and EGYPT to its delta on the MEDITERRANEAN. The river is called the White Nile (Bahr el Abiad) until it reaches KHARTOUM, where it is joined by its main tributary, the Blue Nile (Bahr el Azraq), which rises in ETHIOPIA. (Length 6695 km/4160 miles)

Nîmes a city in southern FRANCE, overlooking the River RHONE. (Pop. 138,000)

Nineveh the excavated remains of the ancient capital of ASSYRIA, near MOSUL in northern IRAQ.

Ningbo a port and industrial city in ZHEJIANG province, in central eastern CHINA. (Pop. 900,000)

Ningxia-Hui Autonomous Region a region of central northern CHINA, south of Inner Mongolia. The capital is YINCHUAN. (60,000 sq km/23,000 sq miles; pop. 3,640,000)

Nis (Nish) a historic city in the east of SERBIA. (Pop. 230,000)

Niue a raised coral island in the South PACIFIC, about 2100 km (1300 miles) northeast of NEW ZEALAND. Discovered by Captain Cook in 1774, it is now a self-governing overseas territory in free association with NEW ZEALAND. The capital is Alofi. (259 sq km/100 sq miles; pop 3032)

Nizhniy Novgorod an industrial city in the RUSSIAN FEDERATION on the River VOLGA, formerly known as Gor'kiy (Gorky). (Pop. 1,392,000)

Nizhniy Tagil an industrial city in the central URAL MOUNTAINS, RUSSIAN FEDERATION. (Pop. 415,000)

Nordkapp *see* **North Cape.**

Nord-Pas de Calais the densely populated industrial and agricultural region in the far north of FRANCE, centring on the LILLE-ROUBAIX-TOURCOING conurbation. (Pop. 3,933,000)

Nordrhein-Westfalen *see* **North Rhineland Westphalia.**

Norfolk (1) a county of EAST ANGLIA, ENGLAND. The county town is NORWICH. (5355 sq km/2068 sq miles; pop. 714,000) **(2)** a port and naval base in the state of VIRGINIA, USA. (Pop. city 279,700/metropolitan area (with NEWPORT NEWS)

1,261,200)

Norfolk Broads (The Broads) a region in EAST ANGLIA, ENGLAND, with a distinctive group of shallow navigable lakes connected by a network of rivers; it is a popular boating and tourist area.

Norfolk Island a small island in the PACIFIC OCEAN, lying 1400 km (875 miles) east of BRISBANE. Discovered by Captain Cook in 1774, it was settled by families of mutineers from HMS *Bounty*, who moved on from PITCAIRN ISLAND in 1856. (35 sq km/13 sq miles; pop. 2500)

Normandy an area of central northern FRANCE, now divided into two regions, Haute Normandie and Basse Normandie. (Pop. 3,006,000)

Norrköping a major industrial seaport of SWEDEN, situated on a BALTIC inlet 160 km (100 miles) southwest of STOCKHOLM. (pop. 118,600)

Northampton the county town of NORTHAMPTONSHIRE. (Pop. 164,000)

Northamptonshire a county in central ENGLAND. The county town is NORTHAMPTON. (2367 sq km/914 sq miles; pop. 547,000)

North Cape (Nordkapp) one of Europe's most northerly points—500 km (310 miles) north of the ARCTIC CIRCLE in NORWAY.

North Carolina a state on the southeastern coast of the USA. The state capital is RALEIGH. (136,198 sq km/52,586 sq miles; pop. 6,255,000)

North Channel a strait between southwest SCOTLAND and northeast IRELAND, 20 km (12 miles) wide at its narrowest; it links the ATLANTIC OCEAN with the IRISH SEA.

North Dakota a state in the west of the USA. The state capital is BISMARCK. (183,022 sq km/70,665 sq miles; pop. 685,000)

North Downs *see* **Downs, The**.

Northern Ireland a province of the UK, occupying most of the northern part of the island of IRELAND. It is divided into six counties. The capital is BELFAST. (14,121 sq km/

5452 sq miles; pop. 1,572,000)

Northern Isles a collective term for the ORKNEY and SHETLAND ISLANDS, lying north of the mainland of SCOTLAND.

Northern Marianas a group of 14 islands in the western PACIFIC which in 1978 became a commonwealth of the USA. The capital is SUSEPE, on the island of SAIPAN.

Northern Rhodesia *see* **Zambia.**

Northern Territory a territory of northern AUSTRALIA. The capital is DARWIN. (13,462,000 sq km/519,770 sq miles; pop. 136,800)

North European Plain a general term for the extensive region of a virtually uninterrupted fertile plain that stretches from the ATLANTIC coast of northern FRANCE, through the Low COUNTRIES and northern GERMANY, along the countries of the southern BALTIC and through western RUSSIAN to the URALS.

North Island the slightly smaller of NEW ZEALAND's two principal islands, but with a population almost three times that of the larger SOUTH ISLAND. (114,685 sq km/44,281 sq miles; pop. 2,323,000)

North Korea *see* **Korea.**

North Land *see* **Severnaya Zemlya**.

North Ossetia *see* **Ossetia**.

North Pole the northernmost point on the earth's axis.

North Rhineland-Westphalia (Nordrhein-Westfalen) the westernmost *länd* (state) of GERMANY, formed in 1946 by the amalgamation of two former Prussian provinces. It is centred on the highly industrialised conurbations of the northern RHINE and RUHR valleys; its capital is Düsseldorf. (34,039 sq km/13,142 sq miles; pop. 17,046,000)

North Sea a comparatively shallow branch of the ATLANTIC OCEAN that separates the BRITISH ISLES from the European mainland.

North Uist an island in the Outer HEBRIDES, off the west coast of SCOTLAND, lying between HARRIS and BENBECULA.

(310 sq km/120 sq miles: pop. 1,399)

Northumberland a county in northeastern ENGLAND. The county town is Morpeth. (5033 sq km/1943 sq miles; pop. 302,000)

Northumbria an ancient Anglo-Saxon region and kingdom that extended in eastern BRITAIN from the Humber to the Firth of FORTH, formed in the 7th century.

North West Cape the extreme northwestern headland of AUSTRALIA, about 1100km (690 miles) north, and slightly west of PERTH, WESTERN AUSTRALIA.

North-West Frontier Province a rugged mountainous province of PAKISTAN, which lies along its border with AFGHANISTAN. (74,52 sq km/28,773 sq miles; pop. 11,061,000)

North West Highlands the large mountainous area of the west Scottish mainland north of the GREAT GLEN, rising to over 1180 m (3870 ft).

Northwest Passage a series of connecting seaways joining the ATLANTIC and PACIFIC OCEANS through CANADA's ARCTIC archipelago; it was first sought by 16th-century navigators as a route to the Orient.

Northwest Territories a vast area of northern CANADA, occupying almost a third of the country's whole land area. The capital is YELLOWKNIFE. (3,246,000 sq km/1,253,400 sq miles; pop. 45,740)

North York Moors an area of heath-covered uplands in NORTH YORKSHIRE, northeastern ENGLAND, close to the densely populated conurbations of West and South Yorkshire; the Moors are a popular recreational area.

North Yorkshire a county in northeastern ENGLAND, formed in 1974 from the former North Riding of YORKSHIRE. (Administrative centre Northallerton; 8309 sq km/ 3241 sq miles; pop 691,100)

Norway occupies the western half of the Scandinavian peninsula in northern EUROPE, and is surrounded to the north, west and south by water. It shares most of its eastern border with SWEDEN. It is a country of spectacular scenery of fjords, cliffs, rugged uplands and forested valleys. Two-thirds of the country is over 600 m/1969 ft and it has some of the deepest fjords in the world. The climate is temperate as a result of the warming effect of the Gulf Stream. Summers are mild and although the winters are long and cold, the waters off the west coast remain ice-free. Agriculture is chiefly concerned with dairying and fodder crops. Fishing is an important industry and the large reserves of forest provide timber for export. Industry is now dominated by petrochemicals based on the reserves of Norwegian oil in the NORTH SEA.

Area : 323,895 sq km (125,056 sq miles)

Population : 4,200,000

Capital : Oslo

Other major cities : Bergen, Trondheim, Stavanger

Form of government : Constitutional Monarchy

Religion : Lutheranism

Currency : Norwegian krone

Norwegian Sea a sea lying between NORWAY, GREENLAND and ICELAND; to the north it joins the ARCTIC OCEAN, and to the south, the ATLANTIC.

Norwich the county town of NORFOLK, in eastern ENGLAND. (Pop. 122,000)

Nottingham the historic county town of NOTTINGHAM-SHIRE, situated on the River TRENT. (Pop. 277,000)

Nottinghamshire a county in the MIDLANDS of ENGLAND. The county town is NOTTINGHAM,. (2164 sq km/836 sq miles; pop. 1,000,000)

Nouakchott the capital city of MAURITANIA, near the ATLANTIC coast. (Pop. 135,000)

Nouméa the capital and chief port of NEW CALEDONIA. (Pop. 85,000)

Nova Scotia a province on the eastern coast of CANADA. The capital is HALIFAX. (52,841 sq km/20,401 sq miles; pop. 847,000)

Novaya Zemlya (New Land) an almost uninhabited pair of islands, separated by a narrow channel, in the

Russian Arctic between the Barents and Kara Seas. (81,400 sq km/31,400 sq miles; pop 400)

Novgorod an industrial and historic town 155 km (95 miles) south of St Petersburg in the Russian Federation. Founded as a city in AD859, it is generally regarded as the cradle of Russian civilization. It began as an important trading post on the Viking route to Constantinople, and by the Middle Ages it rivalled Moscow as the country's most important town. (Pop. 215,000)

Novi Sad (Ujvidek; Neusatz) a city on the River Danube and the capital of Vojvodina, an autonomous province of Serbia. (Pop. 257,700)

Novokuznetsk an industrial city in central southern Siberia. (Pop. 572,000)

Novosibirsk a major industrial city in central Russian Federation. (Pop. 1,386,000)

Novosibirskiye Ostrova *see* **New Siberian Islands**.

Nubia an ancient region of northeastern Africa, centred on the Nile River between Aswan and Khartoum.

Nubian Desert a desert of a mainly sandstone plateau in northeastern Sudan, between the Nile valley and the Red Sea.

Nuku'alofa the capital and main port of Tonga. (Pop. 21,000)

Nullarbor Plain a huge, dry and treeless (the name is from the Latin for "no trees") plain which borders the Great Australian Bight, in Western and Southern Australia.

Nuremberg (Nürnberg) a city in Bavaria, central southern Germany. (Pop. 486,000)

Nürnberg *see* **Nuremberg**.

Nusa Tenggara *see* **Lesser Sunda Islands**.

Nuuk *see* **Godthåb**.

Nyasa, Lake *see* **Malawi, Lake**.

Nyasaland *see* **Malawi**.

O

Oahu the third largest of the islands of HAWAII, where the state capital, HONOLULU, and PEARL HARBOUR are located. (1549 sq km/598 sq miles; pop. 797,400)

Oakland a port on SAN FRANCISCO BAY in central western CALIFORNIA, USA. (Pop. city 351,900/metropolitan area 1,871,400)

Oberammergau a village in BAVARIA in southwest GERMANY, famed for the Passion play which it puts on every ten years. (Pop. 4800)

Oberösterreich *see* **Upper Austria**.

Ob', River a river in the RUSSIAN FEDERATION which rises near the border with MONGOLIA and flows northwards to the KARA SEA. (Length 5570 km/3460 miles)

Obuasi a gold-mining town in the Ashanti region of south-central GHANA (formerly the Gold Coast); it produces 75 per cent of the country's gold output. (Pop. 47,400)

Oceania a general term used to describe the central and southern islands of the PACIFIC OCEAN including those of AUSTRALIA and NEW ZEALAND. (8,900,000 sq km/3,400,000 sq miles; pop. 25,800,000)

Odense the third largest city of DENMARK and administrative centre for the island of FUNEN; it was the birthplace of the author of fairytales Hans Christian Andersen (1805-75). (Pop. 170,200)

Oder, River a river in central EUROPE rising in the CZECH REPUBLIC and flowing north and west to the BALTIC SEA; it forms part of the border between GERMANY and POLAND. (Length 912 km/567 miles)

Odessa a major BLACK SEA port in the UKRAINE. (Pop. 1,113,000)

Offaly a county in the center of the Republic of IRELAND. The county town is Tullamore. (1998 sq km/771 sq miles; pop. 58,300)

Ogaden a desert region of southeastern ETHIOPIA, claimed by SOMALIA.

Ogbomosho a historic Yoruba city and busy industrial centre, lying on the Western Uplands of southwestern NIGERIA. (Pop. 514,000)

Ohio a MIDWEST state of the USA, with a shoreline on Lake ERIE. The capital is COLUMBUS. (106,765 sq km/41,220 sq miles; pop. 10,744,00)

Ohio River a river in the eastern USA, formed at the confluence of the Allegheny and Monongahela Rivers. It flows west and south and joins the MISSISSIPPI at Cairo, ILLINOIS. (Length 1575 km/980 miles)

Okavango Basin *or* **Delta** a swampy inland delta basin of the KAVANGO River, occupying a large area of northwest BOTSWANA. In good rainy seasons it drains into the vast Makgadikgadi Pans, 200 km (125 miles) to the southeast. (10,360 sq km/4000 sq miles)

Okavango, River see **Kavango (Cubango), River**.

Okayama a commercial city in southwest HONSHU Island, JAPAN. (Pop. 572,400)

Okhotsk, Sea of a part of the northwestern PACIFIC OCEAN bounded by the KAMCHATKA peninsula, the KURIL islands, and the east coast of SIBERIA.

Okinawa the main island of the RYUKYU ISLANDS, lying in the EAST CHINA SEA about 500 km (310 miles) southwest of JAPAN, to whom it belongs. It was captured, after fierce fighting, by US troops in 1945—a turning point in World War II. (1176 sq km/454 sq miles; pop. 1,072,200)

Oklahoma a state in the southwest of the USA. The state capital is OKLAHOMA CITY. (173,320 sq km/66,919 sq miles; pop. 3,301,000)

Oklahoma City the state capital of OKLAHOMA. (Pop. city 443,200/metropolitan area 962,600)

Öland a long and low-lying island off the southeast BALTIC coast of SWEDEN. It is linked to the mainland by a 6-km (4-mile) long bridge. (1345 sq km/520 sq miles; pop. 23,800)

Olinda a beautifully conserved old colonial city, founded by the Portuguese in 1537, just north of RECIFE in north-eastern BRAZIL. It is famed for its annual Mardi Gras carnival. (Pop. 282,000)

Olumouc a historic market town and former 11th-12th-century capital of MORAVIA, in the east of the present-day CZECH REPUBLIC.(Pop. 104,300)

Olympia (1) the original site of the Olympic Games, centring upon a temple to Zeus, on the PELOPONNESE in south-western GREECE. **(2)** a port and the state capital of WASHINGTON, on the west coast of the USA. (Pop. city 29,200/metropolitan area 138,300)

Olympus, Mount a group of mountains in central mainland GREECE, the home of the gods of ancient Greek myth. The highest peak is Mytikas (2917 m/9570 ft).

Omaha a city in eastern NEBRASKA, U.S.A. (Pop. city 334,000/metropolitan area 607,400)

Oman situated in the southeast of the Arabian peninsula, Oman is a small country in two parts. It comprises a small mountainous area, overlooking the Strait of HORMUZ, which controls the entrance to The GULF, and the main part of the country, consisting of barren hills rising sharply behind a narrow coastal plain. Inland the hills extend into the unexplored "Empty Quarter" in SAUDI ARABIA. Oman has a desert climate with exceptionally hot and humid conditions from April to October. Only 0.1% of the country is cultivated, the main produce being dates. The economy is almost entirely dependent on oil which provides 90% of its exports. Oman has some deposits of copper and there is a smelter at Sohar.

Area : 212,457 sq km (82,030 sq miles)
Population : 2,000,000
Capital : Muscat (Musqat)
Form of government : Monarchy (sultanate)
Religion : Ibadi Islam, Sunni Islam

Oman

Currency : Rial Omani

Oman, Gulf of a branch of the ARABIAN SEA leading to the Strait of HORMUZ.

Omdurman a city situated across the River NILE from KHARTOUM, the capital of SUDAN. (Pop. 526,300)

Omsk an industrial city in central western SIBERIA, on the Trans-Siberian Railway. (Pop. 1,094,000)

Onega, Lake (Onezhskoye Ozero) the second largest lake in EUROPE, after Lake LADOGA, situated in the north-west of the RUSSIAN FEDERATION. It is connected by canal to the BALTIC SEA, WHITE SEA, and the VOLGA. (9720 sq km/ 3375 sq miles)

Onitsha a major trading centre and communications focus at one of the few bridges on the lower NIGER River in south-central NIGERIA (Pop. 262,100)

Ontario a province of central CANADA. The capital is TORONTO. (1,068,582 sq km/412,580 sq miles; pop. 8,625,000)

Ontario, Lake the smallest and most easterly of the GREAT LAKES; it drains into the ST LAWRENCE River. (19,550 sq km/7550 sq miles)

Oporto (Porto) a port in north-west PORTUGAL, and the country's second largest city after LISBON. (Pop. 330,200)

Oran (Wahran) a MEDITERRANEAN port and the second largest city of ALGERIA. (Pop. 670,000)

Orange Free State a landlocked province in central SOUTH AFRICA, with its capital at BLOEMFONTEIN. (127,993 sq km/49,405 sq miles; pop. 2,080,000)

Orange, River the longest river in southern AFRICA, rising in LESOTHO and flowing west to the ATLANTIC. (Length 2090 km/1299 miles)

Oranjestad (1) the capital of ARUBA, and an important port. (Pop. 10,100) **(2)** the capital of ST EUSTATIUS, and a port. (Pop. 1200)

Oregon a state in the northwest of the USA, on the PACIFIC. The state capital is SALEM. (251,180 sq km/96,981 sq miles; pop. 2,687,000)

Ore Mountains (Erzebirge; Krosnéhory) the forested range forming the northwestern border of the CZECH REPUBLIC with GERMANY. They rise to 1244 m (4081 ft) and still have workable deposits of mineral ores. It is a popular resort area.

Øresund (The Sound) the deepest and most easterly channel linking the KATTEGAT and NORTH SEA to the BALTIC, passing between ZEALAND and the SKÅNE peninsula of SWEDEN. (Length 140 km/90 miles; narrowest width 4 km/2.5 miles)

Orient, The a general term referring collectively to the countries east of the Mediterranean, or alternatively the whole of the eastern hemisphere.

Orinoco, River a river in northern South AMERICA. It rises in southern VENEZUELA and flows west, then north and finally east to its delta on the ATLANTIC. It forms part of the border between COLOMBIA and Venezuela. (Length 2200 km/1370 miles)

Orissa an eastern state of INDIA. The capital is Bhubaneswar. (155,707 sq km/60,103 sq miles; pop. 26,370,300)

Orkney Islands a group of some 90 islands off the northeast coast of SCOTLAND; they have some of the best preserved prehistoric sites in EUROPE including the famous Skara Brae (2000 BC). The capital is Kirkwall. (976 sq km/377 sq miles; pop. 19,000)

Orlando a city in central FLORIDA, and the focus for visitors to Walt DISNEY WORLD and Cape CANAVERAL. (Pop. city 137,100/metropolitan area 824,100)

Orléans a city in north central FRANCE, on the River LOIRE. (Pop. 225,000)

Orontes, River the river flowing through HOMS and HAMAH in SYRIA. (Length 384 km/238 miles)

Oruro a city and surrounding department set in the ANDES of west-central BOLIVIA; it is a major mining centre, producing half the country's tin output as well as other minerals. It is also famed for its annual Mardi Gras carnival. (Pop. city 132,200/department 385,200)

Osaka a port on south HONSHU Island, and the third largest city in JAPAN after TOKYO and YOKOHAMA. (Pop. 2,636,300)

Osijek a city in eastern CROATIA, on the DRAVA River. It was formerly called Esseg. (Pop. 158,800)

Oslo the capital of NORWAY, and its main port, in the southeast of the country. From 1624 to 1925 it was called Christiania (or Kristiania). (Pop. city 448,800/ metropolitan area 566,500)

Ossetia (1), North one of the 16 autonomous republics of the RUSSIAN FEDERATION, lying on the northern slopes of the central CAUCASUS. The capital city is Alagir. **(2), South** an autonomous republic of GEORGIA, lying on the southern side of the Caucasian watershed from North Ossetia. The capital city is Tskhinvali.

Ostend (Oostende; Ostende) a Flemish-speaking resort, port and ferry terminal on the NORTH SEA coast of BELGIUM. (Pop. 72,000)

Ostrava a coal-mining and manufacturing city in Czech SILESIA, the main industrial region in the northeast of the Republic. It is the birthplace of the psychiatrist Sigmund Freud (1856–1939) and the composer Leos Janácek (1854–1928). (Pop. 323,700)

Ostrova Vrangelya *see* **Wrangel Island**.

Otago a district and former province in the southeast of SOUTH ISLAND, NEW ZEALAND, founded by Scottish settlers in the mid-19th century. The chief town is DUNEDIN.

Otranto, Strait of the waterway separating the heel of ITALY from ALBANIA.

Ottawa the capital of CANADA, in eastern ONTARIO, on the OTTAWA River. (Pop. 718,000)

Ottawa, River a river of central CANADA which flows into the ST LAWRENCE at MONTREAL. (Length 1271 km/790 miles)

Ouagadougou the capital of BURKINA, situated in the centre of the country. (Pop. 286,500)

Oujda an important communications centre in the extreme northeast of MOROCCO, near the border with ALGERIA. (Pop. 260,000)

Oulu (Uleåborg) a seaport and largest city in northern FINLAND, near the Swedish border and at the head of the Gulf of BOTHNIA; it is mainly involved in the timber industry. (Pop. 96,400)

Ovamboland (Owambo) a homeland, in the north interior of NAMIBIA, of the country's largest ethnic group, the Ovambos or Wambo, who are mainly herdsmen working this savanna plateau. (51,800 sq km/20,000 sq miles; pop.545,000)

Oviedo a steel making city in northern SPAIN, capital of the province of ASTURIAS. (Pop. 190,100)

Oxford an old university city, and county town of OXFORDSHIRE, ENGLAND. (Pop. 117,000)

Oxfordshire a county in southern central ENGLAND. The county town is OXFORD. (2611 sq km/1008 sq miles; pop. 558,000)

Oxus, River *see* **Amudar'ya, River.**

Oyo a Yoruba town lying on the Oyo Plains of southwest NIGERIA, about 170 km (105 miles) north and slightly east of LAGOS; it is a trading centre for tobacco and cotton. (Pop. 180,700)

P

Paarl an Afrikaner town at the centre of SOUTH AFRICA's main wine-making region, about 56 km (35 miles) northeast of CAPE TOWN. (Pop.59,100)

Pacific Ocean the largest and deepest ocean on Earth, situated between ASIA and AUSTRALIA to the west and the AMERICAS to the east. (165,384,000 sq km/63,838,000 sq miles)

Padang a port and the capital of West SUMATRA, INDONESIA, on the west coast. (Pop. 480,900)

Padua a historic city in VENETO, northeast ITALY. (Pop. 228,700)

Pagan the ruined 11th-century capital of BURMA, 160 km (100 miles) southwest of MANDALAY.

Pago Pago the capital and chief port of American SAMOA, situated on Tutuila island. (Pop. 3000)

Painted Desert a desert of colourful rocks in northern ARIZONA, USA (19,400 sq km/7500 sq miles)

Paisley an industrial town in central STRATHCLYDE, southwestern SCOTLAND; it developed as a major textile centre in the 19th century, and became famous for its Paisley-pattern shawls. (Pop. 84,789)

País Vasco *see* **Basque Provinces**.

Pakistan lies just north of the Tropic of Cancer and has as its southern border the ARABIAN SEA. The valley of the INDUS river splits the country into a highland region in the west, and a lowland region in the east. In the north are some of the world's highest mountains. The peak K2 (8611 m/28,250 ft) lies in KASHMIR, a territory to which INDIA also lays claim. A weak form of tropical monsoon climate occurs over most of the country and conditions in the north and west are arid. Temperatures are high everywhere in summer but winters are cold in the mountains. Most agriculture is subsistence, with wheat and rice as the main crops. Cotton is the main cash crop, but the cultivated area is restricted because of waterlogging and saline soils. Pakistan's wide range of mineral resources have not been extensively developed and industry concentrates on food processing, textiles and consumer goods.

Area : 796,095 sq km (307,372 sq miles)

Population : 105,400,000

Capital : Islamabad

Other major cities : Faisalabad, Hyderabad, Karachi, Lahore

Form of government : Federal Islamic Republic

Religion : Sunni Islam, Shia Islam

Currency : Pakistan rupee

Palau *see* **Belau.**

Palawan a narrow sword-shaped island in the southwestern part of the PHILIPPINES archipelago, lying between the SULU and SOUTH CHINA SEAS. (11,785 sq km/ 4550 sq miles; pop. 300,100)

Palembang a port and the capital of South SUMATRA, on the southeast coast. (Pop. 787,200)

Palencia an ancient walled town of 3rd-century BC origin in north-central SPAIN; it is the home of the country's oldest university, founded in 1185. (Pop. 75,000)

Palenque the ruins of one of the great Mayan cities in southern MEXICO.

Palermo the capital of SICILY, ITALY, on the northwest coast. (Pop. 718,900)

Palestine a disputed area of the MIDDLE EAST which encompassed the modern countries of ISRAEL and parts of JORDAN and EGYPT.

Palm Beach a resort on an island off the east coast of FLORIDA, USA, with the manufacturing centre of West Palm Beach on the mainland opposite. (Pop. Palm Beach

10,700/metropolitan area 692,200)

Palma (Palma de Mallorca) The capital of MAJORCA and of the BALEARIC ISLANDS. (Pop. 304,400)

Palma, La *see* **Canary Islands.**

Palmerston North a market and university town in the southern part of NORTH ISLAND, NEW ZEALAND. (Pop. 60,100)

Palmyra an ancient ruined city in SYRIA. Its Biblical name is Tadmor.

Pamir a region of high plateaux in central Asia which straddles the borders of TAJIKISTAN, AFGHANISTAN and CHINA.

Pampas the flat grasslands of central ARGENTINA.

Pamplona a city in northeastern SPAIN, famous for its bull-running festival in July. (Pop. 183,100)

Panama is located at the narrowest point in Central AMERICA. Only 58 km (36 miles) separates the CARIBBEAN SEA from the PACIFIC OCEAN at Panama, and the PANAMA CANAL which divides the country is the main routeway from the Caribbean and ATLANTIC to the Pacific. The climate is tropical with high temperatures throughout the year and only a short dry season from January to April. The country is heavily forested and very little is cultivated. Rice is the staple food. The economy is heavily dependent on the Canal and income from it is a major foreign currency earner. The country has great timber resources, and mahogany from these is an important export. Other exports are shrimps and bananas.

Area : 77,082 sq km (29,761 sq miles)

Population : 2,320,000

Capital : Panama City

Other major cities : San Miguelito, Colón

Form of government : Republic

Religion : RC

Currency : Balboa

Panama Canal a canal 64 km (40 miles) long that runs through the centre of PANAMA, linking the CARIBBEAN to the PACIFIC. It was completed in 1914.

Panama City the capital of PANAMA, situated at the

Pacific end of the PANAMA CANAL. (Pop. 502,000)

Panama, Isthmus of the narrow neck of land (only 58 km/36 miles at its narrowest) that separates the CARIBBEAN SEA and ATLANTIC OCEAN from the PACIFIC OCEAN, and links the North and South parts of AMERICA.

Pan American Highway an international highway system linking North and South AMERICA, running some 27,350 km (17,000 miles) from northwest ALASKA to SANTIAGO in CHILE.

Panay *see* **Visayan Islands.**

Pangaea *see* **Gondwanaland**.

Papal States the historical temporal domain of the Popes, in central ITALY, from AD756 until the unification of the country in 1870, since when the VATICAN CITY remains the only vestige.

Papeete the capital of FRENCH POLYNESIA, on the northwest coast of TAHITI. (Pop. 62,700)

Papua New Guinea in the southwest PACIFIC, comprises the eastern half of the island of NEW GUINEA, together with hundreds of islands of which NEW BRITAIN, BOUGAINVILLE and New Ireland are the largest. The country has a mountainous interior surrounded by broad swampy plains. The climate is tropical with high temperatures and heavy rainfall. Subsistence farming is the main economic activity although some coffee, cocoa and coconuts are grown for cash. Timber is cut for export and fishing and fish processing industries are developing. Minerals such as copper, gold, silver and oil form the mainstay of the economy. The country still receives valuable aid from AUSTRALIA, who governed it before independence.

Area : 462,840 sq km (178,703 sq miles)

Population : 3,800,000

Capital : Port Moresby

Form of government : Constitutional Monarchy

Religion : Protestantism, RC

Currency : Kina

Paracel Islands a group of islands lying some 300 km (185 miles) east of Vietnam, owned by China but claimed by Vietnam.

Paraguay, located in central South America, is a country without a coastline and is bordered by Bolivia, Brazil and Argentina. The climate is tropical with abundant rain and a short dry season. The River Paraguay splits the country into the Chaco, a flat semi-arid plain on the west, and a partly forested undulating plateau on the east. Almost 95% of the population live east of the river, where crops grown on the fertile plains include cassava, sugar cane, maize, cotton and soya beans. Immediately west of the river, on the low Chaco, are huge cattle ranches which provide meat for export. The world's largest hydro-electric dam has been built at Itaipú and cheap power from this has stimulated industry. Industry includes food processing, vegetable oil refining, textiles and cement.

Area : 406,752 sq km (157,047 sq miles)

Population : 4,160,000

Capital : Asunción

Other major city : Ciudad Alfredo Stroessner

Form of government : Republic

Religion : RC

Currency : Guaraní

Paraguay, River a major river of South America. It rises in Brazil and flows south through Paraguay to join the Parana River. (Length 1920 km/1190 miles)

Paramaribo the capital, principal city and main port of Suriname. (Pop. 180,000)

Parana, River the second largest river in South America after the Amazon. It rises in Brazil and flows south to join the River Plate. (Length 4200 km/2610 miles)

Paris the capital of France, in the north of the country, on the River Seine. (Pop. city 2,188,900/ Greater Paris 8,761,700)

Parma a historic city in northern Italy, in Emilia-Romagna.

(Pop. 176,800)

Páros an island in the CYCLADES group, GREECE. (194 sq km/75 sq miles; pop. 7400)

Pasadena a city in southwest CALIFORNIA, USA. (Pop. 125,000)

Pascua, Isla de *see* **Easter Island.**

Passchendaele (Passendale) a village in FLANDERS, northwest BELGIUM; it was the scene of heavy fighting during the third battle of YPRES in World War I. (Pop. 4000)

Patagonia a cold desert in southern ARGENTINA and CHILE.

Patna the capital of the state of BIHAR, in northeast INDIA, on the River GANGES. (Pop. 918,900)

Patras a port and the main city of the PELOPONNESE, GREECE. (Pop. 154,000)

Pau a tourist resort and industrial capital of the Pyrénées-Atlantiques département in southwest FRANCE; it was the historical seat of the kings of Navarre. (Pop. 135,700)

Pavlodar a fast-growing food-processing town of northeastern KAZAKHSTAN, centred on a fertile basin of the upper IRTYSH River. (Pop. 309,000)

Paysandú the third largest city of URUGUAY; it is a port on the Uruguay River in the west of the country. (Pop. 71,000)

Pays de la Loire a region in western FRANCE, on the Bay of BISCAY; it is a generally low-lying, fertile area, drained by the LOIRE River and its tributaries. (32,083 sq km/12,387 sq miles; pop. 2,931,000)

Peace River a river in western CANADA, a tributary of the Slave/MACKENZIE River, rising in BRITISH COLUMBIA. (Length 1923 km/1195 miles)

Pearl Harbor a harbour and naval base on OAHU, HAWAII; the Japanese attack on the US fleet in 1941 drew the USA into World War II.

Pécs the main city of southwest HUNGARY. (Pop. 174,500)

Peeblesshire *see* **Borders.**

Pegu the main centre of a rice and sugar-growing area

northeast of RANGOON, BURMA; it was formerly a national capital and seat of the Mon Kingdom (1250–1757). (Pop. 254,800)

Peipus, Lake (Chudskoye Ozero) a lake straddling the border between ESTONIA and the extreme west of the RUSSIAN FEDERATION; it drains northwards to the Gulf of FINLAND. (3512 sq km/1356 sq miles)

Peking *see* **Beijing.**

Pelée, Mount an active volcano on MARTINIQUE, which destroyed the town of St Pierre in 1902. (1397 m/4583 ft)

Peloponnese a broad peninsula of southern GREECE, joined to the northern part of the country by the isthmus of CORINTH.

Pemba a clove-growing island in the INDIAN OCEAN, off the coast of TANZANIA of which it is now a part; it was formerly a British protectorate with ZANZIBAR (1890-1963). (985 sq km/380 sq miles; 250,000)

Pembrokeshire *see* **Dyfed.**

Penang a state of west MALAYSIA comprising Penang Island and the mainland province of Wellesley.

Pennines a range of hills that runs down the middle of northern ENGLAND from the border with SCOTLAND to the MIDLANDS, rising to 894 m (2087 ft) at Cross Fell.

Pennsylvania a state of the northeastern USA situated mainly in the APPALACHIAN MOUNTAINS. The capital is HARRISBURG. (117,412 sq km/45,333 sq miles; pop. 11,853,000)

Pentland Firth an important shipping channel, of notoriously rough waters, between the northern tip of mainland SCOTLAND and the ORKNEY ISLANDS.

Pereira a market town of a coffee-growing region in the ANDES of central COLOMBIA. (Pop. 265,000)

Perm' an industrial port on the Kama River in the western URALS of the RUSSIAN FEDERATION. It was known as Molotov 1940-57. (Pop. 1,049,000)

Perpignan a cathedral town in southwestern FRANCE. (Pop. 140,000)

Persepolis the capital of ancient Persia, southeast of TEHRAN, destroyed by Alexander the Great in 330BC.

Persia *see* **Iran.**

Persian Gulf *see* **Gulf, The**

Perth (1) the state capital of WESTERN AUSTRALIA, which includes the port of Freemantle. (Pop. 969,000). **(2)** a city and former capital of SCOTLAND, 55 km (35 miles) north of EDINBURGH. (Pop. 42,000)

Perthshire a former county of SCOTLAND, now divided between CENTRAL REGION and TAYSIDE.

Peru is located just south of the Equator, on the PACIFIC coast of South AMERICA. The country has three distinct regions from west to east: the coast, the high sierra of the ANDES, and the tropical jungle. The climate on the narrow coastal belt is mainly desert, while the Andes are wet, and east of the mountains is equatorial with tropical forests. Most large-scale agriculture is in the oases and fertile, irrigated river valleys that cut across the coastal desert. Sugar and cotton are the main exports. Sheep, llamas, vicuñas and alpacas are kept for wool. The fishing industry was once the largest in the world but recently the shoals have become depleted. Peru's main source of wealth is oil, but new discoveries are needed as present reserves are near exhaustion. In general, the economy has recently been damaged due to the declining value of exports, natural disasters and guerrilla warfare.

Area : 1,285,216 sq km (496,235 sq miles)

Population : 22,330,000

Capital : Lima

Other major cities : Arequipa, Callao, Cuzco, Trujillo

Form of government : Republic

Religion : RC

Currency : Sol

Perugia a beautifully preserved Renaissance city and present-day cultural centre set in the APENNINES in north-central ITALY. (Pop. 142,200)

Peshawar a historic town in northwest PAKISTAN at the

foot of the KHYBER PASS. (Pop. 555,000)

Petra an ancient ruined city, founded in about 1000BC in southern JORDAN, and carved out of pink limestone.

Petrograd *see* **St Petersburg.**

Petropavlovsk a timber town on the TRANS-SIBERIAN RAILWAY in northern KAZAKHSTAN. (Pop. 222,000)

Petropavlovsk-Kamchatskiy a PACIFIC whaling port and naval base on the southeast coast of the KAMCHATKA peninsula, in the far east of the RUSSIAN FEDERATION. (Pop. 241,000)

Petrozavodsk an industrial town and capital of the KARELIA REPUBLIC in the far northwest of the RUSSIAN FEDERATION, lying on the western shore of Lake ONEGA. (Pop. 247,000)

Philadelphia a port and city in southeast PENNSYLVANIA, the fourth largest city in the USA. (Pop. city 1,688,700/ metropolitan area 4,768,400)

Philippines comprise a group of islands, in the western PACIFIC, which are scattered over a great area. There are four main groups, LUZON and MINDORO to the north, the VISAYAN ISLANDS in the centre, MINDANAO and the SULU ARCHIPELAGO in the south, and Palawan in the southwest. MANILA, the capital, is on Luzon. Most of the island group is mountainous and earthquakes are common. The climate is humid with high temperatures and high rainfall. Typhoons are frequent. Rice and maize are the main subsistence crops and coconuts, sugar cane, pineapples and bananas are grown for export. Copper is a major export and there are deposits of gold, nickel and petroleum. Major industries include textiles, food processing, chemicals and electrical engineering.

Area : 300,000 sq km (115,830 sq miles)

Population : 60,500,000

Capital : Manila

Other major cities : Cebu, Davao, Quezon City

Form of government : Republic

Religions : RC, Aglipayan, Sunni Islam

Currency : Philippine peso

Phnom Penh the capital of CAMBODIA, in the south of the country. (Pop. 500,000)

Phoenicia an ancient maritime country at the eastern end of the MEDITERRANEAN, on the coastal plains of what is present-day LEBANON; as a leading trading nation, it reached its height between 1200 and 1000BC.

Phoenix the state capital of ARIZONA, USA. (Pop. city 853,300/metropolitan area 1,714,800)

Phuket an island and its chief town lying on the ANDAMAN SEA side of the Isthmus of KRA in southern THAILAND; its beautiful coastal scenery attracts many tourists. (Pop. town 86,800/island 146,400)

Picardy (Picardie) a northern region of FRANCE lying between PARIS and ARTOIS. The chief town is AMIENS. (19,399 sq km/7490 sq miles; pop. 1,740,000)

Piedmont (Piemonte) a region of northwest ITALY. The main town is TURIN.

Pierre the capital of SOUTH DAKOTA, USA. (Pop. 121,400)

Pietermaritzburg a city in eastern SOUTH AFRICA and capital of NATAL. (Pop. 180,000)

Pigs, Bay of (Bahia de Cochinos) a bay on the south coast of CUBA where exiled Cubans, backed by the USA, made a disastrous invasion attempt in 1961.

Pilbara an iron-rich mining area in WESTERN AUSTRALIA, centred on the HAMERSLEY RANGE about 1200 km (750 miles) north of PERTH.

Pilsen *see* **Plzen.**

Pindhos the massive mountain range that forms the backbone of GREECE, extending from ALBANIA in the north and falling away into the Gulf of CORINTH; it rises to 2637 m (8657 ft) in Smolikas.

P'ing-tung an industrial and commercial centre in the south of TAIWAN. (Pop. 300,000)

Piraeus the main port of GREECE, close to ATHENS, on the AEGEAN SEA. (Pop. 196,400)

Pisa a city in northwestern ITALY on the River ARNO,

famous for its leaning bell tower. (Pop. 104,300)

Pitcairn Island an island and British colony in the south PACIFIC, where mutineers from H.M.S. *Bounty* settled (after 1790).

Pittsburgh an industrial city in western PENNSYLVANIA, USA. (Pop. city 402,600/metropolitan area 2,172,800)

Planalto Brasil *see* **Brazilian Highlands**.

Plate, River (Rio de la Plata) the huge estuary of the PARANA and URUGUAY Rivers in southeast South AMERICA, with URUGUAY to the north and ARGENTINA to the south.

Platte, River an east-flowing river in NEBRASKA, USA, formed by the confluence of the North and South Platte Rivers, which rise in WYOMING and COLORADO. The historic 19th-century Oregon Trail followed the Platte and North Platte valleys as a route to the west for early settlers.

Plenty, Bay of the broad inlet on the north coast of the North Island of NEW ZEALAND.

Plovdiv a major market town in BULGARIA. (Pop. 373,000)

Plymouth (1) a port and naval base in southwest ENGLAND and the place from which the Pilgrim Fathers set sail in the *Mayflower* in 1620. (Pop. 255,000). **(2)** the capital of the island of MONTSERRAT. (Pop. 3200) **(3)** a town in MASSACHUSETTS, which has grown from the first European settlement in NEW ENGLAND, established by the Pilgrim Fathers of the *Mayflower*. (Pop. 37,100)

Plzen (Pilsen) an industrial city in western BOHEMIA, CZECH REPUBLIC. Pilsner lager beer was first produced here in 1842. (Pop. 174,100)

Po Hai *see* **Bo Hai**.

Pohnpei (Ponape) the island on which KOLONIA, the capital of the Federated States of MICRONESIA, stands.

Pointe-à-Pitre the main port of GUADELOUPE. (Pop. 23,000)

Poitiers a strategically located gap town and capital of Vienne département in western FRANCE; it was the site of a famous English victory over the French in 1256, during the Hundred Years' War. (Pop. 107,700)

Poitou-Charentes a largely rural region of western FRANCE, lying mainly between the POITIERS gap and the GIRONDE estuary. (Pop. 1,568,000)

Pojezierze Mazurskie *see* **Masuria**.

Poland is situated on the North European Plain. It borders GERMANY to the west, the CZECH REPUBLIC and SLOVAKIA to the south and BELARUS and UKRAINE to the east. Poland consists mainly of lowlands and the climate is continental, marked by long severe winters and short warm summers. Over one-quarter of the labour force is involved in agriculture which is predominantly small scale. The main crops are potatoes, wheat, barley, sugar beet and fodder crops. The industrial sector of the economy is large scale. Poland has large deposits of coal and reserves of natural gas, copper and silver. Vast forests stretching inland from the coast supply the paper and furniture industries. Other industries include food processing, engineering and chemicals.

Area : 312,677 sq km (120,725 sq miles)
Population : 37,930,000
Capital : Warsaw (Warszawa)
Other major cities : Gdansk, Kraków, Lódz, Wroclow
Form of government : Republic
Religion : RC
Currency : Zloty

Poles'ye *see* **Pripet Marshes**.

Polynesia the largest of the three island divisions of the PACIFIC, the others being MICRONESIA and MELANESIA. The group includes SAMOA, the COOK, SOCIETY and MARQUESAS Islands, and TONGA.

Pomerania a historical region straddling present-day northeast Germany and northwest POLAND, on the BALTIC coast.

Pompeii an ancient city near NAPLES which was smoth-ered by ash from an eruption of VESUVIUS in AD79.

Ponape *see* **Pohnpei.**

Pondicherry the former capital of French INDIA, in the

southeast of the country, founded in 1683 and governed by France until 1954. (Pop. 251,400)

Ponta Delgada a port and the capital of the Azores, on São Miguel Island. (Pop. 21,200)

Poona (Pune) a historic and industrial city east of Bombay, in western India. (Pop. 1,203,400)

Popocatépetl a volcano, twinned with Ixtacihuatl, 65 km (40 miles) southeast of Mexico City. (5452 m/17,887 ft)

Po, River the longest river in Italy, flowing across the north of the country from the Alps across a fertile plain to the Adriatic Sea. (Length 642 km/405 miles)

Port-au-Prince the main port and capital of Haiti. (Pop. 888,000)

Port Elizabeth a port and industrial city in Cape Province, South Africa. (Pop. 585,400)

Port Gentil the main port of Gabon in west-central Africa; founded in the late 19th century to export hardwoods, it is now a main centre of the country's oil industry. (Pop. 108,000)

Port Harcourt the second port of Nigeria after Lagos. (Pop. 288,900)

Port Jackson the great natural harbour also called Sydney Harbour, in southwest Australia.

Portland (1) a port on the Atlantic coast of the USA, in Maine. (Pop. city 61,800/metropolitan area 210,000). **(2)** a port on the Williamette River in Oregon, USA. (Pop. city 365,900/metropolitan area 1,340,900)

Port Louis the capital and main port of Mauritius, on the east coast of the island. (Pop. 160,000)

Port Moresby the capital and main port of Papua New Guinea, in the southeast. (Pop. 126,000)

Porto *see* **Oporto.**

Porto Alegre a port and regional capital of southern Brazil. (Pop. city 1,126,000)

Port of Spain the capital and chief port of Trinidad and Tobago. (Pop. city 62,700/metropolitan area 443,000)

Porto Novo the administrative capital of Benin. (Pop. 209,000)

Port Said the port at the MEDITERRANEAN end of the SUEZ CANAL, EGYPT. (Pop. 342,000)

Portsmouth a port and major naval base in southern ENGLAND. (Pop. 192,000)

Port Stanley the capital of the FALKLAND ISLANDS. (Pop. 1000)

Port Sudan the largest port of SUDAN, developed early in the 20th century on the RED SEA coast, some 640 km (400 miles) northeast of KHARTOUM. (Pop. 205,000)

Portugal, in the southwest corner of EUROPE, makes up about 15% of the Iberian peninsula. The most mountainous areas of Portugal lie to the north of the river TAGUS. In the northeast are the steep sided mountains of Tras-os-Montes and south of this is the DOURO valley, which runs from the Spanish border to OPORTO, on the ATLANTIC coast. South of the Tagus river is the Alentajo, with its wheat fields and cork plantations, and this continues to the hinterland of the ALGARVE with its beautiful groves of almond, fig and olive trees. Agriculture employs one-quarter of the labour force, and crops include wheat, maize, grapes and tomatoes. Manufacturing industry includes textiles and clothing for export, and footwear, food processing and cork products. Tourism, particularly in the south, is the main foreign currency earner.

Area : 92,389 sq km (35,671 sq miles)

Population : 10,300,000

Capital : Lisbon (Lisboa)

Other major cities : Braga, Coimbra, Oporto, Setúbal

Form of government : Republic

Religion : RC

Currency : Escudo

Port-Vila the capital and chief port of VANUATU. (Pop. 17,500)

Posen *see* **Poznan.**

Potenza the main market and administrative town of the impoverished BASILICATA region of the south of ITALY; it has several new state-aided industries. (Pop. 62,500)

Potosí an old colonial town founded by the Spaniards in 1546; it lies at an altitude of 3978 m (13,050 ft) in the south of BOLIVIA. Its rich heritage was based on its silver mines, which although long exhausted have been replaced by other mineral extraction. (Pop. 103,200)

Potsdam a city just 25 km (16 miles) southwest of BERLIN, GERMANY. (Pop. 137,700)

Powys a county in mid-WALES created in 1974 out of Breconshire, Montgomeryshire, and Radnorshire. The administrative centre is Llandrindod Wells. (5077 sq km/ 1960 sq miles; pop. 111,000)

Poznan (Posen) a historic city in central western POLAND. (Pop. 571,000)

Prague (Praha) the capital and principal city of the CZECH REPUBLIC, situated on the Vltava River. (Pop. 1,235,000)

Praia the capital of CAPE VERDE. (Pop. 4055)

Prairies *see* **Great Plains.**

Prato an industrial city about 16 km (10 miles) northwest of FLORENCE in north-central ITALY. (pop. 161,700)

Pressburg *see* **Bratislava.**

Preston an industrial centre and country town of LANCASHIRE, lying at the head of the Ribble estuary in northwest ENGLAND. (Pop. 87,000)

Pretoria the administrative capital of SOUTH AFRICA, 48 km (30 miles) north of JOHANNESBURG in the TRANSVAAL. (Pop. 739,000)

Prince Edward Island the smallest of the provinces of CANADA, an island in the Gulf of ST LAWRENCE. The provincial capital is Charlottetown. (5660 sq km/2185 sq miles; pop. 123,000)

Prince George the main commercial and industrial town of central BRITISH COLUMBIA, western CANADA, lying at an important junction of routes in the ROCKY MOUNTAINS. (Pop. 67,600)

Prince Rupert an important port on the northern part of BRITISH COLUMBIA's coast, and PACIFIC terminus of the

Canadian National Railway.

Principe *see* **São Tomé and Principe.**

Pripet Marshes (Pripyat Marshes; Poles'ye) the biggest swamp and peat bog in Europe, lying in southern BELARUS and northern UKRAINE, along the Priper river. It is densely forested and almost uninhabited.

Pristina the capital of the autonomous province of KOSOVO in SERBIA. (Pop. 216,000)

Prokop'yevsk the chief coal-mining centre of the KUZNETSK BASIN in south-central SIBERIA of the RUSSIAN FEDERATION. (Pop. 274,000)

Provence a historical MEDITERRANEAN region of southeast FRANCE, lying between the RHÔNE river and the Italian border.

Providence a port, and the state capital of RHODE ISLAND, USA. (Pop. city 154,100/metropolitan area 1,095,000)

Province-Alpes-Côtes d'Azur the most southeasterly of the 21 regions of FRANCE, administered from its main city, MARSEILLE. (31,4000 sq km/12,125 sq miles; pop. 3,860,100)

Prussia a historical state of GERMANY, centring on its capital, BERLIN.

Puebla a major city 120 km (75 miles) southeast of MEXICO CITY, and the capital of a state of the same name. (Pop. city 835,000)

Pueblo a steel-making city in southeastern COLORADO, USA. (Pop. 124,900)

Puerto Cortés the largest port in HONDURAS, situated in the extreme northwest corner of the country; its main export is bananas. (Pop. 62,500)

Puerto Rico is the most easterly of the Greater ANTILLES and lies in the CARIBBEAN between the DOMINICAN REPUBLIC and the US VIRGIN ISLANDS. It is a self-governing commonwealth in association with the USA and includes the main island, Puerto Rico, the two small islands of Vieques and Culebra and a fringe of smaller uninhabited islands. The climate is tropical, modified slightly by cooling sea breezes. The main mountains on Puerto Rico are the Cordillera Central, which reach 1338 m (4390 ft) at the peak of Cerro de Punta. Dairy farming is the most important agricultural activity but the whole agricultural sector has been overtaken by industry in recent years. Tax relief and cheap labour encourages American businesses to be based in Puerto Rico. Products include textiles, clothing, electrical and electronic goods, plastics and chemicals. Tourism is another developing industry.

Area : 8897 sq km (3435 sq miles)

Population : 3,196,520

Capital : San Juan

Form of government : Self-governing Commonwealth (USA)

Relgion : RC, Protestantism

Currency : US dollar

Puglia (Apulia) a region of southeast ITALY. The regional capital is BARI. (19,250 sq km/7500 sq miles; pop. 3,848,000)

Pune *see* **Poona.**

Punjab (1) a state in northwestern INDIA. The capital is CHANDIGARH. (50,362 sq km/19,440 sq miles; pop. 16,789,000) **(2)** a fertile province in the north of PAKISTAN. The capital is LAHORE.(205,344 sq km/79,283 sq miles; pop. 47,292,000)

Punta Arenas the world's southernmost city and a major port on the north shore of the Strait of MAGELLAN in southern CHILE. (Pop. 70,000)

Pusan a major port, and the second largest city in SOUTH KOREA after SEOUL. (Pop. 3,160,000)

Putumayo, River a river of northwest South AMERICA, rising in the ANDES and flowing southeast to join the AMAZON. (Length 1900 km/1180 miles)

Pyongyang (Pyeongyang) an industrial city and the capital of North KOREA. (Pop. 1,700,000)

Pyrénées a range of mountains that runs from the Bay of BISCAY to the MEDITERRANEAN, along the border between FRANCE and SPAIN. The highest point is Pico d'Aneto (3404 m/11,170 ft).

Q

Qaanaaq *see* **Thule**.

Qacentina *see* **Constantine**.

Qatar is a little emirate which lies halfway along the coast of The GULF. It consists of a low barren peninsula and a few small islands. The climate is hot and uncomfortably humid in summer and the winters are mild with rain in the north. Most fresh water comes from natural springs and wells or from desalination plants. The herding of sheep, goats and some cattle is carried out and the country is famous for its high quality camels. The discovery and exploitation of oil has resulted in a high standard of living for the people of Qatar. The Dukhan oil field has an expected life of forty years and the reserves of natural gas are enormous. In order to diversify the economy, new industries such as iron and steel, cement, fertilizers, and petrochemical plants have been developed.

Area : 11,000 sq km (4247 sq miles)

Population : 371,863

Capital : Doha (Ad Dawhah)

Form of government : Monarchy

Religion : Wahhabi Sunni Islam

Currency : Qatari riyal

Qattara Depression a huge sunken area of the WESTERN DESERT of EGYPT, consisting of soft sand, salt marshes and brackish ponds, impassable to vehicles. (18,000 sq km/ 7000 sq miles; lowest point. 13...m/4...ft) below sea level).

Qazvin (Kasvin) a historic town in northwest IRAN. (Pop. 244,300)

Qena (Qinà) a market town on the east bank of the NILE, about 50 km (30 miles) north of LUXOR. (pop. 93,700)

Qeqertarsuaq *see* **Disko**.

Qilian Shan a mountian range rising from the extreme northeast of the Tibetan Plateau, with peaks exceeding 4000 m (13,000 ft) and its highest reaching 6346 m (20,819)

Qingdao a city in Shangdong province in northeastern China. (Pop. 1,300,000)

Qinghai a province of northwestern China. The capital is Xining. (720,000 sq km/280,000 sq miles; pop. 3,720,000)

Qinhai Hu a large salt lake lying 3000 m (10,000 ft) above sea level in Qinhai province of central China. (5957 sq km/2300 sq miles)

Qiqihar a manufacturing city in Heilongjiang province, China. (Pop. 1,000,000)

Qom (Qum) a holy city in central northern Iran. (Pop. 424,100)

Quebec the largest province of Canada, in the east of the country, and also the name of the capital of the province. The majority of the population are French-speaking. (1,358,000 sq km/524,300 sq miles; pop. province 6,438,000/city 164,580)

Queen Charlotte Islands a group of some 150 islands lying 160 km (100 miles) off the west coast of Canada. (9790 sq km/3780 sq miles; pop. 5620)

Queen Charlotte Strait a waterway, some 26 km (16 miles) wide, between the northeastern coast of Vancouver Island and the mainland of Canada.

Queensland the northeastern state of Australia. The state capital is Brisbane. (1,272,200 sq km/591,200 sq miles; pop. 2,488,000)

Quelimane a port on the central part of the Mozambique coast, notorious for the slave trade in the 18th and 19th centuries; it has one of the world's largest coconut plantations, and exports copra, sisal and many other subtropical products. (Pop. 71,800)

Quemoy *see* **Chin-men Tao**.

Quercy a former province of southwestern France, around Cahors.

Quetta the capital of the province of BALUCHISTAN, PAKISTAN. (Pop. 285,000)

Quetzaltenango the second city of GUATEMALA, a university and industrial town lying 2335 m (7660 ft) above sea level on the fertile slopes of a volcano. The city's name means "Place of the Quetzal," after the rare jungle bird worshipped by the Maya Indians. (Pop. 96,100)

Quezon City a major city and university town, now a part of Metro MANILA, and the administrative capital of the PHILIPPINES from 1948 to 1976. (Pop. 1,165,000)

Quimper a sardine-fishing port, tourist centre, and capital of FINISTÈRE départment at the end of the BRITTANY peninsula of northwestern FRANCE. (Pop. 60,200)

Quito the capital of ECUADOR, lying just south of the Equator, 2850 m (9350 ft) high in the ANDES. (Pop. 1,110,000)

Qum *see* **Qom.**

Qwaqwa a non-independent black homeland in SOUTH AFRICA occupied by South Sotho people, bordering LESOTHO. (Pop. 305,000)

R

Rabat the capital of MOROCCO, in the northwest, on the ATLANTIC coast. (Pop. 520,000)

Radnorshire *see* **Powys.**

Radom a historic manufacturing town at an important crossroads of routes in south-central POLAND. (Pop. 201,100)

Ragusa *see* **Dubrovnik.**

Rainier, Mount *see* **Cascade Range.**

Rajasthan a state of northwest INDIA. The state capital is JIAPUR. (342,239 sq km/132,104 sq miles; pop. 34,261,000)

Rajshahi a university town and silk-industry centre, lying on the GANGES River in western BANGLADESH. (Pop. 254,000)

Raleigh the state capital of NORTH CAROLINA, USA. (Pop. city 169,300/metropolitan area 609,300)

Rancagua the capital of the Libertador region of central CHILE. It was the scene in 1814 of an important battle between the Spaniards and troops led by the country's liberator, Bernardo O'Higgins (1778-1842). (Pop. 143,000)

Ranchi an industrial town in the state of BIHAR, INDIA. (Pop. 502,800)

Rand, The *see* **Witwatersrand.**

Rangoon (Yangon) the capital of BURMA, and an important port on the mouth of the Rangoon River. (Pop. 2,549,000)

Rarotonga the largest of the COOK ISLANDS, with the capital of the islands, Avarua, on its north coast. (67 sq km/26 sq miles; pop. 9500)

Ras al Khaymah one of the UNITED ARAB EMIRATES, in the extreme northeast, on the MUSANDAM peninsula. (1036 sq km/400 sq miles; pop. 83,000)

Ravenna a city in northeastern ITALY, noted for its Byzantine churches. (Pop. 136,500)

Rawalpindi a military town of ancient origins in northern PAKISTAN. (Pop. 928,000)

Reading a university, industrial and county town of BERKSHIRE, lying on the River THAMES in southern ENGLAND, 60 km (37 miles) west of LONDON. (Pop. 139,000)

Recife a city and regional capital on the eastern tip of Brazil. (Pop. 1,205,000)

Red Basin *see* **Sichuan Pendi.**

Red River (1) a river of the southern USA, rising in TEXAS and flowing east to join the MISSISSIPPI. (Length 1639km/ 1018miles). **(2) (Song Hong; Yuan Jiang)** a river that rises in southwest CHINA and flows southeast across the north of VIETNAM to the Gulf of TONGKING. (Length 800 km/ 500 miles)

Red Sea a long, narrow sea lying between the Arabian Peninsula and the coast of northeast AFRICA. In the north it is connected to the MEDITERRANEAN SEA by the SUEZ CANAL.

Regensburg a historic university town, tourist centre and port on the DANUBE River, in BAVARIA, GERMANY. (Pop. 129,000)

Reggio di Calabria a port on the toe of southern ITALY. (Pop. 177,700)

Reggio nell'Emilia a town of Roman origins in northeastern ITALY. (Pop. 130,300)

Regina the capital of the province of SASKATCHEWAN, CANADA. (Pop. 164,000)

Reims *see* **Rheims.**

Renfrewshire *see* **Strathclyde.**

Rennes a industrial city in northeastern France. (Pop. 241,300)

Reno a gambling centre in NEVADA, USA. (Pop. city 105,600/ metropolitan area 211,500)

Réunion an island to the east of MADAGASCAR, an overseas department of France. The capital is SAINT-DENIS. (2515 sq km/970 sq miles; pop. 530,000)

Reykjavik the capital and main port of ICELAND, on the southwest coast. (Pop. 87,300)

Reynosa a town in northeastern MEXICO, on the border with the USA. (Pop. 347,000)

Rheims (Reims) a historic city in FRANCE, and the centre of the production of champagne. (Pop. 204,000)

Rheinland-Pfalz *see* **Rhineland-Palatinate**.

Rhine (Rhein, Rhin, Rijn), River one of the most important rivers of EUROPE. It rises in the Swiss ALPS, flows north through GERMANY and then west through the NETHERLANDS to the NORTH SEA. (Length 1320km/825miles)

Rhineland-Palatinate (Rhineland-Pfalz) the *Land* (state) of GERMANY that stretches along the west bank of the RHINE River, south of BONN. It was ruled by the Counts Palantinate of the Holy Roman Empire from the 10th to the 19th centuries. (19,832 sq km/7657 sq miles; pop. 3,641.000)

Rhode Island the smallest state in the USA. The state capital is PROVIDENCE. (3144 sq km/1214 sq miles; pop. 968,000)

Rhodes (Rodhos) the largest of the DODECANESE group of islands belonging to GREECE. (1399 sq km/540 sq miles; pop. 88,500)

Rhodesia *see* **Zimbabwe**.

Rhodope Mountains (Rodopi Planina) a forested mountain range occupying the southwestern corner of BULGARIA and forming a natural barrier up against the borders with GREECE and MACEDONIA.

Rhondda a valley town in MID-GLAMORGAN, South WALES, developed in the 19th century as a major coal-mining centre. (Pop. 81,725)

Rhône-Alpes a large region in eastern FRANCE, which is mainly mountainous and is centred on the middle section of the RHÔNE-SAONE river-valley system. It rises to the edge of the MASSIF CENTRAL in the east and through foothills to the ALPS in the west. (43,698 sq km/16,872 miles; pop. 5,016,000)

Rhône, River a major river of EUROPE, rising in the Swiss ALPS and flowing west into FRANCE, and then south to its delta on the Golfe de LION. (Length 812 km/505 miles)

Rhum *see* **Rum**.

Richmond the state capital of VIRGINIA. (Pop. city 219,100/ metropolitan area 796,100)

Ridings, The *see* **Yorkshire.**

Riga a BALTIC port, and the capital of LATVIA. (Pop. 875,000)

Rijeka (Fiume) a port on the ADRIATIC, in CROATIA. (Pop. 193,000)

Rijn, River *see* **Rhine, River.**

Rimini a popular resort on the ADRIATIC SEA, northeastern ITALY. (Pop. 129,500)

Rio Bravo *see* **Rio Grande.**

Rio de Janeiro a major port and former capital (1763–1960) of BRAZIL, situated in the southeast of the country. (Pop. 5,094,000)

Rio Grande (Rio Bravo) a river of North AMERICA, rising in the state of COLORADO, USA, and flowing southeast to the Gulf of MEXICO. For much of its length it forms the border between the USA and MEXICO. (Length 3078 km/ 1885 miles)

Rioja, La an autonomous region south of the BASQUE COUNTRY of SPAIN, famous for its fine wine. (Pop. 254,000)

Río Muni the mainland part of EQUATORIAL GUINEA, formerly known as Mbini. (26,017 sq km/10,043 sq miles; pop. 241,000)

Riviera the MEDITERRANEAN coastal region between CANNES in FRANCE and LA SPEZIA, in ITALY, containing some of EUROPE's most popular resorts.

Riyadh (Ar Riyad) the capital and commercial centre of SAUDI ARABIA, founded on an oasis. (Pop. 300,000)

Road Town the capital of the British VIRGIN ISLANDS. (Pop. 3000)

Roca, Cabo da a cape sticking out into the ATLANTIC in

central PORTUGAL, to the west of LISBON, the western-most point of mainland EUROPE.

Rochdale an industrial town 16km (10 miles) north of MANCHESTER in northwest ENGLAND. It was formerly a major centre of the LANCASHIRE cotton industry and was the birthplace of the Cooperative Movement in 1844. (Pop. 93,000)

Rochester(1) a city in northern NEW YORK STATE, lying just south of Lake ONTARIO at the heart of AMERICA's fruit and market-garden belt. (Pop. city 242,600/metropolitan area 989,000) **(2)**see **Medway Towns**.

Rockall a tiny, rocky, uninhabited island lying 400 km (250 miles) west of IRELAND, and claimed by the UK.

Rockhampton a city in the centre of a coastal agricultural and coal-mining region of QUEENSLAND, AUSTRALIA, lying on the Tropic of Capricorn. It is known as the country's beef capital, having two of its largest meat-processing plants. (Pop. 50,100)

Rocky Mountains (Rockies) a huge mountain range in western North AMERICA, extending some 4800 km (3000 miles) from BRITISH COLUMBIA in CANADA to NEW MEXICO in the USA.

Rodhos see **Rhodes**.

Rodopi Planina see **Rhodope Mountains**.

Romania apart from a small extension towardss the BLACK SEA, Romania is almost a circular country. It is located in southeast EUROPE and bordered by UKRAINE, HUNGARY, SERBIA and BULGARIA. The CARPATHIAN MOUNTAINS run through the north, east and centre of Romania and these are enclosed by a ring of rich agricultural plains which are flat in the south and west but hilly in the east. The core of Romania is Transylvania within the Carpathian arc. Romania has cold snowy winters and hot summers. Agriculture in Romania has been neglected in favor of industry but major crops include maize, sugar beet, wheat, potatoes and grapes for wine. There are now severe food shortages. Industry is state owned and includes mining, metallurgy, mechanical engineering and chemicals. Forests support timber and furniture making industries in the Carpathians.

Area : 237,500 sq km (91,699 sq miles)

Population : 23,000,000

Capital : Bucharest (Bucuresti)

Other major cities : Brasov, Constanta, Timisoara

Form of government : Republic

Religions : Romanian Orthodox, RC

Currency : Leu

Rome (Roma) the historic capital of ITALY, on the River TIBER, in the centre of the country near the west coast. (Pop. 2,831,300)

Rosario an industrial and commercial city on the River PARANA in ARGENTINA. (Pop. 935,500)

Roscommon a county in the northwest of the Republic of IRELAND, with a county town of the same name. (2462 sq km/950 sq miles; pop. county 54,500)

Roseau the capital of DOMINICA. (Pop. 17,000)

Roskilde a university town, west of COPENHAGEN on the island of ZEALAND, that has remained one of DENMARK's principal cultural centres since its foundation in the 10th century; it has been the burial place of the Danish monarchy for over 600 years. (Pop. 48,300)

Ross and Cromarty a former county of northwest SCOTLAND which includes many islands; part of the HIGHLAND region.

Ross Ice Shelf the largest body of floating ice in the world, lying at the head of ROSS SEA on the PACIFIC side of ANTARCTICA. It is estimated to be as big as FRANCE in area, and it varies in thickness between 400 and 750 m (1300-2460 ft). It moves seawards at about 1000 m (3280 ft) a year, breaking up at its outer edge to produce huge icebergs and leaving cliffs on the shelf up to 70 m (230 ft) high.

Ross Sea a large branch of the ANTARCTIC OCEAN, south of NEW ZEALAND.

Rostock a major port on the BALTIC coast of GERMANY. (Pop. 242,000)

Rostov-na-Donau (Rostov-on-Don) A major industrial city on the River DON, near the northwestern extremity of the Sea of AZOV in southeastern RUSSIAN FEDERATION. (Pop. 983,000)

Rotherham an industrial city on the River Don in north-central ENGLAND, just north of SHEFFIELD in SOUTH YORKSHIRE. (Pop. 82,000)

Rotterdam the largest city in the NETHERLANDS and the busiest port in the world. (Pop. city 558,800/ Greater Rotterdam 1,024,700)

Roubaix *see* **Lille-Roubaix-Tourcoing.**

Rouen a port on the River SEINE in northern FRANCE. (Pop. 385,800)

Rousillon *see* **Languedoc-Rousillon.**

Rovaiemi a city in northern FINLAND, often called "the capital of LAPPLAND"; it is a commercial and tourist centre lying some 160 km (100 miles) north of the port of OULU on the Gulf of BOTHNIA.(Pop. 30,300)

Roxburghshire *see* **Borders.**

R.S.F.S.R. *see* **Russian Soviet Federated Socialist Republic.**

Ruapehu an active volcano that is the highest point of NORTH ISLAND, NEW ZEALAND, rising to 1797 m (9176 ft), about 230 km (140 miles) northeast of WELLINGTON.

Rub al-Khali the so-called "Empty Quarter," a vast area of sandy desert straddling the borders of SAUDI ARABIA, OMAN and YEMEN. (650,000 sq km/251,000 sq miles)

Rubicon a stream in northern ITALY, which in the time of Julius Caesar formed the boundary between the Roman provinces of Italia and Cisalpine Gaul. In 49BC, Caesar, by "crossing the Rubicon" and marching on Rome, committed himself irrevocably to a civil war, hence the meaning of the expression.

Ruhr, River the river in northwestern GERMANY whose valley forms the industrial heartland of western Germany. It joins the RHINE at DUISBURG. (Length 235 km/146 miles)

Rum (Rhum) the largest and most mountainous of the Small Isles group of the Inner HEBRIDES, off the west coast of SCOTLAND. It is worked as an important conservancy, providing opportunities for ecological and environmental research. (109 sq km.42 sq miles; pop. 17)

Runnymede a meadow on the south bank of the River THAMES, just west of GREATER LONDON, where in 1215 King John of ENGLAND set his seal on the Magna Carta, the charter that set out the rights to justice of the barons, the church and freemen.

Rushmore, Mount a mountain in the Black Hills of SOUTH DAKOTA, USA, noted for the huge heads of four US presidents (Washington, Jefferson, Lincoln, Theodore Roosevelt) which were carved into its flank 1927-41. (170 m/5600 ft)

Russia the old name for the Russian Empire, latterly used loosely to refer to the former USSR or the RUSSIAN FEDERATION.

Russian Federation, The, which is the largest country in the world, extends from Eastern EUROPE through the URAL Mountains east to the PACIFIC OCEAN. The CAUCASUS Range forms its boundary with GEORGIA and AZERBAIJAN, and it is here that the highest peak in Europe, Mt ELBRUS, is located. In the east, SIBERIA is drained towards the ARCTIC OCEAN by the great rivers Ob', Yenisey, LENA and their tributaries. Just to the south of the Central Siberian Plateau lies Lake BAIKAL, the world's deepest freshwater lake. The environment ranges from vast frozen wastes in the north to subtropical deserts in the south. Agriculture is organized into either state or collective farms, which mainly produce sugar beet, cotton, potatoes and vegetables. The country has extensive reserves of coal, oil, gas, iron ore and manganese. Major industries include iron and steel, cement, transport equipment, engineering, armaments, electronic equipment and chemicals. The Russian Federation declared itself independent in 1991.

Area : 17,075,400 sq km (6,592,800 sq miles)

Population : 142,117,000

Capital : Moscow (Moskva)

Other major cities : St Petersburg (formerly Leningrad), Nizhniy Novgorod, Novosibirsk

Form of government : Republic

Religions : Russian Orthodox, Sunni Islam, Shia Islam, RC

Currency : Rouble

Russian Soviet Federated Socialist Republic (R.S.F.S.R.) The former name for the RUSSIAN FEDERATION.

Rutanzige, Lake *see* **Edward, Lake.**

Rutland once the smallest county of ENGLAND, now a part of LEICESTERSHIRE.

Ruwenzori a mountain range on the border between ZAÏRE and UGANDA, also known as the Mountains of the Moon. The highest peak is Mount Ngaliema (Mount Stanley) (5109 m/16,763 ft).

Rwanda is a small republic in the heart of central AFRICA which lies just 2° south of the Equator. It is a mountainous country with a central spine of highlands from which streams flow west to the ZAÏRE river and east to the NILE. Active volcanoes are found in the north where the land rises to about 4500 m (14,765 ft). The climate is highland tropical with temperatures decreasing with altitude. The soils are not fertile and subsistence agriculture dominates the economy. Staple food crops are sweet potatoes, cassava, dry beans, sorghum and potatoes. The main cash crops are coffee, tea and pyrethrum. There are major reserves of natural gas under Lake Kivu in the west, but these are largely unexploited.

Area : 26,338 sq km (10,169 sq miles)

Population : 6,710,000

Capital : Kigali

Form of government : Republic
Religions : RC, Animism
Currency : Rwanda franc

Ryazan an industrial city 175 km (110 miles) southeast of Moscow, RUSSIAN FEDERATION. (Pop. 488,000)

Ryukyu Islands (Nansei-shoto) a chain of islands belonging to JAPAN stretching 1200 km (750 miles) between Japan and TAIWAN. (Pop. 1,366,600)

Rzeszow a modern industrial city situated in the southeast of POLAND; it was developed as part of a postwar rehabilitation programme, and since 1945 its population has quadrupled. (Pop. 134,500)

S

Saarbrücken an industrial city of western GERMANY, near the border with France. (Pop. 189,000)

Saarland one of the smaller *Länder* (states) of GERMANY, situated in the southwest, on the border with the French region of LORRAINE. Since the 17th century, it has been fought over by France and Germany, until its nationality was resolved by plebiscite in the 1950s. It is a hilly, forested region of coalfields, heavy industry and vineyards. The capital is SAARBRÜCKEN (2567 sq km/991 sq miles; pop. 1,064,400)

Sabah the more easterly of the two states of MALAYSIA on northern coast of the island of BORNEO. (73,700 sq km/ 28,450 sq miles; pop. 1,034,000)

Sachsen *see* **Saxony**.

Sachsen-Anhalt *see* **Saxony-Anhalt**.

Sacramento the state capital of CALIFORNIA. (Pop. city 304,100/metropolitan area 1,219,600)

Sacramento, River the longest river in CALIFORNIA, USA. (Length: 560 km/350 miles)

Safi a major seaport on the ATLANTIC coast of MOROCCO. It exports phosphates and the world's biggest supply of sardines. (Pop. 198,000)

Sahara Desert the world's largest desert, spanning much of northern AFRICA, from the ATLANTIC to the RED SEA, and from the MEDITERRANEAN to MALI, NIGER, CHAD and SUDAN.

Sahel a semi-arid belt crossing AFRICA from SENEGAL to SUDAN, separating the SAHARA from tropical Africa to the south.

Saidi an important communications and administrative centre in the ATLAS MOUNTAINS of ALGERIA. (Pop. 60,000)

Saigon *see* **Ho Chi Minh City.**

Saimaa the largest lake in FINLAND, lying in the southeastern part of the country, close to the border with the RUSSIAN FEDERATION. Its shoreline extends for about 15,000 km (9320 miles). It is connected to the Gulf of Finland by a 43-km (27-mile) long canal completed in 1856.

Saint-Denis the capital of RÉUNION island. (Pop. 110,000)

Saint John a port at the mouth of the SAINT JOHN RIVER, on the ATLANTIC coast of NEW BRUNSWICK, CANADA. (Pop. 114,000)

Saint John River a river of the eastern USA, which rises in MAINE and flows northwest through CANADA to the Bay of FUNDY. (Length 673 km/418 miles)

Saipan the largest and most heavily populated of the NORTHERN MARIANAS. The island group's capital, SUSUPE, is on the western side. (122 sq km/47 sq miles; pop. 17,000)

Sakai a historic port and industrial city on south HONSHU Island, JAPAN; it was an independent city state between the 14th and 17th centuries. (Pop. 818,400)

Sakhalin a large island to the north of JAPAN, but belonging to the RUSSIAN FEDERATION. (76,400 sq km/29,500 sq miles; pop. 660,000)

Salamanca an elegant university town in western SPAIN, and the name of the surrounding province. (Pop. town 167,100)

Salamís (1) the ruins of an ancient Greek city on the east coast of CYPRUS; the scene of a naval victory for the Greeks over the Egyptians in 306BC. **(2)** a small island in the Saronic Gulf, just west of PIRAEUS, off which, in 480BC, the Athenians destroyed the Persian fleet; it is now a major Greek naval base. (Pop. 28,600)

Salem (1) a city in MASSACHUSETTS, USA. (Pop. city 38,600/metropolitan area 259,100) **(2)** the state capital of OREGON, USA. (Pop. city 90,300/metropolitan area 255,200)

Salerno a historic seaport in southern ITALY, some 45 km (28 miles) southeast of NAPLES. (Pop. 155,900)

Saloniki (Thessaloníki) the second largest city in GREECE after ATHENS. (Pop. 706,200)

Salta an old colonial city founded in 1582, lying in the far northwest of ARGENTINA at an altitude of 1190 m (3900 ft) in the eastern foothills of the ANDES. It is a mining area and a tourist centre for the many Inca and other pre-Columbian archaelogical sites nearby. (Pop. 260,300)

Salt Desert (Dasht-e Kavir) *see* **Iranian Plateau**.

Salt Lake City the state capital of UTAH. (Pop. city 164,800/metropolitan area 1,025,300)

Salto the second largest city and an important river port of URUGUAY, situated in the northwest of the country, on the border with ARGENTINA. (Pop. 80,000)

Salvador a port on the central east coast of BRAZIL and capital of the state of Bahia, which was also the original name of the town. (Pop. 1,507,000)

Salvador, El *see* **El Salvador.**

Salween, River a river rising in TIBET and flowing south through BURMA, forming part of the border with THAILAND, to the ANDAMAN SEA. (Length 2900 km/1800 miles)

Salzburg a city in central northern AUSTRIA, and the name of the surrounding state, of which it is the capital. (Pop. city 140,000)

Samar the third largest island of the PHILIPPINES. (13,080 sq km/5050 sq miles; pop. 1,100,000)

Samara a major industrial city and port on the River Volga in the RUSSIAN FEDERATION. Founded in 1586, it was renamed Kuybyshev, in 1935, after the Revolutionary leader Valerian Kuybyshev. Its name reverted in 1991. (Pop. 1,251,000)

Samaria the central region of ancient PALESTINE, situated between the MEDITERRANEAN and the JORDAN River, and lying south of GALILEE and north of JUDAEA.

Samarkand an ancient city in UZBEKISTAN. (Pop. 515,000)

Samarra a holy city of the Shiite Muslims lying on the TIGRIS river, in central IRAQ, about 100 km (60 miles) northwest of BAGHDAD. (Pop. 62,000)

Samoa, American an American territory, comprising a group of five islands, in the central South Pacific. The capital is Pago Pago. (197 sq km/76 sq miles; pop. 36,000)

Sámos a Greek island 2 km (1 mile) off the coast of Turkey. It was the birthplace of Pythagoras (*c.* 582–507BC) (Pop. 31,600)

Samsun a port on the Black Sea coast of Turkey, and the name of the surrounding province, of which it is the capital. (Pop. town 280,100)

San'a the capital of Yemen, situated in the middle of the country. (Pop. 210,000)

San Andreas Fault a major crack in the earth's crust that extends in a network of faults for nearly 1000 km (over 600 miles) from northwest California to the Gulf of California. It marks the boundary of the Pacific and North American crustal plates, and their relative movement in opposite directions of about 10mm ($^3/_8$ in) a year makes this area prone to earthquakes.

San Antonio an industrial centre in southern Texas, USA. (Pop. city 842,800/metropolitan area 1,188,500)

San Diego a major port and industrial city in southern California, USA. (Pop. city 960,500/metropolitan area 1,063,900)

San Francisco a Pacific port and commercial centre in California. (Pop. city 712,800/metropolitan area 5,684,600)

San Francisco Bay an inlet of the Pacific Ocean in western California, USA, joined to the ocean by the Golden Gate Strait.

San Jose a city in California, USA, and the focus of "Silicon Valley." (Pop. city 686,200/metropolitan area 1,371,500)

San José the capital of Costa Rica, in the centre of the country. (Pop. 249,000).

San Juan the capital of Puerto Rico, and a major port. (Pop. 435,000)

Sankt Gallen *see* **St Gallen**.

San Sebastián

Sankt Peterburg *see* **St Petersburg.**
San Lorenzo del Escorial *see* **Escorial, El.**

San Luis Potosi an elegant colonial city and provincial capital in north-central MEXICO. (Pop. city 407,000)

San Marino is a tiny landlocked state in central ITALY, lying in the eastern foothills of the APENNINES. It has wooded mountains and pasture land clustered around the limestone peaks of Monte Titano which rises to 739 m (2425 ft). San Marino has a mild MEDITERRANEAN climate. The majority of the population work on the land or in forestry. Wheat, barley, maize and vines are grown, and the main exports are wood machinery, chemicals, wine, textiles, tiles, varnishes and ceramics. Some 3.5 million tourists visit the country each year, and much of the country's revenue comes from the sale of stamps, postcards, souvenirs and duty-free liquor. Italian currency is in general use but San Marino issues its own coins.

Area : 61 sq km (24 sq miles)

Population : 22,746

Capital : San Marino

Form of government : Republic

Religion : RC

Currency : Lira

San Miguel de Tucumán a regional capital in north-western ARGENTINA. (Pop. 497,000)

San Pedro Sula the second largest city in GUATEMALA. (Pop. 398,000)

San Remo an old medieval port, a fashionable resort and a major flower-market town on the Italian RIVIERA. (Pop. 62,100)

San Salvador (1) the capital and major city of EL SALVADOR. (Pop. 884,100) **(2)** a small island in the centre of the BAHAMAS, the first place in the New World reached by Columbus (1492). (Pop. 850)

San Sebastián a port and industrial city in northeastern SPAIN. (Pop. 175,600)

Santa Barbara a resort and industrial centre in southern CALIFORNIA, USA (Pop. city 76,900/metropolitan area 322,800)

Santa Fe the state capital of NEW MEXICO, USA. (Pop. city 52,300/metropolitan area 100,500)

Santander a port and industrial city in northeastern SPAIN. (Pop. 180,300)

Santiago the capital and principal city of CHILE. (Pop. 4,132,000)

Santiago de Compostela a university city and centre of pilgrimage in northwestern SPAIN. (Pop. 93,700)

Santiago de Cuba a port and provincial capital in southern CUBA. (Pop. 345,000)

Santo Domingo the capital and main port of the DOMINICAN REPUBLIC. (Pop. 1,313,000)

Santorini a volcanic island in the CYCLADES group of islands, GREECE. (84 sq km/32 sq miles; pop. 7100)

Santos the largest port in BRAZIL, 60 km (38 miles) southeast of SÃO PAULO. (Pop. 417,000)

São Francisco, River a river of eastern BRAZIL, important for its hydroelectric dams. (Length 2900 km/1800 miles)

São Miguel the largest island in the AZORES. (770 sq km/ 298 sq miles; pop. 131,900)

Saône, River a river of eastern FRANCE which merges with the River RHÔNE at LYONS. (Length 480 km/300 miles)

São Paulo a major industrial city in southeastern BRAZIL, and capital of the state called São Paulo. (Pop. city 8,500,000/metropolitan area 16,000,000)

São Tomé and Príncipe volcanic islands which lie off the west coast of AFRICA. São Tomé is covered in extinct volcanic cones which reach 2024 m (6641 ft) at the highest peak. The coastal areas are hot and humid. Príncipe is a craggy island lying to the northeast of São Tomé. The climate is tropical with heavy rainfall from October to May. 70% of the workforce work on the land, mainly in state-owned cocoa plantations. Small manufacturing industries include food processing and timber products.

Area : 964 sq km (372 sq miles)

Population : 115,600

Capital : São Tomé

Form of government : Republic

Religion : RC

Currency : Dobra

São Tomé the capital of São Tomé and Principe. (Pop. 25,000)

São Vincente, Cabo de (Cape St Vincent) the south-western corner of PORTUGAL.

Sapporo a modern city, founded in the late 19th century as the capital of HOKKAIDO Island, JAPAN. (Pop. 1,543,000)

Saragossa *see* **Zaragoza.**

Sarajevo the capital of BOSNIA-HERZEGOVINA. (Pop. 448,500)

Saransk an industrial town, capital of the republic of Mordovia in the RUSSIAN FEDERATION. (Pop. 301,000)

Saratov an industrial city and river port on the VOLGA, RUSSIAN FEDERATION. (Pop. 894,000)

Sarawak a state of MALAYSIA occupying much of the northwestern coast of BORNEO. (125,204 sq km/48,342 sq miles; pop. 1,323,000)

Sardinia (Sardegna) the second largest island of the MEDITERRANEAN after SICILY, also belonging to ITALY, lying just south of CORSICA. The capital is CAGLIARI. (24,089 sq km/9301 sq miles; pop. 1,633,400)

Sargasso Sea an area of calm water in the ATLANTIC between the WEST INDIES and the AZORES, where seaweed floats on the surface. It is a major spawning ground for eels.

Sarh a trading and industrial town in the deep south of CHAD, lying on an important route used for the export of cattle to the CENTRAL AFRICAN REPUBLIC to the south. (Pop. 65,000)

Sark *see* **Channel Islands.**

Saskatchewan a province of western CANADA, in the

GREAT PLAINS. The capital is REGINA. (651,900 sq km/ 251,000 sq miles; pop. 968,000)

Saskatchewan, River a river of CANADA, rising in the ROCKY MOUNTAINS and flowing westwards into Lake WINNIPEG. (Length 1930 km/1200 miles)

Saskatoon a city on the SASKATCHEWAN RIVER. (Pop. 154,000)

Sassari the second city of SARDINIA, after the capital, CAGLIARI; it is an old university town situated in the northwest corner of the island. (Pop. 119,800)

Satu Mare a manufacturing town at the centre of a rich agricultural region in the northwest corner of ROMANIA. (Pop. 113,600)

Saudi Arabia occupies over 70% of the Arabian Peninsula. Over 95% of the country is desert and the largest expanse of sand in the world, "Rub'al-Khali," is found in the southeast of the country. In the west, a narrow, humid coastal plain along the RED SEA is backed by steep mountains. The climate is hot with very little rain and some areas have no precipitation for years. The government has spent a considerable amount on reclamation of the desert for agriculture, and the main products are dates, tomatoes, water melons and wheat. The country's prosperity, however, is based almost entirely on the exploitation of its vast reserves of oil and natural gas. Industries include petroleum refining, petrochemicals and fertilizers.

Area : 2,149,690 sq km (829,995 sq miles)

Population : 12,000,000

Capital : Riyadh (Ar Riyah)

Other major cities : Mecca, Jeddah, Medina, Ta'if

Form of government : Monarchy

Religions : Sunni Islam, Shia Islam

Currency : Rial

Sault Sainte Marie the twin towns that lie on opposite banks of the St Mary's River between Lakes SUPERIOR and HURON, one in ONTARIO, CANADA (pop. 80,905), the other in MICHIGAN, USA (pop. 14,689).

Savannah the main port of Georgia, USA. (Pop. city 145,400/metropolitan area 323,900)

Savoie (Savoy) a mountainous former duchy in southeast France, which has been a part of France since 1860 and is now divided into two departments, Savoie and Haute Savoie.

Saxony (Sachsen) a southeastern *Land* (state) of Germany, reinstated after reunification in 1990. Its principal cities are Dresden and Leipzig. (18,337 sq km/7080 sq miles; pop. 4,900,000)

Saxony-Anhalt (Sachsen-Anhalt) an east-central *Land* (state) of Germany, reinstated after reunification in 1990. It is centred on the axis between its two main towns—Magdeburg and Halle. (20,445 sq km/7894 sq miles; pop. 3,000,000)

Scafell Pike *see* **Lake District.**

Scandinavia the countries on, or near, the Scandinavian peninsula in northeast Europe, usually taken to include Norway, Sweden, Denmark and Finland.

Scania (Skåne) the snub-nosed southern peninsula and province of Sweden; it has the most prosperous agriculture and densest rural population in the country. It was part of Denmark until 1658. Malmö and Helsingborg are its main cities. (11,280 sq km/4355 sq miles; pop. 1,028,800)

Scapa Flow an anchorage surrounded by the Orkney Islands, famous as a wartime naval base.

Schelde, River a river of western Europe rising in France and then flowing through Belgium and the Netherlands to the North Sea. (Length 435 km/270 miles)

Schlesien *see* **Silesia.**

Schleswig-Holstein the northern-most state of Germany. The capital is Kiel. (Pop. 2,614,000)

Schwarzwald *see* **Black Forest.**

Scilly, Isles of a group of islands off the southwest tip of England. The main islands are St Mary's, St Martin's and Tresco. (Pop. 2000)

Scotland a country of the UK, occupying the northern

part of GREAT BRITAIN. The capital is EDINBURGH. (78,762 sq km/31,410 sq miles; pop. 5,035,000)

Seattle a port in WASHINGTON State, USA. (Pop. city 490,000/metropolitan area 1,677,000)

Sédhiou a market town at the head of a deep river inlet in southern SENEGAL; it trades in numerous tropical products. (Pop. 150,000)

Sedom (Sodom and Gomorrah) a town near the southern end of the DEAD SEA; it is the base for chemical and fertilizer industries using salt and minerals extracted from the sea. The biblical towns of Sodom and Gomorrah are believed to lie beneath the sea near this site.

Ségou a town on the NIGER River in south-central MALI and a stopping place on the route north to the SAHARA. It was the capital of the Bambara civilization from 1660 to 1861. (Pop. 65,000)

Seine, River a river of northern FRANCE, flowing through PARIS to the ENGLISH CHANNEL. (Length 775 km/482 miles)

Sekondi-Takoradi the main port of GHANA and capital of the Western Region. (Pop. 254,000)

Selkirkshire *see* **Borders.**

Selvas the vast equatorial forest region of the AMAZON river basin in South AMERICA, characterized by a dense canopy of tall broad-leaved evergreen trees, epiphytes, lianas, etc.

Semarang a port and textile city on the north coast of JAVA, INDONESIA. (Pop. 503,200)

Sendai a city in the east of HONSHU Island, JAPAN. (Pop. 700,200)

Senegal is a former French colony in West AFRICA which extends from the most western point in Africa, Cape Verde, to the border with MALI. Senegal is mostly lowlying and covered by savanna. The Futa Jalon mountains in the south rise to 1515 m (4971 ft). The climate is tropical with a dry season from October to June. The most densely populated region is in the southwest. Almost 80% of the labour force work in agriculture, growing groundnuts and cotton for export and millet, maize, rice and sorghum as subsistence crops. Senegal has been badly affected by the drought that has afflicted the SAHEL and relies on food imports and international aid.

Area : 196,722 sq km (75,954 sq miles)

Population : 7,170,000

Capital : Dakar

Other major cities : Kaolack, Thies, St Louis

Form of government : Republic

Religions : Sunni Islam, RC

Currency : Franc CFA

Senegal River a West African river that flows through GUINEA, MALI, MAURITANIA, and SENEGAL to the ATLANTIC OCEAN. (Length 1790 km/1110 miles)

Seoul (Soul) the capital of South KOREA, in the northwest of the country. (Pop. 8,364,000)

Sepik River a major river of PAPUA NEW GUINEA. (Length 1200 km/750 miles)

Seram (Ceram) an island in the MALUKU group, INDONESIA. (17,148 sq km/6621 sq miles)

Serbia (Srbija) a land-locked republic, and the largest republic of former YUGOSLAVIA. The capital is BELGRADE. (88,361 sq km/34,107 sq miles; pop. 9,314,000)

Serengeti an extensive, high plain in northern TANZANIA, stretching from the NGORONGORO CRATER northwards to the Kenyan border. It contains vast numbers of wild animals and one of AFRICA's most spectacular game reserves.

Sétif a market town at the centre of a rich farming area in the mountain valleys of northeast ALGERIA, lying on the main road and rail routes between ALGIERS and CONSTATINE. (Pop. 195,000)

Seto Naikai *see* **Inland Sea**.

Sevastopol' a BLACK SEA port of the UKRAINE. (Pop. 335,000)

Severn, River the longest river in the UK, flowing through WALES and the west of ENGLAND. (Length 350 km/220 miles)

Severnaya Zemlya (North Land) a group of ice-covered ARCTIC islands of the RUSSIAN FEDERATION lying off Cape CHELYUSKIN, the northernmost point of ASIA. (37,000 sq km/14,300 sq miles)

Seville (Sevilla) a historic, now industrial city in southern SPAIN, and also the name of the surrounding province. (Pop. city 653,800)

Seychelles are a group of volcanic islands which lie in the western INDIAN OCEAN about 1200 km (746 miles) from the coast of East AFRICA. About forty of the islands are mountainous and consist of granite while just over fifty are coral islands. The climate is tropical maritime with heavy rain. About 90% of the people live on the island of Mahé which is the site of the capital, VICTORIA. The staple food is coconut, imported rice and fish. Tourism accounts for about 90% of the country's foreign exchange earnings and employs one-third of the labour force. The Seychelles are a one party socialist state and Soviet-made missiles have been installed as part of the islands' defense system.

Area : 280 sq km (108 sq miles)

Population : 67,378

Capital : Victoria

Form of government : Republic

Religion : RC

Currency : Seychelles rupee

Sfax the second city and a major port and industrial centre of TUNISIA on the Gulf of GABÈS. It was an ancient Phoenician trading settlement and has a grand mosque dating from AD849. (Pop. 232,000)

's-Gravenhage *see* **Hague, The.**

Shaanxi a province of northwestern CHINA. The capital is XI'AN. (190,000 sq km/73,000 sq miles; pop. 28,070,000)

Shaba the mineral-rich province of southeastern ZAÏRE that was known prior to 1972 as Katanga. The capital city is LUBUMBASHI. (496,964 sq km/191,878 sq miles; pop. 3,823,172)

Shandong a province of northern CHINA, with its capital

at JINAN. (150,000 sq km/58,000 sq miles; pop. 72,310,000)

Shanghai the largest and most westernized city in CHINA. An important port, it is situated on the delta of the CHANG JIANG (Yangtze) River. (Pop. 11,860,000)

Shannon, River a river of the Republic of IRELAND, and the longest river in the BRITISH ISLES. It flows southwest into the ATLANTIC OCEAN near LIMERICK. (Length 386 km/ 240 miles)

Shanxi a province of northern CHINA, with its capital at TAIYUAN. (150,000 sq km/58,000 sq miles; pop. 24,472,000)

Sharjah the fourth largest of the UNITED ARAB EMIRATES. Its capital city is also called Sharjah. (159,000 sq km/ 61,000 sq miles; pop. emirate 184,000/ city 126,000)

Shatt al Arab a waterway flowing into The GULF along the disputed border between IRAN and IRAQ, formed where the Rivers EUPHRATES and TIGRIS converge some 170 km (105 miles) from the coast.

Sheffield a major industrial city in South YORKSHIRE, ENGLAND. (Pop. 545,000)

Shenandoah, River a river, of great significance during the American Civil War, that flows through northern VIRGINIA, USA. (Length 90 km/55 miles)

Shenyang the capital of LIAONING province, CHINA. (Pop. 4,000,000)

Shenzhen a fast-growing city in CHINA, just north of the HONG KONG border and in the largest of the "special economic zones" set up to attract investment from overseas. (Pop. 350,000)

's-Hertogenbosch (Den Bosch; Bois-le-Duc) the capital of the province of Noord Brabant in south-central NETHERLANDS. (Pop. city 89,500/Greater 's-Hertogenbosch 186,600)

Shetland Islands a group of some 100 islands lying 160 km (100 miles) northeast of mainland SCOTLAND. The capital is Lerwick. (1426 sq km/550 sq miles; pop. 28,000)

Shijiazhuang the capital of HEBEI province, CHINA. (Pop. 973,000)

Shikoku the smallest of the four main islands of JAPAN. (Pop. 4,227,200)

Shillong the capital of MEGHALAYA state in northeastern INDIA; lying at nearly 1500 m (4930 ft) up in the Khasi Hills, it was formerly a popular hill resort for British colonial families from BENGAL. (Pop. 174,700)

Shimoneski a deep-sea fishing port on the southwest tip of HONSHU Island, JAPAN. (Pop. 261,700)

Shiraz a provincial capital of IRAN, southeast of TEHRAN. (Pop. 801,000)

Shkodër Lake (Skadarsko Jezero; Lake Scutari) the largest BALKAN lake astride the border between ALBANIA and MONTENEGRO. Near the town of Rijeka Crnojevica, at the lake's northern end, are the remains of the monastery where the first books in the Cyrillic alphabet were printed in 1493. (Area of lake: 391 sq km/143 sq miles)

Shropshire a county of west central ENGLAND; the county town is Shrewsbury. (3490 sq km/1347 sq miles; pop. 390,000)

Siam *see* **Thailand.**

Siberia a huge tract of land, mostly in northern RUSSIAN FEDERATION, that extends from the URAL MOUNTAINS to the PACIFIC coast. It is renowned for its inhospitable climate, but parts of it are fertile, and it is rich in minerals. It is split into two main parts: the West Siberian Plain (Zapadno Sibirskaya Ravnina), and the Central Siberian Plateau (Sredne Sibirskoye Ploskogor'ye).

Sibiu a major industrial and tourist centre of southern TRANSYLVANIA, in central ROMANIA. (Pop. 161,000)

Sichuan (Szechwan) the most heavily populated of the provinces of CHINA, in the southwest of the country. The capital is CHENGDU at the heart of the RED BASIN. (570,000 sq km/220,000 sq miles; pop. 97,740,000)

Sichuan Pendi (Red Basin) a vast region surrounded almost entirely by high mountains in the west of CHINA. It is drained by the CHANG JIANG (YANGTZE) and three of its major tributaries.

Sicily (Sicilia) an island hanging from the toe of ITALY, and the largest island in the MEDITERRANEAN. The capital is PALERMO. (25,708 sq km/9926 sq miles; pop. 5,065,000)

Sidi Bel Abbès an important communications and trading centre in northwestern ALGERIA, which was the headquarters of the French Foreign Legion until independence in 1962. (Pop. 158,000)

Sidi Ifni *see* **Ifni**.

Sidon (Saida) an ancient city of PHOENICIA, and today an important port and third city of LEBANON, lying on its coast, 40 km (25 miles) southwest of BEIRUT. It is the MEDITERRANEAN terminus of the oil pipeline from SAUDI ARABIA. (Pop. 24,700)

Sidra, Gulf of *see* **Sirte, Gulf of**.

Siena (Sienna) a historic town of TUSCANY, in central ITALY. (Pop. 60,500)

Sierra Leone, on the ATLANTIC coast of West AFRICA, is bounded by GUINEA to the north and east and by LIBERIA to the southeast. The coastal areas consist of wide swampy forested plains and these rise to a mountainous plateau in the east. The highest parts of the mountains are just under 2000 m (6562 ft). The climate is tropical with a dry season from November to June. The main food of Sierra Leoneans is rice and this is grown in the swamplands at the coast. In the tropical forest areas, small plantations produce coffee, cocoa and oil palm. In the plateau much forest has been cleared for growing of groundnuts. Most of the country's revenue comes from mining. Diamonds are panned from the rivers and there are deposits of iron ore, bauxite, rutile and some gold.

Area : 71,740 sq km (27,699 sq miles)

Population : 4,140,000

Capital : Freetown

Form of government : Republic

Religion : Animism, Sunni Islam, Christianity

Currency : Leone

Sierra Madre del Sur a mountain range extending along

the central part of the southern coast of MEXICO towards the Isthmus of TEHUANTEPEC, and rising to a height of 3850 m (12,630 ft).

Sierra Madre Occidental the mountain range of western MEXICO.

Sierra Madre Oriental the mountain range of eastern MEXICO.

Sierra Nevada (1) a mountain range in southern SPAIN. **(2)** a mountain range in eastern CALIFORNIA, USA.

Si Kiang *see* **Xi Jiang**.

Sikkim a state in northeastern INDIA. The capital is Gangtok. (7096 sq km/2739 sq miles; pop. 316,400)

Silesia (Schlesien) a region straddling the borders of the CZECH REPUBLIC, GERMANY and POLAND.

Silicon Glen a term applied to the central LOWLANDS of SCOTLAND, stretching from AYR to ARBROATH, because of the relatively high concentration of information technology industries.

Silicon Valley *see* **San Jose**.

Silk Road the ancient trade route from north CHINA through Central ASIA to SAMARKAND and ultimately leading to EUROPE, along which Chinese silk was transported west as early as Roman times. Marco Polo, the 13th-century Venetian explorer, journeyed along the well-used trail to re-establish contact with the ORIENT. Modern roads, partly surfaced, follow the line of the old Silk Road.

Simferopol' the capital and chief market town of the CRIMEA peninsula, in the south of UKRAINE. (Pop. 328,000)

Simla a hill station in HIMACHAL PRADESH, northern INDIA. (Pop. 80,200)

Simpson Desert an arid, uninhabited region in the centre of AUSTRALIA.

Sinai a mountainous peninsula in northeastern EGYPT, bordering ISRAEL, between the Gulf of AQABA and the Gulf of SUEZ.

Sind a province of southeastern PAKISTAN. The capital is KARACHI. (140,914 sq km/54,407 sq miles; pop. 19,029,000)

Singapore, one of the world's smallest yet most successful countries, comprises 60 islands which are located at the foot of the Malay peninsula in South-East ASIA. The main island, Singapore Island, is very low-lying, and the climate is hot and wet throughout the year. Only 3% of the land area is used for agriculture and most food is imported. It is self-sufficient in fish. Singapore has the largest oil refining centre in Asia. The country has a flourishing manufacturing industry for which it relies heavily on imports. Products include machinery and appliances, petroleum, food and beverages, chemicals, transport equipment, paper products and printing, and clothes. The Jurong Industrial Estate on the south of the island has over 1900 factories and employs 107,837 workers. Tourism is an important source of foreign revenue.

Area : 618 sq km (239 sq miles)

Population : 2,690,000

Capital : Singapore

Form of government : Republic

Religions : Buddhism, Sunni Islam, Christianity

Currency : Singapore dollar

Singapore, Strait of an important shipping lane running between the south coast of SINGAPORE island and the Riau Islands of INDONESIA; it links the SOUTH CHINA SEA and the Strait of MALACCA. (105 km/65 miles long; 16km/10 miles wide)

Sinkiang Uygur Autonomous Region *see* **Xinjiang Uygur Autonomous Region.**

Sint Maarten *see* **St Martin.**

Siracusa *see* **Syracuse.**

Síros *see* **Cyclades.**

Sirte (Sidra), Gulf of a huge indent of the MEDITERRANEAN SEA in the coastline of LIBYA.

Sittwe *see* **Akyab.**

Sivas an industrial town in central TURKEY. (Pop. 197,300)

Siwa (Sìwah) an ancient desert caravan village and

modern oasis town in the northern part of EGYPT'S WEST-ERN DESERT, near the border with LIBYA. (Pop. 3600)

Sjaelland *see* **Zealand.**

Skagerrak the channel, some 130 km (80 miles) wide, separating DENMARK and NORWAY. It links the NORTH SEA to the KATTEGAT and BALTIC SEA.

Skiathos the westernmost of the Greek Sporades (DODECANESE) Islands. (Pop. 4200)

Skopje the capital of MACEDONIA, a republic in the south of former YUGOSLAVIA. (Pop. 506,500)

Skye an island off the northwest coast of SCOTLAND; the largest of the Inner HEBRIDES. The main town is Portree. (1417 sq km/547 sq miles; pop. 8000)

Skåne *see* **Scania**.

Slavkov (Austerlitz) a small town in south MORAVIA of the eastern CZECH REPUBLIC; it is the site of Napoleon's greatest victory, in 1805, when he defeated the Russian and Austrian armies. (Pop. 6320)

Slavonia (Slavonija) a part of CROATIA, southeast of ZAGREB, mainly between the DRAVA and Slava Rivers.

Sligo a county on the northwest coast of the Republic of IRELAND, with a county town of the same name. (1796 sq km/693 sq miles; pop. county 55,400)

Slovakia was constituted on January 1, 1993 as a new independent nation, following the dissolution of the 74-year old federal republic of CZECHOSLOVAKIA. Landlocked in central Europe, its neighbours are the CZECH REPUBLIC to the west, POLAND to the north, AUSTRIA and HUNGARY to the south, and a short border with UKRAINE in the east. The northern half of the republic is occupied by the Tatra Mountains which form the northern arm of the CARPATHIAN Mountains. This region has vast forests and pastures used for intensive sheep grazing, and is rich in high-grade minerals. The southern part of Slovakia is a plain drained by the DANUBE and its tributaries. Farms, vineyards, orchards and pastures for stock form the basis of southern Slovakia's economy.

Snake

Area : 49,032 sq km (19,931 sq miles)
Population : 5,013,000
Capital : Bratislava
Other major city : Kovice
Form of government : Republic
Religion : RC
Currency : Koruna

Slovenia is a republic which made a unilateral declaration of independence from former YUGOSLAVIA on 25 June, 1991. Its sovereignty was not recognised by the European Community and the United Nations until early in 1992. It is bounded to the north by AUSTRIA, to the west by ITALY, to the east by HUNGARY, and to the south by CROATIA. Most of Slovenia is situated in the Karst Plateau and in the Julian Alps. Although farming and livestock raising are the chief occupations, Slovenia is very industrialized and urbanized. Iron, steel and aluminium are produced, and mineral resources include oil, coal and mercury. Tourism is an important industry. The Julian Alps are renowned for their scenery, and the Karst Plateau contains spectacular cave systems. The northeast of the republic is famous for its wine production.

Area : 20,251 sq km (7817 sq miles)
Population : 1,891,900
Capital : Ljubljana
Other major cities : Maribor, Celje
Form of government : Republic
Religion : RC
Currency : Tolar

Smederevo a historic, former medieval capital of SERBIA, lying on a bluff overlooking the DANUBE, some 40 km (25 miles) southeast of BELGRADE. Today it is a centre for wine-making as well as heavy engineering. (Pop. 107,400)

Smolensk an industrial city in the RUSSIAN FEDERATION, on the River DNIEPER. (Pop. 326,000)

Smyrna *see* **Izmir.**

Snake, River a major river of the American West, rising

in Yᴇʟʟᴏᴡꜱᴛᴏɴᴇ National Park in northwest Wʏᴏᴍɪɴɢ and flowing 1670 km (1038 miles) west and north to join the Columbia river in Wᴀꜱʜɪɴɢᴛᴏɴ State, before reaching the Pᴀᴄɪꜰɪᴄ Oᴄᴇᴀɴ. It is used for irrigation and to create hydroelectric power.

Snowdonia a mountainous region in the north of Wᴀʟᴇꜱ. The highest peak is Mount Snowdon (1885 m/3560 ft).

Snowy Mountains a range of mountains in southeastern Aᴜꜱᴛʀᴀʟɪᴀ, where the River Snowy has been dammed to form the complex Snowy Mountains Hydroelectric Scheme. The highest peak is Mount Kᴏꜱᴄɪᴜꜱᴋᴏ (2230 m/ 7316 ft).

Sochi a major Bʟᴀᴄᴋ Sᴇᴀ port, spa and resort of the Rᴜꜱꜱɪᴀɴ Fᴇᴅᴇʀᴀᴛɪᴏɴ, just northwest of the border with Gᴇᴏʀɢɪᴀ. (Pop. 307,000)

Society Islands a group of islands at the centre of Fʀᴇɴᴄʜ Pᴏʟʏɴᴇꜱɪᴀ. They are divided into the Windward Islands, which include Tᴀʜɪᴛɪ and Moorea; and the Leeward Islands, which include Raiatea and Bora-Bora. (Pop. 142,000)

Socotra an island in the northwestern Iɴᴅɪᴀɴ Oᴄᴇᴀɴ, belonging to Yᴇᴍᴇɴ. (Pop. 12,000)

Sodom and Gomorrah *see* **Sedom**.

Sofia (Sofiya) the capital of Bᴜʟɢᴀʀɪᴀ, in the west of the country. (Pop. 1,093,800)

Sokoto the capital of Nɪɢᴇʀɪᴀ's second largest state, of the same name, lying in the far northwest of the country. The town was prospering at the end of a Saharan caravan route by the 12th century. In the early 19th century it became the chief town of the Fulani people, and remains their spiritual home today. (Pop. town 144,200/state 4,539,000)

Solent, The a strait in the Eɴɢʟɪꜱʜ Cʜᴀɴɴᴇʟ that separates the Isle of Wɪɢʜᴛ from mainland Eɴɢʟᴀɴᴅ.

Solomon Islands the Solomon Islands lie in an area between 5° and 12° south of the Equator to the east of Pᴀᴘᴜᴀ Nᴇᴡ Gᴜɪɴᴇᴀ, in the Pᴀᴄɪꜰɪᴄ Oᴄᴇᴀɴ. The nation

Somalia

consists of six large islands and innumerable smaller ones. The larger islands are mountainous and covered in forests with rivers prone to flooding. GUADAL-CANAL is the main island and the site of the capital, HONIARA. The climate is hot and wet and typhoons are frequent. The main food crops grown are coconut, cassava, sweet potatoes, yams, taros and bananas. The forests are worked commercially, and the fishing industry is developing with the help of the Japanese. Other industries include palm-oil milling, fish canning and freezing, saw milling, food, tobacco and soft drinks.

Area : 28,896 sq km (11,157 sq mi)

Population : 308,796

Capital : Honiara

Form of government : Constitutional Monarchy

Religions : Anglicanism, RC, other Christianity

Currency : Solomon Island dollar

Solway Firth the 56-km (35-mile) long funnel-shaped inlet of the IRISH SEA between northwest ENGLAND and southwest SCOTLAND.

Somalia is shaped like a large number seven and lies on the horn of AFRICA's east coast. It is bounded north by the Gulf of Aden, south and east by the INDIAN OCEAN, and its neighbours include DJIBOUTI, ETHIOPIA, and KENYA. The country is arid and most of it is low plateaux with scrub vegetation. Its two main rivers, the Juba and Shebelle, are used to irrigate crops. Most of the population live in the mountains and river valleys and there are a few towns on the coast. Main exports are live animals, meat, hides and skins. A few large-scale banana plantations are found by the rivers. Years of drought have left Somalia heavily dependent on foreign aid, and many of the younger population are emigrating to oil-rich Arab states.

Area : 637,657 sq km (246,199 sq miles)

Population : 6,260,000

Capital : Mogadishu

Other major cities : Hargeisa, Baidoa, Burao, Kismaayo
Form of government : Republic
Religion : Sunni Islam
Currency : Somali shilling

Somerset a county in the southwest of ENGLAND; the county town is Taunton. (3458 sq km/1335 sq miles; pop. 440,000)

Somme, River a river of northern FRANCE, the scene of a devastating battle during World War I. (Length 245 km/ 152 miles)

Song Hong *see* **Red River.**

Sorrento a resort town on the southern shore of the Bay of NAPLES, which has been a holiday place since Roman times. (Pop. 17,600)

Sosnowiec a heavy-industry town in POLAND's Upper SILESIA region in the south of the country, near KATOWICE. (Pop. 252,000)

Soul *see* **Seoul.**

Sound, The *see* **Øresund**.

Soúnion, Cape a cape at the southern tip of ATTICA overlooking the the southern AEGEAN SEA, 60 km (37 miles) southwest of ATHENS, GREECE.

Sousse an old walled town, industrial port and major tourist centre on the Gulf of Hammamet, southeast of TUNIS. (Pop. 83,500)

South Africa is a republic that lies at the southern tip of the African continent and has a huge coastline on both the ATLANTIC and INDIAN OCEANS. The country occupies a huge saucer-shaped plateau, surrounding a belt of land which drops in steps to the sea. The rim of the saucer rises in the east, to 3482 m (11,424 ft), in the DRAKENSBERG. In general the climate is healthy with plenty of sunshine and relatively low rainfall. This varies with latitude, distance from the sea, and altitude. Of the total land area 58% is used as natural pasture. The main crops grown are maize, sorghum, wheat, groundnuts and sugar cane.

A drought-resistant variety of cotton is also now grown. It is South Africa's extraordinary mineral wealth which overshadows all its other natural resources. These include gold, coal, copper, iron ore, manganese and chrome ore.

Area : 1,221,037 sq km (471,442 sq miles)

Population : 30,190,000

Capital : Pretoria (Administrative), Cape Town (Legislative)

Other major cities : Johannesburg, Durban, Port Elizabeth, Bloemfontein

Form of government : Republic

Religions : Dutch reformed, Independent African, other Christianity, Hinduism

Currency : Rand

Southampton a major port in southern ENGLAND. (Pop. 206,000)

South Australia a state in central southern Australia, on the GREAT AUSTRALIAN BIGHT. ADELAIDE is the state capital. (984,380 sq km/380,069 sq miles; pop. 1,347,000)

South Carolina a state in the southeast of the USA, with a coast on the ATLANTIC OCEAN. The state capital is COLUMBIA. (80,432 sq km/31,055 sq miles; pop. 3,347,000)

South China Sea an arm of the PACIFIC OCEAN between southeast CHINA, MALAYSIA and the PHILIPPINES.

South Dakota a state in the western USA. The state capital is PIERRE. (199,552 sq km/77,047 sq miles; pop. 708,000)

South Downs *see* **Downs, The**.

Southern Alps a range of mountains on the SOUTH ISLAND of NEW ZEALAND.

Southern Ocean *see* **Antarctic Ocean.**

Southern Rhodesia *see* **Zimbabwe**.

Southern Uplands a hilly region extending over southern SCOTLAND and rising to 840 m (2756 ft) at Broad Law.

South Georgia an island in the South ATLANTIC, and a dependency of the FALKLAND ISLANDS. (3755 sq km/1450 sq km)

South Glamorgan a county in south WALES. The administrative centre is CARDIFF. (416 sq km/161 sq miles; pop. 384,700)

South Island the larger of NEW ZEALAND's two principal islands in area, but having only just over 25 per cent of its population. (151,484 sq km/58,488 sq miles; pop. 852,700)

South Korea *see* **Korea.**

South Orkney Islands a barren group of islands in the South ATLANTIC OCEAN, lying about 1360 km (850 miles) northeast of the ANTARCTIC PENINSULA, uninhabited (apart from research stations); they are part of British Antarctic Territory, although disputed by ARGENTINA. (621 sq km/240 sq miles)

South Pole the most southerly point of the Earth's axis, in ANTARCTICA.

South Sandwich Islands a group of islands in the South ATLANTIC which are dependencies of the FALKLAND ISLANDS. (340 sq km/130 sq miles)

South Shetland Islands an uninhabited, barren group of largely volcanic islands lying north of the ANTARCTIC PENINSULA. Formerly used as sealing and whaling stations, they are now the site for scientific surveys. (4662 sq km/1800 sq miles)

South Tyrol *see* **Trentino-Alto Adige.**

South Uist an island of the Outer HEBRIDES, lying between BENBECULA and BARRA, off the west coast of SCOTLAND. (365 sq km/140 sq miles; pop. 2231)

South West Africa *see* **Namibia**.

South Yemen *see* **Yemen.**

South Yorkshire a metropolitan county in northern ENGLAND comprising the districts of BARNSLEY, ROTHERHAM, DONCASTER and SHEFFIELD. The administrative centre is Barnsley. (1560 sq km/602 sq miles; 1,302,000)

Soviet Union *see* **Union of Soviet Socialist Republics**.

Soweto a group of black townships to the southwest of JOHANNESBURG, SOUTH AFRICA. Its name is an acronym of

South Western Townships. (Pop. 829,400)

Spa a spa town in BELGIUM which was the origin of the
general term "spa." (Pop. 10,000)

Spain is located in southwest EUROPE and occupies the
greater part of the Iberian peninsula, which it shares
with PORTUGAL. It is a mountainous country, sealed off
from the rest of Europe by the PYRÉNÉES, which rise to
over 3400 m (11,155 ft). Much of the country is a vast
plateau, the Meseta Central, cut across by valleys and
gorges. Its longest shoreline is the one that borders the
MEDITERRANEAN SEA. Most of the country has a form of
Mediterranean climate with mild moist winters and hot
dry summers. Spain's principal agricultural products are
cereals, vegetables and potatoes, and large areas are
under vines for the wine industry. Industry represents
72% of the country's export value, and production includes textiles, paper, cement, steel and chemicals. Tourism is a major revenue earner, especially from the resorts
on the east coast.

Area : 504,782 sq km (194,896 sq miles)

Population : 39,540,000

Capital : Madrid

Other major cities : Barcelona, Seville, Zaragosa,
Malaga, Bilbao

Form of government : Constitutional Monarchy

Religion : RC

Currency : Peseta

Spanish Town a city on the southern side of JAMAICA, only
20 km (12 miles) west of the capital, KINGSTON. Founded
by Diego Columbus (son of Christopher) in the 1520s, it
was the national capital until 1872, (Pop. 50,000)

Spencer Gulf the finest natural harbour in South Aus-
TRALIA, lying between the Eyre and Yorke peninsulas.
(320 km/200 miles long; 130 km/80 miles wide)

Spice Islands *see* **Maluku**.

Spithead the deep eastern channel between the Isle of
WIGHT and the mainland of HAMPSHIRE, ENGLAND; it is a

busy shipping lane to PORTSMOUTH and SOUTHAMPTON.

Spitsbergen A large island group in the SVALBARD archipelago, 580 km (360 miles) to the north of NORWAY. (39,000 sq km/15,060 sq miles; pop. 2000)

Split the largest city on the coast of DALMATIA, CROATIA. (Pop. 236,000)

Spokane a city in eastern WASHINGTON State, close to the IDAHO border. It is a market and railway centre. (Pop. city 173,300/metropolitan area 352,900)

Sporades (Sporadhes) *see* **Dodecanese.**

Spratly Islands a group of islands in the SOUTH CHINA SEA between VIETNAM and BORNEO. Occupied by JAPAN during World War II, they are now claimed by almost all the surrounding countries.

Springfield (1) the state capital of ILLINOIS, USA. (Pop. city 101,600/metropolitan area 190,100) **(2)** a manufacturing city in MASSACHUSETTS, USA. (Pop. city 150,300/ metropolitan area 515,900)

Srbija *see* **Serbia.**

Sredne Russkayo Vozvyhennost *see* **Central Russian Uplands**.

Sredne Sibirskoye Ploskogor'ye *see* **Central Siberian Plateau**.

Sri Lanka is a teardrop-shaped island in the INDIAN OCEAN, formerly called CEYLON, and lying south of the Indian peninsula from which it is separated by the Palk Strait. The climate is equatorial with a low annual temperature range but it is affected by both the northeast and southwest monsoons. Rainfall is heaviest in the southwest while the north and east are relatively dry. Agriculture engages 47% of the work force and the main crops are rice, tea, rubber and coconuts. Amongst the chief minerals mined and exported are precious and semiprecious stones. Graphite is also important. The main industries are food, beverages and tobacco, textiles, clothing and leather goods, chemicals and plastics. Attempts are being made to increase revenue from tourism.

St Croix

Area : 65,610 sq km (25,332 sq miles)
Population : 16,810,000
Capital : Colombo
Other major cities : Dehiwela-Mt. Lavinia, Moratuwa, Jaffna
Form of government : Republic
Religions : Buddhism, Hinduism, Christianity, Sunni Islam
Currency : Sri Lankan rupee

Srinagar the capital of the state of JAMMU AND KASHMIR, northern INDIA. (Pop. 606,000)

St Barthélémy a small island dependency of GUADELOUPE. (Pop. 3000)

St Christopher (St Kitts) and Nevis The islands of St Christopher (popularly known as St Kitts) and Nevis lie in the LEEWARD group in the eastern CARIBBEAN. In 1983 it became a sovereign democratic federal state with Elizabeth II as head of state. St Kitts consists of three extinct volcanoes linked by a sandy isthmus to other volcanic remains in the south. Around most of the island sugar cane is grown on fertile soil covering the gentle slopes. Sugar is the chief export crop but market gardening and livestock are being expanded on the steeper slopes above the cane fields. Industry includes sugar processing, brewing, distilling and bottling. St Kitts has a major tourist development at Frigate Bay. Nevis, 3 km (2 miles) south, is an extinct volcano. Farming is declining and tourism is now the main source of income.

Area : 261 sq km (101 sq miles)
Population : 43,410
Capital : Basseterre
Form of government : Constitutional Monarchy
Religions : Anglicanism, Methodism
Currency : East Caribbean dollar

St Croix the largest of the US VIRGIN ISLANDS. The main town is Christiansted. (218 sq km/84 sq miles; pop. 50,000)

St-Etienne an industrial city 50 km (30 miles) southwest of LYONS, FRANCE. (Pop. 319,500)

St Eustatius (Statia) an island of the NETHERLANDS ANTILLES, in the LEEWARD ISLANDS. The capital is ORANJESTAD. (Pop. 1500)

St Gallen (Sankt Gallen) a cotton-making town in northeast SWITZERLAND. (Pop. 76,000)

St George's the capital of GRENADA, and the island's main port. (Pop. 30,800)

St Georges Channel a strait between WALES and IRELAND, linking the ATLANTIC OCEAN with the southern part of the IRISH SEA. (Length *c.* 160 km/100 miles; width up to 145 km/90 miles)

St Helena a remote island and British colony in the South ATLANTIC. Napoleon Bonaparte was exiled here by the British from 1815 until his death in 1821. (122 sq km/47 sq miles; pop. 5500)

St Helena Dependencies the islands of ASCENSION and TRISTAN DA CUNHA are so-called dependencies of ST HELENA, a British colony.

St Helens a glass-making industrial town in MERSEYSIDE, northwest ENGLAND. (Pop. 98,769)

St Helens, Mount an active volcano in the CASCADE RANGE of western WASHINGTON State, USA. It erupted in 1980, causing widespread destruction. (2549 m/8364 ft)

St John the smallest of the main islands of the US VIRGIN ISLANDS. (52 sq km/20 sq miles; pop. 2400)

St John's (1) the capital and main port of ANTIGUA. (Pop. 30,000). **(2)** a port and the capital of NEWFOUNDLAND, CANADA. (Pop. 155,000)

St Kilda (Hirta) a remote, steep, rocky island lying some 56 km (35 miles) west of NORTH UIST in the ATLANTIC OCEAN. It has been uninhabited since 1930, apart from army personnel manning its radar station, and research scientists; it has the highest sea cliffs in GREAT BRITAIN.

St Kitts and Nevis *see* **St Christopher and Nevis.**

St Lawrence Seaway a navigable waterway that links

the GREAT LAKES, via the ST LAWRENCE River, to the ATLANTIC OCEAN.

St Lawrence, Gulf of an arm of the ATLANTIC OCEAN in northeastern CANADA, into which the ST LAWRENCE River flows.

St Lawrence, River a commercially important river of southeast CANADA, which flows northeast from Lake ONTARIO to the Gulf of ST LAWRENCE, forming part of the border between Canada and the USA. (Length 1197 km/ 744 miles)

St Louis a city in eastern MISSOURI, USA, on the River MISSISSIPPI. (Pop. city 429,300/metropolitan area 2,398,400)

St Lucia is one of the Windward Islands in the eastern CARIBBEAN. It lies to the south of MARTINIQUE and to the north of ST. VINCENT. It was controlled alternately by the French and the British for some two hundred years before becoming fully independent in 1979. St Lucia is an island of extinct volcanoes and the highest peak is 950 m (3117 ft). In the west are the peaks of Pitons which rise directly from the sea to over 750 m (2461 ft). The climate is wet tropical with a dry season from January to April. The economy depends on the production of bananas and, to a lesser extent, coconuts. Production, however, is often affected by hurricanes, drought and disease. Tourism is becoming an important industry and CASTRIES, the capital, is a popular calling point for cruise liners.

Area : 622 sq km (240 sq miles)

Population : 146,600

Capital : Castries

Form of Government : Constitutional Monarchy

Religion : RC

Currency : East Caribbean dollar

St Martin one of the LEEWARD ISLANDS in the southeastern CARIBBEAN. It is divided politically into two, one a part of GUADELOUPE (France); the other (Sint Maarten) a part of the NETHERLANDS ANTILLES. The capital of the French side is Marigot; of the Dutch side Philipsburg. (54 sq km/21 sq miles; pop. 24,000)

St Paul the state capital of MINNESOTA, twinned with the adjoining city of MINNEAPOLIS. (Pop. city 265,900/ metropolitan area 2,230,900)

St Petersburg (Sankt Peterburg) a former capital of RUSSIA and the current RUSSIAN FEDERATION second-largest city. It is an industrial city, important cultural centre and major port on the BALTIC SEA. From 1914-24 it was known as Petrograd; then, until 1991, Leningrad.

St Pierre and Miquelon two islands to the south of NEWFOUNDLAND, CANADA, which are an overseas territory administered by FRANCE. (240 sq km/93 sq miles; pop. 6100)

St Thomas the principal tourist island of the US VIRGIN ISLANDS. The capital is CHARLOTTE AMALIE. (83 sq km/32 sq miles; pop. 44,000)

St Vincent and the Grenadines St Vincent is an island of the Lesser Antilles, situated in the eastern CARIBBEAN between ST LUCIA and GRENADA. St Vincent is separated from Grenada by a chain of some 600 small islands known as the Grenadines, the northern islands of which form the other part of the country. The largest of these islands are Bequia, MUSTIQUE, Canouan, Mayreau and Union. The climate is tropical, with very heavy rain in the mountains. St Vincent Island is mountainous and a chain of volcanoes runs up the middle of the island. The volcano, Soufrière (1234 m/4049 ft), is active and its last eruption was in 1979. Farming is the main occupation on the island. Bananas for the UK are the main export, and it is the world's leading producer of arrowroot starch. There is little manufacturing and the government is trying to promote tourism.

Area : 388 sq km (150 sq miles)

Population : 113,950

Capital : Kingstown

Form of government : Constitutional Monarchy

Religions : Anglicanism, Methodism, RC
Currency : East Caribbean dollar

St Vincent, Cape *see* **São Vincente, Cabo de.**

Staffordshire a Midlands county of England. The county town is Stafford. (2716 sq km/1949 sq miles; pop. 1,018,000)

Stalingrad *see* **Volgograd**.

Stanley Falls *see* **Boyoma Falls.**

Stanley *see* **Port Stanley**.

Stanley, Mount *see* **Ngaliema, Mount.**

Stanleyville *see* **Kisangani.**

Stara Planina *see* **Balkan Mountains**.

Statia *see* **St Eustatius.**

Stavanger a major port in the southwest of Norway, which now acts as the main national servicing town for the North Sea oil industry. (Pop. 92,000)

Steiermark *see* **Styria**.

Stellenbosch the second oldest European settlement in South Africa, lying 40 km (25 miles) west of Cape Town, at the centre of a fruit and wine-producing area. It has an Afrikaans university. (Pop. 37,700)

Steppes, The *see* **Kirghiz Steppe.**

Sterea Ellas-Evvoia the mountainous central region of Greece, south of Thessaly and Epirus, bounded by the Aegean Sea to the east and the Ionian Sea to the west. It includes Athens and the classical centres of Delphi and Thebes. (24,500 sq km/9572 sq miles; pop. 4,127,200)

Stettin *see* **Szczecin.**

Stewart Island the largest of New Zealand's off-shore islands, separated from the tip of South Island by the Foveaux Strait. (1746 sq km/674 sq miles; pop. 600)

Stirling a historic town, with a new university, built around an ancient castle on a rocky outcrop, guarding the valley of the River Forth in Central Region, Scotland. (Pop. 39,000)

Stockholm the capital of Sweden, and an important port on the Baltic Sea. (Pop. 1,435,500)

Stockton-on-Tees a town in the county of CLEVELAND, ENGLAND. (Pop. 173,000)

Stoke-on-Trent a major city in the "Potteries" of the MIDLANDS of ENGLAND. (Pop. 250,000)

Stonehenge an important prehistoric stone circle on Salisbury Plain, WILTSHIRE, southern ENGLAND; it was constructed between 2750 and 1300BC, and is believed to have had religious and astronomical purposes.

Store Bælt (Great Belt) the central channel through the Danish archipelago, with the islands of FUNEN and LANGELAND to the west and ZEALAND and LOLLAND to the east. EUROPE's longest bridge is being built across it. (Length 115 km/71 miles; width 11-35 km/7-22 miles)

Strasbourg an industrial city and river port in eastern FRANCE, the capital of the ALSACE region, and the seat of the European Parliament. (Pop. 378,500)

Stratford-upon-Avon a town in WARWICKSHIRE, ENGLAND, the home of William Shakespeare (1564–1616). (Pop. 22,000)

Strathclyde an administrative region (and ancient kingdom) in western SCOTLAND, with its administrative centre in GLASGOW. It was created in 1975 out of the former counties of Ayrshire, Lanarkshire, Renfrewshire, Bute, Dunbartonshire and parts of Stirlingshire and Argyll. (13,856 sq km/5350 sq miles; pop. 2,373,000)

Stromboli an island with an active volcano in the EOLIAN ISLANDS, to the north of SICILY. (Pop. 400)

Stuttgart a major industrial centre and river port of the NECKAR river in southwestern GERMANY. (Pop. 600,000)

Styria (Steiermark) the forested mountainous state of southeast AUSTRIA, noted for its mining and metal industries. The capital city is GRAZ. (16,384 sq km/6326 sq miles; pop. 1,187,512)

Sucre the legal capital of BOLIVIA. (Pop. 70,000)

Sudan is the largest country in AFRICA, lying just south of the Tropic of Cancer in northeast Africa. The country covers much of the upper NILE basin and in the north the river winds through the Nubian and Libyan deserts, forming a palm-fringed strip of habitable land. The climate is tropical and temperatures are high throughout the year. In winter, nights are very cold. Rainfall increases in amount from north to south, the northern areas being virtually desert. Sudan is an agricultural country, subsistence farming accounting for 80% of production. Cotton is farmed commercially and accounts for about two-thirds of Sudan's exports. Sudan is the world's greatest source of gum arabic used in medicines and inks. This is the only forest produce to be exported.

Area : 2,505,813 sq km (967,494 sq miles)

Population : 25,560,000

Capital : Khartoum (El Khartum)

Other major cities : Omdurman, Khartoum North, Port Sudan

Form of government : Republic

Religions : Sunni Islam, Animism, Christianity

Currency : Sudanese pound

Sudbury a major nickel-mining centre in south-central ONTARIO, CANADA, some 370 km (230 miles) northwest of TORONTO. (Pop. 88,717)

Sudd a vast swampland on the White NILE in SUDAN.

Sudetenland *see* **Sudety.**

Sudety (Sudetenland) a mountainous region straddling the border between the CZECH REPUBLIC and POLAND.

Suez (El Suweis) a town situated at the southern end of the SUEZ CANAL. (Pop. 195,000)

Suez Canal a canal in northeast EGYPT, linking the MEDITERRANEAN to the RED SEA. It was completed in 1869.

Suez, Gulf of a northern arm of the RED SEA that leads to the SUEZ CANAL.

Suffolk a county in EAST ANGLIA, ENGLAND. The county town is Ipswich. (3800 sq km/1467 sq miles; pop. 619,000)

Sulawesi (Celebes) a large, hook-shaped island in the centre of INDONESIA. (179,370 sq km/69,255 sq miles; pop. 10,409,600)

Sullom Voe a deep coastal inlet in the north of the Mainland island of SHETLAND, off northern SCOTLAND. It is the site of a major NORTH SEA oil-transhipment terminal with pipeline connections to the large oilfields of the East Shetland Basin.

Sulu Archipelago a chain of over 400 islands off the southwest PHILIPPINES, stretching between the Philippines and BORNEO.

Sulu Sea a part of the PACIFIC OCEAN which lies between the PHILIPPINES and BORNEO.

Sumatra the main island of western INDONESIA. (473,607 sq km/182,860 sq miles; pop. 28,016,200)

Sumba one of the LESSER SUNDA ISLANDS, INDONESIA, to the south of SUMBAWA and FLORES. (11,153 sq km/4306 sq miles; pop. 251,100)

Sumbawa one of the LESSER SUNDA ISLANDS, INDONESIA, between LOMBOK and FLORES. (15,448 sq km/5965 sq miles; pop. 195,000)

Sun City a modern holiday complex in the BOPHUTHATSWANA homeland in the northeast of SOUTH AFRICA.

Sunda Islands *see* **Lesser Sunda Islands.**

Sundarbans a region of dense mangrove swamp and jungle on the numberous islands and estuary peninsulas of the huge delta formed by the GANGES, BRAHMAPUTRA and Meghna Rivers coming close to each other at their mouths; it sits astride BANGLADESH and West BENGAL in INDIA and is an area teeming with wildlife, including the Bengal tiger.

Sunda Strait the strait, 26 km(16 miles) across at its narrowest, which separates JAVA and SUMATRA.

Sunderland an industrial town in TYNE AND WEAR, ENGLAND. (Pop. 200,000)

Sundsvall a major timber port and processing town on the Gulf of BOTHNIA coast of SWEDEN. (Pop. 93,200)

Superior, Lake the largest and most westerly of the GREAT LAKES. (82,400 sq km/31,800 sq miles)

Surabaya the second largest city of INDONESIA after JA-

KARTA, on the northeast coast of JAVA. (Pop. 2,470,000)

Surat a port on the west coast of INDIA, in western GUJARAT. (Pop. 913,800)

Suriname is a republic in northeast South AMERICA, bordered to the west by GUYANA, to the east by GUIANA, and to the south by BRAZIL. The country, formerly a Dutch colony, declared independence in 1975. Suriname comprises a swampy coastal plain, a forested central plateau, and southern mountains. The climate is tropical with heavy rainfall. Temperatures at PARAMARIBO average 26-27°C all year round. Rice and sugar are farmed on the coastal plains but the mining of bauxite is what the economy depends on. This makes up 80% of exports. Suriname has resources of oil and timber but these are so far underexploited. The country is politically very unstable and in need of financial aid to develop these resources.

Area : 163,265 sq km (63,037 sq miles)

Population : 416,839

Capital : Paramaribo

Form of government : Republic

Religions : Hinduism, RC, Sunni Islam

Currency : Suriname guilder

Surrey a county of central southern ENGLAND. The county town is Guildford. (1655 sq km/639 sq miles; pop. 1,012,000)

Surtsey a volcanic-ash island that rose from the sea off the south coast of ICELAND in 1963; it was named after Surtr, the god of fire in Norse mythology.

Sussex an ancient kingdom of the South Saxons in southeast ENGLAND, and until 1974 a county, since when it was split in two. *See* **East Sussex** and **West Sussex.**

Susupe the capital of the NORTHERN MARIANAS, on the island of SAIPAN. (Pop. 8000)

Sutherland *see* **Highland**.

Sutlej a major Asian river that rises in the HIMALAYAS of southwest TIBET and flows some 1370 km (850 miles) west into INDIA and southwest through the PUNJAB to join the Chenab and then the INDUS rivers to the ARABIAN SEA.

Suva the capital and main port of FIJI. (Pop. city 74,000/ metropolitan area 133,000)

Suzhou a city in JIANGSHU province, CHINA. (Pop. 900,000)

Svalbard an archipelago in the ARCTIC OCEAN to the north of NORWAY, which includes SPITSBERGEN. A convention (1920) granted sovereignty to Norway, but all signatories can exploit the mineral reserves. (62,049 sq km/23,958 sq miles; pop. 3500)

Sverdlovsk *see* **Yekaterinburg.**

Swansea a port in south WALES. (Pop. 168,000)

Swaziland is a landlocked hilly enclave almost entirely within the borders of the Republic of SOUTH AFRICA. The mountains in the west of the country rise to almost 2000 m (6562 ft), then descend in steps of savanna towards hilly country in the east. The climate is subtropical moderated by altitude. The land between 400 m (1312 ft) and 850 m (2789 ft) is planted with orange groves and pineapple fields, while on the lower land sugar cane flourishes in irrigated areas. Asbestos is mined in the northwest of the country. Manufacturing includes fertilizers, textiles, leather and tableware. Swaziland attracts a lot of tourists from South Africa, mainly to its spas and casinos.

Area : 1736 sq km (6704 sq miles)

Population : 681,059

Capital : Mbabane

Other major cities : Big Bend, Manzini, Mhlume

Form of government : Monarchy

Religion : Christianity, Animism

Currency : emalangeni

Sweden is a large country in northern EUROPE which makes up half of the Scandinavian peninsula. It stretches from the BALTIC SEA north, to well within the ARCTIC CIRCLE. The south is generally flat, the north mountainous, and along the coast there are 20,000 or more islands and islets. Summers are warm but short and winters are long and cold. In the north snow may lie for four to seven months. Dairy farming is the predominant agricultural activity. Only 7% of Sweden is cultivated, with the emphasis on fodder crops, grain and sugar beet. About 57% of the country is covered in forest, and the sawmill, wood pulp and paper industries are all of great importance. Sweden is one of the world's leading producers of iron ore, most of which is extracted from within the Arctic Circle. Other principal industries are engineering and electrical goods, motor vehicles and furniture making.

Area : 449,964 sq km (173,731 sq miles)

Population : 8,500,000

Capital : Stockholm

Other major cities : Göteborg, Malmö, Uppsala, Orebro

Form of government : Constitutional Monarchy

Religion : Lutheranism

Currency : Krona

Switzerland is a landlocked country in central EUROPE, sharing its borders with FRANCE, ITALY, AUSTRIA, LIECHTENSTEIN and GERMANY. The ALPS occupy the southern half of the country, forming two main east-west chains divided by the rivers RHINE and RHÔNE. The climate is either continental or mountain type. Summers are generally warm and winters cold, and both are affected by altitude. Northern Switzerland is the industrial part of the country and where its most important cities are located. BASLE is famous for its pharmaceuticals and ZÜRICH for electrical engineering and machinery. It is also in this region that the famous cheeses, clocks, watches and chocolates are produced. Switzerland has huge earnings from international finance and tourism.

Area : 41,293 sq km (15,943 sq miles)

Population : 6,700,000

Capital : Berne (Bern)

Other major cities : Zürich, Basle, Geneva, Lausanne

Form of government : Federal republic

Religions : RC, Protestantism

Currency : Swiss franc

Sydney the largest city and port in AUSTRALIA, and the capital of NEW SOUTH WALES. (Pop. 3,332,600)

Syracuse (1) a city in the centre of NEW YORK State. (Pop. city 164,200/metropolitan area 650,000). **(2) (Siracusa)** an ancient seaport on the east coast of SICILY, ITALY. (Pop. 119,200)

Syrdar'ya, River a river of central ASIA, flowing through KAZAKHSTAN to the ARAL SEA. (Length 2860 km/1780 miles)

Syria is a country in southwest ASIA which borders on the MEDITERRANEAN SEA in the west. Much of the country is mountainous behind the narrow fertile coastal plain. The eastern region is desert or semi-desert, a stony inhospitable land. The coast has a Mediterranean climate with hot dry summers and mild wet winters. About 50% of the workforce get their living from agriculture, sheep, goats and cattle are raised, and cotton, barley, wheat, tobacco, fruit and vegetables are grown. Reserves of oil are small compared to neighbouring IRAQ but it has enough to make the country self-sufficient and provide three quarters of the nation's export earnings. Industries such as textiles, leather, chemicals and cement have developed rapidly in the last 20 years.

Area : 185,180 sq km (71,498 sq miles)

Population : 11,300,000

Capital : Damascus (Dimashq)

Other major cities : Aleppo, Homs, Lattakia, Hama

Religion : Sunni Islam

Currency : Syrian pound

Szczecin (Stettin) a port in northwest POLAND. (Pop. 390,200)

Szechwan *see* **Sichuan.**

T

Table Mountain a flat-topped mountain overlooking CAPE TOWN on Table Bay in southwest SOUTH AFRICA. (1087 m/3567 ft)

Tabriz a city in northwest IRAN. (Pop. 599,000)

Tacoma a port at the head of Puget Sound, in WASHINGTON State, on the PACIFIC coast of the USA. (Pop. city 159,400/ metropolitan area 515,800)

Tadmor *see* **Palmyra**.

Tadzhikistan *see* **Tajikistan**.

Taegu the third largest city of South KOREA, in the southeast of the country. (Pop. 1,608,000)

Taejan (Daejeon) a modern manufacturing city rehabilitated after the Korean War (1950-53); it lies 150 km (95 miles) south of SEOUL. (Pop. 651,800)

Tafilalt (Tafilet) the largest Saharan oasis in MOROCCO, comprising 50 km (30 miles) of villages and date palm groves, located in the south-central part of the country. (1375 sq km/530 sq miles; pop. 70,000)

Tagus (Tajo; Tejo), River a major river of southwest EUROPE, which rises in eastern SPAIN and flows west and southwest through PORTUGAL to the ATLANTIC OCEAN west of LISBON. (Length 1007 km/626 miles)

Tahiti the largest of the islands of FRENCH POLYNESIA in the South PACIFIC. The capital is PAPEETE. (1005 sq km/388 sq miles; pop. 96,000)

T'aichung a major commercial and agricultural centre in western TAIWAN. (Pop. 1,608,000)

Taimyr Peninsular (Poluostrov Taymyr) the large northernmost mainland extension of the RUSSIAN FEDERATION, lying in north-central SIBERIA, and between the

KARA and LAPTEV seas.

T'ainan a city in southwest TAIWAN. (Pop. 595,000)

T'aipei the capital and largest city of TAIWAN, in the very north of the island. (Pop. 2,272,000)

Taiwan is an island which straddles the Tropic of Cancer in East ASIA. It lies about 160 km (99 miles) off the southeast coast of mainland CHINA. It is predominantly mountainous in the interior, the tallest peak rising to 3997 m (13,114 ft) at Yu Shan. The climate is warm and humid for most of the year. Winters are mild and summers rainy. The soils are fertile, and a wide range of crops, including tea, rice, sugar cane and bananas, is grown. Taiwan is a major international trading nation with some of the most successful export-processing zones in the world, accommodating domestic and overseas companies. Exports include machinery, electronics, textiles, footwear, toys and sporting goods.

Area : 36,179 sq km (13,969 sq miles)

Population : 20,300,000

Capital : Taipei

Other major cities : Kaohsiung, Taichung, Tainan

Form of government : Republic

Religions : Taoism, Buddhism, Christianity

Currency : New Taiwan dollar

Taiwan Strait the stretch of water that separates Taiwan from mainland CHINA.

Taiyuan the capital of SHANXI province, CHINA. (Pop. 1,838,000)

Taiz (Ta'izz) the second largest city of YEMEN, lying at the centre of an important coffee-growing area, high in the hills of the southwest (Altitude 1700 m/5577 ft; pop. 123,000)

Tajikistan, a republic of southern central former USSR, declared itself independent in 1991. It is situated near the Afghani and Chinese borders. The south is occupied by the PAMIR mountain range, whose snow-capped peaks dominate the country. More than half the country lies over 3000 m (9843 ft). Most of the country is desert or semi-desert, and pastoral farming of cattle, sheep, horses and goats is important. Some yaks are kept in the higher regions. The lowland areas in the Fergana and AMUDAR'YA valleys are irrigated so that cotton, mulberry trees, fruit, wheat and vegetables can be grown. The Amudar'ya river is also used to produce hydro-electricity for industries such as cotton and silk processing. The republic is rich in deposits of coal, lead, zinc, oil and uranium, which are now being exploited.

Area : 143,100 sq km (55,250 sq miles)

Population : 5,100,000

Capital : Dushanbe

Form of Government : Republic

Religion : Shia Islam

Currency : Rouble

Taj Mahal *see* **Agra**.

Tajo see Tagus.

Takamatsu an industrial city and ferry port in northeast SHIKOKU Island, JAPAN. (Pop. 327,000)

Takasaki a city in central HONSHU Island, regarded as the gateway to the JAPAN ALPS. (Pop. 231,800)

Taklimakan Shamo the largest desert in CHINA, consisting mainly of sand, in the west of the country.

Takoradi *see* **Sekondi-Takoradi.**

Tallahassee the state capital of FLORIDA, USA. (Pop. city 112,000/metropolitan area 207,600)

Tallinn a port on the BALTIC SEA, and the capital of ESTONIA. (Pop. 458,000)

Tamale a market town and capital of the Northern Region of GHANA, lying at the centre of the Volta river basin. (Pop. 219,200)

Tambov an industrial city on the plain of the DON River in the RUSSIAN FEDERATION, southeast of Moscow. It was founded as a fort in 1636 to defend the capital against the Tatars. (Pop. 290,000)

Tamil Nadu a state in southeast INDIA. The state capital is MADRAS. (130,357 sq km/50,839 sq miles; pop. 48,298,000)

Tammerfors *see* **Tampere**.

Tampa a port and resort on the west coast of FLORIDA, USA. (Pop. city 275,000/metropolitan area 1,811,000)

Tampere (Tammerfors) the second largest city in FINLAND after HELSINKI, in the southwest of the country. (Pop. 167,000)

Tampico an oil-refining city and resort on MEXICO's Gulf coast. (Pop. 401,000)

Tana (Tsana), Lake a lake in the mountains of northwest ETHIOPIA, and the source of the Blue NILE. (3673 sq km/1418 sq miles)

Tanganyika *see* **Tanzania**.

Tanganyika, Lake the second largest lake in AFRICA after Lake VICTORIA, in the GREAT RIFT VALLEY, between TANZANIA and ZAÏRE, although BURUNDI and ZAMBIA also share the shoreline. (32,893 sq km/12,700 sq miles)

Tangier (Tanger) a port on the north coast of MOROCCO, on the Strait of GIBRALTAR. (Pop. 188,000)

Tangshan an industrial and coal-mining city in HEBEI province, CHINA. (Pop. 1,087,000)

Tanta a cotton and wool-processing town in the centre of the NILE delta, in northern EGYPT. (Pop. 285,000)

Tanzania lies on the east coast of central AFRICA and comprises a large mainland area and the islands of Pemba and ZANZIBAR. The mainland consists mostly of plateaux broken by mountainous areas and the east African section of the GREAT RIFT VALLEY. The climate is very varied and is controlled largely by altitude and distance from the sea. The coast is hot and humid, the central plateau drier, and the mountains semi-temperate. 80% of Tanzanians make a living from the land, but productivity is low and there is no surplus from the crops, mainly maize, that they grow. Cash crops include cotton and coffee. The islands are more successful agriculturally and have important coconut and clove plantations.

Tanzania's mineral resources are limited and of low grade, and there are few manufacturing industries.

Area : 945,087 sq km (364,898 sq miles)

Population : 24,800,000

Capital : Dodoma

Other major cities : Dar es Salaam, Zanzibar, Mwanza, Tanga

Form of government : Republic

Religions : Sunni Islam, RC, Anglicanism, Hinduism

Currency : Tanzanian shilling

Tara, Hill of *see* **Navan**.

Tarabulus *see* **Tripoli.**

Taranaki the rich dairying district that occupies the southeastern peninsula of NORTH ISLAND, NEW ZEALAND. (9720 sq km/3753 sq miles; pop. 105,200)

Taranto a port and naval base on the south coast of ITALY, on the Gulf of TARANTO. (Pop. 245,000)

Taranto, Gulf of an inlet of the MEDITERRANEAN SEA between the "toe" and the "heel" of ITALY.

Tarawa the main atoll and capital of the group of islands forming KIRIBATI. (Pop. 23,000)

Tarim Pendi a vast basin in Central ASIA bounded by the massive mountains of ALTUN SHAN, KARAKORAM and TIAN SHAN. The TAKLIMAKAN desert lies at the heart of the basin. (Area 530,000 sq km/205,000 sq miles)

Tarragona a port of ancient origins on the MEDITERRANEAN coast of northeastern SPAIN, and the name of the surrounding province. (Pop. city 111,700)

Tarsus an agricultural centre in southeast TURKEY, the birthplace of St Paul. (Pop. 160,000)

Tartu an old university town in east-central ESTONIA, founded by the Swedish king, Gustav II Adolf, in 1632. (Pop. 110,000)

Tashkent the capital of UZBEKISTAN, in the northeast, near the border with KAZAKHSTAN. (Pop. 1,987,000)

Tasman Bay a wide inlet on the north coast of SOUTH ISLAND, NEW ZEALAND, where in 1770 Captain James Cook recorded evidence of Maori cannibalism.

Tasman Sea a branch of the PACIFIC OCEAN that separates AUSTRALIA and NEW ZEALAND.

Tasmania an island state to the south of AUSTRALIA, separated from the mainland by the BASS STRAIT. The capital is HOBART. (68,332 sq km/26,383 sq miles; pop. 435,000)

Tatar Republic (Tatarstan) an autonomous republic of the RUSSIAN FEDERATION, southwest of MOSCOW, around the River VOLGA. In 1992 it voted to become a sovereign state. The capital is KAZAN'. (68,000 sq km/26,250 sq miles; pop. 394,000)

Tatra Mountains a range of mountains that lines the border between POLAND and SLOVAKIA The highest peak is Gerlachovka (2663 m/8737 ft).

Tatung *see* **Datung.**

Taupo, Lake the largest stretch of inland water in NEW ZEALAND, situated in the centre of NORTH ISLAND. (Area 606 sq km/234 sq miles)

Taurus Mountains (Tords Daglari) a major east-west range of 3000-m (10,000-ft) plus mountains that runs along the MEDITERRANEAN coast of the ANATOLIA peninsula of TURKEY. Mount Erciyas Dagi, at 3916 m (12,848 ft), is the highest peak.

Tayside an administrative region of SCOTLAND formed in 1975 out of the former counties of Angus, Kinrossshire and part of Perthshire. The administrative centre is DUNDEE. (7511 sq km/2900 sq miles; pop. 392,000)

Tbilisi the capital of GEORGIA, in the centre of the republic. (Pop. 1,140,000)

Tegucigalpa the capital of HONDURAS, in the south of the country. (Pop. 473,700)

Tehran the capital of IRAN, in the central north of the country. (Pop. 6,000,000)

Tehuantepec, Isthmus of the narrowest part of southern MEXICO, with the Bahía de CAMPECHE to the north and the Gulf of Tehuantepec, an arm of the PACIFIC

OCEAN, to the south.

Tejo *see* **Tagus**.

Tel Aviv-Jaffa the largest city of ISRAEL, former capital and the main financial centre. It was combined with the old port of Jaffa in 1950. (Pop. 324,000)

Telford a new town in SHROPSHIRE, west-central ENGLAND, designated in 1963. (Pop. 103,786)

Tenerife the largest of the CANARY ISLANDS. The capital is Santa Cruz. (2058 sq km/795 sq miles; pop. 558,000)

Tennessee a state in southern central USA. The state capital is NASHVILLE. (109,412 sq km/42,244 sq miles; pop. 4,762,000)

Tennessee, River a river which flows southwest from the APPALACHIAN MOUNTAINS of NORTH CAROLINA and then through ALABAMA, TENNESSEE and KENTUCKY to join the OHIO RIVER. It is an important source of irrigation and hydro-electric power. (Length 1049km/ 652miles)

Tevere, River *see* **Tiber**.

Texas a state in the southwest of the USA, bordering MEXICO. It is the nation's second largest state. The capital is AUSTIN. (678,927 sq km/262,134 sq miles; pop. 16,370,000)

Thailand, a kingdom about the same size as FRANCE located in South-East ASIA; it was known as Siam until 1939, and from 1945 to 1949, and it is the only nation in the region to have remained free from foreign colonial rule. It is a tropical country of mountains and jungles, rain forests and green plains. Central Thailand is a densely populated, fertile plain and the mountainous Isthmus of Kra joins southern Thailand to MALAYSIA. Thailand has a subtropical climate with heavy monsoon rains from June to October, a cool season from October to March, and a hot season from March to June. The central plain of Thailand contains vast expanses of paddy fields which produce enough rice to rank Thailand as the world's leading exporter. The narrow southern peninsula is very wet, and it is here that rubber is produced.

Thailand is the world's third largest exporter of rubber.
Area : 513,115 sq km (198,114 sq miles)
Population : 55,900,00
Capital : Bangkok (Krung Thep)
Other major cities : Chiengmai, Hat Yai, Songkhla
Form of government : Constitutional Monarchy
Religions : Buddhism, Sunni Islam
Currency : Baht

Thailand, Gulf of a branch of the SOUTH CHINA SEA lying between the Malay peninsula and the coasts of THAILAND, CAMBODIA and VIETNAM.

Thames, River a major river of southern ENGLAND flowing eastwards from its source in the Cotswold Hills, past LONDON to its estuary on the NORTH SEA. (Length 338 km/ 210 miles)

Thar Desert a desert in northwest INDIA, covering the border between RAJASTHAN and PAKISTAN.

Thebes the ruins of an ancient city on the River NILE in central EGYPT. It was the capital of Ancient Egypt for about 1000 years from 1600BC.

Thessaloníki *see* **Saloniki.**

Thessaly (Thesalia) the rural central region of GREECE, centred on a large plain, bounded by MACEDONIA in the north, STEREA ELLÁS-EVVOIA to the south, and the AEGEAN SEA to the east. (12,939 sq km/5382 sq miles: pop. 695,700)

Thimphu (Thimbu) the capital of BHUTAN, in the west of the country. (Pop. 8922)

Thon Buri a city on the west side of the River CHAO PHRAYA, oppposite BANGKOK, in THAILAND. (Pop. 919,000)

Thousand Islands a group of over 1000 islands scattered in the upper ST LAWRENCE River, between the USA and CANADA.

Thrace (1) a historical region that sits astride the borders of modern BULGARIA, GREECE and TURKEY **(2) (Trakiyska Nizina)** the part of BULGARIA north of the RHODOPE MOUNTAINS, which became known as Eastern Rumelia and was ceded from the Ottoman Empire in 1885. **(3)**

(Thraki) a modern Greek region, sometimes called Western Thrace to distinquish it from the Turkish part, which covers 8578 sq km (3312 sq miles) and has a population of 345,200 **(4)** Turkish, or Eastern, Thrace corresponds to European Turkey, covers 23,973 sq km (9256 sq miles) and has a population of 4,325,300.

Thule (Qaanaaq) the northernmost settlement on GREEN-LAND, lying on the northwest coast, some 1530 km (950 miles) from the NORTH POLE. It is the site of an airport, a weather station and a large US military base. (Pop.800)

Thunder Bay a port in western ONTARIO, CANADA, at the western end of Lake SUPERIOR, created in 1970 by the amalgamation of Port Arthur and Fort William. (Pop. 121,380)

Thuringia (Thüringen) one of the 16 *Länder* (states) of GERMANY, lying in the east-central part of the country; it was reinstated after reunification in 1990. It is centred on its chief town, ERFURT. (16,251 sq km/6275 sq miles; pop. 2,500,000)

Tian Shan (Tien Shan) a major mountain range on the northwestern flank of the TARIM basin in Central ASIA, and on the border of KYRGYZSTAN and north-western CHINA, where it rises to 7439 m (24,406 ft).

Tianjin (Tientsin) a major industrial city in HEBEI province, the third largest city in CHINA after SHANGHAI and BEIJING. (Pop. 7,390,000)

Tiber (Tevere), River a river of central ITALY, rising to the east of FLORENCE and flowing south to ROME and then to the MEDITERRANEAN SEA. (Length 405 km/252 miles)

Tibet (Xizang Autonomous Region) a region of south-west CHINA, consisting of a huge plateau high in the HIMALAYAS. Formerly a Buddhist kingdom led by its spiritual leader, the Dalai Lama, it was invaded by China in 1950 and has been gradually desecrated. (1,221,600 sq km/471,660 sq miles; pop. 1,893,000)

Tibetan Plateau (Xizang Gaoyuan) the biggest and highest plateau in the world, a vast, largely uninhabited, highland region of extremely harsh climatic conditions, with temperatures rarely rising above freezing. (1,760,000 sq km/679,500 sq miles; average height 4000 m/15,000 ft above sea level)

Tientsin *see* **Tianjin.**

Tierra del Fuego the archipelago at the southern tip of South AMERICA, belonging to ARGENTINA and CHILE and separated from the mainland by the Strait of MAGELLAN.

Tigrey (Tigray; Tigre) a province of northern ETHIOPIA, bordering ERITREA, whose people have been fighting a separatist war against the central government. The capital is Mekele. (Pop. 2,045,000)

Tigris, River a major river of the MIDDLE EAST, rising in eastern TURKEY, flowing through SYRIA and IRAQ and joining the EUPHRATES to form a delta at the SHATT AL ARAB waterway as it enters The GULF. (Length 1900 km/1180 miles)

Tijuana a border city and resort in northwest MEXICO, at the northern end of the BAJA CALIFORNIA. (Pop. 567,000)

Timbuktu (Tombouctou) a town in central MALI at the edge of the SAHARA DESERT. (Pop. 20,000)

Timisoara an industrial city in southwest ROMANIA. (Pop. 288,000)

Timor an island at the eastern end of the LESSER SUNDA ISLANDS, INDONESIA. The eastern half of the island was a possession of PORTUGAL, but was annexed in 1975 by Indonesia. (30,775 sq km/11,883 sq miles; pop. 3,085,000)

Timor Sea the arm of the INDIAN OCEAN between the northwest coast of AUSTRALIA and the island of TIMOR.

Tipperary a county in the south of the Republic of IRELAND. It includes the town of Tipperary, but Clonmel is the county town. (4255 sq km/1643 sq miles; pop. 135,000)

Tiranë (Tirana) the largest city and the capital of ALBANIA, in the centre of the country. (Pop. 220,000)

Tiree a low-lying island of the Inner HEBRIDES, situated 3 km (2 miles) southwest of COLL, off the west coast of

SCOTLAND. (78 sq km/30 sq miles; pop. 761)

Tirgu Mures an industrial town and Hungarian-speaking cultural centre in northern TRANSYLVANIA, ROMANIA (Pop. 138,000)

Tirol *see* **Tyrol**.

Tiruchiràppalli (Trichinopoly) an industrial city in central TAMIL NADU in southern INDIA. (Pop. 609,500)

Titicaca, Lake the largest lake in South AMERICA, in the ANDES, on the border between BOLIVIA and PERU. (8135 sq km/3141 sq miles)

Titograd a postwar new town and capital of MONTENEGRO, lying 20km (12 miles) north of Lake SHKODËR. It was named in 1946 after the former Yugoslavian Leader, Marshal Tito (1892-1980).

Tobago an island to the northeast of TRINIDAD, forming part of the republic of TRINIDAD and TOBAGO. (Pop. 40,000)

Togo is a tiny country with a narrow coastal plain on the Gulf of GUINEA in West AFRICA. Grassy plains in the north and south are separated by the Togo Highlands, which run from southwest to northeast and rise to nearly 1000 m (3281 ft). High plateaux, mainly in the more southerly ranges, are heavily forested with teak, mahogany and bamboo. Over 80% of the population are involved in agriculture with yams and millet as the principal crops. Coffee, cocoa and cotton are grown for cash. Minerals, especially phosphates, are now the main export earners. Togo's exports are suffering from the recession in its major markets in Western EUROPE.

Area : 56,785 sq km (21,925 sq miles)

Population : 3,400,000

Capital : Lomé

Form of government : Republic

Religions : Animism, RC, Sunni Islam

Currency : Franc CFA

Tokelau an island group in the South PACIFIC composed of three atolls, which in 1948 was included in the territorial boundaries of NEW ZEALAND. (11 sq km/4 sq miles; pop. 1600)

Tokyo the capital of JAPAN, a port on the east coast of HONSHU Island. Its original name was Edo (until 1868). (Pop. city 8,353,700/Greater Tokyo 11,680,000)

Toledo (1) a historic city of central SPAIN, on the River TAGUS. (Pop. 60,100). **(2)** a city and GREAT LAKE port in OHIO, USA. (Pop. city 343,900/metropolitan area 610,800)

Tomsk an industrial Siberian city on the OB' river in the central RUSSIAN FEDERATION. (Pop. 467,000)

Tonga is situated about 20° south of the Equator and just west of the International Date Line in the PACIFIC OCEAN. It comprises over 170 islands and only about one-fifth of them are inhabited. It comprises a low limestone chain of islands in the east and a higher volcanic chain in the west. The climate is warm with heavy rainfall. The government owns all the land, and males can rent an allotment for growing food. Yams, cassava and taro are grown as subsistence crops, and fish from the sea supplements their diet. Bananas and coconuts are grown for export. The main industry is coconut processing.

Area : 750 sq km (290 sq miles)
Population : 95,200
Capital : Nuku'alofa
Form of government : Constitutional Monarchy
Religions : Methodism, RC
Currency : Pa'anga

Tongking (Tonkin) *see* **Mien Bac.**

Tonle Sap a lake in central CAMBODIA which swells and quadruples in size when the River MEKONG floods. (In flood 10,400 sq km/4000 sq miles)

Topeka the state capital of KANSAS, USA. (Pop. city 119,000/metropolitan area 159,000)

Torbay a popular resort on the south DEVON coast, in southwest ENGLAND. It was created in 1968 by the merger of Torquay and two neighbouring coastal towns. (Pop. 115,582)

Torino *see* **Turin.**

Toronto the largest city of CANADA, and the capital of

ONTARIO, situated on Lake Ontario. (Pop. 2,999,000)

Torres Strait the strait which separates the northeastern tip of AUSTRALIA from NEW GUINEA.

Tortola the main island of the British VIRGIN ISLANDS.

Toscana *see* **Tuscany.**

Toulon a major naval base and port in southeast FRANCE, on the MEDITERRANEAN. (Pop. 418,000)

Toulouse a city of southwest FRANCE, on the GARONNE River. (Pop. 551,000)

Touraine a former province of northwest FRANCE, around TOURS.

Tourane *see* **Da Nang**.

Tourcoing *see* **Lille-Roubaix-Tourcoing**.

Tours a town in western FRANCE, on the River LOIRE. (Pop. 268,000)

Townsville the administrative, commericial and industrial capital and chief port of northern QUEENSLAND. lying on the CORAL SEA coast some 1125 km (700 miles) northwest of BRISBANE. (Pop. 86,100)

Trabzon (Trebizond) a port on the BLACK SEA in northeastern TURKEY. (Pop. 156,000)

Trafalgar, Cape the southwestern tip of SPAIN; the waters off the Cape were the scene of a decisive British naval victory over the French in 1805, during which Admiral Lord Nelson was killed.

Trans Amazonian Highway a postwar network of roads stretching some 4800 km (3000 miles) across north-central BRAZIL; it was developed to open up the interior of the vast AMAZON river basin.

Transantarctic Mountains a vast range that splits ANTARCTICA into its western and eastern regions by extending 3200 km (2000 miles) from Victoria Land to the WEDDELL SEA, reaching a height of over 4500 m (14,750 ft)

Trans-Canada Highway the world's longest national road, running for a total of 8000 km (5000 miles) from St JOHN'S, NEWFOUNDLAND, in the east to VICTORIA, BRITISH COLUMBIA, in the west. It was completed in 1962.

Transcaucasia the region that straddles the CAUCASUS and the boundary between ASIA and EUROPE, stretching from the BLACK SEA to the CASPIAN SEA. It includes the countries of ARMENIA, AZERBAIJAN, GEORGIA, and the extreme southern European part of the RUSSIAN FEDERATION.

Trans Siberian Railway the world's longest railway line, extending over 9300 km (5780 miles) from MOSCOW to the PACIFIC ports of VLADIVOSTOK and NAKHODKA in the far east of the RUSSIAN FEDERATION. The main Siberian link was built between 1891 and 1905. A 3200-km (2000-mile) nothern extension to Sovetskaya Gavan was opened up in 1984.

Transkei a Bantu homeland in eastern CAPE PROVINCE, SOUTH AFRICA, declared independent by South Africa in 1976. The capital is Umtata. (41,000 sq km/15,831 sq miles; pop. 3,300,000)

Transvaal a province of northern SOUTH AFRICA. The capital is PRETORIA. (Pop. 8,950,500)

Transylvania a region of central and northwestern ROMANIA.

Transylvanian Alps (Carpatii Meridionali) a mountain range in southern ROMANIA that is the southwestern sweep of the CARPATHIANS; the highest peak is Mount Negoiu, at 2548 m (8360 ft).

Trebizond *see* **Trabzon.**

Trent, River is the main river of the MIDLANDS of ENGLAND, flowing northeast from Staffordshire to the HUMBER. (Length 270 km/170 miles)

Trentino-Alto Adige a mountainous region in the ALPS of northern ITLAY, including South Tyrol, which was ceded from AUSTRIA in 1919, and now forms the provinces of BOLZANO and Trento. (13,613 sq km/5256 sq miles; pop. 877,800)

Trenton a city in eastern USA on the Delaware River in western NEW JERSEY, of which it is the capital. British troops were defeated here (1776) during The American

War of Independence. (Pop. 92,124)

Trichinopoly *see* **Tiruchiràppalli.**

Trieste a port on the ADRIATIC SEA in northeast ITALY, close to the border with SLOVENIA. (Pop. 251,000)

Trinidad and Tobago form the third largest British Commonwealth country in the WEST INDIES and are situated off the ORINOCO Delta in northeastern VENEZUELA. The islands are the most southerly of the Lesser ANTILLES. Trinidad consists of a mountainous Northern Range in the north and undulating plains in the south. Tobago is more mountainous. The climate is tropical with little variation in temperatures throughout the year and a rainy season from June to December. Trinidad is one of the oldest oil-producing countries in the world. Output is small but provides 90% of Trinidad's exports. Sugar, coffee and cocoa are grown for export, but imports of food now account for 10% of total imports. Tobago depends mainly on tourism to make a living.

Area : 5130 sq km (1981 sq miles)

Population : 1,240,000

Capital : Port-of-Spain

Form of government : Republic

Religions : RC, Hinduism, Anglicanism, Sunni Islam

Currency : Trinidad and Tobago dollar

Tripoli (Tarabulus) (1) the capital and main port of LIBYA, in the northwest. (Pop. 620,000). **(2)** a port in northern LEBANON. (Pop. 175,000)

Tripolitania the smallest but most productive of LIBYA's three historical regions, lying along the MEDITERRANEAN coastal plain in the western part of the country; it supports 75 per cent of the population (*c.*3,200,000).

Tristan da Cunha a group of four remote, volcanic islands in the middle of the South ATLANTIC OCEAN, which form part of the ST HELENA DEPENDENCIES. (100 sq km/40 sq miles; pop. 325)

Trivandrum a port on the southern tip of INDIA, and the state capital of KERALA. (Pop. 520,000)

Trondheim the third largest city of NORWAY, after OSLO and BERGEN, and its old medieval capital. It is a major port, lying on the Tronheimsfjord in the central part of the country.

Trossachs a forested mountain lakeland area centring on Loch Katrine, 40km (25 miles) north of GLASGOW, SCOTLAND. Renowned for its scenic beauty, the area was made famous by the romantic description of the Scottish novelist, Sir Walter Scott (1771–1832).

Troy (Ilion; Ilium) the site at the southern end of the DARDANELLES, in north-west Anatolian TURKEY, of nine ancient cities, each of which was built on the ruins of its predecessor. The seventh was the scene of the Trojan War (13th century BC) on which the famous "Wooden Horse" story in Homer's epic poem, the *Iliad,* was based.

Trujillo a city and provincial capital in northwest PERU. (Pop.750,000)

Tsana, Lake *see* **Tana, Lake.**

Tsushima Strait *see* **Korea Strait.**

Tuamotu Archipelago a group of about 80 coral islands, extending over more than 1250 km (800 miles) in the south-east PACIFIC OCEAN, lying in FRENCH POLYNESIA, to the east and north-east of TAHITI. (land area 860 sq km/ 332 sq miles; pop. 8537)

Tubuai Islands a chain of small islands stretching over about 1400 km (850 miles) in the south-east PACIFIC OCEAN, lying in FRENCH POLYNESIA to the south of TAHITI. They were discovered by Captain Cook in 1777 and annexed by FRANCE in 1860. (Land area 173 sq km/67 sq miles; pop. 5208)

Tucson a city in southern ARIZONA, USA. (Pop. city 365,400/ metropolitan area 594,800)

Tulsa a city in northeastern OKLAHOMA, on the ARKANSAS River. (Pop. 375,000/metropolitan area 725,000)

Tunis the capital and main port of TUNISIA. (Pop. 550,000)

Tunisia is a North African country which lies on the south coast of the MEDITERRANEAN SEA. It's bounded by ALGERIA to the west and LIBYA to the south. Northern Tunisia consists of hills, plains and valleys. Inland mountains separate the coastal zone from the central plains before the land drops down to an area of salt pans and the SAHARA DESERT. Climate ranges from warm temperate in the north, to desert in the south. 40% of the population are engaged in agriculture, producing wheat, barley, olives, tomatoes, dates and citrus fruits. The mainstay of Tunisia's modern economy, however, is oil from the Sahara, phosphates, and tourism on the Mediterranean coast.

Area : 163,610 sq km (63,170 sq miles)

Population : 7,750,000

Capital : Tunis

Other major cities : Sfax, Bizerta, Djerba

Form of government : Republic

Religion : Sunni Islam

Currency : Tunisian dinar

Turin (Torino) a major industrial town on the River Po, and the capital of the PIEDMONT region, in northwest ITALY. (Pop. 1,103,500)

Turkestan (Turkistan) an extensive region of Central ASIA between SIBERIA in the north and TIBET, INDIA, AFGHANISTAN and IRAN in the south. It is split into West Turkestan which includes TURKMENISTAN, UZBEKISTAN, KYRGYZSTAN, TAJIKISTAN and the southern part of KAZAKHSTAN, and East Turkestan consisting of the Chineses autonomous region of XINJIANG UYGUR.

Turkey with land on the continents of EUROPE and ASIA, Turkey forms a bridge between the two. It guards the sea passage between the MEDITERRANEAN and the BLACK SEA. Only 5% of its area, Thrace, is in Europe and the much larger area, known as ANATOLIA, is in Asia. European Turkey is fertile agricultural land with a Mediterranean climate. Asiatic Turkey is bordered to the north by the Pontine Mountains and to the south by the Taurus Mountains. The climate here ranges from Mediterranean to hot summers and bitterly cold winters in the central plains. Agriculture employs over half the workforce. Major crops are wheat, rice, tobacco and cotton. Manufacturing industry includes iron and steel, textiles, motor vehicles and Turkey's famous carpets. Hydroelectric power is supplied by the TIGRIS and EUPHRATES. Tourism is a fast-developing industry.

Area : 779,452 sq km (300,946 sq miles)

Population : 50,670,000

Capital : Ankara

Other major cities : Istanbul, Izmir, Adana, Bursa

Form of government : Republic

Religion : Sunni Islam

Currency : Turkish lira

Turkmenistan, a central Asian republic of the former USSR, declared itself a republic in 1991. It lies to the east of the CASPIAN SEA and borders IRAN and AFGHANISTAN to the south. Much of the west and central areas of Turkmenistan are covered by the sandy KARA KUM Desert. The east is a plateau, which is bordered by the AMUDAR'YA river. The climate is extremely dry, and most of the population live in oasis settlements near the rivers. Agriculture is intensive around the settlements and consists of growing cereals, fruit, cotton and rearing Karakul sheep. There are rich mineral deposits, especially natural gas. Silk, oil and sulphur are also produced.

Area : 488,100 sq km (186,400 sq miles)

Population : 3,600,000

Capital : Ashkhabad

Form of government : Republic

Religion : Sunni Islam

Currency : Rouble

Turks and Caicos Islands a British colony in the northeastern WEST INDIES consisting of some 14 main islands. The capital is Cockburn Town on Grand Turk. (430 sq km/166 sq miles; pop. 7400)

Turku (Åbo) a port in southwest FINLAND, on the Gulf of

BOTHNIA. (Pop. 161,400)

Tuscany (Toscana) a region of central western ITALY. The capital is FLORENCE. (Pop. 3,600,000)

Tuva Republic (Tuvinia) a mineral rich, but remote, autonomous republic of the RUSSIAN FEDERATION on the border of north-west MONGOLIA. The capital is Kyzyl. (170,500 sq km/65,800 sq miles; pop. 276,000)

Tuvalu is located just north of FIJI, in the South PACIFIC, and consists of nine coral atolls. The group was formerly known as the Ellice Islands, and the main island and capital is Funafuti. The climate is tropical with temperatures averaging 30°C and annual rainfall ranges from 3000–4000 mm (118–157 inches). Coconut palms are the main crop and fruit and vegetables are grown for local consumption. Sea fishing is extremely good and although largely unexploited licenses have been granted to JAPAN, TAIWAN and South KOREA to fish the local waters. Most export revenue comes from the sale of elabourate postage stamps to philatelists.

Area : 26 sq km (10 sq miles)

Population : 8229

Capital : Funafuti

Form of government : Constitutional Monarchy

Religion : Protestantism

Currency : Australian dollar

Tver an industrial city on the navigable part of the River VOLGA, RUSSIAN FEDERATION, 160 km (100 miles) northwest of MOSCOW. Founded in 1181, it was renamed Kalinin in 1932 after Mikhail Kalinin, the Soviet president 1937–46. Its name reverted to Tver in 1991. (Pop. 437,000)

Tyne and Wear a metropolitan county in northeast ENGLAND, created in 1974 out of parts of Durham and Northumberland. The administrative centre is SUNDERLAND. (540 sq km/208 sq miles; pop. 1,145,000)

Tyrol (Tirol) a province of western AUSTRIA, in the ALPS. The capital is Innsbruck. (Pop. 586,200)

Tyrone a county in the west of NORTHERN IRELAND. The county town is Omagh. (3266 sq km/1260 sq miles; pop. 160,000)

Tyrrhenian Sea a part of the MEDITERRANEAN SEA between SICILY, SARDINIA, and mainland ITALY.

Tyumen' a western Siberian town of the RUSSIAN FEDERATION, lying some 300 km (185 miels) east of YELATERINBURG. Founded in 1586 it was the first Russian town to be built east of the URALS. Today it is the industrial centre of a rich oil and natural gas producing region. (Pop. 411,000)

U

UAE *see* **United Arab Emirates.**

Ubangi, River one of the main tributaries of the ZAÏRE River, flowing 2250 km (1400 miles) westwards and southwards from its Uele headwaters in UGANDA to form the boundaries of ZAÏRE with the CENTRAL AFRICAN REPUBLIC and the CONGO.

Udaipur a historic city in southern RAJASTHAN, INDIA. (Pop. 233,000)

Udmurt Republic one of the 16 autonomous republics of the RUSSIAN FEDERATION, lying in the mid-Kama basin in the west-central part of the country. The capital is Izhevsk. (42,100 sq km/16,250 sq miles; pop. 1,529,000)

Ufa an industrial city and capital of BASHKIRIA, in the RUSSIAN FEDERATION. (Pop. 1,048,000)

Uganda is a landlocked country in east central AFRICA. The Equator runs through the south of the country, and for the most part it is a richly fertile land, well watered, with a kindly climate. In the west are the RUWENZORI Mountains, which rise to over 5000 m (16,405 ft) and are snow-capped. The lowlands around Lake VICTORIA, once forested, have now mostly been cleared for cultivation. Agriculture employs over three quarters of the labour force, and the main crops grown for subsistence are plantains, cassava and sweet potatoes. Coffee is the main cash crop and accounts for 90% of the county's exports. Attempts are being made to expand the tea plantations in the west, to develop a copper mine and to introduce new industries to KAMPALA, the capital.

Area : 235,880 sq km (91,073 sq miles)

Population : 17,000,000

Capital : Kampala
Other major cities : Jinja, Masaka, Mbale
Form of government : Republic
Religions : RC, Protestantism, Animism, Sunni Islam
Currency : Uganda shilling

Ujjain a major city of early Hindu civilization in north-central INDIA; it is one of the seven Hindu holy cities. (Pop. 282,200)

Ujung Padang a major port in the southwest of SULAWESI, INDONESIA. It was formerly known as Makassar. (Pop. 709,000)

Ujvidek *see* **Novi Sad.**

UK *see* **United Kingdom.**

Ukraine, formerly a Soviet socialist republic, declared itself independent of the former USSR in 1991. Its neighbours to the west are POLAND, SLOVAKIA, HUNGARY and ROMANIA, and it is bounded to the south by the BLACK SEA. To the east lies the RUSSIAN FEDERATION and to the north the republic of BELARUS. Drained by the DNEPR, DNESTR, Southern BUG and Donets rivers, Ukraine consists largely of fertile steppes. The climate is continental, although this is greatly modified by the proximity of the Black Sea. The Ukrainian steppe is one of the chief wheat-producing regions of Europe. Other major crops include corn, sugar beet, flax, tobacco, soya, hops and potatoes. There are rich reserves of coal and raw materials for industry. The central and eastern regions form one of the world's densest industrial concentrations. Manufacturing industries include ferrous metallurgy, machine building, chemicals, food processing, gas and oil refining.

Area : 603,700 sq km (233,100 sq miles)
Population : 51,700,000
Capital : Kiev
Other major cities : Dnepropetrovsk, Donetsk, Kharkov, Odessa
Form of government : Republic

United Arab Emirates

Religions : Russian Orthodox, RC

Currency : Rouble

Ul'yanovsk a city of the eastern URALS, in the RUSSIAN FEDERATION, on the River VOLGA. (Pop. 525,000)

Ulan Bator (Ulaanbaatar) the capital of MONGOLIA, in the central north of the country. (Pop. 440,000)

Ulan-Ude the capital of the BURYAT REPUBLIC, in the RUSSIAN FEDERATION. (Pop. 330,000).

Ulster one of the four ancient provinces into which IRELAND was divided, covering the north. It is often used to refer to NORTHERN IRELAND, but three counties of Ulster are in the Republic of Ireland (DONEGAL, MONAGHAN and CAVAN).

Umbria a land-locked region of central, eastern ITALY, bordering TUSCANY. (Pop. 816,000).

Umm al Qaywayn one of the seven UNITED ARAB EMIRATES, on The GULF. Its capital is also called Umm al Qaywaym. (518 sq km/200 sq miles; pop. emirate 14,000/town 3000)

Union of Soviet Socialist Republics (USSR; Soviet Union) the former superpower that was the world's largest state until its break-up in 1991, following the rapid decline in Communist power.

United Arab Emirates (UAE) the United Arab Emirates is a federation of seven oil-rich sheikdoms located in The GULF. As well as its main coast on the Gulf, the country has a short coast on the Gulf of OMAN. The land is mainly flat sandy desert except to the north on the peninsula where the Hajar Mountains rise to 2081 m (6828 ft). The summers are hot and humid with temperatures reaching 49°C, but from October to May the weather is warm and sunny with pleasant, cool evenings. The only fertile areas are the emirate of RAS AL KHAYMAH, the coastal plain of AL FUJAYRAH and the oases. ABU DHABI and DUBAI are the main industrial centers and, using their wealth from the oil industry, they are now diversifying industry by building aluminium smelters, cement factories and steel-rolling mills. Dubai is the richest state in the world.

Area : 83,600 sq km (32,278 sq miles)

Population : 1,600,000

Capital : Abu Dhabi

Other major cities : Dubai, Sharjh, Ras al Khaymah

Form of government : Monarchy (emirates)

Religion : Sunni Islam

Currency : Dirham

United Kingdom (UK) situated in northwest EUROPE, the United Kingdom of GREAT BRITAIN and NORTHERN IRELAND, comprises the island of Great Britain and the northeast of Ireland, plus many smaller islands, especially off the west coast of SCOTLAND. The south and east of Britain is low-lying, and the PENNINES form a backbone running through northern ENGLAND. Scotland has the largest area of upland, and WALES is a highland block. Northern Ireland has a few hilly areas. The climate is cool temperate with mild conditions and an even annual rainfall. The principal crops are wheat, barley, sugar beet, fodder crops and potatoes. Livestock includes cattle, sheep, pigs and poultry. Fishing is important off the east coast. The UK is primarily an industrial country, although the recent recession has left high unemployment and led to the decline of some of the older industries, such as coal, textiles and heavy engineering. A growing industry is electronics, much of it defence-related.

Area : 244,100 sq km (94,247 sq miles)

Population : 57,240,000

Capital : London

Other major cities : Birmingham, Manchester, Glasgow, Liverpool

Form of government : Constitutional Monarchy

Religion : Anglicanism, RC, Presbyterianism, Methodism

Currency : Pound sterling

United States of America (USA) stretches across cen-

tral north AMERICA, from the ATLANTIC OCEAN in the east
to the PACIFIC OCEAN in the west, and from CANADA in the
north to MEXICO and the Gulf of Mexico in the south. It
consists of fifty states, including outlying ALASKA, northwest of Canada, and HAWAII in the Pacific Ocean. The
climate varies a great deal in such a large country. In
Alaska there are polar conditions, and in the Gulf coast
and in Florida conditions may be subtropical. Although
agricultural production is high, it employs only 1.5% of
the population because primarily of its advanced technology. The USA is a world leader in oil production. The
main industries are iron and steel, chemicals, motor
vehicles, aircraft, telecommunications equipment, com-
puters, electronics and textiles. The USA is the richest
and most powerful nation in the world.

Area : 9,372,614 sq km (3,618,766 sq miles)

Population : 249,630,000

Capital : Washington D.C.

Other major cities : New York, Chicago, Detroit,
Houston, Los Angeles, Philadelphia, San Diego, San
Francisco

Form of government : Federal Republic

Religion : Protestantism, RC, Judaism, Eastern
Orthodox

Currency : US dollar

Upper Austria (Oberösterreich) the hilly, well-forested
northern state of AUSTRIA, which is primarily agricultural. Its main towns are LINZ, its capital, and Steyr.
(11,978 sq km/4625 sq miles; pop. 1,270,426)

Upper Egypt an ancient kingdom based on that part of
EGYPT southwards, up the NILE, from CAIRO to the present-
day SUDAN border. Union with LOWER EGYPT in 3100BC
began 30 dynasties of Pharaohs who ruled all Egypt until
Greek conquest in 332BC.

Upper Volta *see* **Burkina.**

Uppsala an old university town in eastern central SWE-
DEN. (Pop. 154,000)

Ural Mountains (Urals, Uralskiy Khrebet) a mountain range in western RUSSIAN FEDERATION. Running north to south from the ARCTIC to the ARAL SEA, the Urals form the traditional dividing line between EUROPE and ASIA. The highest point is Mount Narodnaya (1894 m/ 3500 ft).

Uruguay is one of the smallest countries in South AMERICA. It lies on the east coast of the continent, to the south of BRAZIL, and is bordered to the west by the Uruguay river, Rio de la Plata to the south, and the ATLANTIC OCEAN to the east. The country consists of low plains and plateaux. In the southeast, hills rise to 500 m (1641 ft). About 90% of the land is suitable for agriculture but only 10% is cultivated, the remainder being used to graze vast herds of cattle and sheep. The cultivated land is made up of vineyards, rice fields and groves of olives and citrus fruits. Uruguay has only one major city in which half the population live. The country has no mineral resources, oil or gas, but has built hydroelectric power stations at Palmar and Salto Grande.

Area : 177,414 sq km (68,500 sq miles)

Population : 3,100,000

Capital : Montevideo

Form of government : Republic

Religions : RC, Protestantism

Currency : Uruguayan nuevo peso

Ürümqi (Urumchi) the capital of the XINJIANG AUTONOMOUS REGION of northwest CHINA. (Pop. 1,200,000)

USA *see* **United States of America.**

USSR *see* **Union of Soviet Socialist Republics**.

US Virgin Islands *see* **Virgin Islands, US.**

Utah a state in the west of the USA. The state capital is SALT LAKE CITY. (212,628 sq km/82,096 sq miles; pop. 1,645,000)

Utrecht a historic city in the central NETHERLANDS. (Pop. city 231,000/Greater Utrecht 498,900)

Utsunomiya a modern industrial centre in east HONSHU

Island, JAPAN, some 95 km (60 miles) north of TOKYO. (Pop. 405,400)

Uttar Pradesh the most populous state of INDIA, in the north of the country. The capital is LUCKNOW. (294,364 sq km/113,654 sq miles; pop. 110,865,000)

Uummannarsuaq *see* **Farewell, Cape**.

Uzbekistan, a central Asian republic of the former USSR, declared itself independent in 1991. It lies between KAZAKHSTAN and TURKMENISTAN and encompasses the southern half of the ARAL SEA. The republic has many contrasting regions. The TIAN SHAN region is mountainous, the Fergana region is irrigated and fertile, the KYZLKUM Desert is rich in oil and gas, the lower Amudar'ya river region is irrigated and has oasis settlements, and the Usturt Plateau is a stony desert. Uzbekistan is a major cotton producer, and Karakul lambs are reared for wool and meat. Its main industrial products are agricultural machinery, textiles and chemicals.

Area : 449,500 sq km (173,546 sq miles)

Population : 20,300,000

Capital : Tashkent

Other major city : Samarkand

Form of government : Republic

Religion : Sunni Islam

Currency : Rouble

V

Vaal, River a major river of southern AFRICA, which rises in the DRAKENSBERG and flows some 1160 km (720 miles) westwards through SOUTH AFRICA, forming the boundary between TRANSVAAL and the ORANGE FREE STATE, and then across CAPE PROVINCE to join the ORANGE River near KIMBERLEY.

Vaasa (Vasa) an industrial town and seaport of west-central FINLAND, lying on the Gulf of BOTHNIA. It was the provisional national capital in 1918. (Pop. 54,400)

Vadodara (Baroda) an industrial city in southeast GUJARAT, INDIA. (Pop. 745,000)

Valencia (1) a port on the MEDITERRANEAN coast of SPAIN, and the capital of the province of the same name. (Pop. city 752,000). **(2)** An industrial city in northern VEN-EZUELA. (Pop. 540,000)

Valenciennes a former lace-making, now metal-manu-facturing, town in norther FRANCE, close to the Belgian border. (Pop. 350,600)

Valladolid an industrial city in northwest SPAIN. (Pop. city 330,200)

Valle d'Aosta a French-speaking region of northwest ITALY. The capital is AOSTA. (Pop. 114,000)

Valletta the capital of MALTA. (Pop. 14,000)

Valparaíso the main port of CHILE, in the centre of the country. (Pop. 267,000)

Van, Lake a salt lake in eastern TURKEY. (3675 sq km/1419 sq miles)

Vancouver a major port and industrial centre in south-east BRITISH COLUMBIA, CANADA, on the mainland opposite

VANCOUVER ISLAND with access to the Pacific Ocean. (Pop. 1,268,000)

Vancouver Island the largest island off the PACIFIC coast of North AMERICA, in southwest CANADA. The capital is VICTORIA. (32,137 sq km/12,408 sq miles; pop. 390,000)

Vänern the largest lake of SWEDEN, lying in the southwest of the country. (5586 sq km/2157 sq miles)

Vanuatu, formerly known as the New Hebrides, is located in the western PACIFIC, southeast of the SOLOMON ISLANDS and about 1750 km (1087 miles) east of AUSTRALIA. About eighty islands make up the group. Some of the islands are mountainous and include active volcanoes. The largest islands are Espírtu Santo, Malekula and Efate, on which the capital Vila is sited. Vanuatu has a tropical climate which is moderated by the southeast trade winds from May to October. The majority of the labour force are engaged in subsistence farming, and the main exports include copra, fish and cocoa. Tourism is becoming an important industry.

Area : 12,189 sq km (4706 sq miles)

Population : 142,630

Capital : Vila

Form of government : Republic

Religion : Protestantism, Animism

Currency : Vatu

Varanasi (Benares) a holy Hindu city on the banks of the River GANGES in UTTAR PRADESH, northeastern INDIA. (Pop. 798,000)

Vatican City State lies in the heart of ROME on a low hill on the west bank of the river TIBER. It is the world's smallest independent state and headquarters of the Roman Catholic Church. It is a walled city made up of the Vatican Palace, the Papal Gardens, St Peter's Square and St Peter's Basilica. The state has its own police, newspaper, coinage, stamps and radio station. The radio station, "Radio Vaticana," broadcasts a service in thirty-four languages from transmitters within the Vatican

City. Its main tourist attractions are the frescoes of the Sistine Chapel, painted by Michelangelo Buonarroti (1475–1564). The Pope exercises sovereignty and has absolute legislative, executive and judicial powers.

Area : 44 hectares (108.7 acres)

Population : 1000

Capital : Vatican City (Citta del Vaticano)

Form of government : Papal Commission

Religion : RC

Currency : Vatican City lira

Vatnajökull the largest ice sheet in the Northern Hemisphere outside GREENLAND. Lying in southeast ICELAND, parts of it are more than 2000 m (6560 ft) high, with the thickness of the ice nearly 1000 m (3280 ft) in places. (8538 sq km/3296 sq miles)

Veglia *see* **Krk.**

Venda a two-part Bantu homeland in northeastern TRANSVAAL that was declared independent by the South African government in 1979. The capital is Thohoyandou. (6500 sq km/2510 sq miles; pop. 435,000)

Veneto a region of northeastern ITALY, centring upon VENICE. (Pop. 4,367,000)

Venezia *see* **Venice.**

Venezuela forms the northernmost crest of South AMERICA. Its northern coast lies along the CARIBBEAN SEA and it is bounded to the west by COLUMBIA and to the southeast and south by GUYANA and BRAZIL. In the northwest a spur of the ANDES runs southwest to northeast. The river ORINOCO cuts the country in two, and north of the river run the undulating plains known as the Llanos. South of the river are the Guiana Highlands. The climate ranges from warm temperate to tropical. Temperatures vary little throughout the year and rainfall is plentiful. In the Llanos area cattle are herded across the plains, and this region makes the country almost self-sufficient in meat. Sugar cane and coffee are grown for export but petroleum and gas account for 95% of export earnings. The oil fields lie in the north-west near LAKE MARACAIBO, where there are over 10,000 oil derricks.

Area : 912,050 sq km (352,143 sq miles)

Population : 9,250,000

Capital : Caracas

Other major cities : Maracaibo, Valencia, Barquisimeto

Form of government : Federal Republic

Religion : RC

Currency : Bolívar

Venice (Venezia) a historic port built on islands at the head of the ADRIATIC SEA in northeastern ITALY. The principal thoroughfares are canals. (Pop. 346,000)

Ventiane (Viangchan) the capital of LAOS, on the River MEKONG in the north-east of the country, near the border with THAILAND. (Pop. 177,000)

Verde, Cape (Cap Vert) the westernmost point of AFRICA, situated in SENEGAL on a peninsula between the GAMBIA and Senegal Rivers.

Verdun a fortified town, lying on the Meuse river in northeast FRANCE; it was the scene of the longest and most severe battle (1916) of World War I, in which the French repelled a major German offensive. In AD843 a treaty was agreed here to divide up the Holy Roman Empire amongst three grandsons of Charlemagne.

Vermont a state in the northeast of the USA, bordering CANADA. The state capital is MONTPELIER. (24,887 sq km/ 9609 sq miles; pop. 535,000)

Verona a historic and industrial city in VENETO, northern ITALY. (Pop. 260,000)

Versailles a town just to the west of PARIS, FRANCE, which grew up around the palace built there by Louis XIV in the 1660s. (Pop. 96,000)

Vesterålen an island group in northern NORWAY, lying just northeast of the LOFOTEN Islands. The main port and capital is Harstad. (2400 sq km/927 sq miles; pop. 34,000)

Vesuvius an active volcano to the southeast of NAPLES, in southwest ITALY, notorious for having buried POMPEII in ash during an eruption in AD79. (1281 m/4203 ft)

Viangchan *see* **Vientiane.**

Victoria (1) a state in southeastern AUSTRALIA. The state capital is MELBOURNE. (227,620 sq km/87,884 sq miles; pop. 4,054,000). **(2)** a port on the southeastern coast of VANCOUVER ISLAND, southwest CANADA, and the capital of BRITISH COLUMBIA. (Pop. 233,000). **(3)** former port and capital of HONG KONG, in the northwest of Hong Kong Island. (Pop. 1,026,900) **(4)** the capital of the SEYCHELLES, on the island of Mahé. (Pop. 25,000)

Victoria Falls (Mosi-oa-Toenja) one of the greatest waterfalls in the world, where the River ZAMBEZI tumbles some 108 m (355 ft), on the border between ZAMBIA and ZIMBABWE. The local name for the falls means "the Smoke that Thunders" referring to the clouds of spray that soar 500 m (1600 ft) above the chasm. David Livingstone, the Scottish missionary and explorer, was the first European to see them in 1855.

Victoria, Lake the largest lake in AFRICA, and the second largest freshwater lake in the world after Lake SUPERIOR. Its shoreline is shared by UGANDA, KENYA and TANZANIA. (69,485 sq km/26,828 sq miles)

Vienna (Wien) the capital of AUSTRIA, on the River DANUBE, in the northeast of the country. (Pop. 1,531,000)

Vietnam is a long narrow country in southeast ASIA which runs down the coast of the SOUTH CHINA SEA. It has a narrow central area which links broader plains centered on the RED and MEKONG rivers. The narrow zone, now known as MIEN TRUNG, is hilly and makes communications between north and south difficult. The climate is humid with tropical conditions in the south and subtropical in the north. The far north can be very cold when polar air blows over Asia. Agriculture employs over three quarters of the labour force. The main crop is rice but cassava, maize and sweet potatoes are also grown for domestic consumption. Rubber, tea and coffee are grown for export. Major industries are food processing, textiles, cement, cotton and silk manufacture. Vietnam, however, remains underdeveloped and is still recovering from the ravages of many wars this century.

Area : 331,689 sq km (128,065 sq miles)

Population : 65,000,000

Capital : Hanoi

Other major cities : Ho Chi Minh City, Haiphong

Form of government : Socialist Republic

Religion : Buddhism, Taoism, RC

Currency : Dong

Vijayawanda a city at the head of the KRISHNA River delta in southeast INDIA; it is the focus of an ancient working irrigation-canal system. (Pop. 543,000)

Villahermosa a major oil town in the south of MEXICO, and capital of Tabasco state. (Pop. 250,900)

Villmanstrand *see* **Laappeeranta**.

Vilnius the capital of LITHUANIA. (Pop. 536,000)

Vinson Massif the highest peak in ANTARCTICA, rising to 5140 m (16,863 ft) at the southern end of the ANTARCTIC PENINSULA.

Virginia a state in the east of the USA, with a coast on the ATLANTIC OCEAN. The capital is RICHMOND (103,030 sq km/ 39,780 sq miles; pop. 5,706,000).

Virgin Islands, British a British Crown colony in the eastern CARIBBEAN, to the east of PUERTO RICO. The British islands are in the east of the Virgin Island group. Sixteen of the islands are inhabited, including Virgin Gorda and TORTOLA, the site of the capital, ROAD TOWN. (103 sq km/ 50 sq miles; pop. 12,000)

Virgin Islands, US a territory of the USA in the eastern CARIBBEAN, to the east of PUERTO RICO. The US islands are in the west and south of the Virgin Island group. The main islands are ST JOHN, ST CROIX and ST THOMAS, the site of the capital, CHARLOTTE AMALIE. (344 sq km/133 sq miles; pop. 100,000)

Visayan Islands a group of islands in the center of the PHILIPPINES, which includes NEGROS, CEBU, Leyte, Masbate,

Bohol, Panay and Samar.

Vistula, River a river of central and northern POLAND, flowing northwards through CRACOW and WARSAW to the BALTIC SEA. (Length 1090 km/677 miles)

Vitoria a historic BASQUE town, and capital of the Álava province, about 60km (35 miles) southeast of the Bay of BISCAY port of BILBAO. (Pop. 192,800)

Vlaanderen *see* **Flanders.**

Vladimir a tourist city in the RUSSIAN FEDERATION, lying about 160km (100 miles) east of MOSCOW; it is famed for its fine kremlin, its fortified Golden Gate. and its two 12th-century cathedrals. (Pop. 326,000)

Vladivostok a major port on the Pacific coast in the far east of the RUSSIAN FEDERATION, 50 km (30 miles) from the border with CHINA. (Pop. 590,000)

Vlissingen *see* **Flushing.**

Vojvodina an autonomous province in the north of SERBIA. The capital is NOVI SAD. (21,506 sq km/8301 sq miles; pop. 2,035,000)

Volcano Islands *see* **Kazan-rettó**.

Volga, River a largely navigable river of western RUSSIAN FEDERATION, flowing south from its source, to the northeast of MOSCOW, to the CASPIAN SEA. It is the longest river in EUROPE. (Length 3690 km/2293 miles)

Volgograd a port and major industrial city on the River VOLGA. It was called Stalingrad from 1925 to 1961; it was the site of a critical World War II battle in 1942 when the Russians beat back the advancing German armies. (Pop. 990,000)

Volta, Lake a major artificial lake that occupies much of eastern GHANA, formed by the damming of the Volta River. (8480 sq km/3251 sq miles)

Volta, River a river in GHANA, fed by the Black Volta and the White Volta, which flows south to the Bight of BENIN. It was dammed to form Lake VOLTA. (Length, including lake, 480 km/298 miles)

Voralberg the smallest and most westerly state of AUS-

TRIA, noted for its spectacular Alpine scenery, which attracts an active tourist trade. The capital is Bregenz (2601 sq km/1004 sq miles; pop. 307,900)

Voronezh an industrial city 450 km (280 miles) south of Moscow, Russian Federation. (Pop. 842,000)

Voroshilovgrad *see* **Lugansk**.

Vosges a range of block mountains on the western French side of the Rhine valley, opposite their counterpart block of the Black Forest to the east in Germany

W

Wadi Halfa an important communications town in north-central SUDAN, on the border with EGYPT. It lies at the southern end, and was partly submerged by the creation, of Lake NASSER; ferries connect Sudan's road and rail system with Egypt's at ASWAN.

Wahran *see* **Oran.**

Waikato, River the longest river in NEW ZEALAND, flowing northwest from the centre of North Island to the TASMAN SEA. (Length 350 km/220 miles)

Waikiki Beach a popular surfing resort area on south-eastern OAHU, near HONOLULU, in HAWAII, USA.

Wales a principality in the southwest of GREAT BRITAIN, forming a part of the UK CARDIFF is the capital. (20,768 sq km/8017 sq miles; pop. 2,749,600)

Wallis and Fortuna Islands three small islands forming an overseas territory of FRANCE in the southwest PACIFIC, to the northeast of FIJI. The capital is Mata-Utu. (367 sq km/143 sq miles; pop. 13,500)

Walvis Bay a small enclave port, midway along the coast of NAMIBIA, that is part of SOUTH AFRICA, although administered as Namibia's main outlet.

Wanke *see* **Hwange**.

Warsaw (Warszawa) the capital of POLAND, on the River VISTULA, in the eastern central part of the country. (Pop. 1,641,000)

Warwickshire a county of central ENGLAND. The county town is Warwick. (1981 sq km/765 sq miles; pop. 475,000)

Wash, The a shallow inlet formed by the NORTH SEA in the coast of East Anglia, between the counties of LINCOLN-SHIRE and NORFOLK.

Washington a state in the northwest of the USA, on the border with CANADA, and with a coast on the PACIFIC. The capital is OLYMPIA. (172,416 sq km/66,570 sq miles; pop. 4,409,000)

Washington D.C. the capital of the USA, on the Potomac River. It stands in its own territory, called the District of Columbia (D.C.), between the states of VIRGINIA and MARYLAND, close to the ATLANTIC coast. (179 sq km/69 sq miles; pop. city 622,800/metropolitan area 3,429,400)

Waterford a county in the south of the Republic of IRELAND. The county town is also called Waterford. (1838 sq km/710 sq miles; pop. county 89,000)

Waterloo a town in central BELGIUM, 16 km (10 miles) south of BRUSSELS, which commemorates the great battle of Waterloo in 1815, when the French emperor Napoleon was decisively defeated by the British under the Duke of Wellington, with crucial support from the Prussians.

Weald, The a rich agricultural region, formerly forested, that lies in southeastern ENGLAND between the North and South DOWNS.

Weddell Sea an arm of the South ATLANTIC OCEAN, lying in the sweep of the ANTARCTIC PENINSULA. (800,000 sq km/308,880 sq miles)

Weimar a historic city in southern central GERMANY. (Pop. 65,000)

Wellington the capital of NEW ZEALAND and a port in the south-west of North Island. (Pop. 342,000)

Weser, River a river in the northwest of GERMANY, flowing through BREMEN and BREMERHAVEN to the NORTH SEA. (477 sq km/196 sq miles)

Wessex a historic Anglo-Saxon region of south and southwestern ENGLAND, which had become the most powerful English kingdom by the 10th century. Thomas Hardy (1840-1928) used the name to cover DORSET, the setting for his works.

West Bank a piece of disputed territory to the west of the River JORDAN, including a part of JERUSALEM, which was taken by Israel from Jordan in the Arab-Israeli war of 1967, and has been occupied by Israel since then. New Israeli settlements here have incited growing resentment among the Palestinian population. (5858 sq km/2262 sq miles)

West Bengal a state in eastern India, bordering Bangladesh. Calcutta is the capital. (88,752 sq km/34,258 sq miles; pop. 54,581,000)

West End, The a non-specific term used to describe that part of west-central London, England, containing the capital's main shopping and entertainment areas.

Western Australia a state occupying much of the western half of Australia. The capital is Perth. (2,527,636 sq km/975,920 sq miles; pop. 1,300,000)

Western Desert the northeastern part of the Sahara that lies within Egypt, west of the Nile River. Apart from the mountainous southwest area, it is generally low and undulating sand desert, with several extensive oases and wind-scoured depressions, as at Qattara.

Western Ghats a mountain range that provides the high west flank of the Deccan Plateau of southern India; it runs parallel to the Malabar Coast of the Arabian Sea, and rises to its highest peak, Anai Mudi, 2695 m (8841 ft).

Western Isles the regional island authority covering the Outer Hebrides of western Scotland. The administrative centre is Stornaway, on the Isle of Lewis. (2900 sq km/1120 sq miles; pop. 32,000)

Western Sahara a disputed territory of western Africa, with a coastline on the Atlantic Ocean. Consisting mainly of desert, it is rich in phosphates. It was a Spanish overseas province until 1975 and is now claimed by Morocco, against the wishes of an active separatist movement. The main town is Laâyoune (El Aaiún). (266,770 sq km/103,000 sq miles; pop. 200,000)

Western Samoa lies in the Polynesian sector of the Pacific Ocean, about 720 km (447 miles) northeast of Fiji.

It consists of seven small islands and two larger volcanic islands, Savai'i and Upolu. Savai'i is largely covered with volcanic peaks and lava plateaux. Upolu is home to two-thirds of the population and the capital APIA. The climate is tropical with high temperatures and very heavy rainfall. The islands have been fought over by the Dutch, British, Germans and Americans, but they now have the lifestyle of traditional Polynesians. Subsistence agriculture is the main activity, and copra, cocoa and bananas are the main exports. Many tourists visit the grave of the Scottish writer Robert Louis Stevenson (1850–94) who died here and whose home is now the official home of the king.

Area : 2831 sq km (1093 sq miles)

Population : 163,000

Capital : Apia

Form of government : Constitutional Monarchy

Religion : Protestantism

Currency : Tala

West Flanders *see* **Flanders**.

West Glamorgan a county in South WALES, created in 1974 from part of Glamorgan and the borough of SWANSEA, with Swansea as the administrative centre. (817 sq km/315 sq miles; pop. 368,000)

West Indies a general term for the islands of the CARIBBEAN SEA.

West Lothian *see* **Lothian**.

Westmeath a county in the central north of the Republic of IRELAND. The county town is Mullingar. (1764 sq km/681 sq miles; pop. 61,500)

West Midlands a metropolitan county of central ENGLAND, created in 1974, with its administrative centre in BIRMINGHAM. (889 sq km/347 sq miles; pop. 2,658,000)

West Siberian Plain *see* **Siberia**.

West Sussex a county in southeast ENGLAND, comprising the western part of the former county of SUSSEX; the main administrative centre is CHICHESTER. (1989 sq km/768 sq miles; pop. 658,562)

West Virginia a state of eastern USA. The capital is CHARLESTON. (62,341 sq km/24,070 sq miles; pop. 1,936,000)

West Yorkshire a metropolitan county of northern ENGLAND which includes the heavily populated and industrialized districts of BRADFORD, LEEDS, Calderdale, Kirklees and Wakefield, the last being the chief administrative centre. (2039 sq km/787 sq miles; pop. 2,037,510)

Wexford a county in the south-east of the Republic of IRELAND. The county town is also called Wexford. (2352 sq km/908 sq miles; pop. county 13,293)

Whitehorse the capital of YUKON TERRITORY, lying at the upper limit of navigation on the Yukon River and just over 80km (50 miles) north of the border with BRITISH COLUMBIA. (Pop. 14,800)

White Sea an arm of the BARENTS SEA off the northwest of the RUSSIAN FEDERATION, which is almost enclosed by the bulge of the KOLA peninsula.

Whitney, Mount a mountain in the Sequoia National Park in eastern CALIFORNIA, with the highest peak in the USA outside ALASKA. (4418 m/14,495 ft)

Wichita a city in southern KANSAS, USA, on the ARKANSAS River. (Pop. city 283,500/metropolitan area 428,600)

Wicklow a county in the southwest of the Republic of IRELAND. The county town is also called Wicklow. (2025 sq km/782 sq miles; pop. county 87,000)

Wien *see* **Vienna.**

Wiesbaden an old spa town in western GERMANY, and capital of the state of HESSEN. (Pop. 272,000)

Wight, Isle of an island and county off the south coast of ENGLAND, separated from the mainland by the SOLENT. Famous for its chalk cliffs, especially The Needles, a line of white chalk stacks off the western tip. The county town is Newport. (380 sq km/147 sq miles; pop. 120,000)

Wiltshire a county in central southern ENGLAND. The county town is Trowbridge. (3481 sq km/1344 sq miles; pop. 510,000)

Winchester a historic city in southern ENGLAND, and the county town of HAMPSHIRE. (Pop. 31,000)

Windermere the largest lake in ENGLAND, and a town beside it, in the LAKE DISTRICT in the northwest of the country. (Lake length 17 km/10.5 miles)

Windhoek the capital and main industrial centre of NAMIBIA, lying at the heart of the country, surrounded by the Auas Mountains. (Pop. 105,000)

Windsor (1) one of AUSTRALIA's oldest settlements, founded in 1810, some 50 km (30 miles) northwest of SYDNEY. (Pop. 15,400) **(2)** an industrial city in the extreme south of CANADA, across the US border from DETROIT. (Pop.246,110). **(3)** a royal English town on the THAMES, west of LONDON, with its famous castle. (Pop. 31,000)

Windward Islands *see* **Leeward and Windward Islands.**

Winnipeg the capital of MANITOBA, CANADA, in the south of the state. (Pop. 585,000)

Winnipeg, Lake a lake in the south of MANITOBA, CANADA, which drains into HUDSON BAY via the Nelson River. (23,553 sq km/9094 sq miles)

Winterthur an industrial town in northeastern SWITZERLAND; it manufactures locomotives and textiles. (Pop. 90,000)

Wirral a peninsula in northwest ENGLAND, lying between the estuaries of the MERSEY and Dee Rivers.

Wisconsin a state in the north central USA, bordering Lake SUPERIOR and Lake MICHIGAN. The state capital is MADISON. (141,061 sq km/54,464 sq miles; pop. 4,775,000)

Witwatersrand (The Rand) a major gold-mining and industrial area of south TRANSVAAL, SOUTH AFRICA.

Wollongong a major port and industrial centre in NEW SOUTH WALES, AUSTRALIA, 80 km (50 miles) south of SYDNEY. (Pop. 235,000)

Wolverhampton an old industrial town in the WEST MIDLANDS of ENGLAND. (Pop. 255,000)

Woomera a small town in the interior of SOUTH AUSTRALIA, near to which is the space communications station operated jointly by Australia and the US. (Pop. 4100)

Worcestershire *see* **Hereford and Worcester.**

Wrangel Island (Ostrova Vrangelya) an isolated ARCTIC island off the coast of the extreme northeastern RUSSIAN FEDERATION, of which it is part. It is mountainous, snow-covered tundra, and home to many polar bears. (7300 sq km/2800 sq miles).

Wroclaw (Breslau) an industrial city on the River ODER in south-west POLAND. (Pop. 631,000)

Wuhan (Hankow) the capital of HUBEI province, southeast CHINA. (Pop. 3,885,000)

Wuppertal a textile-manufacturing city in northwestern GERMANY, famous for its overhead monorail system, developed prewar as the world's first. (Pop. 380,000)

Wuxi a silk and cotton textile centre in east-central CHINA, 120 km (75 miles) west of SHANGHAI. (Pop. 1,000,000)

Wyoming a state in the west of the USA. The state capital is CHEYENNE. (253,597 sq km/97,914 sq miles; pop. 509,000)

X

Xiamen (Amoy) a port on an island off the east coast of CHINA, in FUJIAN province. One of the first treaty ports opened to European trade (1842). (Pop. 1,006,000)

Xi'an (Sian) an ancient city and capital of SHAANXI province in east-central CHINA. It is renowned for the spectacular archaeological site of the "terracotta army" of some 7000 life-size figures discovered in 1974. (Pop. 2,020,000)

Xi Jiang (Si Kiang) the third longest river in CHINA, flowing across the southwest of the country from YUNNAN to its delta on the SOUTH CHINA SEA near GUANGZHOU (Canton). (Length 2300 km/1437 miles)

Xining an industrial city and the capital of QINGHAI province, in western CHINA. (Pop. 860,000)

Xinjiang (Sinkiang) Uygur Autonomous Region a region of northwest CHINA, bordering MONGOLIA, the RUSSIAN FEDERATION, AFGHANISTAN, PAKISTAN and INDIA. It is also known as Dzungaria. The capital is ÜRÜMQI. (1,646,799 sq km/635,829 sq miles; pop. 12,830,000)

Xizang Autonomous Region *see* **Tibet.**

Xizang Gaoyuan *see* **Tibetan Plateau.**

Y

Yakut Republic (Yakutia; Yakutsk) the largest of the 16 autonomous republics of the RUSSIAN FEDERATION, occupying a vast area (almost the size of Western EUROPE) in east-central SIBERIA, centred on the LENA river basin. It consists mainly of barren sub-ARCTIC plains, uplands and marshy coniferous forests. The climate is very severe, and it includes the world's coldest places, with temperatures below -60°C (-76°F). Herding reindeer and fur trapping are the main occupations. It is minerally rich and has 25 per cent of the world's diamonds—so far not fully exploited. The capital is Yakutsk. (3,103,200 sq km/ 1,198,150 sq miles; pop. republic 965,000/city 175,000)

Yamoussoukro the new capital of CÔTE D'IVOIRE, in the centre of the country. (Pop. 45,000)

Yamuna (Jumna), River a major river of north INDIA, a tributary of the GANGES. (Length 1376 km/855 miles)

Yangon *see* **Rangoon.**

Yangtze Kiang *see* **Chang Jiang.**

Yannina (Ioannina) the main town of the EPIRUS region of western GREECE, lying on a promontory in Lake Ioanminon at a height of 520 m (1708 ft) and overlooked by the PINDHOS MOUTAINS. (Pop. 44,800)

Yaoundé the capital of CAMEROON, in the southwest of the country. (Pop. 500,000)

Yaren the capital of NAURU. (Pop. 400)

Yaroslav *see* **Jaroslaw**.

Yaroslavl' an industrial city and river port on the VOLGA, about 240 km (150 miles) northeast of MOSCOW. (Pop. 623,000)

Yazd (Yezd) a Persian carpet-making and wool and silk

fabric-manufacturing town, lying on the edge of the SALT DESERT in central IRAN. (Pop. 193,000)

Yekaterinburg an industrial city to the east of the URAL MOUNTAINS, RUSSIAN FEDERATION. It was called Ekaterinburg before 1924 and Sverdlosk from 1924 to 1992. (Pop. 1,288,000)

Yellowknife a city on the GREAT SLAVE LAKE, CANADA, and capital of the NORTHWEST TERRITORIES. (Pop. 11,077)

Yellow River *see* **Huang He.**

Yellow Sea a branch of the PACIFIC OCEAN between the north-east coast of CHINA and the peninsula of KOREA.

Yellowstone an area mainly in the northwest corner of WYOMING, USA, that contains many unusual geological formations, thermal springs, mud pots, and over 200 geysers, including Old Faithful, which erupts regularly about every hour. It is the site of the oldest and largest National Park in the US, established in 1872.

Yemen is bounded by SAUDI ARABIA in the north, OMAN in the east, the Gulf of ADEN in the south, and the RED SEA in the west. The country was formed after the unification of the previous Yemen Arab Republic and the People's Democratic Republic of Yemen (South Yemen) in 1989. Most of the country comprises rugged mountains and trackless desert lands. The country is almost entirely dependent on agriculture even though a very small percentage is fertile. The main crops are coffee, cotton, millet, sorghum and fruit. Fishing is an important industry. Other industry is on a very small scale. There are textile factories, and plastic, rubber and aluminium goods, paints and matches are produced. Modernization of industry is slow because of lack of funds.

Area : 195,000 sq km (75,290 sq miles)
Population : 12,000,000
Capital : Sana'a, Commercial Capital : Aden
Form of government : Republic
Religion : Zaidism, Shia Islam, Sunni Islam
Currency : Riyal and dinar

Yerevan an industrial city and the capital of ARMENIA, close to the border with TURKEY. (Pop. 1,114,000)

Yinchuan the capital of NINGXIAHUI AUTONOMOUS REGION, in north central CHINA. (Pop. 635,000)

Yogyakarta (Jogjakarta) a city of south central JAVA, and a cultural centre. (Pop. 40,000)

Yokohama the main port of JAPAN, and the country's second largest city after neighbouring TOKYO, on the southeast coast of HONSHU Island. (Pop. 3,012,900)

York a historic English cathedral city in NORTH YORKSHIRE, having visible associations with Roman, Viking and Industrial Revolution heritage. (Pop. 103,000)

York, Cape the northernmost point on the Australian mainland, lying in QUEENSLAND, across the TORRES STRAIT from PAPUA NEW GUINEA. The Cape York Peninsula, on which it stands, extends for about 800 km (500 miles) between the CORAL SEA and the Gulf of CARPENTARIA.

Yorkshire an old county of northeast ENGLAND which used to be divided into the East, West and North Ridings. In 1974, however, the county was redivided into North Yorkshire (administrative centre Northallerton; 8309 sq km/3207 sq miles; pop. 666,000); West Yorkshire (administrative centre Wakefield; 2039 sq km/787 sq miles; pop. 2,038,000); and South Yorkshire (administrative centre Barnsley; 1560 sq km/602 sq miles; pop. 1,302,000).

Yorkshire Dales (The Dales) a picturesque area of northern ENGLAND covering the NORTH YORKSHIRE valleys of several rivers that flow eastwards from the PENNINES (eg. Swaledale and Wensleydale); they were made popular by the novels of James Herriot.

Yorubaland the traditional homeland of the Yoruba people, occupying most of southern NIGERIA, west of the NIGER River. It is mainly a fertile coastal plain, producing tropical products, and is intensely populated, with many villages, towns and large industrial cities.

Yucatán a state on a broad peninsula of southeast MEXICO. (Pop. 1,100,000)

Yugoslavia, which was created in 1918, became a single federal republic after World War II under the leadership of Marshal Tito (1892–1980). The six constituent republics were SERBIA, CROATIA, SLOVENIA, BOSNIA-HERZEGOVINA, MACEDONIA and MONTENEGRO. Yugoslavia today refers only to the republics of Serbia, Montenegro and Macedonia, the other republics having declared independence in 1992. It is likely that Macedonia may follow suit. The economy is largely agricultural, but exports include chemicals, machinery, textiles and clothing. The main languages are Serbo-Croat and Macedonian.

Area : 127,886 sq km (49,377 sq miles)

Population : 11,807,098

Capital : Belgrade (Beograd)

Other major cities : Nis, Skopje, Titograd

Form of government : Federal Republic

Religions : Eastern Orthodox

Currency : Dinar

Yukon Territory a mountainous territory in northwest CANADA centring upon the River Yukon and including the River KLONDIKE. The capital is WHITEHORSE. (536,372 sq km/207,076 sq miles; pop. 23,500)

Yünnan a province in southwestern CHINA. The capital is KUNMING. (436,200 sq km/168,400 sq miles; pop. 34,000,000)

Yunnan Plateau a mountainous area of southwest CHINA, embracing the great ranges and canyons of the Qam'do region. It enjoys a mild temperate climate.

Z

Zagreb the capital of CROATIA. (Pop. 1,180,000)

Zagros Mountains a mountain range in southwest IRAN, running parallel to the border with IRAQ. The highest point is Zard Kuh (4548 m/14,918 ft).

Zaïre situated in west central AFRICA; it was formerly the Belgian Congo prior to independence in 1960. Zaïre is a vast country with a short coastline of only 40 km (25 miles) on the ATLANTIC OCEAN. Rain forests, which cover about 55% of the country, contain valuable hardwoods such as mahogany and ebony. The country is drained by the river Zaïre and its main tributaries. Mountain ranges and plateaux surround the Zaïre Basin, and in the east the RUWENZORI Mountains overlook the lakes in the GREAT RIFT VALLEY. In the central region the climate is hot and wet all year but elsewhere there are well-marked wet and dry seasons. Agriculture employs 75% of the population yet less than 3% of the country can be cultivated. Grazing land is limited by the infestation of the tsetse fly. Cassava is the main subsistence crop, and coffee, tea, cocoa, rubber and palms are grown for export. Minerals, mainly copper, cobalt, zinc and diamonds, account for 60% of exports.

Area : 2,345,409 sq km (905,562 sq miles)

Population : 34,140,000

Capital : Kinshasa

Other major cities : Lubumbashi, Mbuji-Mayi, Kananga

Form of government : Republic

Religion : RC, Protestantism, Animism

Currency : Zaïre

Zaïre (Congo), River a major river of central AFRICA (the second longest river in Africa after the NILE) and, with its tributaries, forming a massive basin. It rises as the Lualaba in the south of Zaïre, then flows north and northwest, and finally southwest, forming the border between Zaïre and the CONGO before entering the ATLANTIC OCEAN. (Length 4800 km/3000 miles)

Zambezi, River a river of southern AFRICA. It rises in ZAMBIA, then flows south to form the border with ZIMBABWE, and then southeast across MOZAMBIQUE to the INDIAN OCEAN. (Length 2740 km/1700 miles)

Zambia (formerly the British colony of Northern Rhodesia, prior to independence in 1964), situated in central AFRICA, is made up of high plateaux. Bordering it to the south is the ZAMBEZI river, and in the southwest it borders on the KALAHARI DESERT. It has some other large rivers, including the Luangwa, and lakes, the largest of which is Lake BANGWEULU. The climate is tropical, modified somewhat by altitude. The country has a wide range of wildlife, and there are large game parks on the Luangwa and Kafue rivers. Agriculture is underdeveloped and most foodstuffs have to be imported. Zambia's economy relies heavily on the mining of copper, lead, zinc and cobalt. The poor market prospects for copper, which will eventually be exhausted, make it imperative for Zambia to develop her vast agricultural potential.

Area : 752,614 sq km (290,584 sq miles)

Population : 8,500,000

Capital : Lusaka

Other major cities : Kitwe, Ndola, Mufulira

Form of government : Republic

Religion : Christianity, Animism

Currency : Kwacha

Zanzibar an island lying just off the east coast of AFRICA, in the INDIAN OCEAN. Settled by Arab traders, it was a major commercial centre by the 17th century. It became a British protectorate in 1890, and joined neighbouring

Tanganyika in 1964 to form the independent republic of Tanzania. The main town is the port also called Zanzibar. (2461 sq km/950 sq miles; pop. 556,000)

Zapadno Sibirskaya Ravnina *see* **Siberia**.

Zaporozh'ye a major industrial city on the River Dnieper in the Ukraine. (Pop. 844,000)

Zaragoza (Saragossa) a historic and industrial city in northeastern Spain, on the River Ebro, and the name of the surrounding province. (Pop. city 590,000)

Zealand (Sjaelland) the largest island of Denmark, on which the capital, Copenhagen, is sited. (7014 sq km/2708 sq miles; pop. 1,855,500)

Zelle *see* **Celle**.

Zemlya Frantsa Iosita *see* **Franz Josef Land**.

Zermatt a popular ski resort in southwest Switzerland, close to the Matterhorn. (Pop. 3200)

Zhangjiakou a city in Hebei province, in northeast China. (Pop. 630,000)

Zhejiang a province of eastern China, with a coast on the East China Sea. The capital is Hangzhou. (102,000 sq km/ 39,780 sq miles; pop. 37,920,000)

Zhengzhou the capital of Henan province, in east central China. (Pop. 1,271,000)

Zibo an industrial city in Shangdong province, northeastern China. (Pop. 2,000,000)

Zimbabwe is a landlocked country in southern Africa. It was the British self-governing colony of Southern Rhodesia until 1965, and then known as Rhodesia, under the Unilateral Declaration of Independence (UDI) by the European controlled government until full independence in 1980. It is a country with spectacular physical features and is teeming with wildlife. It is bordered in the north by the Zambezi river, which flows over the mile-wide Victoria Falls before entering Lake Kariba. In the south, the River Limpopo marks its border with South Africa. Most of the country is over 300 m (984 ft) above sea level, and a great plateau between 1200 m (3937 ft) and 1500 m

(4922 ft) occupies the central area. Massive granite outcrops, called *kopjes*, also dot the landscape. The climate is tropical in the lowlands and subtropical in the higher land. About 75% of the labor force are employed in agriculture. Tobacco, sugar cane, cotton, wheat and maize are exported and form the basis of processing industries. Tourism is a major growth industry.

Area : 390,580 sq km (150,803 sq miles)

Population : 9,370,000

Capital : Harare

Other major cities : Bulawayo, Mutare, Gweru

Form of government : Republic

Religion : Animism, Anglicanism, RC

Currency : Zimbabwe dollar

Zuiderzee (Zuyder Zee) a former inlet of the NORTH SEA in the north coast of the NETHERLANDS. It was sealed off by a dam in 1932, and a major land reclamation development created the polderlands; the remaining water area is now the fresh water IJSSELMEER.

Zululand *see* **KwaZulu.**

Zürich the largest city in SWITZERLAND, in the northeast of the country, and a major industrial and financial centre. (Pop. 422,000)

Appendices

The World's Vital Statistics

Age: Approx 4600 million years.

Weight: Approx 5.976 x 10²¹ tonnes

Diameter: Pole to Pole through the centre of the Earth 12,713 km (7900 miles);across the Equator through the centre of the Earth 12,756 km (7926 miles).

Circumference: Around the Poles 40,008 km (24,861 miles); around the Equator 40,091 km (24,912 miles)

Area: *Land* 148,326,000 sq km (57,268,700 sq miles)—29% of total surface; *Water* 361,740,000 sq km (139,667,810 sq miles)—71% of total surface

Volume: 1,084,000 million cubic km (260,160 million cubic miles)

Volume of the oceans: 1321 million cubic km (317 million cubic miles)

Average height of land: 840 m (2756 ft) above sea level

Average depth of ocean: 3808 m (12,493 ft) below sea level.

Density: 5.52 times water

Mean temperature: 22°C (72°F)

Length of year: 365.25 days

Length of one rotation: 23 hours 56 minutes

Mean distance from Sun: 149,600,000 km (92,960,000 miles)

Mean velocity in orbit: 29.8 km (18.5 miles) per second

Escape velocity: 11.2 km (6.96 miles) per second

Atmosphere: Main constituents: nitrogen (78.5%), oxygen (21%)

Crust: Main constituents: oxygen (47%), silicon (28%), aluminium (8%), iron (5%)

Known satellites: One (The Moon)

Continents

	Highest Point		Area	
	metres	feet	sq km	sq miles
Asia	8848	29,028	43,608,000	16,833,000
Africa	5895	19,340	30,335,000	11,710,000
North &				
Central America	6194	20,320	25,349,000	9,785,000
South America	6960	22,834	17,611,000	6,798,000
Antarctia	5140	16,863	14,000,000	5,400,000
Europe	5642	18,510	10,498,000	4,052,000
Oceania	4205	13,796	8,900,000	3,400,000

Oceans

	Max. Depth		Area	
	metres	feet	sq km	sq miles
Pacific	11,033	36,198	165,384,000	63,838,000
Atlantic	8381	27,496	82,217,000	31,736,000
Indian	8047	26,401	73,481,000	28,364,000
Arctic	5450	17,880	14,056,000	5,426,000

Principal Mountains of the World

Name (location)	Height (m)	Height (ft)
Everest (Tibet-Nepal)	8848	29,028
Godwin-Austen *or* **K2** (India)	8611	28,250
Kangchenjunga (Nepal-India)	8586	28,170
Makalu (Nepal)	8463	27,766
Dhaulagiri (Nepal)	8167	26,795
Nanga Parbat (India)	8125	26,657
Annapurna	8091	26,545
Gosainthan (Tibet)	8012	26,286
Nanda Devi (India)	7816	25,643
Kamet (India)	7756	25,446
Namcha Barwa (Tibet)	7756	25,446
Gurla Mandhata (Tibet)	7728	25,355
Kongur (China)	7720	25,325
Tirich Mir (Pakistan)	7691	25,230
Minya Kanka (China)	7556	24,790
Kula Kangri (Tibet)	7555	24,784
Muztagh Ata (China)	7546	24,757
Kommunizma (Tajikistan)	7495	24,590
Pobedy (Kyrgyzstan-China)	7439	24,406
Chomo Lhar (Bhutan-Tibet)	7313	23,992
Api (Nepal)	7132	23,399
Lenina (Kyrgyzstan-Tajikistan)	7134	23,405
Acongagua (volcano) (Argentina)	6960	22,834
Ojos del Salado (Argentina)	6908	22,664
Tupungato (Argentina-Chile)	6801	22,310
Mercedario (Argentina)	6770	22,211
Huascarán (Peru)	6769	22,205
Llullaillaco (Chile)	6723	22,057
Neradas de Cachi (Argentina)	6720	22,047
Kailas (Tibet)	6714	22,027
Incahuasi (Argentina)	6709	22,011

Appendices

Name (location)	Height (m)	Height (ft)
Tengri Khan (Kyrgyzstan)	6695	21,965
Sajama (Bolivia)	6542	21,463
Illampu (Bolivia)	6485	21,276
Antofalla (volcanic) (Argentina)	6441	21,129
Illimani (Bolivia)	6402	21,004
Chimborazo (volcanic) (Ecuador)	6310	20,702
Cumbre de la Mejicana (Argentina)	6249	20,500
McKinley (Alaska)	6194	20,320
Copiapo or Azifre (Chile)	6080	19,947
Logan (Yukon, Canada)	5951	19,524
Cotopaxi (volcanic) (Ecuador)	5896	19,344
Kilimanjaro (volcanic) (Tanzania)	5895	19,340
Ollagüe (Chile-Bolivia)	5868	19,250
Cerro del Potro (Argentina-Chile)	5830	19,127
Misti (volcanic) (Peru)	5822	19,101
Cayambe (Ecuador)	5797	19,016
Huila (volcanic) (Colombia)	5750	18,865
Citlaltepi (Mexico)	5699	18,697
Demavend (Iran)	5664	18,582
Elbrus (volcanic) (Russian Fed.)	5642	18,510
St Elias (volcanic) (Alaska, Canada)	5489	18,008
Popocatepetl (volcanic) (Mexico)	5452	17,887
Cerro Lejfa (Chile)	5360	17,585
Foraker (Alaska)	5304	17,400
Maipo (volcanic) (Argentina-Chile)	5290	17,355
Ixtaccihuati (volcanic) (Mexico)	5286	17,342
Lucania (Yukon, Canada)	5228	17,150
Tomila (volcanic) (Colombia)	5215	17,109
Dykh Tau (European Russian Fed.)	5203	17,070
Kenya (Kenya)	5200	17,058
Ararat (Turkey)	5165	16,945
Vinson Massif (Antarctica)	5140	16,863
Kazbek (volcanaic) (Georgia)	5047	16,558
Blackburn (Alaska)	5037	16,523
Jaya (Irian Jaya, Indonesia)	5030	16,502

Name (location)	Height (m)	Height (ft)
Sanford (Alaska)	4941	16,208
Klyucheveyskava (Russian Fed.)	4750	15,584
Mont Blanc (France-Italy)	4808	15,774
Domuyo (volcanic) (Argentina)	4800	15,748
Vancouver (Alaska-Yukon, Canada)	4786	15,700
Trikora (West Irian, Indonesia)	4750	15,584
Fairweather (Alaska-British Columbia, Canada)	4670	15,320
Monte Rosa (Switzerland-Italy)	4634	15,203
Ras Dashen (Ethiopia)	4620	15,158
Belukha (Kazakhstan)	4506	14,783
Markham (Antartica)	4350	14,271
Meru (volcanic) (Tanzania)	4566	14,979
Hubbard (Alaska-Yukon)	4557	14,950
Kirkpatrick (Antarctica)	4528	14,855
Karisimbi (volcanic) (Rwanda-Zaire)	4508	14,787
Weisshorn (Switzerland)	4505	14,780
Matterhorn/Mont Cervin (Switzerland-Italy)	4477	14,690
Whitney (California)	4418	14,495
Elbert (Colorado)	4399	14,431
Massive Mount (Colorado)	4397	14,424
Harvard (Colorado)	4396	14,420
Rainier or Tacoma (Washington)	4392	14,410
Williamson (California)	4382	14,375
La Plata (Colorado)	4371	14,340
Blanca Peak (Colorado)	4364	14,317
Uncompahgre (Colorado)	4361	14,306
Crestone (Colorado)	4356	14,291
Lincoln (Colorado)	4354	14,284
Grays (Colorado)	4351	14,274
Evans (Colorado)	4347	14,260
Longs (Colorado)	4345	14,255
White (California)	4343	14,246
Colima (volcanic) (Mexico)	4340	14,236

Appendices

Name (location)	Height (m)	Height (ft)
Shavano (Colorado)	4337	14,229
Princeton (Colorado)	4327	14,196
Yale (Colorado)	4327	14,196
Elgon (volcanic) (Uganda-Kenya)	4321	14,176
Shasta (volcanic) (California)	4317	14,162
Grand Combin (Switzerland)	4314	14,153
San Luis (Colorado)	4312	14,146
Batu (Ethiopia)	4307	14,130
Pikes Peak (Colorado)	4301	14,110
Snowmass (Colorado)	4291	14,077
Culebra (Colorado)	4286	14,070
Sunlight (Colorado)	4284	14,053
Split (California)	4283	14,051
Redcloud (Colorado)	4278	14,034
Finsteraarhorn (Switzerland)	4274	14,022
Wrangell (Alaska)	4269	14,005
Mount of the Holy Cross (Colorado)	4266	13,996
Humphreys (California)	4259	13,972
Ouray (Colorado)	4254	13,955
Guna (Ethiopia)	4231	13,881
Mauna Kea (Hawai)	4205	13,796
Gannet (Wyoming)	4202	13,785
Hayes (Alaska)	4188	13,740
Fremont (Wyoming)	4185	13,730
Sidley (Antarctica)	4181	13,717
Mauna Loa (volcanic) (Hawai)	4169	13,677
Jungfrau (Switzerland)	4158	13,642
Kings (Utah)	4124	13,528
Kinabalu (Sabah)	4102	13,455
Cameroon (volcanic) (Cameroon)	4095	13,435
Fridtjof Nansen (Antarctica)	4068	13,346
Tacaná (volcanic) (Mexico-Guatemala)	4064	13,333
Bernina (Switzerland)	4049	13,284
Summit (Colorado)	4046	13,272

Name (location)	Height (m)	Height (ft)
Waddington (British Columbia, Canada)	4042	13,262
Lister (Antarctica)	4025	13,205
Cloud Peak (Wyoming)	4016	13,176
Yu Shan (Taiwan)	3997	13,113
Truchas (New Mexico)	3994	13,102
Wheeler (Nevada)	3981	13,058
Robson (British Columbia, Canada)	3954	12,972
Granite (Montana)	3902	12,799
Borah (Idaho)	3858	12,655
Baldy (New Mexico)	3848	12,623
Monte Viso (Italy)	3847	12,621
Kerinci (volcanic) (Sumatra)	3805	12,483
Grossglockner (Austria)	3797	12,460
Erebus (volcanic) (Antarctica)	3794	12,447
Excelsior (California)	3790	12,434
Fujiyama (volcanic) (Japan)	3776	12,388
Cook (New Zealand)	3753	12,313
Adams (Washington)	3752	12,307
Lanín (volcanic) (Argentina-Chile)	3740	12,270
Teyde or Tenerife (Canary Islands)	3718	12,198
Mahameru (volcanic) (Java)	3676	12,060
Assiniboine (British Columbia-Alberta, Canada)	3618	11,870
Hood (volcanic) (Orego)	3428	11,245
Pico de Aneto (Spain)	3404	11,168
Rheinwaldhorn (Switzerland)	3402	11,161
Perdido (Spain)	3352	10,997
Etna (volcanic) (Sicily)	3323	10,902
Baker (Washington)	3286	10,778
Lassen (volcanic) (California)	3188	10,457
Dempo (volcanic) (Sumatra)	3159	10,364
Siple (Antarctica)	3100	10,170
Montcalm (France)	3080	10,105
Haleakala (volcanic) (Hawaii)	3058	10,032

Appendices

Name (location)	Height (m)	Height (ft)
St. Helens (Washington)	2950	9677
Pulog (Philippines)	2934	9626
Tahat (Algeria)	2918	9573
Shishaldin (volcanic) (Aleutian Islands)	2862	9387
Roraima (Brazil-Venezuela-Guyana)	2810	9219
Ruapehu (volcanic) (New Zealand)	2797	9175
Katherine (Egypt)	2637	8651
Doi Inthanon (Thailand)	2594	8510
Galdhöpiggen (Norway)	2469	8100
Parnassus (Greece)	2457	8061
Olympus (Washington)	2425	7954
Kosciusko (Australia)	2230	7316
Harney (South Dakota)	2208	7242
Mitchell (North Carolina)	2038	6684
Clingmans Dome (North Carolina-Tennessee)	2025	6642
Washington (New Hampshire)	1917	6288
Rogers (Virginia)	1807	5927
Marcy (New York)	1629	5344
Cirque (Labrador)	1573	5160
Pelée (volcanic) (Martinique)	1463	4800
Ben Nevis (Scotland)	1344	4409
Vesuvius (volcanic) (Italy)	1281	4203

Principal Rivers of the World

Name (location)	Length (km)	(miles)
Nile (Africa)	6695	4160
Amazon (South America)	6516	4050
Yangtze (Chang Jiang) (Asia)	6380	3965
Mississippi-Missouri (North America)	6019	3740
Ob-Irtysh (Asia)	5570	3460
Yenisel-Angara (Asia)	5553	3450
Hwang Ho (Huang He) (Asia)	5464	3395
Zaïre (Africa)	4667	2900
Mekong (Asia)	4426	2750
Amur (Asia)	4416	2744
Lena (Asia)	4400	2730
Mackenzie (North America)	4250	2640
Niger (Africa)	4032	2505
Paraná (South America)	4000	2485
Missouri (North America)	3969	2466
Mississippi (North America)	3779	2348
Murray-Darling (Australia)	3750	2330
Volga (Europe)	3686	2290
Madeira (South America)	3203	1990
St. Lawrence (North America)	3203	1990
Yukon (North America)	3187	1980
Indus (Asia)	3180	1975
Syr Darya (Asia)	3079	1913
Darling (Australia)	3057	1900
Salween (Asia)	3060	1901
Rio Grande (North America)	3034	1885
São Francisco (South America)	2897	1800
Danube (Europe)	2850	1770
Brahmaputra (Asia)	2840	1765
Euphrates (Asia)	2815	1750
Pará-Tocantins (South America)	2752	1710

Appendices

Name (location)	Length (km)	(miles)
Kolyma (Asia)	2600	1600
Ganges (Ganga) (Asia)	2525	1568
Arkansas (North America)	2350	1460
Colorado (North America)	2330	1450
Xi Jiang (Asia)	2300	1437
Dnepr (Europe)	2285	1420
Negro (South America)	2254	1400
Aldan (Asia)	2242	1393
Irrawaddy (Asia)	2150	1335
Ohio (North America)	2102	1306
Orange (Africa)	2090	1299
Kama (Europe)	2028	1260
Xingú (South America)	2012	1250
Columbia (North America)	1950	1210
Juruá (South America)	1932	1200
Peace (North America)	1923	1195
Tigris (Asia)	1900	1180
Don (Europe)	1870	1165
Pechora (Europe)	1814	1127
Araguaya (South America)	1771	1100
Snake (North America)	1670	1038
Red (North America)	1639	1018
Churchill (North America)	1610	1000
Marañón (South America)	1610	1000
Pilcomayo (South America)	1610	1000
Ucayali (South America)	1610	1000
Uruguay (South America)	1610	1000
Magdalena (South America)	1529	950
Oka (Europe)	1481	920
Canadian (North America)	1459	906
Godavari (Asia)	1465	910
Parnaíba (South America)	1449	900
Dnestr (Europe)	1411	877
Brazos (North America)	1401	870
Fraser (North America)	1370	850

	Length	
Name (location)	*(km)*	*(miles)*
Salado (South America)	1368	850
Rhine (Europe)	1320	825
Narmada (Asia)	1288	800
Tobol (Asia)	1288	800
Athabaska (North America)	1231	765
Pecos (North America)	1183	735
Green (North America)	1175	730
Elbe (Europe)	1160	720
Ottawa (North America)	1121	696
White (North America)	1111	690
Cumberland (North America)	1106	687
Vistula (Europe)	1090	677
Yellowstone (North America)	1080	671
Donets (Europe)	1079	670
Tennesse (North America)	1050	652
Loire (Europe)	1012	629
Tagus (Europe)	1007	626
Tisza (Europe)	997	619
North Platte (North America)	995	618
Ouachita (North America)	974	605
Sava (Europe)	940	584
Neman (Europe)	937	582
Oder (Europe)	910	565
Cimarron (North America)	805	500
Gila (North America)	805	500
Gambia (Africa)	483	300

Principal Waterfalls of the World

Name (location)	Height (m)	(ft)
Angel (Venezuela)	979	3212
Yosemite (California) (including upper, central and lower falls, and rapids)	740	2,425
Kukenaãm (Guyana)	610	2,000
Sutherland (New Zealand)	581	1904
Wolloomombie (Australia)	519	1700
Ribbon (California)	492	1612
Upper Yosemite (California)	436	1430
Gavarnie (France)	422	1384
Tugela (South Africa)	412	1350
Takkakau (British Columbia)	366	1200
Staubbach (Switzerland)	300	984
Trümmelbach (Switzerland)	290	950
Middle Cascade (California)	278	910
Vettisfoss (Norway)	271	889
King Edward VIII (Guyana)	256	840
Gersoppa (India)	253	830
Skykjefos (Norway)	250	820
Kajeteur (Guyana)	226	741
Kalambo (Zambia)	222	726
Maradalsfos (Norway)	199	650
Maletsunyane (South Africa)	192	630
Bridalveil (California)	189	620
Multnomah (Oregon)	189	620
Vöringfoss (Norway)	182	597
Nevada (California)	181	594
Terni (Italy)	180	590
Skjeggedalsfoss (Norway)	160	525
Marina (Guyana)	153	500
Aughrabies (South Africa)	147	480

		Height
Name (location)	*(m)*	*(ft)*
Tequendama (Colombia)	131	427
Guaíra (Brazil-Paraguay)	114	374
Illilouette (California)	113	370
Victoria (Zambia and Zimbabwe)	108	355
Kegon-no-tali (Japan)	101	330
Lower Yosemite (California)	98	320
Cauvery (India)	98	320
Vernal (California)	97	317
Virginia (North West Territories	96	315
Lower Yellowstone (Wyoming)	94	308
Churchill (Labrador)	92	302
Reichenbach (Switzerland)	91	300
Sluiskin (Washington)	91	300
Lower Gastein (Austria)	86	280
Paulo Alfonso (Brazil)	84	275
Snoqualmie (Washington)	82	268
Seven (Colorado)	81	266
Montmorency (Quebec)	77	251
Handegg (Switzerland)	76	250
Taughannock (New York)	66	215
Iguassú (Brazil)	64	210
Shoshone (Idaho)	64	210
Upper Gastein (Austria)	63	207
Comet (Washington)	61	200
Narada (Washington)	52	168
Niagara (New York-Ontario)	51	167
Tower (Wyoming)	41	132
Stora Sjöfallet (Sweden)	40	131
Kabalega (Uganda)	40	130
Upper Yellowstone (Wyoming)	34	109